Preparing Personnel
to Work wit'
with Sev

Preparing Personnel to Work with Persons with Severe Disabilities

edited by

Ann P. Kaiser, Ph.D.
Department of Special Education
George Peabody College for Teachers
Vanderbilt University
Nashville, Tennessee

and

Celane M. McWhorter, M.Ed.
Office of Government Relations
The Association for Persons with Severe
  Handicaps
Alexandria, Virginia

·P·A·U·L·H·
BROOKES
PUBLISHING C°   Baltimore • London • Toronto • Sydney

Paul H. Brookes Publishing Co., Inc
P.O. Box 10624
Baltimore, Maryland 21285-0624

Typeset by The Composing Room of Michigan, Inc., Grand Rapids, Michigan
Manufactured in the United States of America by
St. Mary's Press, Hollywood, Maryland.

Library of Congress Cataloging-in-Publication Data
Preparing personnel to work with persons with severe
disabilities /
    edited by Ann P. Kaiser and Celane M. McWhorter.

    p.   cm.
    ISBN 1-55766-051-4 :
    1. Handicapped children—Education—United States—
Congresses.   2. Special education—United States—
Congresses.   I. Kaiser, Ann P.   II. McWhorter, Celane M.,
1944–
LC4005.P73   1990
371.9′0973–dc20   90–1403
                                                                    CIP

Contents

Contributors vii

Acknowledgments ix

Introduction   Focusing on the Future in Preparing Personnel to Work
with Persons with Severe Disabilities
Ann P. Kaiser 1

Part I   CURRENT PERSPECTIVES

Chapter 1   Building Our Capacity to Meet the Needs of Persons
with Severe Disabilities: Problems and Proposed
Solutions
Martha E. Snell 9

Chapter 2   National Needs and Resources: Available Databases
Mack L. Bowen 25

Chapter 3   Current Federal Policies Affecting Personnel Preparation
Celane M. McWhorter 47

Chapter 4   An Analysis of the Part D Program and the Relationship
to Preparation of Personnel to Educate Individuals
with Severe Handicaps
*Margaret J. McLaughlin, Carol H. Valdivieso,
and Barbara Stettner-Eaton* 75

Chapter 5   The Politics of Higher Education and Personnel
Preparation
Herbert J. Rieth 91

Part II   SPECIFIC NEEDS IN PERSONNEL PREPARATION

Chapter 6   Meeting Personnel Needs in Early Intervention
Philippa H. Campbell 111

Chapter 7   Preparation of Personnel to Work with Students
with Complex Health Care Needs
Donna H. Lehr 135

Chapter 8   Training Needs of Physical and Occupational Therapists
Who Provide Services to Children and Youth
with Severe Disabilities
*Jennifer York, Beverly Rainforth, and
Winnie Dunn* 153

v

Chapter 9   Teaching Personnel to Use State-of-the-Art,
             Nonaversive Alternatives for Dealing
             with Problem Behavior
             Ian M. Evans 181
Chapter 10   Preparing Personnel to Work in Community
             Support Services
             Julie Ann Racino 203
Chapter 11   Preparation of Supported Employment Personnel
             Paul Sale 227
Part III   MODELS OF PERSONNEL PREPARATION THAT
             WORK
Chapter 12   An Applied Research Model for Teacher Preparation
             in the Education of Persons with Severe Disabilities
             David L. Gast and Mark Wolery 243
Chapter 13   Personnel Preparation for a Community Intensive Model
             of Instruction
             Lori Goetz, Jacki Anderson, and Kathy Doering 271
Chapter 14   The Iowa Model of Personnel Preparation
             Greg A. Robinson 289
Chapter 15   A Generic In-Service Training Model
             H.D. Bud Fredericks and Torry Piazza Templeman .. 301
Chapter 16   Contemporary Policy and Best Practice
             Celane M. McWhorter and Ann P. Kaiser 319
Chapter 17   National Needs and Resources: A Commentary
             Steven F. Warren 329

Index 337

Contributors

Jacki Anderson, Ph.D.
California State University, Hayward
Department of Educational Psychology
Hayward, California 94542

Mack L. Bowen, Ph.D.
Department of Specialized Educational
  Development
Fairchild Hall
Illinois State University
Normal, Illinois 61761

Philippa H. Campbell, Ph.D.
Family Child Learning Center
Children's Hospital Medical Center of
  Akron
281 Locust Street
Akron, Ohio 44308

Kathy Doering, M.A.
Department of Special Education
San Francisco State University
4 Tapia Drive
San Francisco, California 94132

Winnie Dunn, Ph.D., O.T.R.
University of Kansas–Medical Center
Occupational Therapy Department
4013 Hirch Hall
39th & Rainbow Boulevard
Kansas City, Kansas 66103

Ian M. Evans, Ph.D.
Department of Psychology
State University of New York–
  Binghamton
Binghamton, New York 13901

H.D. Bud Fredericks, Ph.D.
Oregon State System of Higher
  Education
Teaching Research Division
Western Oregon State College
345 North Monmouth Avenue
Monmouth, Oregon 97361

David L. Gast, Ph.D.
Department of Special Education
570 Aderhold Hall
University of Georgia
Athens, Georgia 30602

Lori Goetz, Ph.D.
San Francisco State University
612 Font Street
San Francisco, California 94132

Ann P. Kaiser, Ph.D.
Department of Special Education
George Peabody College for Teachers
Vanderbilt University
Nashville, Tennessee 37203

Donna H. Lehr, Ph.D.
Associate Professor
Department of Special Education
Boston University
605 Commonwealth Avenue
Boston, Massachusetts 02215

Margaret J. McLaughlin, Ph.D.
University of Maryland
Institute for the Study of Exceptional
  Children and Youth
Department of Special Education
1308 Benjamin Building
College Park, Maryland 20742

Celane M. McWhorter, M.Ed.
Office of Government Relations
The Association for Persons with
  Severe Handicaps
1511 King Street
Alexandria, Virginia 22314

Julie Ann Racino, M.A.
Research and Training Center on
  Community Integration
Center on Human Policy
200 Huntington Hall
Syracuse University
Syracuse, New York 13244–2340

Beverly Rainforth, Ph.D., P.T.
State University of New York–
  Binghamton
School of Education and Human
  Development
Division of Education
P.O. Box 6000
Binghamton, New York 13902–6000

Herbert J. Rieth, Ed.D.
Department of Special Education
Box 328 Peabody
Vanderbilt University
Nashville, Tennessee 37203

Greg A. Robinson, Ed.D.
Consultant Mental Disabilities
Iowa Bureau of Special Education
Grimes State Office Building
Des Moines, Iowa 50319

Paul Sale, Ed.D.
Rehabilitation Research and Training
  Center on Supported Employment
Virginia Commonwealth University
1314 West Main Street
Richmond, Virginia 23284–2011

Martha E. Snell, Ph.D.
Curry School of Education
Department of Curriculum, Instruction,
  and Special Education
Room 236,Ruffner Hall
405 Emmet Street
University of Virginia
Charlottesville, Virginia 22903

Barbara Stettner-Eaton, Ph.D.
Office of Special Education Programs
Division of Educational Services
U.S. Department of Education
400 Maryland Avenue, SW
MS 2732
Washington, DC 20202

Torry Piazza Templeman, M.A.
Oregon State System of Higher
  Education
Teaching Research Division
Western Oregon State College
345 North Monmouth Avenue
Monmouth, Oregon 97361

Carol H. Valdivieso, M.A.
National Information Center for
  Children and Youth with Handicaps
7926 Jones Branch Drive
McLean, Virginia 22102

Steven F. Warren, Ph.D.
Department of Special Education
Box 328 Peabody
Vanderbilt University
Nashville, Tennessee 37203

Mark Wolery, Ph.D.
Department of Special Education
College of Education
University of Kentucky
229 Taylor Building
Lexington, Kentucky 40506–0001

Jennifer York, Ph.D., P.T.
University of Minnesota
Institute on Community Integration
6 Patee Hall
150 Pillsbury Drive, SE
Minneapolis, Minnesota 55455

Acknowledgments

The production of this book and of the 1987 Conference on the Preparing of Personnel to Work with Persons Who Are Severely Handicapped was a collaborative effort in the finest sense.

Resources for the conference were contributed by the Research and Training Center on Community Integration, Center on Human Policy at Syracuse University, Peabody College of Vanderbilt University and the John F. Kennedy Center for Research on Mental Retardation at Vanderbilt University. Steve Taylor, Director of the Policy Center and Dean Willis Hawley of Peabody College of Vanderbilt University generously shared their limited resources to make this conference possible.

The support and guidance of Naomi Karp, Project Officer at the National Institute on Disability and Rehabilitation Research, in obtaining funding and organizing the conference, was essential to its success. The Kennedy Center staff, especially Jan Rosemergy and Vickie Williams, provided superb conference management. Angele Thomas, Education Program Specialist in the Office of Special Education Programs, provided inspiration and invaluable advice on the planning of the conference and the book. Norm Howe, then Acting Director, Division of Personnel Preparation at the Office of Special Education Programs, gave generously of his time in helping us design the original plan for the conference. Carol Westlake was our valued collaborator and assistant in every aspect of conference planning.

In addition to the persons whose contributions are contained in this volume, faculty from Peabody College and representatives from the Tennessee Department of Education participated in the conference: Everett Hill, James Lent, Sam Odom, Richard Shores, Joleta Reynolds, and Mary McEvoy. Dara Howe provided us with an important perspective on parent concerns. We greatly appreciated the contributions of each of these participants to the conference; their comments are often reflected in the contents of individual chapters in this volume.

The production of this book was the result of Rebecca Hendrix's careful word processing and infinite patience with revisions and reconsiderations. We are most grateful for her many hours of work and her ever-cheerful demeanor.

We are very fortunate to work in organizations that provide flexibility and support for the projects we believe to be important. We gratefully acknowledge the many obvious and less obvious contributions of the Department of Special Education at Vanderbilt and The Association for Persons With Severe Handicaps to our efforts.

This book is for Molly, Emily, and Kay

Preparing Personnel to Work with Persons with Severe Disabilities

Introduction

Focusing on the Future in Preparing Personnel to Work with Persons with Severe Disabilities

Ann P. Kaiser

Personnel preparation is a critical investment in the future of persons with severe disabilities. As a field, our goal is the enhancement of services for the immediate and long-term future. As a society, we have made a formal commitment to the education of all children in the form of legislative mandates. If we are to fulfill our societal commitment and meet our professional goals, we must address and support personnel preparation as an ongoing process. It is essential that we work together to design high quality personnel preparation programs that reflect the changing needs in the field of disabilities and the emerging knowledge base and best practices.

In October 1987, a group of researchers, teacher trainers, administrators and parents held a conference at Vanderbilt University to discuss state-of-the-art practices in personnel preparation for professionals working in the area of severe disabilities and to focus on directions for the future. Participants with varied expertise in personnel program development, evaluation, and administration, and with a shared belief that appropriate education for all children is closely linked to the ability to provide training for personnel who will educate these children and support them in their communities, combined their talents to examine alternatives for the future. During

1

the 2 days of the conference, participants addressed national needs and resources, current critical issues in training, effective models of personnel preparation, and strategies for the future. The individual chapters contained in this volume represent the content of those discussions and reflect the best thinking of the individual authors as influenced by the group's discussion during the conference.

While many issues related to training personnel to work with individuals with severe disabilities are discussed in this volume, we are aware that not every important issue is addressed here. A comprehensive volume on personnel preparation would certainly have more chapters addressing the training required to work with individuals with particular disabilities and training models for all types of personnel who provide services and support for these individuals. While we acknowledge the importance of a very large set of issues and professional training concerns, we have chosen to focus on national and state policy issues as well as specific training strategies; thus, we have limited the range of specific training needs addressed in this volume.

STRATEGIES FOR THE FUTURE

In the course of the conference, three strategies for ensuring the future of personnel preparation in the area of severe disabilities emerged across presentations and discussions.

First, *personnel preparation must be made an explicit priority for local, state, and federal funding and program planning.* The critical relationship between personnel preparation and the successful provision of appropriate services for persons with severe disabilities was apparent in nearly every presentation. While there are currently policies and specific legislative mandates supporting personnel preparation as a priority for funding across federal agencies (see Chapter 2 by Mack L. Bowen, Chapters 3 and 16 by Celane M. McWhorter, and Chapter 4 by Margaret J. McLaughlin and her colleagues), continuing concerns for the level of funding, the specific authorizing legislation, and limited resources for in-service training were frequently cited. Furthermore, while the federal mandates are clear in their intent, if not generous in the provision of fiscal support, at the state and local levels, there are fewer mandates for personnel preparation and there are inconsistent patterns of funding across states and within states. In particular, the analysis of state level needs for personnel, the development of comprehensive preservice and in-service training programs, and the evaluation of personnel training efforts must be undertaken. These activities will be ensured only if there is widespread recognition by educators, legislators, and community members that the future of education for persons with severe disabilities depends on the adequacy of personnel preparation.

Second, *collaboration is key to all aspects of effective personnel preparation.* Collaboration and networking across federal agencies, state agencies, and institutions of higher education are essential in using the federal funds currently available to support preservice and in-service training. Within each state, ongoing collaborative planning by representatives of the state and the institutions of higher education that provide training is needed as the basis for the development of comprehensive systems of personnel development. While this concept is not new, few states have fully developed the type of collaborative relationships that have led to effective statewide training programs. Iowa's model of personnel development (described by Greg A. Robinson in Chapter 14) exemplifies the benefits of long-term, invested collaboration among state departments, training universities and colleges, and public schools.

Collaboration within the university is needed to provide the broad based, interdisciplinary training that forms the basis for preschool, school-age, and post-school services as indicated in Chapter 6 by Philippa H. Campbell, in Chapter 1 by Martha E. Snell, and in Chapter 11 by Paul Sale. Collaboration among professionals will be essential in developing community-based services and for ensuring that specific behavioral interventions are both ethically and procedurally reflective of current values and technologies. In Chapter 10, Julie Ann Racino describes an emerging model of community-based supports for persons with severe disabilities. In doing so, she points out the need for new types of collaboration to ensure successful community work, living, and recreation. Chapter 9 by Ian M. Evans provides an excellent discussion of the use of nonaversive intervention as an ethical and technologically advanced approach to intervention for persons with problem behavior and points out how scientific knowledge across disciplines must form the basis for innovation in service delivery. Administrative and instructional goals within the university must be addressed in a collaborative manner as well. As Herbert J. Rieth indicates in Chapter 5, the future of programs for training personnel in severe disabilities will depend to a considerable extent on new collaborative efforts within and across university departments to support training programs for personnel working in this area.

Collaboration with communities was an emergent theme of Chapter 13 by Lori Goetz and her colleagues in their description of the San Francisco model of community-referenced instruction, and in the discussions of early childhood services, community-based supports and supported employment. As special education services become a part of the mainstream of community activities, we must seek to build the linkages within communities that will support the long-term goal of full functional integration as well as the immediate goals of better prepared personnel with a community orientation.

The third strategy is the *construction and maintenance of long-term systems for ensuring the continued training of professionals in state-of-the-art practices*. This strategy becomes workable only when we have established personnel preparation as a priority and have begun to establish collaboration in training efforts at all levels. Professionals in the field of severe disabilities are challenged to stay abreast of the changing instructional technology and values base of the field. The master's level training program described by David L. Gast and Mark Wolery in Chapter 12 introduces teachers to research-based knowledge by training them to critically use and conduct research in conjunction with classroom teaching. Innovative in-service training strategies, such as those described by H.D. Bud Fredericks and Torry Piazza Templeman in Chapter 15, provide a beginning toward establishing a tradition of continuing dynamic training for professionals. It is critical that we prepare new teachers for the ongoing nature of their education and that we present continued training as a valuable, worthwhile, and expected aspect of professional development. Research on adult learning and on the successful experiences of corporations and other professional fields must be utilized as part of the effort to change both the strategies for and the attitudes toward in-service training. Innovation and research in this area clearly are among the most pressing needs for the 1990s if we are to both retain our teaching staffs and train the numbers of personnel to meet the needs of new populations and new programs.

In addition to the three strategies above, there is a clear need to build a better, more accurate, and more accessible data base that describes the numbers of individuals who require specific special education services and the types of personnel we have available to provide those services. Such a data base is both a political necessity in arguing for the need to prepare personnel and a programmatic necessity for effective planning at the state and local levels.

We must be open to innovation and change. In particular, we must consider the newer options that technology provides for training personnel. We must listen to our constituencies—to parents, to teachers, to other professionals we train, and to the persons with severe disabilities we intend to serve. Effective services must continue to be defined by the success in meeting the needs of individuals. Evaluations of effectiveness must guide our change and development.

Throughout the conference and in many of the chapters presented in this volume, the need for political awareness and political involvement as a basis for developing programs is a recurrent theme. We have come to understand that now, more than at any other time in our history, political process in developing legislation, in establishing programmatic priorities, and in allocating funds is an essential determinant of our future. Wise policy development requires clear thinking about our values base, knowledgeable interactions with policy makers, a solid empirical data base for decision-making, and the willingness of the field to continue to engage at all levels in the political process. Professionals, parents, and people with disabilities must collaborate to influence this process at both the state and the national levels.

The agenda for the future is a long one. There is much work to be done in developing models, building collaborative arrangements, securing funding for our efforts, and in actually providing high quality, state-of-the-art training to professionals in the area of severe disabilities. We are at a critical juncture in defining the success of education for all children and in establishing the community as the basis for services to persons with severe disabilities. The challenge is considerable, but as the contents of this volume indicate, so are our talents, our energy, and our commitments.

I

CURRENT PERSPECTIVES

Building Our Capacity to Meet the Needs of Persons with Severe Disabilities

Problems and Proposed Solutions

Martha E. Snell

Undoubtedly, the single most influential factor in transforming the quality of existing programs for people with severe disabilities is personnel. When professional staff have mastered the knowledge and competencies important to their role and accept the fact that their learning is unfinished, and further, when they operate from a set of values consistent with the importance of the individual student or client, then "best practices" come within reach. Yet, the goal of providing best practices is not easily attained. Meyer, Eichinger, and Park-Lee (1987) found in a survey of experts in the field of severe disabilities that 123 features were indicative of program quality and these features clustered into five different factors: integration, home-school cooperation, staff development, data-based instruction, and functional skills for criterion environments. Attainment of quality services for people with severe disabilities requires that a variety of professionals with competency in many program areas provide the needed services.

The special education teacher has been the professional with the most responsibility for influencing the future for school-age persons. However, if integrated school programs are to be a reality, this responsibility must be shared by many more people, including "regular" educators and building principals; along with therapists and allied personnel, such as preschool and infant teachers; and later, job coaches. When students grow into adults and leave school, the professionals who worked with them continue to be important to them. Many of us who are concerned with best practices are teacher trainers specializing in the area of school-age persons with severe disabilities. Just as we have had little influence over the training and development of regular education personnel, we also have evolved separately from the preparation of staff who will serve our students during their adult years. These personnel include job coaches, vocational rehabilitation counselors, sheltered workshop staff, day training program personnel, residential program staff in group homes and supervised apartment programs, staff in foster homes, personnel in nursing facilities and other institutions, and people working in recreation programs serving the general public and recreation programs for special populations only. Because preparation of *these* personnel is essential to the adult lives of persons with severe disabilities, their talents also pose an urgent concern for the field. This chapter focuses on current problems in personnel preparation and some ways in which personnel training can be strengthened in the future to ensure better and more consistent services.

PROBLEMS DERIVING FROM AGE- AND DISCIPLINE-BASED PERSONNEL PREPARATION

Two major criteria are used to organize the training of personnel: the age of the person with disabilities and the responsible service-providing agency. The chronological age of students or clients certainly influences what skills are needed by the professional staff who work with them, but in the field of severe disabilities, the criteria of age and agency divisions of services have produced some undesirable effects. For example, the major age-based service-delivery groups have been: 1) infants and toddlers, 2) school-age students, and 3) adults. As schools have come to practice what public law promotes in terms of serving the age group 3–21 years, preschoolers (ages 3–5) with disabilities are viewed more as "school-age," as are young adults ages 18–21 years. Yet preschoolers and young adults who do not have disabilities have *not* been the business of schools. Still, most special educators have stuck rigidly to the school setting instead of looking to age-appropriate locations like community day care and preschools for those under 5 years or community colleges for young adults. Teacher trainers for these younger and older groups have been urged to broaden their focus beyond that only of special education to include professional staff from agencies serving infants and adults as co-trainers in an effort to facilitate the cross-agency transitions that students and their families must make (Everson & Moon, 1987; Hains, Fowler, & Chandler, 1988). The following three sections address these and related personnel problems that derive from age- and discipline-based training programs.

Personnel Serving School-Age
Persons with Severe Disabilities

Perhaps the biggest personnel dilemma facing schools now and in the 1990s is the widespread existence of two separate systems of education: regular and special. In the enthusiastic pursuit of developing special services, we have separated students with defined disabilities from those who are "typical" or nonspecial. Natural diversity of school population is drastically limited during school hours based on the belief that students with disabilities cannot learn in regular classrooms and particularly that students with more severe disabilities require special classes and centers. With this division has come the separation of educators and administrators into two major groups. Rarely does personnel preparation meaningfully overlap between these two groups; thus, over time, the separation of regular and special education is reinforced (Lilly, 1989). Furthermore, in their separate evolution, the basic designs within special education and regular education are often incongruent: there are pronounced differences in terms of curricula, scheduling, teaching methods, and at times even transportation. These differences act as barriers to the unification of educational programs to serve all students.

Placement data across most states indicate that referral to special education generally means permanent placement in special education; few students move from special education to the regular classroom (Lipsky & Gartner, 1989a). Data on placements in least restrictive environments (LRE) in 1988 (*Tenth Annual Report to Congress,* 1988, Table 10, p. 30) indicate that students labeled mentally retarded, multihandicapped, orthopedically handicapped, visually handicapped, or deaf-blind have the highest percentages of placement in separate public school buildings where only students with disabilities are in attendance (10%–19%), with students labeled mentally retarded and multihandicapped having the highest separate class placement (56% and 43% respectively). Furthermore, Danielson and Bellamy's (1989) analysis of LRE data shows enormous state-to-state variation in the use of separate facilities for students with disabilities. While Congress clearly was interested in normalizing services for students who have disabilities with the passage of Public Law 94-142, the Education for All Handicapped Children Act, 1975, the current statistics seem to reflect placement according to convenience or locally traditional patterns of educational placement rather than placement based upon individually determined needs and the law's LRE principle which says:

> To the maximum extent appropriate, handicapped children, including children in public or private institutions or other care facilities, are educated with children who are not handicapped, and that special classes, separate schooling, or other removal of handicapped children from regular educational environments occurs only when the nature or severity of the handicaps is such that education in regular classes with the use of supplementary aide and services cannot be achieved satisfactorily. [20 U.S.C. 1415(5) (b)]

Many special educators have built a strong case for the benefits of joining forces with regular education. Brown and his colleagues (Brown, Long, Udvari-Solner, Davis, et al., 1989; Brown, Long, Udvari-Solner, Schwarz, et al., 1989; Sailor, 1989) have reasoned that such a union would enable all students to attend their "home school," thereby facilitating skill generalization, development of friendships between peers with disabilities and those without, more positive attitudes toward people with disabilities, and the improvement of communication between home and school. Biklen (1985) has shown that stronger teams of educators are formed when all teachers work together under a single building administrator. Lilly (1989) predicts that the elimination of learning deficit-based approaches to the education of children and to teacher preparation will enable special educators to have some influence on the future reform of education. How these reforms would influence teacher preparation is a question not easily nor simply answered. But Lilly (1989) explains that a unitary system of teacher preparation would meet the needs of most students, while specialists also would be prepared to assist teachers in their education of students having sensory or movement limitations: "All teachers would be expected to teach children and to assist each other in meeting individual students' needs" (p. 147). Furthermore, Lilly emphasizes the need for increased decision-making and accountability at the level of the classroom and school and less regulation from higher levels. Most authors in the literature agree that the first steps toward changing the separate patterns of personnel preparation will be the most difficult.

Personnel Serving Very Young Children with Severe Disabilities

Public Law 99-457, the Education of the Handicapped Act Amendments of 1986 (specifically Part H), has significantly influenced preparation of personnel serving infants and toddlers. The most obvious influence has been to create a need for trained teachers and related-services staff for very young children with disabilities. Current survey data from across the country indicate that 88.4% of the states report shortages of special education personnel trained to serve the youngest group of children with disabilities, those ages birth to 3 years (Miesels, Harbin, Modigliani, & Olson, 1987, cited in Smith & Powers, 1987). Another influence on personnel preparation concerns the consistency with which states implement the federal regulations for personnel preparation. Unlike administration of programs for older children under PL 94-142, PL 99-457 allows different states to house their educational programs for infants and toddlers in different state departments. Currently, in about one-third of all states and territories in the United States, departments of education are responsible for implementing the special educational programs to these very young children with disabilities (J. Thiele, personal communication, August 23, 1989). In almost an equal number of states, departments of health oversee the administration of Part H of PL 99-457, while about six to seven states place this responsibility in departments of human services or social welfare, and three to four states have an interagency council that supervises implementation of these educational programs (J. Thiele, personal communication, August 23, 1989). Even at the federal level, multiple agencies in two departments (the Departments of Education, and Health and Human Services) are charged with the responsibility to implement the legislation.

This division of responsibility at both state and federal levels appears likely to complicate consistency in enforcement of federal standards for certification and licensing of teachers and related-services staff (Hurley, 1989). It is possible, however, that more creative service-delivery models and more complete services will result given the involvement of a broader set of agencies and federal programs. For example, at the federal level, the Office of Special Education Programs (OSEP, in the Department of Education) and the Division of Maternal and Child Health (in the Department of Health and Human Services) have collaborated in their funding of personnel preparation programs in university settings to include physicians along with teachers and related-services professionals (Department of Education, 1989).

Several other issues that directly or indirectly influence personnel preparation for very young children with disabilities warrant attention. The first issue is the problem of supply and demand. From 1987–1989 the number of applications submitted to and funded by the Department of Education for programs to prepare personnel to serve very young children with disabilities has more than doubled, with about one quarter of all awards made in 1989 in this area of emphasis (J. Thiele, personnel communication, August 23, 1989). This increase in training programs clearly is needed (Smith & Powers, 1987). The second issue is the variation in professional requirements between federal programs serving young children with special needs. For example, Head Start teachers are not required to be certified by departments of education, while teachers hired under PL 99-457 are required to have a bachelor's degree plus state certification. This imbalance can create staffing problems between programs as Head Start teachers seek improvement in salary and job conditions. Furthermore, the frequent vacancies for occupational and physical therapists in PL 99-457 programs indicates that the working conditions, pay, and professional control may be less desirable than in more traditional employment settings like hospitals (Smith & Powers, 1987).

Another issue likely to have an impact, though less directly, on personnel preparation in programs for personnel serving very young children with disabilities is the actual location of the program. Some have feared that the weak LRE language in the law coupled with agency responsibility varying from state to state will mean that new programs for infants and toddlers with disabilities will not be located in integrated community settings where children can be served alongside their nondisabled peers (Snell, 1987). If these children are to lead normalized lives, services for infants and toddlers with special needs must be provided primarily in their own homes, with their babysitters, or in their daycare settings alongside nondisabled peers and family members. Though the issue of a program's location is separate from preparation of its personnel, the two issues become interrelated once a program exists (Lilly, 1989). If the service location is a hospital or a separate center serving only special groupings of people, it becomes more difficult to work with the child's parents and to initiate the concept of normalized educational services. Personnel trained to work with young students, parents, and other care providers in natural community locations will find separate, "handicapped only" settings less advantageous to the techniques of service provision they have learned; children's skill generalization will be adversely affected as will communication with parents. Finally, the transition into an integrated school program at age 3 or age 5 is likely to be less natural if a child's first "least restrictive" environment was in a segregated location (Fowler, 1982; Hains et al., 1988).

Personnel Serving
Adults with Severe Disabilities

Typically, when an individual reaches adulthood the responsible agencies change from the state education departments, during the school years, to departments of mental health and mental retardation. These departments also may have overseen early intervention programs, but their responsibility was disrupted during the school years, eliminating the possibility of continuous case management across a person's life span. The Department of Education is not an exception to this practice of dividing clients by age, although the formation of the Office of Special Education and Rehabilitative Services (OSERS) was an attempt to reduce the problems caused by such divisions.

The primary federal law influencing personnel preparation for adults with severe disabilities is the Vocational Rehabilitation Act of 1986. However, with the exception of standards for rehabilitation engineers, this act does not specify personnel preparation standards as do PL 94-142 and PL 99-457. The Vocational Rehabilitation Act (PL 98-221) did formalize the concept of supported work, and as a result, the role of the job coach or the employment training specialist has evolved. During the 1980s, training programs for these personnel have developed within existing rehabilitation counselor programs and sometimes within special education departments to prepare staff for these direct service roles (Bellamy, Rhodes, Mank, & Albin, 1988). Other personnel working with adults who have severe disabilities are trained through a combination of programs in mental health and counseling, psychology, vocational rehabilitation, nursing, and social work.

While state regulations for adult services may address staffing loads and ratios in settings like sheltered workshops and adult activity centers, state regulations typically do not set minimum competencies for the staff in these settings. In Virginia, direct service staff serving adults with severe disabilities are paid less than certified teachers in schools (although institutional staff may not be). The job demands on adult services staff may be similar to demands on secondary teachers, but *direct services staff* tend to have less training, their training typically is in fields of sociology and psychology, not education, they have far fewer training requirements, and they generally obtain more training from the agency they are employed by, but with enormous variation in the quality and type of training from agency to agency (Everson, personal communication, August 23, 1989). *Professional staff* in management positions of adult service agencies typically have training in education and may have moved to their positions from school system jobs. The turnover in adult services direct care staff is high in most states (e.g., 45% in Virginia), reportedly due to low salary and little opportunity for advancement. Inevitably high turnover means a sacrifice in the quality of services (Everson, personal communication, August 23, 1989).

Several factors will have a strong influence on the quality of future preparation of personnel to work with adults having more severe disabilities. The first two factors are interrelated: the lack of professionalization for supported employment staff positions and the low salaries of persons in these positions which typically are far less than those of public school teachers (Buckley, Albin, & Mank, 1988; Renzaglia, 1986; Rusch, 1986). If salaries were increased along with professional preparation programs and requirements, the high turnover for these jobs that now exists probably would decline and the quality of programs would improve (Buckley et al., 1988). Without these changes in salary and professional standards, fewer people will seek careers in adult services, and universities will take less interest in developing training programs. Without changes in pay and improved professional standards, technical assistance, the third factor, will remain the primary vehicle for training adult services staff. But there is an absence of talented consultants who can provide quality in-service training to direct care personnel (Rusch, Mithaug, & Flexor, 1986). Everson, in her research at the Rehabilitation Research and Training Center on Supported Employment at Virginia Commonwealth University, has found that there are few consultants who have direct experience in the provision of current best practices for adults with severe disabilities (Everson, personal communication, August 23, 1989). This third factor poses a challenge for personnel preparation programs.

Summary

Several problems result from the age, discipline, and service agency organizational approach to personnel preparation:

1. *Change and innovation across the age range are more difficult.* For example, to the extent that philosophies such as nonaversive treatment and integration are accepted by special educators and built into educators' curricula, the practice of these philosophies is facilitated during the school years. These practices are unlikely to extend beyond the lower or the upper school-age boundaries simply because only educators have been exposed fully to these philosophies.

2. *Professional skills training for personnel who work with different age groups differ radically.* The differences in focus of training exacerbates problems in transitions between service systems for both very young children entering the educational system and young adults leaving school and beginning community services. Academic disciplines tend toward differentiation of professional roles rather than toward team work of service personnel across the life span to address the whole person, which is the approach that typifies best practices.

3. *Families may become confused and disenchanted with professionals and the service system.* As individuals with disabilities move from one set of professionals to the next as they cross age boundaries, their families must deal with procedural changes, philosophical differences, new staff, knowledge gaps, different supervision patterns, and various funding sources. These changes in agencies responsible for services over time cause families to fight the same battles repeatedly, to use up precious time and energy, and often to become disillusioned with the service-delivery system when their children reach adulthood and may need family support the most (Dokecki & Heflinger, 1989; Hains et al., 1988; Turnbull, Turnbull, Bronicki, Summers, & Roeder-Gordon, 1989).

4. *Ultimately, individuals with disabilities suffer from the inconsistencies across treatment approaches, skills, values, and success criteria held by various professionals.* Although inconsistencies also exist in services pro-

vided within the three age groups—from teacher to teacher and later from one vocational staff member to the next—it is the abrupt and major changes in staff, services, and procedures that occur as students pass through these rigid age groupings from infancy to school-age and from school-age to adulthood that are most problematic.

FOUR POTENTIAL SOLUTIONS

Four potential solutions might address the problems just discussed:

1. Training personnel to facilitate transitions between service groupings
2. Creating university-based interdisciplinary training programs for all personnel who will work with people with severe disabilities
3. Investing in innovative strategies for case management
4. Teaching a common values base

Teaching Transition

The concept of transition is one of the most promising solutions to the personnel preparation problems related to rigid age and discipline boundaries. Vocational experts have popularized the valuable concept of transition from school to work (Wehman, Moon, Everson, Wood, & Barcus, 1988). Students do not make the passage from their 21st year to their 22nd year without great effort by the school and community and by the family. The same can be said about early life transitions. This concept of transition also needs to be developed and practiced during the passage from the infancy/toddler years to school-age. Fowler and her colleagues (Fowler, 1982; Hains et al., 1988) have laid the groundwork with their research on preschool-kindergarten transitions in special education.

Successful transitions require that professionals communicate and negotiate with each other and with the family in order to plan together for the changes that will occur in the child's or adult's future (Wehman et al., 1988). Skills in communication and negotiation with other professionals and with families, and skills in future planning typically are not taught in the course of teacher preparation, although they may be taught in some of the other helping professions. Adding these skills to professional preparation programs, along with realistic, practical opportunities to use them, will be necessary if a transition model is to be used successfully.

Cross-Discipline Training

Another strategy to reduce the age- and discipline-bound nature of personnel preparation involves faculty in university programs sharing personnel preparation responsibilities across disciplines which can be done without special education sacrificing "ownership" of training programs. One common example of shared training is practiced when teachers are taught by occupational and physical therapists, not special educators, to position and handle students with movement difficulties. But there are many other areas in which shared training would improve the professional preparation. Examples of topics in which special educators need assistance from others often include, but are not limited to, the following:

1. Effective and sensitive communication with other professionals and families
2. Managing teams of professionals and leading them toward client-centered programs
3. Future planning with families
4. The structure and functions of agencies providing services to families across the child's age span (i.e., contact information, service characteristics, methods of procurement, cost)
5. Medical information necessary for the health and safety of students with the most profound disabilities
6. Effective methods to teach other adults (e.g., role release and knowledge sharing)
7. Legal rights and basic strategies for pursuing them
8. Strategies for administrative and systems change

Sharing across disciplines or "role release" in the preparation of personnel is a two-way process, with special education both giving and receiving input from other disciplines (Rainforth & York, 1987). Sharing is not simply a matter of inviting guest speakers from other disciplines to make presentations in discipline-based classes. Shared training must include planning by instructors from different disciplines so that the information from the "outside" discipline is made compatible with the philosophies and other practices applied in the education of people with severe disabilities.

In the 1970s and early 1980s, when I first involved occupational therapists and physical therapists in a class I taught on positioning, handling, and self-care skills, I found that while students learned about movement disorders and mastered techniques to facilitate movement in their students from these therapists, they were also presented with some real contradictions to the approaches I valued. For example, the therapists often passed on very negative views of the potential of clients with "serious cognitive delays" in addition to orthopedic problems. They used age-inappropriate materials and nonfunctional tasks to illustrate training in fine motor skills. Over a period of several years, while I vastly improved my lifting and positioning skills, the therapists also learned from their involvement with the course content I presented. They began to address the importance of the student's chronological age, to include a rationale for teaching only functional skills, to consider the role of partial participation and skill adaptation, to see the relationship of integrated therapy to skill generalization, and to value the offering of choices to students. Shared training resulted in infiltration of values from special education into a related discipline, thus closing one of the gaps that exist in the preparation of personnel who work with people having disabilities.

Case Management

The concept of case management needs to be updated to match contemporary values and service-delivery patterns. If a person with a severe disability and his or her family could be accompanied across the life span by a "professional advocate" who could mobilize resources to meet the client's needs (Dunst & Trivette, 1989), perhaps the repeated battles for services not only would be fewer, but would be fought with more consistency, require less energy from families, and have more desirable outcomes. Case management is hardly a new concept, with its roots dating back to the casework practices of social workers in the early 1900s (Dunst & Trivette, 1989). Its inclusion in Part H of the reauthorization of the Education of the Handicapped Act (PL 99-457, the Education of the Handicapped Act Amendments, 1986), along with the individualized family service plan (IFSP), is an indication of the importance that Congress placed upon the "system's" responsibility to strengthen and support the family "in ways that make them more capable of mobilizing resources to meet their needs and those of their children" (Dunst & Trivette, 1989, p. 97). The value that good case management could have for families is not limited to the preschool years, but would continue through the school years and into adulthood as the family continued to obtain services from many different agencies for their son or daughter with severe disabilities and faced the vocational, leisure, and residential issues of the post-school period.

Dokecki and Heflinger (1989) link case management with advocacy, even though the Part H does not mention the advocacy capacity of case management. When successful, case management should prevent the fragmentation and dehumanization that goes along with being "referred around" and "falling between the cracks" of the special education service systems (Dokecki & Heflinger, 1989, p. 72). Also, professional advocates might reduce or mediate the confrontations between other professionals and the parents they represent. Such case managers would need cross-discipline training to be able to interact effectively with the wide range of professionals the family encounters across time. Careful consideration must be given to those who would train these advocates and how training would be accomplished. The addition of these professionals whose work would span all age periods *and* disciplines might lessen the age and discipline boundaries faced by people with severe disabilities and their families.

Preparing Professionals with Values

One method of ensuring the quality of professionals' skills through the passage of time is to teach them a set of human values that is the basis for best practices. While professionals with a strong values base, in addition to a current knowledge and skill base, will never be immune to the need to update their knowledge, they will have a foundation for taking appropriate action in new situations and at any other time when areas of their professional preparation are incomplete or outdated (Lipsky & Gartner, 1989b). Kaiser and Hemmeter (1989) have illustrated how values-based decision-making is an essential aspect of working with families. Their values-based assumptions included statements like: "Communities are enhanced by the full participation of children with handicaps and their families," and "interventions should not separate children and families from their community" (p. 78). From these values-based assumptions, questions were posed about the intervention: Is the intervention demeaning or divisive to anyone? "Does the intervention increase heritage, mutual aid, and community-building?" (p. 78). One could easily use values-based assumptions to support interventions within the context of the home and community, while segregated settings would be devalued as divisive to the family. Kaiser and Hemmeter's listing includes many values with versatility across the life span and exemplifies how the knowledge base applied in personnel preparation can be improved with a complimentary values base. Teaching values in academe is sometimes *de*valued and confused with teaching subjectivity in place of objective knowledge. When personnel preparation competencies do not include acquiring a values base, professionals are left with many incomplete rules for being competent professionals.

In 1987 at the annual meeting of the Association for Behavior Analysis (ABA) in Nashville, Tennessee, several individuals spoke of the organization's emerging position paper on the rights of clients with developmental disabilities. In this paper, about a dozen basic rights were set forth by the ABA committee on the right to treatment. Many members responded to their call for comments. One item in the list of rights concerned the individual's right to interact with others, but there was no mention of who these others might be beyond staff members. When suggestions were made to extend this interaction right to include peers who do not have disabilities and to add the concept of integration as a basic right, the response by several panel members was directed toward the value of integration. The response was something along the lines that the data are not all in on integration . . . we don't really know whether integrated programs or, for that matter, programs with lower staff-client ratios, are really better programs.

In our lifetimes, not *all* the evidence necessary will be available to convince many of our professional peers of the validity of some practices that are critical to individuals with severe disabilities, including integration, supported employment, nonaversive approaches, the effects of labeling, and so forth. In the midst of limited empirical evidence, we must address the gray areas of intervention where evidence or social validation is weak or lacking *and* where the professionals we prepare frequently must make decisions. First, we must caution professionals-in-training about uncritically applying *all* that research has demonstrated. Second, we must inform them on the problems of choosing inaction when the data for or against the available choices are incomplete. An alternative approach is to teach professionals to apply knowledge that is consistent with the values they hold about the lives of people with severe disabilities. When professionals appreciate the relationship between the knowledge of their discipline and the values they hold for clients with severe disabilities, they will make fewer erroneous decisions.

SUMMARY

The roles that teachers of students with severe disabilities must fill have expanded enormously in the 1980s. The Vocational Rehabilitation Act Amendments of 1986 have added work in supported employment to the job descriptions of those responsible for older students, and PL 99-457 has added more intensive work with families and infants for teachers in early intervention. Still, the preparation of professionals working across the life span with persons having severe disabilities is characterized by rigid age, discipline, service, and agency boundaries that result in problems for all. In the future, personnel preparation must be characterized by efforts to reduce the boundaries existing between regular and special education *and* between behavior professionals trained to work with infants, those working with school-age students, and those working with adults who have severe disabilities and their families. Methods to accomplish this goal include: 1) increased use of transition planning; 2) preparing professionals to communicate and negotiate with other professionals and with families; 3) using the concept of shared training across disciplines that involves two-way exchange and infiltration of knowledge and values between university faculty; 4) the case manager as a professional advocate for families; and 5) the teaching of values to professional personnel *along with* knowledge to guide their decision-making when evidence is incomplete or outdated, or in the absence of guidelines to protect the rights of persons with severe disabilities.

REFERENCES

Bellamy, G.T., Rhodes, L.E., Mank, D.M., & Albin, J.M. (1988). *Supported employment: A community implementation guide.* Baltimore: Paul H. Brookes Publishing Co.

Biklen, D. (1985). *Achieving the complete school: Strategies for effective mainstreaming.* New York: Teachers College Press.

Brown, L., Long, E., Udvari-Solner, A., Davis, L., VanDeventer, P., Ahlgren, C., Johnson, F., Gruenewald, L., & Jorgensen, J. (1989). The Home School: Why students with severe intellectual disabilities must attend the schools of their brothers, sisters, friends, and neighbors. *Journal of The Association for Persons with Severe Handicaps, 14*(1) 1–7.

Brown, L., Long, E., Udvari-Solner, A., Schwarz, P., VanDeventer, P., Ahlgren, C., Johnson, F., Gruenewald, L., & Jorgensen, J. (1989). Should students with severe intellectual disabilities be based in regular or in special education classrooms in home schools? *Journal of The Association for Persons with Severe Handicaps, 14*(1) 8–12.

Buckley, J., Albin, J.M., & Mank, D.M. (1988). Competency-based staff training for supported employment. In G.T. Bellamy, L.E. Rhodes, D.M. Mank, & J.M. Albin (Eds.), *Supported employment: A community implementation guide* (pp. 229–245). Baltimore: Paul H. Brookes Publishing Co.

Danielson, L.C., & Bellamy, G.T. (1989). State variation in placement of children with handicaps in segregated environments. *Exceptional Children, 55,* 448–455.

Department of Education and the Department of Health and Human Services. (January, 1989). *Meeting the needs of infants and toddlers with handicaps: Federal resources, services, and coordination efforts in the Departments of Education and Health and Human Services.* Washington: Government Printing Office.

Dokecki, P.R., & Heflinger, C.A. (1989). Strengthening families of young children with handicapping conditions. In J.J. Gallagher, P.L. Trohanis, & R.M. Clifford (Eds.), *Policy implementation and PL 99-457: Planning for young children with special needs* (pp. 59–84). Baltimore: Paul H. Brookes Publishing Co.

Dunst, C.J., & Trivette, C.M. (1989). An enablement and empowerment perspective of case management. *Topics in Early Childhood Special Education, 8*(4), 87–102.

Everson, J.M., & Moon, M.S. (1987). Transition services for young adults with severe disabilities: Defining professional and parental roles and responsibilities. *Journal of The Association for Persons with Severe Handicaps, 12*(2) 87–95.

Fowler, S. A. (1982). Transition from preschool to kindergarten for children with special needs. In K.E. Allen & E.M. Gpeta (Eds.), *Early childhood education: Special problems, special solutions* (pp. 309–334). Rockville, MD: Aspen Systems Corporation.

Hains, A.H., Fowler, S.A., & Chandler, L.K. (1988). Planning school transitions: Family and professional collaboration. *Journal of the Division for Early Childhood, 12,* 108–115.

Hurley, O.L. (1989). Implications of PL 99-457 for preparation of preschool personnel. In J.J. Gallagher, P.L. Trohanis, & R.M. Clifford (Eds.), *Policy implementation and PL 99-457: Planning for young children with special needs* (pp. 133–145). Baltimore: Paul H. Brookes Publishing Co.

Kaiser, A.P., & Hemmeter, M.L. (1989). Value-based approaches to family intervention. *Topics in Early Childhood Special Education, 8*(4), 72–86.

Lilly, S.M. (1989). Teacher preparation. In D.K. Lipsky & A. Gartner (Eds.), *Beyond separate education: Quality education for all* (pp. 143–157). Baltimore: Paul H. Brookes Publishing Co.

Lipsky, D.K., & Gartner, A. (1989a). The current situation. In D.K. Lipsky & A. Gartner (Eds.), *Beyond separate education: Quality education for all* (pp. 3–24). Baltimore: Paul H. Brookes Publishing Co.

Lipsky, D.K., & Gartner, A. (1989b). Building the future. In D.K. Lipsky & A. Gartner (Eds.), *Beyond separate education: Quality education for all* (pp. 255–290). Baltimore: Paul H. Brookes Publishing Co.

Meyer, L.H., Eichinger, J., & Park-Lee, S. (1987). A validation of program quality indicators in educational services for students with severe disabilities. *Journal of The Association for Persons with Severe Handicaps, 12,* 251–263.

PL 94-142, The Education for All Handicapped Children Act, 1975, 20 U.S.C. 1415 (5) (B).

Rainforth, B., & York, J. (1987). Integrating related services in community instruction. *Journal of The Association for Persons with Severe Handicaps, 12*(3) 190–198.

Renzaglia, A. (1986). Preparing personnel to support and guide emerging contemporary service alternatives. In F.R. Rusch (Ed.), *Competitive employment issues and strategies* (pp. 303–316). Baltimore: Paul H. Brookes Publishing Co.

Rusch, F.R. (1986). *Competitive employment issues and strategies.* Baltimore: Paul H. Brookes Publishing Co.

Rusch, F.R., Mithaug, D.E., & Flexor, R.W. (1986). Obstacles to competitive employment and traditional program options for overcoming them. In F.R. Rusch (Ed.), *Competitive employment issues and strategies* (pp. 7–21). Baltimore: Paul H. Brookes Publishing Co.

Sailor, W. (1989). The educational, social and vocational integration of students with the most severe disabilities. In D.K. Lipsky & A. Gartner (Eds.), *Beyond separate education: Quality education for all* (pp. 53–74). Baltimore: Paul H. Brookes Publishing Co.

Smith, B.J., & Powers, C. (1987). Issues related to developing state certification policies. *Topics in Early Childhood Special Education, 7*(3), 12–23.

Snell, M.E. (1987, September). Serving young children with special needs and their families and PL 99-457. *TASH Newsletter,* p. 1–2.

Tenth annual report to Congress on the implementation of the Education of the Handicapped Act. (1988). Washington, DC: U.S. Department of Education.

Turnbull, H.R., Turnbull, A.P., Bronicki, G.J., Summers, J.A., & Roeder-Gordon, C. (1989). *Disability and the family: A guide to decisions for adulthood.* Baltimore: Paul H. Brookes Publishing Co.

Wehman, P., Moon, M.S., Everson, J.M., Wood, W., & Barcus, J.M. (1988). *Transition from school to work: New challenges for youth with severe disabilities.* Baltimore: Paul H. Brookes Publishing Co.

2

National Needs and Resources

Available Databases

Mack L. Bowen

"A wise man will make more opportunity than he finds" (Bacon, 1625). One might paraphrase that statement to say, a wise government will make more opportunity than it finds. Accordingly, this chapter outlines the opportunities and national resources that the federal government makes available to meet the training needs of personnel for the education of children and youth with disabilities.

On October 8, 1986, PL 99-457, the Education of the Handicapped Act Amendments was enacted; this was the reauthorization of the original Education of the Handicapped Act, 1970, PL 91-230. Part D (Training Personnel for the Education of the Handicapped [CFDA 84.029, Sections 631 and 632]) of PL 99-457 authorizes support to increase the quantity and improve the quality of personnel available to educate children with handicaps.

Personnel preparation assistance authorized under Section 631, as designed by Congress, is administered by the Department of Education through the Division of Personnel Preparation (DPP) within the Office of Special Education and Rehabilitative Services (OSERS). In each fiscal year

The author wishes to thank M. Angele Thomas and Norman D. Howe, both of the Division of Personnel Preparation, Office of Special Education Programs, United States Department of Education, for their assistance in the preparation of this chapter in their private capacity. No official support or endorsement by the Department of Education is intended or should be inferred.

approximately 1200 training grant applications are submitted for consideration under this authority. Typically, the department provides support for over 800 new and continuation projects that train special education teachers and administrators, related-services personnel, leadership personnel, volunteers, and parents to assist children and youth with disabilities to receive a free, appropriate, public education. Personnel training is provided at the associate baccalaureate, master's, specialist, and doctoral levels.

Prior to fiscal year 1989 no funds were specifically authorized for the training of personnel to work with low-incidence disabilities, such as severe/profound mental retardation. However, as of this date and continuing with fiscal year 1990, training funds have been authorized for the preparation of personnel to work with students with low-incidence handicaps (CFDA 84.029A). A discussion concerning the funding mechanism of this and other personnel training priorities and how the funds are obtained follows.

PRIORITY SPENDING FOR SECTION 631

For distributing funds under Section 631, the Department of Education annually identifies specific training priorities (U.S. Department of Education, 1989). These funding priorities include the following categories:

Preparation of Special Educators for Careers in Special Education and Early Intervention supports projects designed to provide preservice training of personnel, including special education teachers, special education administrators and supervisors, speech-language pathologists, audiologists, adaptive physical educators, vocational educators, and infant intervention specialists.

Preparation of Related-Services Personnel supports projects that are designed to provide preservice preparation of individuals who provide developmental, corrective, and other supportive services that assist infants, toddlers, children, and youth with handicaps to benefit from special education. Training may extend to paraprofessional personnel, therapeutic recreation specialists, health service providers, physical therapists, occupational therapists, and other related-services personnel.

Preparation of Leadership Personnel supports projects that are designed to provide preservice doctoral and post-doctoral preparation of personnel such as administrators, supervisors, researchers, and teacher trainers.

Preparation of Personnel for Transition of Youth with Handicaps to Adult and Working Life supports projects designed to provide preservice preparation. Personnel may be prepared to provide short- and long-term transitional services, long-term employment services, or instruction in community and school settings with secondary school students.

Preparation of Personnel to Provide Early Intervention Services to Infants and Toddlers with Handicaps supports projects designed to provide preservice preparation of individuals who serve infants and toddlers with handicaps or those who are at high risk for having handicaps. Personnel may be prepared to provide short- or long-term services that extend into a child's preschool program.

Preparation of Personnel for Special Populations of Infants, Toddlers, Children, and Youth with Handicaps supports the preservice preparation of early intervention, special education, and related-services personnel who will serve special populations of infants, toddlers, children, and youth with handicaps. The training may include preparation of personnel to work with children with handicaps from minority groups, children with limited English proficiency, and those from disadvantaged groups.

Preparation of Personnel to Work in Rural Areas supports projects designed to provide preservice training of personnel who will serve infants, toddlers, children, and youth with handicaps in rural areas, including training of personnel to work with parents, teachers, and administrators in a rural environment.

Preparation of Personnel for Low-Incidence Handicapped Students supports preservice preparation of special educators and early intervention personnel who serve infants, toddlers, children, and youth with low-incidence handicaps in a designated state or geographic area. Training may focus on preparation of personnel to work with students with severe handicaps, including intense physical or mental problems; deaf-blindness and other multiple handicaps; serious emotional disturbance; and other health impairments, including autism and chronic or acute health problems.

Special Projects may be funded to support preservice and in-service training activities that include development, evaluation, and distribution of imaginative or innovative approaches to personnel preparation, and the development of materials to prepare personnel to educate or provide early intervention services to individuals with disabilities. This priority may also be used to support projects of national significance for the preparation of personnel needed to serve individuals with disabilities.

Parent Projects support parent organizations as defined in the statute and regulations for the purposes of providing training and information to parents of children and youth with disabilities and to volunteers who work with parents to enable those individuals to participate more effectively with professionals in meeting the educational needs of children and youth who have disabilities.

EXAMPLES OF FUNDED PROJECTS

A number of projects that focus on the preparation of personnel in the area of severe and profound handicapping conditions have been funded through the training priorities described above. The following discussion provides examples of such projects funded in these priority competitions during FY 1989. Program descriptions are adapted from a Division of Personnel Preparation program overview related to the training of individuals with severe and profound handicaps prepared by Thomas (1989).

CFDA 84.029B—Special Educators

The University of Vermont received a grant to prepare master's level educators of school-age learners with severe handicaps in need of intensive special education. Through working relationships with the Center for Developmental Disabilities, the State Interdisciplinary Team for Intensive Special Education, and the Vermont Special and Compensatory Education Unit, an interdisciplinary, competency-based preservice intensive special education master's degree program will be provided for educators of school-age learners with severe handicaps. The program expects to train approximately 10 intensive special educators a year.

CFDA 84.029F—Related Services

The University of Nebraska Medical Center requested funding to support the development and implementation of an educational and practicum sequence in handicapped and at-risk infant/toddler specialization for school psychologists. The project will provide coursework and supervised, competency-based experiences in community, hospital, and clinic settings for students in the University of Nebraska School Psychology Program.

CFDA 84.029E—Special Populations

Georgetown University received a grant to support an interdisciplinary preservice training program to provide services to medically fragile infants and their families. The focus of the training is on developing a specific knowledge base and clinical skills geared to birth to 3-year-old medically fragile infants and their families. Trainees will be drawn from professional degree programs in occupational therapy, physical therapy, speech pathology, special education, psychology, nursing, and social work. Five trainees will be selected yearly for a 6-month to 1-year clinical affiliation. They will be provided a variety of didactic and clinical experiences with medically fragile infants and their families.

CFDA 84.029G—Transition

The C.W. Post Campus of Long Island University received funding to establish a master's degree program in special education with concentrations in autism and severe developmental disabilities, community integration, and transition from school to work. The program will focus on the preparation of teachers to facilitate the transition from school to adult living and employment for students with autism and severe developmental disabilities. It will also include interdisciplinary coursework and practical experiences, with an emphasis on interagency collaboration.

CFDA 84.029J—Rural

The University of Colorado at Denver requested funding to develop, implement, and evaluate an Integration Facilitator, Severe/Profound Needs rural personnel preparation project. This project expects to prepare 60 integration facilitators for rural and small school districts in Colorado over a 5-year period. The primary role of these teachers will be to train, develop, and participate in building-level support teams for students with severe/profound needs at the preschool, elementary, and secondary levels.

CFDA 84.029Q—Infants and Newborns

The University of Arkansas for Medical Sciences and the Department of Communicative Disorders at Little Rock will provide graduate level preservice training for speech/language pathologists with special focus on infants with handicaps or at risk for handicapping conditions and their families. Speech/language pathologists will specialize in communication assessment techniques and intervention strategies appropriate with infants or toddlers and their families. A primary objective is to address existing and anticipated shortages of personnel qualified to provide services to children birth to 3 with severe communication delays, and their families.

CFDA 84.029H—State Education Agencies

The Michigan Department of Education, Special Education Services will provide a central clearinghouse to build awareness, prepare staff, and inform the field on training, research, and demonstration of promising curricula that lead to adoption of innovative practices, such as use of technology, using exemplary practices, use of new teaching approaches, and use of new materials. The project will establish the structure of a Special Education Instructional Resource Network to provide training for the use of program guides for students with visual impairments, hearing impairments, and severe mental impairments. It will also disseminate a model to improve interagency cooperative planning for transition of students to adult life. The publication and distribution of a statewide curriculum newspaper to approximately 15,000 professionals throughout Michigan will serve as the major vehicle for dissemination of information.

CFDA 84.029K—Special Projects

The Kansas Department of Education requested funding to establish and maintain a statewide in-service project that would provide training in functional applications of microcomputer technology for Kansas LEA (local education agency) personnel currently providing direct educational services to children and youth with moderate and severe disabilities who are served in programs for children and youth with mental handicaps and severe, multiple handicaps who are identified as trainable. The primary purposes of the project are: 1) to train personnel to improve and increase the number of functional applications involving technology available to these students, and 2) to create a network of personnel who will support continued expansion of technological applications after the project is completed. The project will be implemented by the Kansas State Department of Education, the University of Kansas Department of Special Education, and the Capper Foundation, a private agency that provides assessment and training in the area of assistive technology for persons with disabilities.

CFDA 84.029D—Leadership

The Division of Special Education and Rehabilitation at Syracuse University sought funding to prepare leadership personnel qualified to address emerging issues in school integration for students with severe disabilities. Four students per year will be enrolled in the program. Upon completion of the program, trainees will be able to: 1) examine emerging school integration issues utilizing quantitative and qualitative research methodologies; 2) develop, evaluate, and advocate for models that successfully integrate students with disabilities into regular schools and classes; 3) teach university classes and supervise students in practica; 4) provide consultation and technical assistance to districts and state education agencies; and 5) collaborate with school districts, state education agencies, parent groups, and other groups for the purpose of developing policies to improve integration opportunities for students with disabilities.

CFDA 84.029A—Low Incidence

A project was approved for the University of Northern Colorado to prepare master's degree level teachers to work with students who have profound disabilities. Eighteen teachers are projected to be trained during the course of the project and will be certified as teachers of students with profound needs. Teacher certification in the area of profound impairments has only recently been introduced in Colorado, and there is a critical shortage of teachers who have the skills needed to provide educational services in this area. Recruitment for trainees will focus on regular education teachers in the state of Colorado who are seeking additional certification so that they may better meet the educational needs of students with profound disabilities.

Section 632

Section 632 of the Education of the Handicapped Act Amendments directs the Secretary of Education to award a grant of sufficient size and scope to *each state education agency* that applies for either preservice or in-service training funds. This is a departure from the past when SEAs competed for funding. The discretion in awards now exists only in regard to the amount of money awarded and the length of the award. Section 632 of the legislation also authorized the Assistant Secretary to announce an additional priority that would be competitive among the SEAs for preservice training.

OSEP STANDARDS IN SPECIAL EDUCATION PERSONNEL PREPARATION

A good teacher can make an important difference in a child's progress in school. The professional literature provides a wealth of support for this assumption (Carnegie Forum's Task Force on Teaching as a Profession, 1986; Darling-Hammond, 1988; Pugach, 1987; Smith, Smith-Davis, Cross, & Morsink, 1986). Functionally, quality personnel preparation programs are, in the final analysis, those programs that produce graduates who make a difference in the lives of children with disabilities. Concern for training effective teachers is not limited to the field of special education. Similar concerns are apparent in the national debate on general educational improvement. Teacher preparation is at the heart of both school reform programs and efforts to avoid predicted teacher shortages.

Two questions arise in pursuing the development of criteria for quality: 1) what kinds of personnel preparation programs produce skilled teachers, and 2) how should OSEP structure its grant programs in personnel preparation to stimulate the development of such programs?

OSEP has taken these concerns as a challenge to formulate regulations that will: 1) improve the quality of personnel preparation efforts so that graduates are equipped with the skills needed to improve the quality of services received by children with disabilities, and 2) target federal resources in areas of present and projected need so that personnel shortages are eliminated or avoided. Current guidelines in application for new awards for the training of personnel to work with persons with disabilities (U.S. Department of Education, 1988) specifically require the applicant to address the following quality issues: 1) the impact that training will have on the quality of personnel prepared, 2) evidence of significant need for improvement in the quality of personnel, 3) qualifications of the project director and key training personnel, 4) quality of practicum training settings, 5) recruitment of well-qualified students, and 6) quality of design of the project and the plan of operation. These issues are evaluated specifically by peer reviewers.

Strategies for improved distribution of targeted personnel preparation funds to reduce and avoid shortages of specific personnel have included giving state education agencies a greater role in identifying projects that address their needs; collecting data on national needs through a separate federally funded project, separating the review of applications so that ranking for quality and for needs are done independently by specialists in each area, and holding competitions by region to ensure equitable distribution of funds.

ADDRESSING PERSONNEL SHORTAGES

The success of personnel preparation programs ultimately will be measured by the extent to which graduates are qualified for job vacancies that exist in the nation's schools. The tie between program quality and personnel needs has long been of importance to OSEP, and PL 99-457 underscores the importance of that relationship. Job vacancies exist because of attrition in the field, normal turnover in staffing, program expansion, program upgrading, demographic shifts, and other such factors. Identifying and anticipating these changes in personnel needs are critical to the successful operation of training programs and are a wise investment of personnel preparation funds by OSEP.

Targeting resources in the personnel preparation program for existing and projected staffing needs, in order to avoid shortages in particular locations and specialty areas, is a foremost concern for OSEP and for the field of special education. To encourage data-based decision-making, the PL 99-457 amendments, Part D, Section 631 (a) (2) (A) state that in making grant awards, ". . . the Secretary shall base the determination of such grants on information relating to the present and projected need for the personnel to be trained based on identified state, regional or national shortages, and the capacity of the institution or agency to train qualified personnel" (PL 99-457, Education of the Handicapped Act Amendments of 1986, S.2294, p. 220).

If personnel preparation programs are to be efficient and effective, they must accurately respond to personnel needs. Ideally, programs would not only respond to current needs data, but would also anticipate shifts in personnel needs and have the capacity to alter their programs on the basis of changing needs. As a result of appropriately targeted training programs, local education agencies would be able to readily and consistently recruit trained individuals. Personnel shortages related to specific geographical considerations should be addressed through such training programs. Geographical determinants are also an additional consideration in a national training effort and thus a necessary dimension to address when supporting training programs.

OSEP's ability to target personnel preparation resources in order to reduce or avoid shortages depends to some degree on how well personnel preparation applications utilize state, regional, and national needs data to describe personnel shortages in special education. Some of the specific needs-related information that is requested on training project applications, and that is subsequently used as selection criteria in current application guidelines, include the following: 1) the extent to which the training will have a significant impact on critical state, regional, or national needs in the quality or quantity of personnel serving infants, toddlers, children, and youth with disabilities; 2) what that significance of the personnel needs to be addressed have to the provision of special education, related services, and early intervention services; 3) evidence of critical personnel shortages in targeted speciality or geographic areas drawn from various indicators of need that are demonstrated to be relevant, reliable, and accurate; 4) significant need as evidenced by comparisons of actual and needed skills of personnel in targeted specialty or geographic areas; and 5) the impact the proposed project will have on the targeted need, including the projected number of graduates from the project each year.

Applicant Information

To define personnel needs, OSEP's personnel preparation program now relies on data submitted by applicants. These data are expected to support proposed training activities by relating needs defined in the state's Comprehensive System of Personnel Development (CSPD) to the proposed program. Differences among states in the development and use of the CSPD cause decisions about relative need in different programs or geographical areas to be extremely difficult. OSEP uses the peer review process to evaluate the needs data presented in each application. Reviewers are asked to rate the extent to which applicants have documented a need for the proposed training activities. The results of this strategy for evaluating need have been questioned. In some instances, due to variations in applicants' documenting of needs, training funds have become concentrated in some states and specialty areas, while there is relatively little local support allocated in other locations and geographical regions.

Utilization of needs data in making decisions about training priorities will help target some personnel shortages. However, data relevant to programs preparing personnel to work with students with severe handicaps are limited. A lack of data exists related to: 1) the number of children and youth with severe handicaps (Thomas & Halloran, 1987), and 2) the number of teachers who work with these students and the number of teachers in training to work in the severe handicaps sub-area of special education. There appears to be no accurate national compilation of data that documents the number of students with severe disabilities specifically. In part, this is a problem of definition. A nationally agreed upon and used definition of persons with severe handicaps is much needed (Switzky, Haywood, & Rotatori, 1982; TASH, 1987). Until an accepted definition of "severe handicap" is used to identify those students within the total special education population, program applicants, teacher trainers, and researchers must continue to use the more general data to describe the prevalence of handicapping conditions, as illustrated in Table 2.1.

Similarly, a critical need exists for data on the number of teachers needed to work with students with severe handicaps. It is also imperative to know how the numbers of teachers employed and needed have changed over time. In Table 2.2, data concerning percent of change in the number of special education teachers employed and needed during the years 1982–1986 are presented. The 10 areas of handicapping conditions tracked annually by OSEP are represented but do not reflect the number of children who have severe handicaps. Table 2.3 provides an example of the number of additional teachers needed both nationally and for one state in 1985–1986. Again, teachers of children and youth with severe handicaps are not specifically identified. The assumption can be made that the number of students with severe handicaps and the number of teachers employed and needed to work with them are somehow embedded within one or more of the existing 10 handicapping conditions typically reported. It should be noted that each state education agency may identify the severe/profound handicaps population differently, such as by age, by severity, as a subcategory within mental retardation, or as having multiple handicaps. Specific data relevant to the identification of the population with severe handicaps and the associated personnel training needs, currently depends entirely on reports from the professional community of teachers, teacher trainers, and researchers who work with this population, and professional association advocates.

Needs Data: Requirements for New Applicants

Growing public and legislative attention is being directed toward matching training funds to areas where there is a documented need for training and toward reporting benefits or products of training efforts resulting from the available dollars. Because existing information about numbers of students with different handicapping conditions varies considerably across states and is not consistently reported across OSEP competitions, the data-based needs statement supporting individual applications is a critical part of the successful application for federal training funds. Applicants should include an intensive review in the "extent of need" section for each proposed project.

To be successful, an application for funding under Section 631 (Training Personnel for the Education of the Handicapped) must: 1) contain a well-developed rationale for training that is based on identified state, regional, and/or national shortages; 2) address specific, identified personnel shortages; 3) state how the project relates to the identified personnel needs; 4) identify the impact and benefits of training to be gained by meeting the identified personnel needs; 5) include quantifiable data to substantiate the stated need for preservice training, such as actual and projected data on

Table 2.1. Percentage of school enrollment served as students with handicaps, for school years 1976–1977 and 1982–1983 through 1985–1986

Handicapping condition	1976–1977	1982–1983	1983–1984	1984–1985	1985–1986
Learning disabled	1.79	4.40	4.57	4.72	4.73
Speech impaired	2.84	2.86	2.86	2.90	2.86
Mentally retarded	2.16	1.92	1.84	1.84	1.68
Emotionally disturbed	0.64	0.89	0.91	0.96	0.95
Other health impaired	0.32	0.13	0.13	0.18	0.17
Multihandicapped	—	0.07	0.07	0.18	0.22
Hard of hearing and deaf	0.20	0.18	0.18	0.18	0.14
Orthopedically impaired	0.20	0.14	0.14	0.15	0.14
Visual handicaps	0.90	0.07	0.07	0.08	0.07
Deaf-blind	—	0.01	0.01	0.01	0.01
Total all conditions	8.24	10.76	10.89	11.19	10.97

The above percentages generally represent children from birth to age 20 served under Chapter 1 of ECIA (SOP) and children ages 3–21 years old served under EHA-Part B as a percentage of the students enrolled in prekindergarten through grade 12.

The above information was compiled from the first through the ninth reports of the *Annual report to Congress on the implementation of the Education of the Handicapped Act*, Division of Innovation and Development, OSERS/OSEP, United States Department of Education. Washington, DC: Author.

Table 2.2. Number of special education teachers employed and needed to serve children with handicaps, ages 0–21, for school years 1982–1983 through 1985–1986

Handicapping condition	1982–1983	1983–1984	1984–1985	1985–1986
Learning disabled				
Employed	82,625	89,756	102,395	111,785
Needed	9,669	4,772	7,800	10,785
Speech impaired				
Employed	19,632	20,000	36,612	39,747
Needed	1,212	1,443	2,511	3,504
Mentally retarded				
Employed	61,452	58,727	61,832	61,411
Needed	3,484	3,426	4,671	5,014
Emotionally disturbed				
Employed	29,967	28,225	32,027	32,747
Needed	2,881	2,798	4,322	4,701
Hard of hearing and deaf				
Employed	8,224	7,253	7,992	8,200
Needed	1,488	759	773	679
Multihandicapped				
Employed	5,240	5,769	8,637	9,078
Needed	913	621	618	868

Handicapping condition	1982–1983	1983–1984	1984–1985	1985–1986
Orthopedically impaired				
Employed	4,383	4,643	4,240	4,681
Needed	376	303	243	446
Other health impaired				
Employed	3,079	3,174	10,445	3,376
Needed	498	481	1,299	230
Visually handicapped				
Employed	3,275	3,047	2,995	3,261
Needed	335	289	296	342
Deaf/blind				
Employed	898	786	396	298
Needed	30	123	38	46
Noncategorical				
Employed	25,305	24,919	*	*
Needed	800	2,090	*	*
Total all conditions				
Employed	241,079	247,791	274,519	291,954
Needed	21,638	17,103	22,852	27,474

*Noncategorical data not collected or reported in the ninth and tenth annual reports.

The above information was compiled from the sixth through the ninth reports of the *Annual report to Congress on the implementation of the Education of the Handicapped Act*, Division of Innovations and Development, OSERS/OSEP, United States Department of Education. Washington, DC: Author.

Table 2.3. Number of special education teachers employed and needed, 1985–1986, State of Virginia

Handicapping conditions	Employed	Needed	Percent needed as a percentage of employed	Percent of total needed
Learning disabled	3,013	814	27.0	49.7
Mentally retarded	1,450	271	18.7	16.5
Emotionally dis-turbed	732	228	31.1	13.9
Speech impaired	798	199	24.9	12.1
Hard of hearing and deaf	163	36	22.1	2.2
Multihandicapped	112	42	37.5	2.5
Orthopedically im-paired	51	15	29.4	0.9
Other health im-paired	34	15	44.1	0.9
Visually handi-capped	75	20	26.6	1.2
Deaf-blind	2	0	—	—
Total teachers	6,431	1,638	25.5	99.9

The above information was compiled from data contained in the *Tenth annual report to Congress on the implementation of the Education of the Handicapped Act.* (1988). Division of Innovation and Development, OSERS/OSEP, United States Department of Education. Washington, DC: Author.

teacher vacancies, pupil/teacher ratios in the need area, number of uncertified personnel hired, number of new teacher positions filled, teacher attrition rate, and number of students with handicaps presently served in the need area; and 6) include a comparison ratio of new hires (new or additional teacher positions filled) to the total population of students with handicaps in the state's service area.

The application also may include: 7) self-developed data, such as: a) surveys and samples of state and local school district need; b) institution/agency data reporting number of graduates in the area of need, requests for trained personnel, placement patterns, graduates and number of unfilled positions; and c) a description of how the institution/agency has responded to the training need, such as development of new curricula or training programs, hiring of additional staff, increased number of graduates or increased in-service activities. The application should: 8) state the projected number of students that will be trained or certified in the need area for a period of time (e.g., in 3 years), as well as the number of students trained in the previous 3 years, where applicable (i.e., a comparison of the number of graduates expected from the programs to the number of graduates hired in previous years).

The application should also: 9) discuss the benefits of the proposed training to the field (e.g., How will this training benefit children and youth with handicaps? How will current practices in the need area benefit or change as a result of the proposed training?) Finally, the application should 10) review the current professional literature that pertains to the stated training need, including data and other information that substantiates a rationale for personnel need in the specialty area.

Taken together, these aspects of the need statements should demonstrate the applicant's response to the intent of the present mandate that personnel be trained on the basis of need. Related data also can be used to strengthen the needs statement. For example, census data, general teacher shortage data, and CPSD data can be analyzed to estimate numbers of students with severe disabilities and numbers of personnel required to serve them.

Census Data   Several types of data derived from census information, such as the *Current Population Reports* (Bureau of the Census, 1982), can be used in developing the needs statement, including population projections for various school-age populations, the prevalence of handicapping conditions, and teacher employment data. For example, population projection data could be integrated with available data on students with special needs in order to establish a basis for demonstrating the need for personnel in given areas of handicap.

Teacher Shortage and Attrition Data   In analyzing data on the employment of teachers in the 10 categories of handicap tracked by the Office of Special Education Programs, Bowen (1987) found that the number of teachers employed and needed in these categories increased in six areas and decreased in four others. The six areas in which the number of teachers increased over a 5-year period are learning disability, speech and language impairments, emotional disturbance, multiple handicaps, orthopedic handicaps, and deaf/blindness. The four categories in which the number of teachers decreased were mental retardation, hearing impairments, other health impairments, and visual impairments. The number of teachers employed in the latter group decreased below 1976–1977 levels, a fact that should be of concern to policy makers and university faculty. Similar findings were observed by Smith-Davis (1985) who reported the most critical teacher shortages in areas related to physical and emotional disabilities, severe behavioral disabilities and mental retardation, sensory disabilities, and personnel to work in special education at the secondary school level and in rural settings.

Beyond the number of personnel needed and hired as indicators of teacher shortage, two other major factors that appear to be closely related to the shortfall of personnel are the decrease in new degree awards and teacher attrition. In a 10-year review of special education degree awards, Bowen (1988) found: 1) a consistent drop of 500–1,000 special education teachers being graduated per year; 2) a diminution of degrees conferred across all degree levels and categories; and 3) a rapid reduction of the total number of degrees awarded in special education. Furthermore, there is some evidence that special education teachers in general, and teachers in certain areas of disability in particular, have a higher attrition rate than the national average of all teachers. Smith-Davis, Burke, and Noel (1984) report that, although 10 times as many teachers were hired for children with severe disabilities in 1984–1985 as were employed in 1975–1976, the attrition rate for these personnel is 30%, compared to 6% for all teachers and 12% for all special education teachers. Grosenick and Huntze (1982) report that the attrition rate for teachers of students with behavioral disorders has been reported as high as 54%. Personnel working in special education at the secondary school level and in rural settings also are lacking (Smith-Davis, 1985).

Annual Reports to Congress on the Implementation of the Education of the Handicapped Act   Each year a comprehensive report is prepared by the Division of Innovation and Development, a division within the Office of Special Education Programs, and sent to Congress. Data in the report are compiled from the responses to a standard set of questions sent to each state director of special education. The first report was prepared on 1976–1977 data and the most recent is the 11th report. The reports are an invaluable source of data, covering such topics as number of students served in each of 10 handicapping conditions, number of teachers employed and needed, number of related-services personnel employed and needed, and state and national compilations of data.

National Clearinghouse for Professions in Special Education   The National Clearinghouse for Professions in Special Education was mandated by Congress through PL 99-457 and was initially funded in fiscal year 1988. The clearinghouse, through its Supply/Demand Analysis Center, collects, monitors, and reviews a wide range of relevant information concerning the supply and need for special education professionals. A wide range of useful publications, in the form of topical papers, is disseminated on such topics as educating personnel from minority groups; measurement of personnel needs in special education; the decline of special education degrees conferred; competency testing; alternative teacher certification; national, regional, and state accreditation profiles; and annotated bibliographies.

State CSPD Documents Each state is required by Congress to produce a CSPD document that details the number of students receiving services, the number of personnel available and their training, and other related information. Prospective applicants would be well advised to obtain a copy of their state's CSPD document and study it prior to and during the development of a proposed training program. Applicants may also wish to consult with their state CSPD coordinator regarding available state data, how the data were collected, and possible interpretations of the data.

The Condition of Education *The Condition of Education* and a companion publication, *Digest of Education Statistics,* are published data studies produced by the staff of the National Center for Education Statistics, Office of Educational Research and Improvement. These publications highlight statistical information concerning regular and special education, teacher supply and demand, attrition studies, and school conditions. For example, *The Condition of Education* (NCES, 1988) tracks, the national need for special education teachers and lists the areas of greatest shortage.

Higher Education General Information Survey The National Center for Education Statistics also publishes the *Higher Education General Information Survey,* which contains results from an annual survey of states and institutions of higher education regarding the number of degrees conferred in higher education. Each state is asked to submit the number of degrees granted at the baccalaureate, master's, and doctoral levels in all fields of education, including all specialty areas in general education and special education. The data are collected by institution from each state. Useful information concerning the number of graduates in the various categories of special education can be obtained if an individual is willing to spend time collating the available figures.

American Society for College and University Staffing (ASCUS) Each year the American Society for College and University Staffing (ASCUS) surveys teacher placement officers in institutions of higher education and publishes relative demand data in a wide variety of teaching fields (Akin, 1987). Teaching fields are rated on a scale of one (least demand) to five (greatest demand) in order to identify teaching fields with considerable teacher shortages in comparison with teaching fields with a surplus of teachers. Special education specialty areas are rated along with other teaching fields. The example in Table 2.4 shows the ASCUS compilation of relative demand by teaching area over a range of several years.

State and University Surveys and Reports Specifically designed and conducted surveys, studies, or research projects that analyze a particular topic or need at the state or institutional level can be most useful in documenting a training need. Data are collected and reported to answer such questions as: 1) where program graduates are employed, 2) how many

Table 2.4. Relative demand by teaching area and year (contiguous forty-eight states)

	1989*	1988*	1987	1986*	1985	1982	1976*
Teaching fields with considerable teacher shortage (5.00–4.25):							
Bilingual Education	4.45	4.35	4.42	4.27	4.12	4.13	—
Special Education–BD	4.40	4.33	4.30	4.20	4.02	3.98	3.42
Special Education–Ment. Handi.	4.29	4.15	3.97	4.25	3.76	3.84	2.87
Special Education–LD	4.26	4.26	4.46	4.23	3.95	4.20	4.00
Speech Pathology/Audio.	4.25	4.00	4.21	4.09	4.01	3.95	3.68
Teaching fields with some teaching shortage (4.24–3.45):							
Special Education–Multi. Handi.	4.14	4.26	3.85	4.25	3.94	3.93	—
Science–Physics	4.12	4.01	4.26	4.44	4.57	4.41	4.04
Special Education–Deaf	4.12	3.91	3.81	3.72	—	—	3.72
Science–Chemistry	4.01	3.96	4.21	4.40	4.42	4.13	3.72
Special Education–Gifted	3.93	3.74	3.88	3.91	3.85	3.81	3.85
Mathematics	3.83	4.00	4.35	4.55	4.71	4.81	3.86
Psychologist (school)	3.79	3.57	3.46	3.43	3.65	3.56	3.09
Language, Mod.–Spanish	3.76	3.59	3.57	3.64	3.43	2.68	2.47
Computer Science	3.75	3.79	3.98	4.22	4.37	—	—
Library Science	3.60	3.56	3.33	3.39	3.49	3.12	—
Data Processing	3.58	3.59	3.81	3.97	4.30	3.86	—
Special–Reading	3.58	3.43	3.45	3.46	3.39	3.73	3.96
Science–Earth	3.55	3.52	3.43	3.86	3.79	3.89	3.44
Language, Mod.–French	3.51	3.43	3.24	3.34	3.31	2.49	2.15
Teaching fields with balance supply and demand (3.44–2.65):							
Science–General	3.43	3.42	3.32	3.82	3.65	—	—
Language, Mod.–German	3.42	3.34	3.15	3.26	3.11	2.48	2.03

Counselor-Elementary	3.40	3.12	3.31	3.04	3.05	2.72	3.15
Science-Biology	3.35	3.37	3.33	3.65	3.58	3.66	2.97
Counselor-Secondary	3.26	3.03	3.24	3.05	3.08	2.79	2.69
Music-Instrumental	3.20	3.00	3.29	3.14	3.29	3.28	3.03
Social Worker (school)	3.03	3.01	2.82	2.77	2.81	2.34	—
Music-Vocal	3.00	2.89	3.11	2.95	3.19	2.95	3.00
English	2.97	3.11	3.02	3.25	3.14	3.21	2.05
Industrial Arts	2.95	3.07	3.24	3.30	3.65	4.36	4.22
Speech	2.95	2.91	2.86	2.72	2.91	2.76	2.46
Agriculture	2.93	2.88	2.81	3.23	3.11	4.36	4.06
Business	2.84	2.90	2.94	3.11	3.32	3.47	3.10
Journalism	2.76	2.91	3.00	2.93	2.74	2.61	2.86
Driver Education	2.71	2.70	2.67	2.46	2.05	2.77	2.44
Teaching fields with some surplus of teachers (2.64–1.85):							
Elementary-Primary	2.63	2.71	2.58	2.70	2.57	2.02	1.78
Elementary-Intermediate	2.62	2.72	2.61	2.78	2.53	2.26	1.90
Home Economics	2.33	2.26	2.16	2.51	2.79	2.43	2.62
Art	2.24	2.35	1.89	2.20	2.04	1.84	2.14
Health Education	2.03	2.02	1.95	1.92	2.08	1.90	2.27
Social Science	1.98	2.00	2.05	2.11	2.17	2.11	1.51
Teaching field with considerable surplus of teachers (1.84–1.00):							
Physical Education	1.78	1.67	1.53	1.60	1.75	1.72	1.74

*Mailings for the 1976, 1986, 1988 and 1989 reports included all teacher placement offices which were members of ASCUS.

5 = Considerable Shortage; 4 = Some Shortage; 3 = Balanced; 2 = Some Surplus; 1 = Considerable Surplus

Akin, J. (1989). *Teacher supply and demand: A recent survey.* Manhattan, KS: American Society for College and University Staffing. Reprinted with permission.

teachers are being hired each year, and 3) how long graduates stay in special education. These data can provide excellent documentation for establishing the need for a training program.

Taken together, the data sources reviewed here represent powerful sources of information for establishing and justifying the basis of need for specific, proposed training programs. Citation of relevant data that support the development of a training program in an area of critical need or shortage can greatly enhance the strength of an application. As stated earlier, the funding of training programs is closely tied to the congressional mandate that training should be related to the present and projected need for personnel identified by state, regional, or national shortages.

CONCLUSION

The focus of this chapter has been the statutes, regulations, and the priorities of the Training Personnel for the Education of the Handicapped program, in particular, the importance and inclusion of needs-based data in grant applications submitted to CFDA 84.029 under Part D of PL 99-457. The basis for a needs data approach is found in the current law, public opinion, and available professional resources. The successful applicant will have utilized a variety of data that document the need for the proposed training program.

REFERENCES

Akin, J. (1989). *Teacher supply and demand: A recent survey.* Manhattan, KS: American Society for College and University Staffing.

Bacon, F. (1625). Of ceremonies and respects (essay). Cambridge, England.

Bowen, M. (1987). *A review of national and state population data related to students receiving special education services, number of special education teachers employed and supply of new teachers.* Unpublished manuscript.

Bowen, M. (1988). *Leadership training in special education: A status analysis.* Washington, DC: National Association of State Directors of Special Education.

Bureau of the Census. (1982). *Current population reports: Population estimates and projections.* Series P-25, No. 922. Washington, DC: Bureau of the Census, U.S. Department of Commerce.

Carnegie Forum's Task Force on Teaching as a Profession. (1986). *A nation prepared: Teachers for the 21st. century.* Princeton: Carnegie Forum on Education and Economy.

Darling-Hammond, L. (1988). *Assessing teacher supply and demand.* Santa Monica, CA: Rand Publications.

Division of Education Services, OSERS/OSEP. (1988). *Tenth annual report to Congress on the implementation of the Education of the Handicapped Act.* Washington, DC: U.S. Department of Education.

Education of the Handicapped Act Amendments, PL 99-457. (1986). S.2294, Part D, Section 631.

Grosenick, J., & Huntze, S. (1982). *National needs analysis in behavior disorders.* Unpublished manuscript, University of Missouri, Department of Special Education, Columbia.

National Center for Education Statistics. (1988). *The condition of education: Elementary and secondary education* (Vol. I). Washington, DC: Office of Educational Research and Improvement, U.S. Department of Education.

Pugach, M. (1987). The national education reports and special education: Implications for teacher education. *Exceptional Children, 53*(4), 308–314.

Smith, D., Smith-Davis, J., Cross, D., & Morsink, C. (1986). *The need for special education leadership training.* Unpublished manuscript, Higher Education Consortium for Special Education Research Committee.

Smith-Davis, J. (1985). Issues in education: Personnel supply and demand in special education. *Counterpoint,* December.

Smith-Davis, J., Burke, P., & Noel, M. (1984). *Personnel to educate the handicapped in America: Supply and demand from a programmatic viewpoint.* College Park, MD: Institute for the Study of Exceptional Children and Youth, Department of Special Education, University of Maryland.

Switzky, H., Haywood, C., & Rotatori, A. (1982). Who are the severely and profoundly mentally retarded? *Education and Training of the Mentally Retarded, 17* (4), 268–272.

The Association for Persons with Severe Handicaps (TASH). (1987). Definitions of severely handicapped. *TASH Newsletter.*

Thomas, M.A. (1989). *Division of Personnel Preparation Program overview: Grant awards supporting the preparation of personnel training individuals with severe and profound handicaps.* Washington, DC: Division of Personnel Preparation, OSERS/OSEP, U.S. Department of Education.

Thomas, M.A., & Halloran, W. (1987). Facts and attitudes about adult services for people with severe disabilities. *American Rehabilitation, 13* (3), 20–25.

United States Department of Education. (1988). New application for grants under training personnel for the education of the handicapped, FY 1989. *Federal Register, 53*(218), 45730–45740.

United States Department of Education. (1989). Application for new awards under certain direct grant programs for Fiscal Year 1990. *Federal Register, 54*(139), 30640–30676.

Current Federal Policies Affecting Personnel Preparation

Celane M. McWhorter

The federal government is a pervasive presence in programs designed to train personnel to work with and support individuals with severe disabilities. Federal money has been targeted to support training in virtually every area that has such personnel.

Federal funding covers only a small portion of the overall costs of personnel training programs. Yet, federal dollars often are essential in establishing new training efforts and maintaining the quality of continuing programs.

The relationship between federal policy and personnel preparation strategies used in the field of severe disability is a complex one. From a strictly fiscal perspective the federal government is highly influential in determining local program designs. However, professionals in the field are likewise influential in defining the parameters of federal policy and priorities for funding. It is difficult to point to the "lead influence." In fact, it is probably true that influence is exerted in both directions. Existing programs are shaped by the federal interpretation of current needs and priorities and by training strategies as represented by professionals and advocates from the field. To the extent that the field identifies well documented needs and exemplary practices, and presents data that indicate success or clear promise of success of these practices, the field influences federal policy. Once the policy for federal spending is set, those seeking federal assistance respond in accordance with that policy. Training programs in the field may be directly or indirectly shaped by the requirements specified in federal regulations associated with the allocation of training funds.

Given the role of federal policy in influencing and supporting program design, it is very important for professionals to understand the federal policy-making process. The purpose of this chapter is to provide an overview of federal resources and to survey the processes that determine the allocation of these resources for personnel preparation.

FEDERAL POLICY-MAKING

There are two major processes involved in federal policy-making: legislative and regulative. The first obviously occurs in the United States Congress and the second in the federal departments.

How a Bill Becomes a Law

There are multiple decision points through which a bill must pass before meeting with success (Oleszek, 1984), and many more bills fail than pass. At every decision point a majority of the voting body (subcommittee, committee, full House or Senate, conference committee) is needed for passage. Typically, compromises occur at every decision point, and a bill can be significantly altered before it is signed into law.

Figure 3.1 is a concise depiction of the legislative process. A successful bill is: 1) introduced; 2) given a committee assignment; 3) given a subcommittee assignment; 4) passed by the subcommittee, typically after hearings are held to gather information from national expertise; 5) passed by the full committee and sent to the House/Senate floor for a vote (note: in the House there is a detour to the Rules committee where the bill is given a rule for floor debate); 6) passed by the full House/Senate and then on to the other body for the same actions, unless it has already been introduced in the other body as a similar measure; 7) sent to a conference committee, made up of senior members of the committees through which it passed in both houses, to iron out the differences in the two versions of the bill; 8) sent back to the House and Senate as a compromise, which is then passed by both; and finally, 9) sent to the president to be signed.

Although the basic mechanics of the process are straightforward, the process rarely is simple. There are many opportunities for waiver of the rules in both the House and the Senate. Behind the scenes negotiations, compromises, and agreements control the process. These are, in many cases, elusive at best to all but the most astute observer. Disability professionals, parents, and other advocates play an important role in the develop-

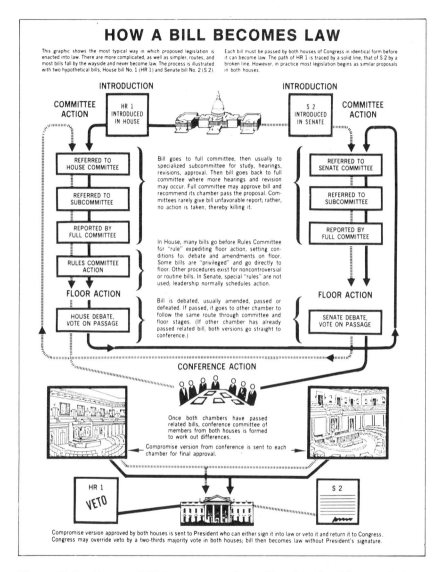

HOW A BILL BECOMES LAW

This graphic shows the most typical way in which proposed legislation is enacted into law. There are more complicated, as well as simpler, routes, and most bills fall by the wayside and never become law. The process is illustrated with two hypothetical bills, House bill No. 1 (HR 1) and Senate bill No. 2 (S 2).

Each bill must be passed by both houses of Congress in identical form before it can become law. The path of HR 1 is traced by a solid line, that of S 2 by a broken line. However, in practice most legislation begins as similar proposals in both houses.

INTRODUCTION		INTRODUCTION

COMMITTEE ACTION

HR 1 INTRODUCED IN HOUSE

S 2 INTRODUCED IN SENATE

COMMITTEE ACTION

REFERRED TO HOUSE COMMITTEE

Bill goes to full committee, then usually to specialized subcommittee for study, hearings, revisions, approval. Then bill goes back to full committee where more hearings and revision may occur. Full committee may approve bill and recommend its chamber pass the proposal. Committees rarely give bill unfavorable report; rather, no action is taken, thereby killing it.

REFERRED TO SENATE COMMITTEE

REFERRED TO SUBCOMMITTEE

REFERRED TO SUBCOMMITTEE

REPORTED BY FULL COMMITTEE

REPORTED BY FULL COMMITTEE

RULES COMMITTEE ACTION

In House, many bills go before Rules Committee for "rule" expediting floor action, setting conditions for debate and amendments on floor. Some bills are "privileged" and go directly to floor. Other procedures exist for noncontroversial or routine bills. In Senate, special "rules" are not used; leadership normally schedules action.

FLOOR ACTION

FLOOR ACTION

HOUSE DEBATE, VOTE ON PASSAGE

Bill is debated, usually amended, passed or defeated. If passed, it goes to other chamber to follow the same route through committee and floor stages. (If other chamber has already passed related bill, both versions go straight to conference.)

SENATE DEBATE, VOTE ON PASSAGE

CONFERENCE ACTION

Once both chambers have passed related bills, conference committee of members from both houses is formed to work out differences.

Compromise version from conference is sent to each chamber for final approval.

HR 1

VETO

S 2

Compromise version approved by both houses is sent to President who can either sign it into law or veto it and return it to Congress. Congress may override veto by a two-thirds majority vote in both houses; bill then becomes law without President's signature.

Figure 3.1. How a bill becomes a law. (Reprinted with permission, *Congressional Quarterly Inc.*)

ment of legislation for special education, rehabilitation, developmental disabilities, and so forth. At every decision point the successful advocates can influence the outcome through concerted grassroots activities and effective representation in Washington.

TYPES OF LEGISLATION

There are three major types of legislation: budget resolution (and in most years the accompanying reconciliation legislation), authorization, and appropriation.

Budget Resolution

The annual budget cycle begins in January/February each year when the president submits a budget proposal to the Congress. The president's proposed budget figures are based on work that begins in the executive branch agencies the previous spring, almost a year before the actual legislative work.

The Congress immediately begins work on the administration's budget with a goal of a budget resolution passed by late spring. The resolution sets spending targets and is used as a blueprint for funding decisions for the following year. In the 1980s the budget began to routinely include reconciliation instructions. Following those instructions, each authorizing committee adjusts the programs for which they are responsible to bring their spending totals in line with the spending targets in the congressional budget.

Authorization

Authorizing legislation establishes the purposes and guidelines for a particular federal activity, thus providing parameters for federal spending (Collender, 1987). Federal dollars can only be spent on programs that have been authorized. In most cases the authority is good for a limited number of years and must be renewed, that is, reauthorized, before the expiration date if the programs funded are to continue with federal support.

Appropriations

Appropriations are based on the authorizations and are guided by the mandates of the budget resolution for the year. The appropriating legislation provides the actual funds for the next fiscal year. Without an appropriation, funds cannot be spent. Without an authorization, funds generally cannot be appropriated. Appropriations often include specific programmatic instructions, known in Washington as "pork."

Both an authorization and appropriation are necessary if a program is to be funded (Collender, 1987). It is not unusual for the appropriation to be less than the authorized level. Most of the funding decisions are strongly influenced by the state of the economy. Since the early 1980s the economic climate has led to more frugal committee decisions.

THE COMMITTEE SYSTEM

The primary work on legislation takes place in committees. These bodies are created to prepare legislation and to conduct investigations into particular areas over which they have been assigned jurisdictional responsibility. This is where the major legislative decisions are made. There are 22 standing committees in the House and 15 in the Senate. Committee assignments are made at the beginning of every new Congress by the Speaker of the House and the Majority Leader of the Senate. The committees for the most part are broken into subcommittees that have even more specialized jurisdiction. For example, special education issues fall within the jurisdiction of the Senate Labor and Human Resources Committee, with the bulk of the expertise and work in this area occurring in the Subcommittee on Disability Policy (previously the Subcommittee on the Handicapped). Special education shares this subcommittee with a limited number of other issue areas, including rehabilitation and developmental disabilities.

Except in very rare instances, committees must pass legislation before it can be considered by the full House or Senate. Committees are the strongest determinants of a bill's future; they have the power to deny initial consideration of a bill; to reject a bill, thus preventing it from moving any further; or to amend it or alter it dramatically. Most lobbying activities occur at the subcommittee or committee levels through personal contacts, letter writing, and other forms of communication with the senators, representatives, and their staffs who serve on these subcommittees and committees.

REGULATION

Once the president has signed a bill into law, it becomes the responsibility of the administrative branch. Professional bureaucrats spend months thoroughly studying the new statutory language as well as any other legislative history that might aid them in gaining a clear understanding of congressional intent and in making interpretations of the statute that will withstand judicial scrutiny. Based on this information, they draft regulations that will "drive" implementation of the law. Legislative history is made up of committee reports accompanying a bill from the committee to the full House or Senate; conference reports that outline compromises made in the conference committees; clarifying statements inserted in the *Congressional Record,* especially colliloquies between two members to clarify intent; and other written records that can be considered official congressional documents.

Draft regulations usually are printed in the *Federal Register* in the form of a "Notice of Proposed Rulemaking" (NPRM), and the public is given the opportunity to review them and provide comments. There is a deadline indicated and comments must be received by that deadline. The bureaucrats then review the comments and determine if changes should be made to the proposed regulations before they are finalized. Once finalized they are again published in the *Federal Register.* The federal department generally develops interim policies that are followed until this process is complete.

Guided by the regulations, spending priorities for most federal disability programs are set on a regular basis. These also are published in the *Federal Register,* providing to the field direction needed to design competitive programs. Finally, the *Federal Register* announces competitions for funds, usually in the form of "Requests for Proposals" (RFP). The RFP includes the priorities and application deadlines.

FEDERAL RESOURCES FOR TRAINING

Federal resources generally can be placed in one of four categories:

1. Directly funded federal training programs provide funds that flow directly from the federal agency to the recipient organization for the explicit purpose of personnel preparation.
2. Discretionary federal training programs provide funds that flow directly from the federal agency to the recipient organization, with federal discretionary authority to include training as a priority for the funding.
3. State optional training programs provide federal funds to the states with an array of options for expenditures, one of which is personnel preparation.
4. Indirectly supported training programs provide federal funds that flow from the federal agency either directly or indirectly to the program for purposes other than personnel training but that result in the opportunity for rich, hands-on training, usually through student involvement with research and demonstration by the program coordinator.

Directly Funded Federal Training Programs

The most apparent federal support comes from those programs that are directly funded by the government with specific training missions. An overview of these resources is found in Table 3.1. (See also Table 3.2.)

Table 3.1 also illustrates the policy-making process from congressional action through program implementation. Statutory language provides the foundation from which all policy is built. The side-by-side reading of the statute, regulations, priorities, and program implementation examples reveals the ways in which the federal agencies build upon the congressional edict. Table 3.1 also includes the 1989 authorization and appropriation levels as a means of demonstrating how the two figures can differ, with the actual funding level (appropriation) often being lower than the amount authorized.

The most readily apparent of the federal training initiatives for individuals are the direct training authorities in the Education of the Handicapped Act, 1970, PL 91-230. There is discretionary training authority in many sections of this act, but only in Part D are funds clearly and exclusively earmarked for personnel training. During the most recent reauthorization of this act, the inadequacy of training funds under Section 631 and Section 632, Training Personnel for the Education of the Handicapped, was a major issue. There was strong advocacy for increased levels of funding.

The Rehabilitation Services Administration (RSA) funds training programs through Title III of the Rehabilitation Act, 1973, PL 93-112. In the late 1980s a portion of this money began to be directed toward training programs for supported employment personnel. Table 3.1 reflects the two RSA programs that have most aggressively sought supported employment personnel training programs: Rehabilitation Long Term Training and Experimental and Innovative Training.

Also, within the Department of Education, training programs are funded by the National Institute on Disability and Rehabilitation Research. The Rehabilitation Research and Training Centers (RRTCs) include a training component, and thus, are included in category one of federal resources even though they are not limited to a training mandate. Likewise, with their core federal funds, the University Affiliated Programs can participate in more than training, but a UAP will not be funded unless there is evidence of strong multidisciplinary training activities.

Discretionary Federal Training Programs

There are a number of programs authorized under the Education of the Handicapped Act that do not include a mandate for personnel training. The authority does, however, for many of these programs provide the Department of Education the discretion to add training as a funding priority in any given year. For example, Section 624, Programs for Severely Handicapped Children, for 1988 and 1989 has included an in-service training priority. Many of these projects have provided valuable training opportunities, especially for personnel already working with individuals with severe disabilities but with little opportunity to remain abreast of the rapidly changing state of the art. Table 3.3 includes an overview of the major federal programs in category two of federal resources. (See also Table 3.2.)

State Optional Training Programs

In addition to the above described federal discretionary funds which are awarded to grant recipients for specific purposes, federal funds are distributed to states under certain authorities for services that are less prescriptive. For example, based on a child count, funds are distributed to states through formulas to provide a free and appropriate education for students within the state who have disabilities (PL 94-142, the Education for All Handicapped Children Act of 1975 and PL 89-313, revised by Chapter 1, Education Consolidation and Improvement Act, 1965, which authorized the State Operated Programs for Handicapped Children). Also distributed by formula are federal funds to the developmental disability planning councils. Medicaid

Table 3.1. Personnel training: Federal programs with specified training function

Agency/ program	Statute	Regulation
Training for the Education of the Handicapped, Department of Education, OSEP Grants for personnel training	Part D, Section 631, EHA. a) (1) The Secretary may make grants, which may include scholarships with necessary stipends and allowances, to institutions of higher education including the university-affiliated facilities . . . and other appropriate nonprofit agencies to assist them in training personnel for careers in special education and early intervention, including (A) special education teaching, including speech-language pathology and audiology, and adaptive physical education, (B) related services to handicapped children and youth in educational settings, (C) special education supervision and administration, (D) special education research, and (E) training of special education personnel and other personnel providing special services and preschool and early intervention services for handicapped children. (b) The Secretary may make grants to institutions of higher education and other appropriate non-profit agencies to conduct special projects to develop and demonstrate new approaches (including the application of new technology) for the preservice training purposes set	34 CFR 318.1. This program serves to increase the quantity and improve the quality of personnel available to serve infants, toddlers, children, and youth with handicaps through— a) The provision of awards to support the preservice training of personnel for careers in special education and early intervention . . . The secretary supports three types of projects under this program: a) Special projects designed to include— (1) Development, evaluation, and distribution of innovative approaches to personnel preparation; (2) Development of materials to prepare personnel to educate or provide early intervention services to infants, toddlers, children and youth with handicaps; and (3) Other projects of national significance for the preparation of personnel needed to serve infants, toddlers, children and youth with handicaps. (b) Development of new programs designed to establish and increase the capacity and quality of preservice training; and (c) Improvement of existing programs designed to maintain and upgrade the

(*continued*)

Table 3.1.   *(continued)*

Priorities	Implementation example	Funding level
(1) Preparation of personnel for careers in special education and early intervention	U. of Oregon, certificate or master's-level preservice for community-based training with students with severe handicaps	1989 Auth: 79.0 1989 Appropr: 67.1 (Total Training)
(2) Preparation of related services personnel	U. of Minnesota, master's- and undergraduate-level, recreation specialists to work in community-based programs for students with severe disabilities	
(3) Preparation of leadership personnel	U. of Wisconsin, doctoral-level preservice, severe communication and behavior disorders	
(4) Preparation of personnel for transition of youth with handicaps to adult and working life	Eastern Montana, master's-level preservice, transitional services for students with severe handicaps	
(5) Preparation of personnel to provide early intervention services to infants and toddlers with handicaps	U. of Maryland, master's-level preservice, early childhood special education	
(6) Preparation of personnel for special populations of infants, toddlers, children and youth with handicaps	Kent State U., master's-level preservice, severe behavior disorders in inner city settings. (Note: such as minority and disadvantaged groups, and limited English proficiency)	
(7) Preparation of personnel to work in rural areas	U. of Kentucky, graduate-level preservice, severe/profound in rural settings	

(continued)

Table 3.1. (*continued*)

Agency/ program	Statute	Regulation
	forth in subsection (a), for regular education, for the training of teachers to work in community and school settings with handicapped secondary school students, and for the inservice training of special education personnel, including classroom aides, related services personnel, and regular education personnel who serve handicapped children and personnel providing early intervention services.	capacity and quality of preservice training.
		34 CFR 318.4 What priorities may the Secretary establish?
		One or more of the following . . .
		(1) Preparation of personnel for careers in special education and early intervention . . .
		(2) Preparation of related services personnel . . .
		(3) Preparation of leadership personnel . . .
		(4) Preparation of personnel for transition of youth with handicaps to adult and working life . . .
		(5) Preparation of personnel to provide early intervention services to infants and toddlers with handicaps . . .
		(6) Preparation of personnel for special populations of infants, toddlers, children, and youth with handicaps . . .
		(7) Preparation of personnel to work in rural areas . . .

(*continued*)

Table 3.1. (*continued*)

Priorities	Implementation example	Funding level
(8) Special projects	Kansas Department of Education, in-service, functional applications of microcomputer technology for LEA personnel working with students with moderate/severe disabilities	
(9) Preparation of personnel for low incidence handicapped students (Specifically: severe handicaps, deaf, blind, serious emotional disturbance, other health impairments).	University of Kansas, master's-level preservice for professionals to work with students with severe-/profound or multiple handicaps or deaf/blindness	

(*continued*)

Table 3.1. (*continued*)

Agency/ program	Statute	Regulation
		(8) Special projects . . . In addition the Secretary may select . . . as a priority the support of preservice preparation of . . . personnel who serve infants, toddlers, children, and youth with low-incidence handicaps . . . (1) Severe handicaps . . . (2) Deaf. (3) Blind. (4) Serious emotional disturbance. (5) Other health impairments, including autism and chronic or acute health problems.
Grants to SEA and Inst. for Traineeships, Department of Education, OSEP	Sec. 632, EHA. The Secretary shall make grants to each State educational agency and may make grants to institutions of higher education to assist in establishing and maintaining preservice and in-service programs to prepare personnel to meet the needs of handicapped infants, toddlers, children, and youth or supervisors of such persons, consistent with the personnel needs identified in the State's comprehensive system of personnel development under section 613.	34 CFR 318.1 (d) Projects to assist State educational agencies in establishing and maintaining, directly or through grants to institutions of higher education, programs for the preservice and in-service training of teachers of handicapped children and youth, or supervisors of such teachers.
Rehabilitation Training, Department of Education, RSA	Title III. Sec. 304, Rehabilitation Act of 1973. (a) The Commissioner may make grants to and contracts with State and public or nonprofit agencies and organizations, including institutions of higher	34 CFR 385.1 What is the Rehabilitation Training Program? (a) The Rehabilitation Training Program is designed to— (1) Increase the supply of qualified personnel

(*continued*)

Table 3.1.   (*continued*)

Priorities	Implementation example	Funding level
No published priorities	Vermont State Education Agency, (1) statewide training assistance grant to support local schools to serve students with special needs, (2) paraprofessional training program through local schools and community college, (3) in-service to work with local school personnel in supporting students with serious emotional disturbance.	Included in total funding levels above.
Published under separate training categories (see below).	See separate training categories, below	1989 Auth: 35.0, 1989 Appropr: 30.5 (Total rehabilitation funding)

(*continued*)

Table 3.1.   *(continued)*

Agency/ program	Statute	Regulation
	education, to pay part of the cost of projects for training, traineeships, and related activities designed to assist in increasing the numbers of qualified personnel trained in providing vocational, medical, social, and psychological rehabilitation services to individuals with handicaps including . . . personnel specifically trained to identify, assess, and meet the individual rehabilitation needs of individuals with severe handicaps.	available for employment in public and private agencies and institutions involved in the vocational rehabilitation of physically and mentally handicapped individuals, especially those individuals with the most severe handicaps. . .
	(b) In making such grants or contracts, funds made available for any years shall be targeted to areas of personnel shortage which may include projects in rehabilitation engineering, rehabilitation medicine, rehabilitation nursing, rehabilitation counseling, . . . specialized personnel in providing employment training for supported employment, other specialized personnel for those individuals who meet the definition of severely handicapped. . .	(b) The Secretary awards financial assistance through five categories of training programs— (1) Rehabilitation Long Term Training; (2) Exprimental and Innovative Training; (3) State Vocational Rehabilitation Unit In-Service Training; (4) Rehabilitation Continuing Education Programs; (5) Rehabilitation Short-Term Training.
Rehabilitation Long Term Training, Department of Education, RSA	Sec. 304, Rehabilitation Act (see above)	34 CFR 386.10 What types of projects are authorized under this program? The Rehabilitation Long-Term Training Program provides financial assistance for— (a) Projects that provide basic or advanced training

(continued)

Table 3.1. (*continued*)

Priorities	Implementation example	Funding level
Priority 1—Rehabilitation Counseling Pro-jects. . .must provide training at the master's degree level that is designed to improve and strengthen the capacity of rehabilitation counselors to serve and place	San Francisco State Univer-sity, master's-level pro-gram for rehabilitation administrators with focus on community collabora-tion	(Included in total reha-bilitation funding level, above)

(*continued*)

Table 3.1.   *(continued)*

Agency/program	Statute	Regulation
		leading to an academic degree in one of those fields of study identified in section 386.1.
		(b) Projects that provide a number of interrelated training activities designed to improve the professional competence of employed rehabilitation workers in one of those fields of study identified in section 386.1 but not directly related to the awarding of an academic degree.
		(c) Projects that provide undergraduate medical students an orientation to the concepts and techniques of rehabilitation medicine.
		(d) Projects that provide support for medical residents enrolled in residency training programs in the specialty of physical medicine and rehabilitation.
		. . .the Secretary will set aside funds and give an absolute preference to applications. . .that address one of the priorities described . . .
Experimental and Innovative Training, Department of Education, RSA	Sec. 304, Rehabilitation Act (see above)	34 CFR 387.1 What is the Experimental and Innovative Training Program? This program is designed— (a) To develop new types of rehabilitation personnel, and to demonstrate the effectiveness of these new types of personnel in

(continued)

Table 3.1. (*continued*)

Priorities	Implementation example	Funding level
individuals with severe disabilities in employment, especially competitive employment, and arrange for independent living rehabilitation services and promote community options for individuals with severe disabilities. (FY 1989)		
This program must address the training of personnel to provide community-based supported employment.	TASH 3-year project to develop demonstration sites for creation of support networks for individuals in supported employment; includes training personnel in the techniques of creating support networks	(Included in total rehabilitation training level, above)

(*continued*)

Table 3.1.   (*continued*)

Agency/ program	Statute	Regulation
		providing rehabilitation services to severely handicapped persons; and
		(b) To develop new and improved methods of training rehabilitation personnel so that there may be a more effective delivery of rehabilitation services by State and other rehabilitation agencies.
		387.10 What types of projects are authorized under this program?
		The Experimental and Innovative Training Program supports time-limited pilot projects through which new types of rehabilitation workers may be trained or through which innovative methods of training rehabilitation workers may be demonstrated.
RRTC Department of Education, NIDRR	Sec. 202, Rehabilitation Act. (a) In order to promote and coordinate research with respect to handicapped individuals and to more effectively carry out the programs under section 104, there is established within the Department of Education, a National Institute on Disability and Rehabilitation Research. . .	34 CFR 352.1 What is the rehabilitation research and training center's program? This program is designed to support the establishment and operation of Rehabilitation Research and Training Centers for the purpose of— (a) Providing training (including graduate training) to research and other rehabilitation personnel and to assist individuals to more effectively provide rehabilitation services; and
	Sec. 204 (a) The Director may make grants to and contracts with States and public or private agencies and organizations, including	

(continued)

Table 3.1. (*continued*)

Priorities	Implementation example	Funding level
(1) Rehabilitation for persons with long-term mental illness; (2) Improving management effectiveness in independent living; (3) Research in policy issues in independent living; (4) Community integration for persons with mental retardation.	Rehabilitation Research and Training Center on Supported Employment, Virginia Commonwealth University Beach Center on Families and Disabilities, University of Kansas Non-Aversive Community Referenced Behavior Management, University of Oregon	1989 Auth: 55.0 1989 Appropr: 52.2

(*continued*)

Table 3.1. (*continued*)

Agency/ program	Statute	Regulation
	institutions of higher education, to pay part of the cost of projects for the purpose of planning and conducting research . . . to assist in the provision of vocational and other rehabilitation services to individuals with disabilities, especially those with the most severe handicaps. . . (b) In addition to carrying out projects under subsection (a) of this section, the Director may make grants to pay part or all of the cost of the following specialized research activites: (1) Establishment and support of Rehabilitation and Training Centers to be operated in collaboration with institutions of higher education for the purpose of (A) providing training (including graduate training) to assist individuals to more effectively provide rehabilitation services, (B) providing coordinated and advanced programs of research in rehabilitation, and (C) providing training (including graduate training) for rehabilitation research and other rehabilitation personnel.	(b) Conducting coordinated and advanced programs of rehabilitation research. 152.10 What types of centers are authorized under this program? (a) Rehabilitation research and training centers must be operated in collaboration with institutions of higher education and must be associated with a rehabilitation service setting which fosters a close working relationship between researchers, service delivery personnel, and service recipients. Each center must conduct a program of research and training activities.
UAP Department of HHS, ADD	Sec. 151, The Developmental Disabilities Assistance and Bill of Rights Act: The purpose of this part is to provide for grants to university facilities to assist in the provision of	45 CFR 1385.5 (1) To ensure quality comprehensive interdisciplinary training, professional staff representing the major disciplines of education, health, psychology, and

(*continued*)

Table 3.1. (*continued*)

Priorities	Implementation example	Funding level
There are no published priorities. However, there is a requirement that there be one UAP in each state before any new UAPs can be established in states where one already exists.	University Affiliated Programs comprise a network of 46 full-service programs and one satellite center, located in major universities and/or teaching hospitals throughout the	1989 Auth: 15.2 Appropr: 12.5

(*continued*)

Table 3.1. (*continued*)

Agency/program	Statute	Regulation
	interdisciplinary training, the conduct of service demonstration programs, and the dissemination of information which will increase and support the independence, producti- vity, and integration into the community of persons with developmental dis- abilities	social work, and holding appropriate university appointments must direct the interdisciplinary train- ing program. (2) The focus of training must be interdisciplinary service and treatment of persons with various ages with developmental dis- abilities and their families. (3) Training must be inte- grated with exemplary services provided by or affiliated with the UAF.

money is reimbursed to states for long-term care services; this is a federal-state match based on the number of individuals served within the state. Such funds distributed to the state from the federal government carry with them requirements that are more general in nature than those in categories one and two. States have the discretion to use some amount of the money from many of these federal-state programs for personnel training.

Indirectly Supported Training Programs

Finally, most research activities have no direct training component and are not viewed as training programs. However, they certainly are to be included in a training discussion. They actually provide excellent hands-on, mentor type opportunities through student involvement in university-based re-search activities.

Table 3.3 includes a listing of programs from categories two, three and four. While not an exhaustive list of these programs, it provides overviews of the major activities that receive federal supports.

For reference purposes the statutory (United States Code:USC) and regulatory citations (Code of Federal Regulations:CFR) are included in Tables 3.1 and 3.3. The Catalogue of Federal Domestic Assistance (CFDA) reference number is also included for readers interested in additional program information. All of these referenced documents are found in most large public libraries.

Table 3.1. (*continued*)

Priorities	Implementation example	Funding level
	United States. The principal focus of UAPs is the interdisciplinary training of physicians, pediatricians and allied professionals ranging from occupational and physical therapists to speech pathologists, child psychologists and social workers. In the 1987 reauthorization funds were authorized for three specific interdisciplinary training functions: early intervention personnel, paraprofessionals in community-based settings, and aging.	

Table 3.2. Glossary of acronyms and abbreviations in Tables 3.1 and 3.3 (in order of appearance)

OSEP:	Office of Special Education
USC:	United States Code
CFR:	Code of Federal Regulations
LEA:	local education agency
Auth:	authorization
Appropr:	appropriation
SEA:	state education agency
RSA:	Rehabilitation Services Administration
RRTC:	Rehabilitation Research and Training Center
NIDRR:	National Institute on Disability and Rehabilitation Research
UAP:	University Affiliated Program
ADD:	Administration on Developmental Disabilities
HHS:	(Department of) Health and Human Services
OHDS:	Office of Human Development Services
ACYF:	Administration on Children, Youth and Families
MCH:	Maternal and Child Health

Table 3.3. Federal programs with training options

Federal agency	Program	References	Training initiatives
Education/OSEP	Regional Resource Centers	Sec. 621, EHA 20 USC 1421 CFDA 84.028	Provides technical assistance to administrators and educators working with students with handicaps. In-service training is possible.
Education/OSEP	Services for Deaf-Blind Youth	Sec. 622, EHA 20 USC 1422 CFDA 84.025	Supports in-service training projects jointly with Sec. 624 to meet personnel needs for services to students who are deaf-blind or have severe handicaps. . . (FY88 priority)
Education/OSEP	Early Education for Handicapped Children	Sec. 623, EHA 20 USC 1423 CFDA 84.024	Supports in-service training grants for infant related personnel highlighting professional and paraprofessional training for work with infants (FY88 priority).
Education/OSEP	Programs for Severely Handicapped Children	Sec. 624, EHA 20 USC 1424 CFDA 84.086	Supports in-service training jointly funded with deaf-blind program (see above); FY90 priorities: Utilization of Innovative Practices for Children with Severe Handicaps/Utilization of Innovative Practices for Children with Deaf-Blindness, highlight in-service training.
Education/OSEP	Research and Demonstration Projects	Sec. 641, EHA Sec. 642, EHA 20 USC 1441 USC 1442 CFDA 84.023	Focuses on research and demonstration. Graduates/undergraduates serve as project assistants in hands-on learning opportunities.
Education/OSEP	State Operated Programs	Chapter 1, ECIA 20 USC 241c CFDA 84.009	Provides supplementary services for children counted under this program rather than under PL 94-142. Supplementary services can be in-service training.

Agency	Program	Authority	Description
Education/NIDRR	Research and Demonstration Projects; Expansion and Innovation Grants; Rehabilitation Engineering Centers	Title II, Rehabilitation Act 29 USC 760 CFDA 84.133	Provides student research assistants with hands-on training opportunities.
Education/NIDRR	State Grants Program for Technology-Related Assistance for Individuals with Disabilities	Title I, PL 100–407 29 USC 2211 CFDA 84.224 (A)	Funds state grants to develop statewide programs of technology-related assistance for individuals with developmental disabilities; state can include a program of training for personnel who work in this area.
Education/RSA	Special Projects Demonstrations (Supported Employment)	Title III Sec. 311, Rehabilitation Act 29 USC 777 CFDA 84.128	Provides for staff training, including supported employment as one of the funded activities.
HHS/ACYF OHDS	Temporary Child Care for Handicapped Children and Crisis Nurseries	Title II PL 99–401 42 USC 5117 CFDA	Funds grants for states to develop respite and crisis nursery services; staff training may be included as a component of the funded projects.

(continued)

Table 3.3. (continued)

Federal agency	Program	References	Training initiatives
HHS/ADD OHDS	Developmental Disabilities	Part B, Developmental Disabilities Assistance and Bill of Rights Act 42 USC 6000 CFDA 13.630	Provides formula grants to each state for activities by developmental disability planning council; personnel training is one of many ways the councils may use their money.
HHS/ADD OHDS	Grants for Projects of National Significance	Part E, Developmental Disability Assistance and Bill of Rights Act 42 USC 6081 CFDA 13.631	Supports specific types of projects of national significance that improve opportunities for individuals with developmental disabilities; projects can include training programs for policymakers.
HHS/MCH	Special Projects of Regional and National Significance	Title V, Social Security Act 42 USC 701 CFDA 13.994	Supports service improvement for mothers and children (including children with handicaps; includes multidisciplinary training of physicians, educators, therapists, and so forth).

72

CONCLUSION

The overview in Table 3.3 represents a small portion of the information available on federal programs relating to personnel training and is in no way exhaustive. Most of the information about specific programs is not static. Each year the Congress makes changes to current statutes which typically result in changes all the way down the federal chain of rules and regulations. While this information was up to date in Fall 1989, by Spring 1990 the Congress will have completed a reauthorization of the discretionary programs under the Education of the Handicapped Act. At that time some of the information included in this chapter may be outdated. Likewise, with the next publication of priorities from any of the federal agencies, some of the information in this chapter could become outdated. It should only be used as a guide to possibilities that the reader will find it necessary to pursue each year for current information. Careful monitoring of newly published regulations and priorities in the *Federal Register* is highly recommended.

REFERENCES

Collender, S. (1987). *The Guide to the Federal Budget.* Washington, DC: The Urban Institute Press.

Congressional Quarterly Inc. (1990). How a bill becomes a law. *CQ's Guide to Current American Government,* Spring, p. 135.

Developmental Disabilities Assistance and Bill of Rights Act, 1987, PL 100-146, Sec. 151.

Education for All Handicapped Children Act, 1975, PL 94-142. Part D, sec. 304, sec. 631, sec. 632.

Oleszek, Walter J. (1984). *Congressional procedures and the policy process.* Washington, DC: CQ Press.

Rehabilitation Act, 1973, PL 93-112, Title III, sec. 202, sec. 204, sec. 304.

4

An Analysis of the Part D Program and the Relationship to Preparation of Personnel to Educate Individuals with Severe Handicaps

Margaret J. McLaughlin,
Carol H. Valdivieso, and
Barbara Stettner-Eaton

If we have learned but one thing from our research and program development efforts in the area of severe disabilities, it is that the success or failure of our policies and practices rests with the quality of those personnel who must eventually implement them. The critical importance of personnel has long been acknowledged by policy makers. In fact, the federal legislation that opened the door to establishing federal policy in special education was Public Law 85-926, enacted in 1958 to authorize grants for training personnel to work with persons with mental retardation. The federal commitment to personnel issues has been maintained through subsequent legislation. Today we have provisions for personnel training in a large number of statutes and regulations in special education, as well as other disability concerns.

One of the oldest and most visible of the federal programs is the current Training Personnel for the Education of the Handicapped (CFDA 84.029D). Known as the Part D program, it is one of the discretionary programs authorized under the Education for All Handicapped Children Act of 1975, PL 94-142. With its legislative roots in the 1958 law, this program has had a major impact on the provision of services to children and youth with disabilities, including those with severe disabilities. It remains a focal point for our efforts to supply quality service providers for children and youth with severe disabilities. As such, it is appropriate to examine what this program currently is doing with respect to these personnel, and more important, what it might be able to do. Accomplishing the analysis, however, requires a review of the original intent of the Personnel Training Program, as well as its accomplishments.

LEGISLATIVE HISTORY OF THE PART D PROGRAM

The enactment of the original legislation stemmed from a realization that there were few professionals committed to training or research in the area of mental retardation and that efforts to develop educational programs for students were being thwarted by the lack of trained personnel. To remedy this situation, Congress passed a law specifically authorizing grants to institutions of higher education (IHEs) for training leadership personnel in mental retardation, and grants to state education agencies (SEAs) for training teachers of students with mental retardation. According to Burke (1976), policy makers viewed the original bill as a temporary boost to existing training efforts. A cadre of professionals would be trained who would in turn train teachers, conduct research, and provide program leadership in mental retardation. It was intended that, once the first people were trained, the legislation could then be phased out.

Not only was the legislation maintained, but legislative support for personnel preparation increased. Subsequent amendments broadened the scope by adding other categories of disability and expanding support to institutions of higher education to provide both undergraduate and graduate training. However, it was not until after the enactment of PL 88-164 in 1963 that the handicapped personnel preparation program began to receive substantial federal support. The funding level for personnel preparation increased from $2.5 million in 1963 to nearly $13 million in fiscal year 1964 (Holland & Noel, 1985). In 1966, PL 89-750, the Elementary and Secondary Education Act Amendments, was enacted, creating Title VI and marking the creation of the Part D personnel training program.

With each amendment or reauthorization, Congress made clear its intent for this program: to prepare a sufficient quantity of quality special educators and other personnel to deliver services to students with handicaps. A statement of the House Committee on Education and labor during the 1983 reauthorization of Part D illustrates the strength of the legislative commitment to federal support for continued personnel training:

> The Committee recognizes that the most critical element in providing effective services to handicapped children is well-prepared special education personnel. Without sufficient numbers of qualified personnel, the nation will always be a step away from the goal of Public Law 94-142, a free appropriate public education for all handicapped children. (Weintraub & Ramirez, 1985, p. 33)

Yet, the passage and continuance of the legislative mandate is only a portion of the Part D story. More important, perhaps, is the administration of the program which has, over the years, shaped the direction and the focus of personnel training efforts in special education across the United States.

PROGRAM ADMINISTRATION

The original graduate fellowship program authorized under PL 85-926 was administered by the Section on Exceptional Children and Youth located in the Office of Education. This was a small, sparsely staffed office whose main purpose was information gathering and dissemination (Riley, Nash, & Hunt, 1978). The section provided only limited administration of the program. In 1963, with the passage of PL 88-164, a Division of Handicapped Children and Youth was created within the Office of Education. The division was abolished within 18 months. However, the training branch from the division remained, reduced to a section and placed under the Division of Personnel Training in the Bureau of Elementary and Secondary Education (Burke, 1976).

Title VI in the 1966 Elementary and Secondary Education Act created the Bureau of Education for the Handicapped which contained a Division for Personnel Preparation. The stability provided by the new organization allowed attention to be focused on the Part D program and provided the context for administrative decision-making.

The earliest program, under PL 85-926, provided graduate fellowships awarded to IHEs to support individual graduate students in mental retardation. Subsequent amendments added a $2,500 support grant to the IHEs which accompanied the fellowships. This additional money was to help the institution provide the resources necessary to train students. With the expansion of the program in 1963 came the fellowship/traineeship program, which included six types of grants: undergraduate traineeships; graduate fellowships; summer session traineeships (generally reserved for in-service training); special study institutes (short-term intensive programs generally reserved for personnel from state education agencies; program development grants (designed to increase the number of personnel preparation programs or to expand existing programs to different levels of training such as from master's level to doctorate); and special projects (planning, development, and evaluation grants for new training models). An IHE could submit separate applications for different types of grants in one or more categorical areas.

Funding for these grants increased from $1 million in FY 1960, which supported 84 IHE fellowships and 92 (SEA) traineeships, to $29.7 million in FY 1970. The impact of the program and its growth were immense. The 84 recipients of the first fellowships represented 19 IHEs; financial support in 1970 was provided to 263 IHEs. According to data collected by Saettler (1969), during the first 8 years following the establishment of the federal grants, an additional 188 IHEs began training programs in special education. Undergraduate program numbers rose from 418 to 774, and the number of graduate programs increased from 381 to 794. One of the most impressive expansions occurred in the area of mental retardation, which had almost a 500% increase in the numbers of undergraduate and graduate training programs. In terms of student enrollments, the greatest increase also was in the area of mental retardation, with 33,309 persons reportedly being trained during the 8-year period.

The success of the program in increasing personnel training programs and personnel in special education is widely acknowledged. However, in the late 1960s, quality, and not just program expansion, began to emerge as a major administrative issue (Heller, 1968). A relatively unique and rigorous set of procedures was developed by the program administrators to ensure that programs funded were indeed of sufficient quality. Advisory review panels of experts in special education were appointed by the United States Commissioner of Education to assist IHEs in developing and evaluating their training programs in special education. These reviewer panels evaluated all areas of the training programs and made recommendations to the Division of Personnel Preparation pertaining to quality and need for improvement.

The staff of the Division for Personnel Training sponsored regional conferences for IHE faculty to discuss the evaluation criteria used in dispensing funds to programs. The division also provided reports and other written guidance about the evaluation process to IHEs that had submitted proposals. Those institutions desiring further funding were required to address the federal evaluation criteria in their proposals. This emphasis on program evaluation and peer review was considered unique among educational programs and a major administrative accomplishment (Heller, 1968).

Unfortunately, this emphasis on evaluation was diluted at the federal administrative level. Evaluations did not address the program's impact on teachers or students, and funding for the evaluation components frequently was excised from grant budgets (Holland & Noel, 1985).

Administrative attempts to increase efficiency in grant processing and cost effectiveness led to the creation in 1971 of Program Assistance Grants (PAGs). The Program Assistance Grants replaced the traineeships/fellowships. These were comprehensive multi-year grants that replaced the annual application required under the previous program and awarded money to programs, not to individual students. Every program was required to have an evaluation component, and funding decisions were to be based on field reader evaluation plus site visits (Balow, 1971). There was opposition on a number of fronts to these new regulations, particularly from existing programs in the area of mental retardation, which had the potential of losing the most training support. Since these programs were among the first established, they had been able to attract the most traineeship/ fellowship applicants and accompanying support money over the years. The new regulations appeared to spread available funds across a potentially larger number of IHEs by encouraging the development of new programs.

With this funding shift from individual students to programs, the division for personnel preparation was able to target funds for priority personnel areas such as rural programs, early childhood, and career education. Over the years, these priorities shifted to reflect current needs of the field. Another intent of the PAG program was to improve personnel planning. Applicants were required to provide evidence that graduates were meeting the educational needs of handicapped children at the local, regional, and/or state level. The push toward accountability and improved personnel planning resulted in additional funding criteria for project applications. However, the goals of determining the extent to which a program met existing needs were never fully realized due to lack of adequate needs data and an inability of the federal program administrators to monitor or assist training programs in developing their evaluations.

The program had much more success in directing training efforts toward specific priorities. Over the years, new programs have been created or expanded to train personnel in new areas. Students with severe handicaps (SH) became a priority area in FY 1975 and remained a priority for almost 10 years. The result has been the creation of new and bigger teacher preparation programs in the area of severe handicaps and thus, more special education teachers to serve students with severe handicaps. Examples of the impact of the success of this funding are the data provided by the Part D program, which indicate that for each year of the severe handicaps priority, approximately 1700 students were trained at the preservice level as a result of Part D funding (Holland & Noel, 1985). (Note that these numbers do not necessarily represent new persons trained each year since training programs are usually multi-year.)

The infusion of Part D funds into IHEs has helped effect educational change in the area of severe handicaps. The funds allowed a focus of attention on this area, enabled research and the development of new instructional approaches, and helped supply the professionals who would apply these innovations.

While the Part D program has been responsive to the needs in the area of severe handicaps, there is some question of whether it will remain responsive. If the program is to maintain a leadership position within the field beyond that of disbursing monies, it must respond to the current realities facing preparation of personnel to work with persons who have severe disabilities.

CURRENT ISSUES

Shortages

The overarching problem facing public school systems is the shortage of special education personnel. While it is true that it is difficult to ascertain the exact magnitude of the problem given the unreliable data, it is also true that the problem represents a significant barrier to service delivery.

One source of personnel data is a national survey of the state education department representatives in all states and the trust territories (N=57 jurisdictions) regarding personnel supply and demand in special education (see McLaughlin, Smith-Davis, & Burke, 1986). The report ranked personnel shortages in all areas. The area of severe and profound disability was found to have the fifth most severe shortage nationally (33 jurisdictions or 58% of the 57 jurisdictions surveyed) reported shortages in this area. In addition, 26 (46%) jurisdictions reported shortages in teachers of students with multiple handicaps. Critical personnel shortages were found in two additional areas affecting services to persons with severe and profound disabilities: early childhood with 32 jurisdictions reporting shortages, and related services (occupational therapy [OT] and physical therapy [PT]) reported severe shortages in 46 and 47 jurisdictions respectively. The majority of these shortages occurred across all jurisdictions, and especially in rural and inner-city areas. Also, 11 states reported that at the time of the survey they did not have a personnel training program specifically in the area of severe and profound disability.

Quality

In addition to inadequate numbers of personnel, the competency of existing personnel also represents a major concern to the field. Initial staffing of programs for students with severe disabilities came from a variety of sources, including voluntary transfers from the surplus of regular education teachers and non-certified college graduates. In addition, many of the earliest training programs were rather unsophisticated. Relatively few professionals understood curriculum and service-delivery models for students with severe disabilities. During this time, the area of severe disabilities was expanding rapidly, and local schools were pressed to hire new teachers and other service-delivery staff. As a result, many of the earliest people electing to work in this area did not necessarily have the knowledge and skill bases for implementing current best practices.

Early curricula generally reflected a developmental or Piagetian approach based on assessment of skill deficits and comparisons with developmental scales and milestones. From these data, instruction was designed to fill the gaps in development. Early teacher training programs did not address issues of preparing students with severe disabilities for participation in daily life activities and providing training in skills needed to survive in the "real world," nor did the activities or knowledge base reflect concepts such as "normalization" and functional skill training that could prepare students for life following school.

Current Programmatic Content   State-of-the-art service delivery to students with severe disabilities has changed dramatically in the 1980s both in terms of curriculum content and placement of services. No longer are educators, or parents, content with training in developmental milestone skills in isolated settings. Instead, the focus is on training students to become active participants in their home communities, working, living, and enjoying recreational activities alongside individuals who do not have disabilities. Public education has the responsibility for providing students who have severe disabilities with the skills necessary to function in today's society. To do this requires well trained professionals who espouse the concepts of functional skill training and integration and are able to infuse them effectively into their instructional programs. Current personnel must understand and be able to demonstrate skills in community-based instruction, behavior management, case management, integrated therapy, and social integration.

The current trend in curriculum for students with severe disabilities is to teach functional skills that are a requisite part of daily life, with instruction occurring in the actual environments in which the skills must be performed. An additional benefit from this type of training is the opportunity to interact with individuals in the general community during the learning activities. Teachers must actively integrate behavior management techniques into the context of ongoing instructional programs, especially as more students with behavior problems return to their district schools. The role of the teacher has become multifaceted in the late 1980s. In addition to providing direct instruction, teachers often assume the role of case manager to coordinate the many professionals, both within and outside education, who provide services. Case management is essential for older students exiting the educational system and for those who have complex medical needs. In addition, due to documented shortages of sufficient numbers of related-service providers and the need to provide ongoing, rather than episodic, therapy, teachers must also assume a support role for specialists. Personnel training programs have a responsibility to respond to the need for preservice training in the new skill areas required by these roles. In addition, professional standards as articulated by state certification or federal funding guidelines must be structured to reinforce and promote the acquisition of these competencies during training. Unfortunately, such a proactive approach is not now apparent in most states.

Certification as a Quality Control   While best practice may demand a range of skills, the educational bureaucracy has not responded to ensure that all who serve persons with severe disabilities do indeed have the necessary skills. Certification policies set by State Departments of Education control entry into the profession as well as the content of training programs. According to the McLaughlin et al. study (1986), states are exerting more control over the field through changes in certification policies. While most states have maintained categorical certification, changes in certification policies since 1982 reflect efforts to increase flexibility in deployment of teachers (McLaughlin & Stettner-Eaton, 1988). For example, one state has a new mental retardation certification that covers all levels of severity, and two states have initiated policies enabling regular educators to become certified in special education without going through a degree program. However, there does appear to be a trend toward creating separate endorsements or otherwise increasing requirements for teachers of students with severe disabilities.

The training programs in institutions of higher education are very responsive to state-mandated standards. Certification requirements established by state education agencies often become the major force behind the course requirements of a teacher training program. A study of faculty in departments of special education conducted by the Institute for the Study of Exceptional Children and Youth (McLaughlin, Valdivieso, Spence, & Fuller, 1988) found that faculty members considered their departments too reactive to certification requirements, and that program quality was often compromised to meet state mandates. For example, faculty often reported that their programs had not added coursework in areas considered important for teaching, such as consulting and communicating with regular educators and related-service personnel, because state requirements "took up all the credit hours."

Changes in certification can create major upheavals in a training program and potentially undermine its quality. In one state included in the higher education study, the state certification office was seriously considering reducing the program in severe disabilities from a master's level program to a program requiring only the bachelor's degree. This was in response to pressure from local school superintendents who needed personnel and wanted them as cheaply as possible. Teacher training programs in the state were concerned because they did not agree with the policy; nonetheless, they would move their departments' graduate programs to the undergraduate major if the state policy changed. Another state had become noncategorical in certification and in the process had spent much time responding to the state's demand for rigorous documentation and alignment of their curricula with the state's competency-based requirements. The training program reorganization had consumed almost 3 years of effort in each IHE, and the faculty interviewed stated that they were unable to focus on teaching. Some faculty questioned the need for this change, other than for the additional flexibility it provided local administrators in hiring and deploying personnel.

A related, but serious quality issue is that of provisional certification. Provisional certification is one of several methods used to respond to the need for teachers. An emergency, out-of-field, or temporary/provisional certificate is used to sanction the employment of teachers who do not meet the state requirements to teach. In the personnel study (McLaughlin et al., 1986), 13 jurisdictions reportedly increased the number of provisional certificates they had issued since 1982, while in 19 jurisdictions the numbers remained the same. In one state, over two-thirds of the special education teaching force had provisional certification.

In-Service Training

The 1986 personnel report (McLaughlin et al., 1986) found that, although in-service training traditionally has been used to retrain teachers who wish to cross disciplines, or regular educators who have mainstreamed students, only recent in-service training has included the upgrading and supplementing of the preservice training of new personnel. In-service topics identified in the personnel study placed information related to students with severe disabilities as a major in-service priority in 23 jurisdictions, ranking eighth in the list of need areas.

The retooling or retraining of special educators to assume new instructional roles absorbed some in-service training resources in approximately one fourth of the jurisdictions. Retraining efforts were reported more often in most areas of low-incidence disabilities and included training teachers of students with mild disabilities to serve students with more severe disabilities. In every instance, the retraining was attributed to the shortage of personnel in severe disabilities and lack of preservice programs in the area. Faculty interviewed in another higher education study (Noel, Valdivieso, & Fuller, 1985) reported that in-service training was not a high priority for them due to insufficient funds and frustration over the effectiveness of the models used. Since federal monies were not available, faculty relied on the SEA to fund their in-service efforts. When state budgets did not make in-service training a priority, and, therefore, did not allocate state monies for it, IHEs no longer provided in-service training.

Issues Related to Personnel Training

A series of related issues have an impact on the preparation of quality teachers for all students with disabilities. One such issue is recruitment. Overall, the number of preservice education majors has declined during the 1980s, and the need for additional new personnel is projected to increase markedly due to a large number of teachers retiring (Feistritzer, 1985). Data on the number of special education preservice majors are not available. Training programs in special education need to be proactive in recruiting but must also utilize strategies that will ensure quality in their trainees.

Another issue is the changing demographics of students enrolling in special education teacher training programs. According to a third study conducted by the Institute for the Study of Exceptional Children and Youth (Spence, Noel, & Boyer-Schick, 1985), the composition of graduate level students appears to be changing. A national survey of special education majors revealed that about two-thirds of the graduate students are returning to school to obtain additional degrees or certification credits in special education in order to increase their salaries and enhance their teaching skills, but not to move on to advanced degrees. Students returning to refine their classroom skills may not need the traditional approach to graduate training. In fact, some faculty in the higher education study (Noel et al., 1985) suggested that new approaches to graduate education were needed, and the seminar model so familiar to graduate education might need to be altered to include more practical, hands-on training.

A final consideration drawn from the Spence et al. (1985) study is that students selected a training program on the bases of reputation and proximity to home (specifically location within a 50-mile radius of home). This information suggests that there is a particular need to ensure that quality training programs addressing the needs of persons with severe disabilities are widely available and geographically dispersed.

CONSIDERATIONS FOR THE CURRENT PART D PROGRAM

Currently, the Part D Training Personnel for the Education of the Handi-capped program remains a very strong force within special education. Given the congressional support and its funding, it is imperative that the Part D program examine its current operations as well as its underlying architecture. Clearly, the major goal of this federal program is to increase the numbers of qualified personnel in special education. While the Congress, in reauthorizing this legislation, has repeatedly recognized that personnel shortages cannot be rectified by this program alone, the program must respond to this need.

Increasing the Supply of Personnel

The 1989 administrative regulations governing the Part D program provide opportunity to increase personnel in the area of severe handicaps. For FY 1989 and FY 1990 the program is to have a separate priority addressing the personnel needs in "preparation of personnel for low-incidence handicapped students." Eleven of these projects were funded in FY 1989 and seven awards are anticipated in FY 1990. In addition, other priority areas in the Part D competition, such as careers in special education, transition, related services, and infants and toddlers can also include children with severe disabilities.

Among the selection criteria specified for the training grants is the requirement that the applicant document need, including both the lack of personnel as well as a lack of training programs in a specified geographic area. Of the 11 FY 1989 projects, all but one were existing programs, and the grants were sought to support or enhance the current training program. Thus, in the 1980s, the Part D program has demonstrated a somewhat greater commitment to increasing personnel supplies in the area of severe handicaps. However, the question is whether the personnel preparation program could be more responsive to the critical teacher shortages in this area.

One suggestion is that the Part D competition include a Program Development Grant priority. That is, a certain amount of funding could be set aside for the purposes of starting new training programs in the area of severe handicaps in states or regions within states that currently have none. The criteria for funding would have to reflect state need for such a program as well as evidence of a lack of a current degree (as opposed to certification only) program in the area of severe handicaps. Obviously, funding criteria would also include quality indicators to ensure that the program would reflect current best practices. The current quality indicators document is but one example of such criteria, but others tailored to specialty areas could also be developed. Finally, program administration of these grants should be intensified to include site visits and provision of other forms of technical assistance to ensure that the programs do indeed get off to a good start. The purpose of creating such a Program Development Priority Grant would be to encourage and enable new programs to be developed without forcing them to compete with experienced and well-established personnel training programs.

In addition to this new Program Development Grant priority, the current system of designating priorities could be continued. Grants under existing priorities could be seen as program enhancement grants. That is, they would be awarded to currently operating training programs for the purpose of expanding training into a new area (e.g., including training in the infant and toddler area in an existing early childhood program or including an emphasis on rural areas or minorities within an established program) or to otherwise improve the quality of existing programs. Enhancement could also be defined in terms of expanding the training capacity of an existing program in order to produce more graduates. Support for expansion could be awarded in the form of increased student stipends or positions for new faculty. In such a program of support, the funding criteria should include demonstration of a training program's performance or track record in producing students, as well as an assessment of the quality of the training provided. In addition, criteria would have to address the quality of the existing program as well as the extent to which new funding would increase the numbers of graduates.

One other area of personnel supply is the area of leadership. In general, this priority remains important to ensure the continuation of a highly skilled cadre of researchers, scholars, teacher trainers, and program administrators. Unfortunately, needs data are almost totally absent in this area. Nonetheless, it is reasonable that the need for leadership training is particularly important in areas seeking program expansion or development. If new training programs in the area of severe handicaps are to be created, there will be a need for new faculty to direct these programs.

The inclusion of post-doctoral support within the leadership training priority is also a valuable component and perhaps should be expanded. The maturation of special education as a field requires that both new and more experienced scholars be provided the opportunity to profit from the infusion of new knowledge. In addition, post-doctoral study could be used to provide opportunities for program administrators in the public schools or other service agencies to return to academe to renew their knowledge.

Enhancing Quality

Merely increasing the numbers of new personnel without regard for quality is counter to the purpose of the Part D program. The statute and the regulations both emphasize the need for programs to prepare well-qualified special education personnel and other service providers. It is particularly important that, in their zeal to increase quantity, program administrators do not neglect quality.

State and professionally recognized standards for the preparation of personnel should be considered the minimum requirements used to judge quality. Program administrators should provide, through proposal guidelines and published evaluation criteria, clearly stated standards for training programs in the various specialty areas. In the area of severe disabilities, these standards should include a clear philosophical basis supporting principles of integration, community-based instruction, and preparation for transition to adult life. Personnel preparation programs applying for funding for training in the area of severe handicaps should present curricula and extensive practicum experiences that clearly reflect the current philosophy and best practices of educating students with severe handicaps.

In a broad way the current evaluation criteria do address these areas. However, further interpretations of the present criteria are necessary to provide even clearer guidance regarding expectations. The ultimate value of proposal guidelines and evaluation criteria will be determined by the quality of the peer reviewers who will determine the degree to which applicants meet the criteria. This is an extremely critical issue and has been an issue almost from the inception of the peer review process. According to one former program head interviewed in the Holland and Noel (1985) study, the recognition of the federal goals for the Part D program . . .

> has been diminished by the use of the egalitarian but ineffective peer review process because peer reviewers in some cases are simply not up to speed with respect to contemporary research, methodology, and field direction. Given the selection process for obtaining reviewers, it is not surprising that many of them are not adequately prepared for such an important job. Over the years the peer review process has been increasingly diluted by an increasing dependence upon representativeness rather than expertness in the review panel. (p. 36)

It is imperative that the federal program administrators examine the current review process and its requirements. Reviewers for any priority competition, as well as specialty areas within a priority, should have knowledge of the current research of best practices in that area. Professional groups within the field can assist in providing names of individuals, but the program administrators must exert some quality control over the review process by selecting people from these lists. There are certainly enough well-trained professionals in the area of severe disabilities, for example, to provide an ample pool of reviewers.

SEAs and Quality Preservice Training

The SEA has a legitimate role in the area of in-service training, and the Part D program has provided support for SEA preservice initiatives. However, there is a need for quality control in the latter area. The use of the SEA monies for preservice training, particularly when such training consists of "summer institutes" and other short-term measures to meet certification requirements, is antithetical to the concept of quality. In the McLaughlin et al. (1986) study, SEAs reported using their Part D funds to provide *ad hoc* training experiences in response to severe personnel shortages. It is incumbent upon the federal program to ensure that SEA monies are used responsibly and that activities that are supported represent the same level of quality required of the IHE preservice training programs.

Increasing In-Service Training

A final consideration regarding the current Part D program concerns the absence of in-service training monies. In the past, the program has supported in-service training grants, and at times, such as during the mid-1970s, the in-service funds surpassed those provided for preservice priorities. Disenchantment with the quality and questionable impact of the in-service programs led to their exclusion from Part D. However, the need for in-service training must be reconsidered in light of current personnel shortages and the rapidly changing content of instructional technology. A balance between in-service and preservice activities must be struck.

As discussed earlier, the need to upgrade skills of professionals currently in service is critical. The need for involvement of the IHE faculty also is critical. Part D funds could be used to facilitate both if program priorities were included that would fund creative collaborative efforts between IHEs and local schools. In addition to adhering to the principles as outlined by Fredericks and Templeman (see Chapter 15, this volume), such collaborative arrangements could enable long-term commitment to staff development rather than episodic in-service training.

One example of such a model of collaboration is the establishment of model schools or centers within a school district that consolidate a number of current exemplary practices or programs and serve as staff development sites for a district or region. Professionals could spend time at the sites observing and actually participating in the programs and could also receive technical assistance on return to their home site. Other models involving cross-site visits and direct technical assistance should be explored. The important point is that there must be a return to in-service training as an effort to upgrade and/or maintain the quality of all individuals who work with students with severe disabilities.

SUMMARY

The establishment of the federal personnel training, or Part D, program has had an overwhelming influence on the direction and solidification of the field of special education. It has enabled the growth and diversification of a number of specialty areas within the field, including the area of severe handicaps. Congress remains confident about the importance of this federal program to the mission of providing quality education to children with handicaps. Furthermore, it is clear that the program itself maintains a position of influence within special education. Thus, it is incumbent upon the administrators of the Part D program to construct a program that provides real leadership in personnel preparation.

A number of considerations have been presented in this chapter. Most are centered around quality. It is critical that the profession of special education as a whole be prodded into defining and ensuring quality in teacher preparation. The process of determining and actively advocating training standards must begin in the area of special education for students with severe disabilities, just as it must begin in all areas of special education. The Part D program can provide the impetus and the context for the establishment of strict and well-defined professional standards in all areas. Through mechanisms such as funding criteria, proposal guidelines, and other forms of professional guidance, the federal program can make teacher preparation a major national initiative. Program funds can be used creatively to assist the profession in defining new areas of teacher preparation. For example, the research and evaluation in teacher training currently is a neglected area for which support could be fostered through a combination of Part D and other program funds.

Finally, the program must remain faithful to its mission of increasing personnel in special education. To this end, the program must address the supports students and programs require in order to meet current and impending personnel shortages. New forms of student assistance or new incentives for IHEs may be necessary. Whatever the strategy, the federal program has the potential and the opportunity to make significant changes in teacher preparation in special education.

REFERENCES

Balow, B. (1971). *Proposal for multiyear funding.* Washington, DC: Bureau of Education for the Handicapped, United States Office of Education.

Burke, P.J. (1976). Personnel preparation: Historical perspective. *Exceptional Children, 43,* 144–147.

Feistritzer, C.E. (1985, August). Commentary by publisher. *Teacher Education Reports,* p. 7.

Heller, H. (1968). Training of professional personnel. *Exceptional Children, 34,* 539–543.

Holland, R.P., & Noel, M.M. (1985). *A review of federal legislation concerning special education personnel preparation.* College Park, MD: Institute for the Study of Exceptional Children and Youth.

McLaughlin, M.J., Smith-Davis, J., & Burke, P.J. (1986). *Personnel to educate the handicapped in America: A status report.* College Park, MD: Institute for the Study of Exceptional Children and Youth.

McLaughlin, M.J., & Stettner-Eaton, B. (1988). *Categorical certification in special education: Does it really make a difference?* Charleston, WV: Appalachia Educational Laboratory.

McLaughlin, M.J., Valdivieso, C.H., Spence, K.L., & Fuller, B.C. (1988). Policy issues confronting special education teacher preparation: A synthesis of four research studies. *Exceptional Children, 55,* 215–221.

Noel, M.M., Valdivieso, C.H., & Fuller, B.C. (1985). *Determinants of teacher preparation: A Study of departments of special education.* College Park, MD: Institute for the Study of Exceptional Children and Youth.

Riley, D., Nash, H., & Hunt, J. (1978). *National Incentives in Special Education.* Washington, DC: National Association of Directors of Special Education.

Saettler, H. (1969). Students in training programs in the education of the handicapped. (Doctoral Dissertation, University of Illinois, Microfilms No. 70–13, 468).

Spence, K.L., Noel, M.M., & Boyer-Schick, K. (1985). *Summary report of a 1985 survey of special education students.* College Park, MD: Institute for the Study of Exceptional Children and Youth.

Weintraub, F.J., & Ramirez, B.A. (1985). *Progress in the education of the handicapped: An analysis of P.L. 98-199, the Education of the Handicapped Amendments of 1983.* Reston, VA: Council for Exceptional Children.

5

The Politics of Higher Education and Personnel Preparation

Herbert J. Rieth

The purpose of this chapter is to discuss the issues and politics in higher education related to providing preservice and in-service programs to prepare personnel to work with persons with severe disabilities. Institutions of higher education (IHEs) are expected to prepare sufficient numbers of well trained personnel to provide effective services to persons with severe disabilities. This training must be done, however, in an organizational system that is fueled primarily by tuition related revenues. Traditionally, in most IHEs, this creates a tension between personnel preparation programs in the area of severe disabilities, which are low-enrollment programs, and institutional priorities for income generation. This chapter identifies and describes some of these tensions and potential strategies to resolve them.

SHORTAGES OF TEACHERS FOR STUDENTS WITH SEVERE DISABILITIES

The education of children with severe disabilities is the greatest legacy of Public Law 94-142 (the Education for All Handicapped Children Act, 1975) because it liberated these children in particular to receive a free, appropriate, public education (Smith-Davis, Burke, & Noel, 1984). While access to education has increased, the shortage of qualified personnel to develop and implement high quality, comprehensive programs remains a major barrier to the improvement of overall program quality. Smith-Davis and colleagues (1984) reported that most of the national jurisdictions that they surveyed had shortages of personnel to teach students with severe mental retardation, severe emotional disturbances, and students with multiple disabilities. In addition, where serious personnel shortages were not reported, information suggested that the personnel are not in demand because of limited public school programming.

The genesis of the shortage of qualified personnel appears to be twofold. First, the number of qualified personnel entering the teaching profession who are interested in teaching students with severe disabilities is decreasing. Second, it is increasingly difficult to retain the teachers once they enter the profession. Smith-Davis et al. (1984) report that attrition of personnel is most problematic in rural districts, where attrition rates as high as 50% are not uncommon. Also, they point out that trained teachers, over the course of their careers, tend to work with students with less severe disabilities because they can obtain the same salary for somewhat less arduous and more immediately gratifying work. Burnout also is a factor that affects teacher attrition. It is an issue particularly among teachers of students with emotional disturbances and severe disabilities, among whom attrition rates are as high as 30% every 3–4 years.

Clearly, the chronic difficulties in attracting and retaining qualified teachers to work with persons with severe disabilities is affecting the quantity and quality of programs for students. Also, data suggest that continuing personnel needs, burnout, and attrition will continue to perpetuate personnel shortages into the foreseeable future. Problems in personnel supply and demand not only influence programming and placement of pupils with disabilities, but also influence the standards that may be used to qualify people to teach these pupils. When supplies are plentiful, the tendency is to screen applicants carefully and select only the best qualified. When supplies are short, as they are currently, selection standards tend to be compromised and lowered overall. Therefore, strategies must be developed to address the shortage of teachers while upholding high standards.

FUNDING PROGRAMS IN THE AREA OF SEVERE DISABILITIES: THE IHE DILEMMA

Professionals sensitive to the teacher shortage press for resources for programs to prepare personnel to work with persons with severe disabilities. They are encountering increasing difficulty, however, in convincing deans of schools of education, who are confronting budget deficits, to invest in training programs in the area of severe disabilities. During the 1980s schools of education have experienced declining enrollments, which have precipitated revenue shortfalls, in turn causing budget reductions, which have brought about program reductions and/or abolition. Now deans must argue to save their own budgets and are not interested in expanding, adding, or sometimes even continuing low-enrollment programs. They are besieged with carefully documented resource requests from a variety of program areas, but given typical budget deficits, they must question allocating resources to programs that do not and/or will not generate enough revenue to equal program costs.

The magnitude of the problem appears to be growing as more IHEs are faced with budgets that fall short of requests for resources. As revenues fail to approximate legitimate requests for resources, IHEs endeavor to diminish program spending. Typically, schools of education, forced into retrenchment because of declining enrollment, are not strategically positioned to leverage additional dollars. More typically, they are hard pressed to stave off further reductions. Therefore, administrators may have difficulty rationalizing the allocation of resources to low-enrollment programs that will not produce enough income to balance expenditures. Programs to prepare personnel to work with children with severe disabilities are typically included among these low-enrollment programs.

FEDERAL FUNDING FOR PROGRAMS IN SEVERE DISABILITIES

Given the existing fiscal context in higher education, how can special educators compete effectively for resources for programs to train personnel to work with persons with severe disabilities? What arguments can special educators develop to persuade deans to perpetuate, enhance, or improve training programs in the area of severe disabilities?

One strategy for obtaining resources that has proven effective for many programs is to pursue federal funds. These funds can be added to IHE funds, to help finance a program in the area of severe disabilities. This strategy is consonant with the federal role of stimulating, with funds, IHE's to develop long-standing, successful programs to prepare special education teachers (Whelan, 1989). Federal funds were designed to be catalytic by stimulating IHEs to commit resources to low-enrollment programs. Federal policy enables an IHE to develop a program by using external funds, and maintain it by establishing a reasonable balance between external funding and internal funding. Clearly, the intent is to reduce federal support once the initial funding period is concluded, with the IHE or state education agency (SEA) absorbing the cost of maintaining the program. Presently, with schools of education struggling financially, fierce competition for internal IHE dollars, and the continuing personnel shortages, it is obvious that the federal financial support must continue for the foreseeable future.

Support for Students

Federal funds are used, principally, for student financial support and to a lesser degree for faculty and general program support. Student financial support, usually stipends and/or tuition payments, has a dual purpose. The first is to facilitate recruiting capable persons to the profession by offering financial inducements through subsidized training. Financial assistance may attract competent personnel to the profession, who, in some cases, may not initially have elected to work with persons with severe disabilities. The second purpose is to make high quality training affordable. In particular, graduate training is a high cost item for most professionals, and financial support reduces the response cost. Overall, student support funds have the dual effect of enhancing the pool of competent well-trained teachers who are increasingly likely to remain in the profession.

The student stipend strategy has benefitted many students by reducing their educational costs. However, persistent personnel shortages, which reflect difficulties in attracting and retaining professionals, coupled with substantial staff development and in-service training needs, underscore the importance of continuing and, preferably, expanding federal involvement in funding personnel preparation programs. The assumption that IHEs will be able to assume the costs of maintaining programs is flawed given the current budget context and the internal competition for funding. Federal support is essential to recruit and to retain competent personnel to ensure that all children receive a high quality, free, and appropriate public education.

The Office of Special Education Programs (OSEP) is the primary funding source to support the preparation of undergraduate, master's, and doctorate degree students to work with students who have disabilities. Program funding has gradually risen from $55.4 million in 1984 to $64 million in 1988 (Bowen, 1988). Unfortunately, during that time period, the funding level of the average award has not risen at a rate consonant with inflation and tuition and stipend increases, and the number of categories of programs funded has increased. This decrease in purchasing power has, in part, required IHEs to search for alternative federal funding sources to support students.

The essential role of student aid in recruiting students has prompted training programs to develop an array of strategies to creatively use federal funds, other than personnel preparation funds, for student stipends (Rieth, 1989). For example, the Handicapped Children's Early Education Program (HCEEP) and model demonstration project funds can be used to hire students to work on project activities related to program training objectives. This synergistic relationship between the project and the student benefits the project through the employment of competent, highly motivated workers and enhances the students' training by providing supervised, high quality training experiences in applied settings.

Other federal agencies, including the National Institutes of Health (NIH) and the Office of Educational Research and Improvement (OERI), provide research, development, and training grant funds that can be used to support a relatively small number of students as research assistants on multidisciplinary research teams. The National Institute for Child Health and Human Development (NICHD) funds primarily basic research that focuses on the study of mental retardation and developmental disabilities. Students work on multidisciplinary research teams containing psychology and special education faculty and students. The focus on multidisciplinary training and on professional collaboration are particularly germane to professionals preparing to work with nonschool-age persons with severe disabilities.

The National Institute of Mental Health (NIMH) also provides research and training funding. The research funding, which focuses exclusively on mental health issues, can be used to employ students as researchers. The funded research ranges from applied to basic research, depending on the agency branch. Students work with multidisciplinary research task forces that include special education and psychology faculty and students. Graduate traineeships are available for master's and doctoral students aspiring to career positions in the mental health profession, such as researcher, clinician, community mental health worker, parent trainer, among others.

IHEs have also supported graduate students as employees on federal grants written by faculty, in cooperation with local education agencies (LEAs) or state education agencies (SEAs). Students work in an agency as tutors or program aides, as teacher trainers, instructional developers, and evaluators, while continuing to prepare to be teachers. Since this funding strategy generally entails a full-time work commitment, it requires students to carefully plan their programs of study to meet project and program requirements simultaneously. In addition, students must spend extensive time off campus, and may be deprived of important interactions with fellow students, faculty, and library facilities. This tradeoff must be considered carefully because it can dilute the quality of the training program.

Support for Faculty

In some cases, federal funds have been used in specific personnel preparation areas to partially or fully support the salaries of faculty hired specifically to teach or to supervise field placements. Funds have been used to finance an array of options including: faculty members' full 9- or 12-month salary, full- or part-salary for a practicum coordinator, faculty members' summer salary, and to pay visiting faculty in specialty training areas. Normally, federal funds are allocated for personnel only after the IHE provides compelling information documenting the necessity of hiring or buying out a faculty member's salary to attain the training program workscope and after the IHE demonstrates that it cannot realistically underwrite the cost. In addition, it is usually incumbent on the institution to provide assurances that the faculty member will be transferred to IHE funds subsequent to the expiration of the federal funds in accordance with the federal policy of stimulating SEAs and IHEs to maintain federal investments in personnel to train personnel to work with persons who have severe disabilities. This policy, however, requires continuous review since the financial context at many institutions is dismal. Therefore, flexible policy is required to accommodate the changing contextual constraints. One federal policy option that deserves further consideration is lengthening grant funding periods to 5 years in order to allow an IHE more time to assume the cost of program maintenance.

Alternatively, federal research, development, and model demonstration funds can be used to buy out portions of faculty salaries, thereby releasing faculty to work on grant activities. For example, faculty members may buy out 50% of their salaries to work on a research grant. The department may negotiate to reinvest funds to hire another faculty member to teach in a personnel preparation program. Alternatively, additional faculty can be hired to augment existing faculty resources to prepare personnel to work with students who have severe disabilities using combinations of research, development, model demonstration, personnel preparation, and IHE funding.

STATE FUNDING FOR PROGRAMS IN SEVERE DISABILITIES

State funds are another resource that can be used to augment IHE funds. State education agencies have access to two categories of federal funds to support training personnel to ameliorate critical shortages. The first is earmarked personnel preparation funds available from the Division of Personnel Preparation (DDP) in the Office of Special Education Programs that is set aside specifically to enable SEAs to address personnel shortage areas. The second involves investing discretionary federal flow-through funds to prepare personnel in order to ameliorate personnel shortages or to fund continuing education programs. Once funded, an SEA has the option of subcontracting the training to IHEs by writing a request for proposals (RFP) to solicit competitive responses from IHEs or to subcontract with specific IHEs qualified to deliver effective training. This pool of funds represents an additional revenue source available, on a competitive basis, to enable IHEs to help alleviate personnel shortages and to upgrade practice by preparing personnel to work with persons with severe disabilities.

State education agencies also have general revenue funds that can be invested in personnel preparation. Funding policies vary across states. Some are designed to mirror the federal policy of stimulating IHEs with funds to develop and maintain programs designed to alleviate general personnel shortages. Other policies are designed to meet specific short-term personnel shortages, which are often transitory and, therefore, require a rather straightforward strategy of contracting for the training and certification of a specific number of professionals.

Frequently, funds are targeted to enable persons teaching on waivers to complete programs of study leading to certification. For example, an SEA may contract with an IHE to train 15 teachers to be certified and competent to teach students with autism. Funds are provided either directly to the IHE with the understanding that they are to be used for student tuition or to the students, who must enroll in a designated university or are free to apply the award to the IHE of their choice. The costs of faculty and program administration are negotiated separately. Some IHEs underwrite faculty salaries with the income produced by course credit income and absorb additional program administration costs. IHEs with more limited fiscal and/or faculty resources may negotiate funds to partially or fully defray program costs. This may involve hiring part-time faculty with specific expertise in the area of severe disabilities or paying the summer salary of a faculty member or practicum coordinator. In most cases, the state policy goal is to use funding to stimulate the IHE to develop a new program to alleviate personnel shortages. These funds can, in some cases, provide leverage to enable a department chair to argue persuasively for the IHE to underwrite the cost of institutionalizing a program required to meet continuing personnel shortages. In other cases, SEA funding support can be combined with federal and IHE funds to maintain existing personnel preparation programs.

Alternatively, SEA funds can be a resource to fund student internships. This strategy involves cooperative agreements between the IHE, SEA, LEA, research and development center, technology center, or federal agency. Typically, students spend 6 months or a year working for a cooperating agency to obtain practical, career-related experience while earning course credit. The internship supplements coursework and practicum activities. This strategy also provides a unique opportunity to evaluate formatively new personnel roles in working with persons with severe disabilities. For example, an SEA might sponsor an internship to allow the trainee to work in a potential employment situation to pilot the development and implementation of a new role (e.g., parent trainer or interagency coordination liaison person). The internship arrangement enables the student to develop, work in, and evaluate the role, while continuing to have access to faculty and agency supervisors who can assist with problem-solving activities related to the role. This strategy has the dual advantage of providing students with an excellent culminating training experience while exploring the development of new roles to enhance the efficacy of services to students with disabilities.

Some SEAs have developed cooperative agreements with IHEs that enable faculty and students to complete important research, development, training, or evaluation tasks for the SEA. The SEA, in return, hires the students or provides grant funds to the IHE for preparing students to teach in critical need areas. This model provides SEAs with a valuable personnel resource pool to resolve pressing professional problems and provides students with funds for advanced training and high quality, well supervised field experiences to enhance their professional skills.

LEAs and IHEs have also engaged in cooperative agreements that provide student support while simultaneously solving specific LEA personnel shortages. For example, the Albuquerque, New Mexico public schools faced severe shortages of special education teachers and middle-level special education program managers (e.g., supervisors and program coordinators). The school system and the University of New Mexico developed a cooperative program whereby teachers with at least 7 years teaching experience who were interested in special education leadership positions were released, with full pay, to pursue a doctoral program at the university. In return, they were expected to supervise two master's degree interns assigned to teach their class, and then to return to the school system as a special education supervisor. In this case, the program enabled the university to recruit talented teachers as doctoral students, to obtain good, reliable practicum student placements, to provide good training for aspiring special education teachers, to build a cadre of community-based researchers, and to build good will. The school system received competent student interns who were carefully supervised and helped solve pressing personnel shortages (Rieth, 1989).

COOPERATIVE IHE-SEA-LEA ARRANGEMENTS

Other IHEs have established cooperative arrangements with school systems whereby students work part-time as staff developers, teacher's aids, substitute teachers, evaluation specialists, curriculum developers, or computer software developers. Some school systems have provided 1- or 2-year leaves of absence to enable selected employees to pursue graduate training. The leave program has been employed to prepare people to teach in shortage areas, prepare people for leadership roles, provide the opportunity to obtain new certifications, and provide skill enhancement opportunities.

Other IHEs and LEAs have established cooperative on- and off-campus–

based degree or topic specific training programs that entail intensive weekend and full-time summer training. The programs are developed in response to local, regional, or statewide personnel shortages. Typically, they entail the SEA providing partial or full tuition support to enable persons to obtain the needed training. The promise of guaranteed numbers of students is justification for training programs to offer courses and programs. These programs allow school systems to enrich the cadre of informed leaders and faculty, while the IHE receives increased enrollment and credit hour production and builds good will by addressing important training needs. Such programs require constant monitoring to maintain rigor and quality since students rarely interact with other students, collaborate with faculty, or have access to research libraries. In addition, practicum placements are often made in off-campus sites that are more difficult to monitor, and practicum placements involving students with severe disabilities are more difficult to arrange during summers. Care must be taken not to sacrifice quality in deference to expeditious teacher training.

Teachers College of Columbia University has developed cooperative programs with several agencies serving children with developmental disabilities (Rieth, 1989). This program allows master's students to complete their internships in the cooperating agencies under the supervision of doctoral students who are paid by the agency. This arrangement allows the agency access to well-trained interns who effectively serve agency clients and have highly trained supervisors. The students obtain valuable practical experience, work on program competencies, and earn financial support.

Other programs have instituted part-time programs in which the students frequently pay their own tuition and enroll in one or two courses a semester plus summer courses. The IHE schedules courses in the late afternoon or early evening to accommodate the teachers, most of whom teach during the day. The tradeoff for employing this strategy is that the students who remain full-time employees and are not necessarily teaching students with severe disabilities have limited or no access to alternative practicum placements. This hinders their preparation to work with students with severe disabilities. Frequently, students work in school districts spread over an extensive geographic area making systematic student supervision a logistical nightmare. Programs attempt to solve these problems by using practicum sites located in institutional settings or by using on-campus summer school sites. Unfortunately, many institutional settings are less than optimal placement options and frequently model behaviors that are not consistent with contemporary thinking regarding least restrictive program options for persons with severe disabilities. Therefore, the above training option should be considered only where students have access to appropriate practicum sites and adequate supervision is available.

Where participating teachers are teaching students with severe disabilities, part-time programs that are field-based and include intensive supervision can produce positive benefits for the teacher trainees. In these programs, the teachers receive training and feedback that is germane to their teaching styles in their classrooms. Therefore, they are not required to transfer information from a university-based setting to their own classroom. Under these conditions, the trainees and the school system benefit because the teacher receives advanced training that will enhance the efficacy of instruction, and the school system enhances the quality of programs provided to students with severe disabilities.

IHE FUNDED STUDENT SUPPORT

The IHE is another source of student support funding. In some cases funds are awarded directly to the department while additional funds are made available through interdepartment competition. The funds are used to provide graduate assistantships, which cover tuition costs and/or monthly stipends. Some programs mix IHE funds and federal funds, with IHE funds used to pay tuition while students work on research, development, or model program grants to earn monthly stipends. Typically, students work from 10 to 20 hours a week for the department and/or grant project. These funds and the activities that they support are integral to most training programs.

Student benefits associated with this approach include opportunities to enhance their coursework with valuable field experience, establish a close mentor relationship with faculty members, complete program competencies, learn to conduct research, and have an opportunity for facilitation of thesis or dissertation research. Benefits accrue where activities are consonant with the students' career aspirations and are monitored closely. Additional benefits include program enrichment and student inspiration to seek additional training for roles as professional leaders. IHE benefits include the development of a pool of competent people to staff grants, in addition to enhanced student support, increased course enrollments, and enhanced student competence.

To work effectively this strategy requires faculty cooperation. Faculty must be willing to employ students on grants, schedule graduate coursework after public school hours to minimize scheduling conflicts, and do problem solving when students require extended training or intensive supervision.

The most compelling argument to obtain IHE resources to support personnel preparation programs is one based on enrollment and credit hour production that equal or exceed program expenditures. Many programs have data available to develop plausible program quality arguments. Few other comprehensive programs preparing personnel to work with persons with severe disabilities have sufficiently large enrollments to argue persuasively that revenues equal program expenditures. Typically, programs capable of making this argument are the sole or the designated training program in a state or region preparing personnel to work with persons with severe disabilities; the state or region is populated densely and enrollment offsets program operation costs. Alternatively, the IHE has external grant and contract support to defray program operating expenses. While this is the best case scenario, it is an infrequent occurrence.

DEVELOPING ALTERNATIVE ARGUMENTS FOR SUPPORTING TRAINING IN THE AREA OF SEVERE DISABILITIES

Low-enrollment programs must shift to alternative arguments if program enrollment data fall short of balancing expenditures. One plausible alternative argument involves shifting the unit of measurement from the program in severe disabilities to the entire special education program. The shift to a larger measurement unit broadens the data base. Such an argument is sensible only when program enrollments are sufficiently large to strengthen the case for resource allocation. The argument is compelling when the smaller enrollment classes can be offset by larger enrollments in other classes. Strategically, this is accomplished by designing a training program that consists of common core courses required of all students combined with specific area content courses. The mix depends on faculty resources, fiscal variables, program quality, and state certification standards. The common core courses may encompass a general introduction to the field of special education, coursework in behavior management, general instructional methods and materials, practica, assessment, and consultation strategies. Specialized training is provided in specific training strands that are coordinated with the core. These may include methods courses, idiosyncratic assessment courses (e.g., motor and language assessment), and practica. The combination of core courses, which are more likely to have larger enrollments, and the specialty courses increases the likelihood of enrollments that allow high quality training and also produce revenue. In addition, the number of courses that are considered core and specialty can be manipulated to regulate enrollments. The range of the combination of core and specialty course are guided by overall program content and the philosophical and procedural congruence of the program components. Therefore, in programs where faculty share common philosophical and methodological beliefs, the core can be expanded to incorporate a coordinated continuum of courses that will link effectively with specialty courses to enable students to acquire required skills. For example, a program faculty that espouses an applied behavior analysis orientation tends to imbed the philosophy in a sequence of closely linked courses that provide students with strong methodological and procedural core skills that transfer to specialty area courses. The ratio of common core courses to specialty courses must be sufficient to produce competent program graduates. Program quality cannot be sacrificed to enhance enrollments.

In cases where enrollments do not support quantitative arguments for a program in severe disabilities, programs must rely solely on qualitative arguments to seek resources. These arguments include: information discussing the quality of the program; related external funding obtained for research; development and training; impact of the training on meeting state personnel shortages; and political impact of the program. The quality of program data attests to the quality of the program graduates, program faculty, national reputation of the program, and/or program content. The quality of program graduates argument may be supported by student satisfaction data, quantitative and qualitative satisfaction data documenting student competency attainment, quantitative and qualitative data from employers, teaching awards earned by program graduates, data documenting efforts of local education agencies to recruit program graduates, and national reputational survey data focused on quality of programs. Additional documentation may include information regarding the national status of the program faculty. Influential information may include the number and impact of publications of the faculty; presence on major state, regional, and national committees; and leadership in state and national professional organizations. Program reputational data may include data reported by professional associations attesting to the quality of the program and/or faculty; indices of the impact of program graduates; survey data documenting perceived excellence; and testimonials from LEA, SEA, and federal leaders regarding the excellence of the program.

Relevant funding information to be presented may include documentation of the number of external funding awards from the SEA, LEA, federal sources, foundations, and corporations. The number of students supported, the amount of tuition revenue earned for the institution, faculty salaries funded, support personnel hired, equipment provided, and the amount of indirect cost funding produced through the department's efforts may also be summarized as evidence of program impact. Since the intent of SEA and federal funds, particularly in the area of training, is to *stimulate* program development with the assumption that the IHE will assume financial responsibility for program maintenance once the grant period expires, attempts to convince IHE officials to invest in program maintenance must start early in the grant period.

Student support and faculty buy-out revenue are particularly important to departments of special education and schools of education; they support general fund activities with no cost to the IHE. Typically, the school contracts with adjunct or part-time faculty for enough salary only to to cover the cost of teaching classes, and the remaining funds, which are released from use for salary, revert to the general fund. As a result of lobbying efforts by faculty, some IHEs have begun to return percentages of both release and indirect cost monies to the department and/or individual faculty members as an inducement for grant acquisition. The return of indirect costs and release money can provide a department flexibility to invest in a program, in faculty development, or in obtaining additional external funding.

Generally, externally funded projects tend to enhance the academic environment and thus, either directly or indirectly benefit university students and the quality of training programs. In addition, external funding can be used as leverage to obtain additional IHE funding. The logic is that the infusion of IHE resources for faculty, students, or staff will help faculty obtain additional external funds and assist the program in attaining national prominence.

Information documenting the importance of the training program in meeting critical personnel needs in the city, region, or state is useful in negotiating resources. Needs survey data collected by IHEs, SEAs, or LEAs that portray the existing need for teachers and other professional personnel, and that project future needs using adjustments for demographic trends and attrition among existing teachers is an important component. Most SEAs conduct a yearly comprehensive system of personnel development (CSPD) survey that provides useful data to document preservice and in-service training needs. Data describing and forecasting staff development or in-service training needs that might result in credit hour production is useful as IHEs develop strategies for enhancing program enrollment while maintaining program quality. The impact of the data may be enhanced by attaching moral arguments documenting the importance of training personnel for roles in working with persons with severe disabilities and their families. Moral arguments suggest that the state has an obligation to provide effective programs for students with severe disabilities. The programs must be taught by competent and certified teachers whom the state is obligated to train or to facilitate hiring.

Supplemental data documenting the impact of trained personnel on enhancing the academic, social, emotional, and financial status of persons with severe disabilities can be used to supplement numerical, qualitative, and moral need arguments. Testimonials provided by LEA, SEA, and/or regional officials may also be useful documentation in arguing for program resources. Publicity provided by local, state, regional, or national media attesting to a program's impact can also be used to supplement the data base. Some IHEs document impact by aggregating the media citations.

COLLABORATIVE IHE TRAINING PROGRAMS

Programs plagued with low enrollment and/or the lack of resources to implement a high quality program might consider developing collaborative training programs. Collaborative programs can vary in form depending on the nature of cooperation and the economic context. One scenario involves faculty from different IHEs cooperating to develop a common curriculum course offering, with teaching responsibilities divided among the IHEs. For example, students might take core and some specialty courses at one IHE and other specialty courses at another. Alternatively, faculty from one IHE might be recruited to teach summer courses or to supervise practica at another IHE. Both institutions share responsibility for training the student and receive the credit hour revenue. However, differences in training and program content philosophies employed by the training institutions are a potential threat to this arrangement. The differences may be negotiable, however, and the economic pressure may assist in overcoming some of these barriers.

While collaborative programming is appealing, it is directly opposed to the spirit of competition that is most pervasive among IHEs. However, as reported in the October 4, 1989 issue of the *Chronicle of Higher Education,* the leaders of the various IHEs in Kansas who were less than cooperative and "spent most of the legislative sessions fighting for their own programs" (p. A22), found a bleak economic environment the incentive needed to wage lobbying campaigns founded upon cooperation. Their cooperation worked to the benefit of all programs. This example suggests that, given the proper set of contextual variables, collaborative activities may be viable in seeking to continue programs to train people to work with persons who have severe disabilities, even in a low-resource environment.

An alternative collaborative arrangement involves forming a consortium of educators to identify IHEs with strong programs in different areas of disability. One IHE might be designated as the lead institution in, for example, severe mental retardation, and thereby obtain resources to develop and implement programs in that area. Another IHE may have strength in rehabilitation training and would be designated as the lead institution in that area. The model can be expanded to a series of low-incidence programs outside of special education to ensure that each institution is assigned lead status in an area of program strength. Students seeking training in a concentration area are directed to specific institutions. Alternatively, IHEs not interested in cooperating are free to continue existing programs.

Another option involves the SEA working in concert with an IHE or a series of IHEs to commit resources to establish a state telecommunication network to provide coursework to teachers in regional sites located around a state. An example of such a system is the Indiana Higher Education Telecommunication System. This telecommunication system links eight regionally distributed branch campuses of the state university system. The system allows courses to originate on one campus and be shown simultaneously to people on other campuses. The system is interactive, thereby allowing questions and discussion. Such a system could be used to broadcast certain coursework in the area of severe disabilities statewide. Teachers have easy access to the conveniently located regional facilities where they can receive specialty coursework. However, practicum experiences are more difficult to coordinate since they require highly trained supervisors as well as sites and supervising teachers who would model exemplary practices. Practicum can be coordinated through a central IHE or through the local campus.

Cooperative agreements between IHEs, SEAs, and LEAs can facilitate precise strategic planning to address state personnel needs and facilitate the coherent, responsive program development at the IHE. It is also conceivable that state personnel needs might be in short supply but the number of newly certified teachers needed may not be sufficient to warrant starting a new program or continuing an existing program. Solution options to such complex situations include engaging in cooperative planning with adjacent states to develop a program in one state and through reciprocal agreements allow teachers to attend an IHE in the adjacent state. For example, the Big Ten Universities have formed a consortium that allows students living in one state to enroll, when a course or program is not offered at their state Big Ten University, at another Big Ten University that offers the course or program. Through this consortium, students only pay in-state tuition. The Big Ten Universities have resolved differences between in- and out-of-state tuition, which is one of the major stumbling blocks to cross-state training consortia. The other major problem is differences in state certification standards. The resolution of this issue requires careful coordination among the participating SEAs.

Another feasible cooperative option to the delivery of instruction is to simply contract with an institution in an adjacent state to have instructors from that state teach at a desired location in the state with the personnel needs. For example, an SEA in a state that does not have a training program in the area of vision might contract with an IHE in an adjacent state with a strong program in this area to provide specialized training for teachers who require certification. The arrangement may involve teachers from the first state attending the cooperating institution for summer sessions in order to obtain the required training. Alternatively, the faculty from the training institution may visit the adjacent state to provide a summer institute or summer session to provide required courses and practicum experiences. Tuition differences are negotiated.

The future may require more cooperative planning among IHEs, SEAs, and LEAs regarding the preparation of personnel to meet state needs. In general, cooperative programming requires: planning among IHEs, SEAs, and LEAs to identify precise needs; to discuss political, turf, and economic implication issues; and to formulate coordinated solutions. Such planning requires a concerted effort to identify actual and projected numbers of personnel needed to serve persons with severe disabilities. These data can help individual institutions identify their capacity to contribute to the SEA's training needs.

UNIVERSITY AND
EXTRA-UNIVERSITY CONTEXTS INFLUENCING
PROGRAMS IN THE AREA OF SEVERE DISABILITIES

The preceding material focused on arguments and strategies designed to obtain resources to implement programs to prepare personnel to work with persons with severe disabilities. In framing these arguments, it is important to understand the context that has an impact on the persons, usually deans, who make the resource allocation decisions. These decisions are made based on a variety of variables, and deans must balance income-generating and deficit-producing programs. Variables including the quality of program, impact on critical state personnel needs, or favorable reviews from SEA officials or state legislators can influence a dean's decision-making matrix. The persuasiveness of the argument and the dean's receptivity depends on variables including: the economic context of the school of education, the status of the school within the university, the financial status of the university, the perception of the quality and reputation of the program, the support of key university or state politicians, and the perception that the program addresses pressing state personnel needs.

The economic context of the school of education is a key variable. A positive climate is one in which revenue and expenditures are balanced and the school does not project imminent budget deficits. Also, the school's profile of income-generating and deficit-producing programs is a key variable. An abundance of justifiably important programs that are deficit-producing will lessen the likelihood of resources for other deficit-producing programs, regardless of the need arguments. Decision-makers are concerned that resources will be drained from thriving income-generating programs, thereby causing them to fail to thrive. A dean might be persuaded to argue the merit of perpetuating important or mandated deficit-producing programs to the central administration. The probability of the dean doing this is influenced by the extent of need, the economic status of the IHE, and the political climate. However, central administration officials must consider, on a larger, university-wide scale, the impact of the dean's argument on the balance of revenue-generating and deficit-producing programs.

As a manager, a dean must balance income-generating and deficit-producing programs, while responding to needs for trained personnel. Where few deficit-producing programs exist, the likelihood of obtaining resources for such a program are better than in universities with several deficit-producing programs. Sometimes a dean can rationalize an investment in a program that is highly justified on a needs basis but might be a deficit-producing program.

The economic climate of the IHE and the school of education, the number of similar programs at other institutions in the state or region, and the need for trained personnel influence resource allocations. The economic climate encompasses the state economy and the funding for higher education within the larger economic system. States with healthy economies, particularly those with budget surpluses, are more likely to be predisposed to invest in higher education. First, one must consider, however, a state's history of investing in higher education. In a state with a balanced or surplus producing economy, requests for program support have a greater likelihood of receiving favorable disposition. In states with less robust economies, resources will be difficult to obtain, although the IHE's resources and the programmatic and financial priorities of the institution will be key determining variables. Second, one must consider the status of the school of education in the IHE. If the school enjoys a good academic reputation, provides important services, and has solid political support, the likelihood of obtaining support is increased.

Geographic context may also have some impact on the options available. States encompassing vast geographic areas expect students to commute substantial distances or make arrangements to transport faculty to regional centers, with students expected to commute to the centers. These arrangements complicate course offerings and student supervision. Clusters of states in geographic proximity can cooperate in establishing interstate cooperative programs modeled on the within-state cooperative model. Cable television networks or satellite networks also can be explored as options to delivering preservice and in-service training to teachers in rural areas.

The disposition of duplicative low-enrollment programs among IHEs in a state is a challenging problem when resources are limited. When resources are relatively plentiful, program reductions, program consolidation, and formation of cooperative programs are rarely considered. As budget resources diminish, program reviews are more frequent, and conscious decisions are required to determine the future of programs. When duplicate programs exist, a number of options must be considered. One option is to obtain an institutional commitment that the program is essential to the state and the IHE will continue to offer the program because it meets a state personnel need. The low enrollment is acknowledged consciously, but the commitment is made to serve the needs of the state. Each IHE must independently decide to make this commitment. Other options involve program reductions, program elimination, or designing cooperative programs. Historically, institutions have competing programs and, in many cases, the competition is healthy; however, the future economic climate, particularly for schools of education, may not allow all IHEs in a state to afford to provide comprehensive programs across all areas of high- and low-incidence disabling conditions. Cooperative solutions will be required.

CONCLUSION

The purpose of this chapter has been to review strategies for acquiring resources to provide high quality programs to prepare personnel to work with persons with severe disabilities. The intent was to identify some of the issues confronting training programs in the area of severe disability, in tuition revenue driven contexts. This chapter was written to provide information to help programs compete effectively for resources and to stimulate the development of alternative resource acquisition strategies.

REFERENCES

Bowen, M. (1988). *Leadership training in special education: A status analysis.* Washington, DC: National Association of State Directors of Special Education.
Cage, M.C. (1989). Optimism returns to higher education in Kansas after nearly a decade of belt tightening. *The Chronicle of Higher Education, 36*(5), A20, A22.
Rieth, H.J. (1989). Graduate student funding sources. In C. Kochhar (Ed.), *Excellence in doctoral leadership training: Special education and related services* (pp. 104–108). Washington, DC: George Washington University.
Smith-Davis, J., Burke, P., & Noel, M. (1984). *Personnel to educate the handicapped in America: Supply and demand from a programmatic viewpoint.* College Park, MD: Institute for the Study of Exceptional Children and Youth, University of Maryland.
Whelan, R. (1989). The federal contribution to doctoral leadership preparation: A perspective on the past and the future. In C. Kochhar (Ed.), *Excellence in doctoral leadership training: Special education and related services* (pp. 2–38). Washington, DC: George Washington University.

II

SPECIFIC NEEDS IN PERSONNEL PREPARATION

6

Meeting Personnel Needs in Early Intervention

Philippa H. Campbell

Early intervention programs for infants and toddlers with disabilities have existed nationwide throughout the 1980s. These programs use varying service-delivery models and are staffed by interdisciplinary personnel with different types of training and expertise (Tjossem, 1976). Available programs vary widely in terms of eligibility of children and families served, location of services, curriculum and program design, and relative focus on family involvement. Typically, existing services have not been provided on the basis of a statewide system of service delivery. Rather, isolated service-provision models have been developed in different locations within a state. Many of the differences among early intervention services may be accounted for by differences in funding and administrative arrangements used to establish and maintain these programs. Existing services have been supported through demonstration projects (e.g., Handicapped Children's Early Education Program; Maternal and Child Health [MCH] funded projects); through private agencies (e.g., United Cerebral Palsy Association [UCP], Association for Retarded Citizens [ARC], and Easter Seal agencies); through state Mental Retardation and Developmental Disabilities (MR/DD) programs; and through public education agencies. Services are, for the most part, either based on a medical model of service delivery, using occupational and physical therapists and speech-language pathologists as primary personnel, or include educators or infant specialists as primary service providers or members of a professional team.

Few personnel in early intervention have been certified, due to a general lack of adoption of standards by states. Even fewer personnel have received training specific to specialization in infants and toddlers with disabilities (Bailey, 1989). A number of developments have created a dramatic and immediate need for qualified early intervention personnel; these include: 1) federal policy changes; 2) changes in service-delivery models; and 3) requirements for new roles for early intervention personnel. These changes significantly alter the numbers and types of new professionals required by early intervention systems and require retraining of existing personnel to perform new roles and responsibilities.

FEDERAL POLICY CHANGES

Significant national needs for well-trained early intervention personnel have resulted from federal legislation designed to ensure appropriate services for children from birth through age 21 years. The 1986 Public Law 99-457, amendments to the Education for All Handicapped Children Act (EHA, Public Law 94-142), and the regulations for this law (June, 1989) establish a federal program to encourage states to develop comprehensive, coordinated, statewide early intervention systems with the purpose of ensuring continuity of services across states. The Program for Infants and Toddlers with Handicaps (Part H of the EHA) will have an impact on both the types of services available for families and their infants and toddlers and the quality of those services. States participating in this federal program are required to address specific issues related to program policy and procedures, infant-toddler and family services, and personnel (Campbell, Bellamy, & Bishop, 1988; Gallagher, Harbin, Thomas, Clifford, & Wenger, 1988; Gallagher, Trohanis, & Clifford, 1989).

States are provided a 5-year phase-in period to plan and implement a comprehensive statewide system of early intervention services that includes 13 components listed in the statute. These components require states to develop Comprehensive Systems of Personnel Development (CSPD), personnel standards, and administrative policies, as well as to initiate coordination of family-focused services, defined by an individualized family service plan (IFSP). Policy studies in the late 1980s indicate that most states are not yet addressing issues of personnel standards or CSPD's (Campbell et al., 1988; Gallagher et al., 1989; Walsh, Campbell, & McKenna, 1988). Yet, issues related to sufficient personnel and well-trained interdisciplinary personnel are cited continually as obstacles to implementing a quality statewide early intervention system (Bailey, 1989; Bricker & Slentz, 1989).

CHANGES IN SERVICE-DELIVERY MODELS

The federal Part H program has made several changes in typical service delivery for infants and toddlers and their families. First, states are required to define the term "at risk" and to determine the extent to which infants and toddlers who are at risk for delay in development will be covered by the state's comprehensive statewide system for early intervention. Because the needs of children within various risk categories are different, the extent to which states address the needs of young children who are biologically or environmentally at risk for developmental delays changes significantly the service-delivery models that will be implemented (Campbell, in press). Therefore, newly developed service-delivery models must be broad enough to address the needs of various types of children and their families.

Second, there are important differences between the service system outlined in the federal Part H program and the systems that traditionally have been provided for infants and toddlers with special needs. Part H requires the development of an individualized family service plan (IFSP) that is different in several key ways from the individualized education program (IEP) used in preschool and school-age services. While both plans are based on the results of assessment strategies, the IFSP is designed to address the needs of *both* infants and their families (Johnson, McGonigel, & Kaufmann, 1989). Early intervention personnel are required to develop and use strategies for determining family needs and strengths in order to develop the IFSP. While many existing early intervention personnel are skilled in infant assessment procedures, few have had either training or experience in determining family needs and strengths.

Third, the new service systems for infants, toddlers, and families are dependent on interdisciplinary teams that include families as members of the team throughout the planning, assessment, and implementation processes of service provision (Johnson et al., 1989). In addition, a wide variety of disciplines are described as early intervention services (e.g., counseling, special instruction, occupational therapy). These features differentiate the Part H program from previous models of service provision that have been either supported under Part B of the Education for all Handicapped Children Act or provided using a medical model (Campbell, in press). Under Part B of the EHA, children are entitled to related services only when provision of the services benefits the child educationally (Dunn, 1989). Services for families (such as counseling) have not been required. In contrast, Part H specifies that infants and families receive those services needed to enhance and promote the development of the infant or toddler and does not specify special education as the base for services, as is the case under Part B.

Fourth, the future service systems for infants, toddlers, and families require coordination among agencies. The federal statute recognizes that no one agency or provider can address all the needs of families and children. Therefore, an interagency IFSP is to be developed for each family and infant to include all the services being provided through all agencies (Johnson et al., 1989). While the IEP has come to be seen as a document that defines services within one agency, the public school, the IFSP will specify services necessary to address family and infant needs across multiple agencies. New and existing personnel will require training through either in-service or preservice programs in many areas including the IFSP process, family skills, and program redesign.

NEW ROLES FOR EARLY INTERVENTION PERSONNEL

The changes in service delivery for families and their infants and toddlers with disabilities will require new roles for early intervention personnel. Most professionals within the early intervention disciplines are trained to function in roles related specifically to the content of their disciplines as applied in direct service with children (Bailey, 1989; McCollum, McLean, McCarten, Odom, & Kaiser, 1989; McCollum & Thorpe, 1988). For example, speech-language pathologists are trained to assess an infant's behavior with respect to communication, speech, and language abilities and to provide direct service to children in need of assistance. Occupational or physical therapists assess posture and movement skills and deliver individualized intervention for children with delays or dysfunction in posture and movement abilities. Professionals will be required to extend direct service roles and participate, with families, as members of teams within early intervention systems. Resulting services may be delivered using a variety of approaches and models of service provision (Dunn & Campbell, in press; York, Rainforth, & Dunn, Chapter 8, this volume). One professional may provide intervention across disciplines (i.e., a transdisciplinary approach) or several professionals may independently provide direct service, monitor interventions delivered by other individuals, and consult regarding other interventions (i.e., an integrated therapy approach). Many professionals may facilitate interventions by sharing general content information with other individuals. For example, a speech-language pathologist may assist infant educators to promote language development of all children within a program. In addition, speech professionals may provide direct therapy, monitor therapist-developed programs, and consult with families and professionals in their own or other disciplines.

A common feature of these approaches and models is that professional expertise is directed to issues involving the infant and young child. One change in roles of professionals will be that they will direct their expertise to the family, as well. New skills, such as family assessment, will be required. More important, there will be a new role for professionals as consultants to parents in their attempts to facilitate the development of their children. Early intervention personnel will be required to work collaboratively with families in planning and identifying desired outcomes for children, as well as in facilitating children's development (Johnson et al., 1989). In addition, professionals will be required to function as members of teams and within team organization structures that also will require changes to adapt to family-centered services. While many of the child-focused and interdisciplinary skills of professionals identified in the past will continue to be needed, preservice, doctoral, and in-service training programs will be required to broaden and define professional roles to ensure competence in family-centered systems (Campbell, in press).

Professionals are likely to perform two new roles within early intervention service systems in addition to reorienting traditional professional roles within a family-centered, team approach to service delivery. One new role requires professionals to function as members of broader interagency teams of professionals. In essence, PL 99-457 requires interagency planning and service provision in order to address the comprehensive needs of families and their infants with disabilities. In-service, doctoral, and preservice training will be required to prepare professionals to coordinate with personnel from other agency disciplines, such as medical personnel (e.g., physicians, nurses), nutritionists, and personnel from other support disciplines who traditionally have not been members of program teams. A second new role derives from the broadened concept of team and relates to skills necessary to perform (and share with families) responsibilities related to service coordination (case management). Case management is a critical element in the new federal legislation. Family needs that are addressed by multiple agencies and specified on one IFSP can be provided adequately only when someone is taking responsibility for coordination. The federal statute suggests that this responsibility is to be that of the early intervention professional who is most knowledgeable about the infant and family. The role of service coordinator has not been the role of most early intervention professionals. Therefore, extensive training will be required to enable existing and new personnel to acquire the competencies and knowledge necessary to perform this vital and critical role.

EARLY INTERVENTION PERSONNEL NEEDS

Only six states were providing public statewide services for infants under Part B of the EHA prior to the passage of PL 99-457 (Campbell et al., 1988). Several others had mandated statewide or entitlement service systems under other agencies (Meisels, Harbin, Modigliani, & Olson, 1989). The remaining states had been either uninvolved in early intervention or addressed the needs of particular infants (of specific categorical or diagnostic categories) through a variety of agencies (e.g., health, developmental disabilities) but did not have statewide systems in place. Federal policy will affect states in varying ways. The overall impact will be to change systems from child-focused assessment and intervention to family-centered services and from single-agency to multiple-agency service-delivery systems. These critical changes require personnel training systems that retrain existing personnel and prepare additional personnel to meet the increased demands for services.

Personnel training needs are addressed traditionally by each state's program administration office, regional and local sources, and university training programs. However, several issues will have an impact on quality personnel training as the Part H Program for Infants and Toddlers with Handicaps is being implemented. First, many aspects of the program are being addressed or developed simultaneously. For example, while the federal legislation requires states to develop personnel standards and a plan for addressing personnel and training needs (the state's Comprehensive System of Personnel Development [CSPD]), most states have not yet addressed these components (Gallagher et al., 1988). Universities seldom offer training in the absence of state certification. Therefore, development of university programs, including hiring or retraining faculty, most often accompanies or follows a state's adoption of personnel standards (Bailey, 1989). A survey conducted by the North Carolina Personnel Preparation Institute (Bailey, Palsha, & Huntington, in press) verified that few universities were preparing personnel to work in early intervention. More important, few indicated that these programs would be developed in the future and cited lack of student demand and lack of qualified faculty as reasons. Less than 20% of the universities surveyed had faculty with any expertise in infancy.

Bailey et al. (in press) surveyed 122 colleges that either had received funding for early intervention training from the Office of Special Education Programs (OSEP) or were included in the National Directory of Special Education Personnel Preparation Programs and indicated an early childhood focus. Of the 59 surveys that were returned, 37 were used for analysis. Those eliminated either never had a focus on infancy or no longer provided training in early childhood education. Only 12 of the universities offered an infancy focus alone, 18 focused on birth to 5 years, and seven specialized in both areas. Most programs were supported by federal funds. Apparently, federal support currently is necessary to enable universities to train doctoral leadership personnel and to develop comprehensive early intervention training programs (Bailey et al., in press). Similar data were published in a review of the 26 early intervention training programs funded by OSEP between 1984 and 1987. Twelve programs trained only related-services personnel and four focused only on special education infant specialists. The remaining provided interdisciplinary training for personnel of a variety of disciplines (Bruder & McLean, 1988). Ten new programs were funded in 1988, with projections for training a total of 78 personnel nationally in the first year. Clearly, several years will be required before appropriate training programs are easily accessible to individuals across the country (Klein & Campbell, 1990). As states prepare to implement the Infant and Toddler Program, there will be states where training programs are not immediately available. Existing and newly developed programs will, of necessity, provide training for a wide variety of personnel who may not obtain employment in the state where training is available (Bailey, 1989; Weiner & Koppelman, 1987).

A second issue regarding early intervention personnel is the differentiation among strategies used to retrain existing personnel, address initial personnel shortages, and maintain an ongoing pool of highly qualified personnel over time. For example, in-service training and on-the-job experience may be used to provide knowledge and skills in the infancy and early childhood areas for personnel who have special education certificates or licenses to practice in particular disciplines, such as occupational or physical therapy (Bailey et al., in press; Humphry & Link, 1989; Weiner & Koppelman, 1987). In-service training also may be a primary vehicle used to maintain highly qualified personnel. University training programs address initial personnel shortages while also maintaining an ongoing pool of highly qualified (and certified) personnel. It is necessary to develop and implement standards and personnel training programs not only for special education personnel, but also for a wide array of other personnel (e.g., occupational and physical therapists, psychologists) who traditionally have been required to meet state licensure requirements to attain public school certification.

Personnel needs cannot be based solely on numbers of required personnel (Smith-Davis, Burke, & Noel, 1984). Rather, the roles of personnel and the skills and competencies required to perform those roles also must be considered. State certification standards are a primary mechanism used within the educational system to ensure that teachers and other educational personnel meet minimum criteria necessary to work with specific populations or age groups. Other professionals who will be employed in early intervention systems traditionally have been licensed to practice within a state rather than certified. Licensure is granted on the basis of successful completion of training and examination requirements and is not specific to particular types of disabling conditions or to individuals of particular ages. Many of the professionals who will provide early intervention services are licensed to practice in a discipline. Licensure in physical and occupational therapy, nursing, speech pathology, psychology, and medicine ensures that individuals possess generalized competencies necessary to practice in a discipline but does not establish specialized competencies that are necessary to work with specific age groups such as infants and toddlers.

Determining Personnel Needs
for Early Intervention Systems

The most accurate estimates of needed personnel are made on the basis of direct counts of the numbers and types of families and infants who are in need of or who are receiving services. However, federal and state data bases for numbers of infants and toddlers being served currently are not accurate. In part, this inaccuracy is due to the phase-in implementation of the Part H program and, in part, to multiple criteria, variations in services provided, and timeliness of reported data. For example, data reported in the *Tenth Annual Report to Congress* (1988) indicate a nationwide total of 32,693 infants and toddlers (ages 0–2 years) served during the 1985–1986 school year under Part B of the Education for All Handicapped Children Act (EHA-B). Data for infants and toddlers served under other federal education administered programs, such as ESEA (PL 89-313, the Elementary and Secondary Education Act Amendments, 1965); federal health or human services programs (e.g., Administration on Developmental Disabilities); state funding; or private third party billing (e.g., Medicaid, EPSDT [Early and Periodic Screening, Diagnosing, and Treatment], CCS [Crippled Children's Services] insurance) are unknown (Gallagher et al., 1988; Gallagher et al., 1989). Neither the Office of Special Education Programs nor any other federal agency has required states to collect and report data concerning personnel needs or shortages. States were required by OSEP in fiscal year 1989 only to estimate the numbers of infants and toddlers who were believed to be receiving services. Most states reported duplicated counts of infants and toddlers due to lack of synthesized data systems and coordinated funding for statewide programs (Gallagher et al., 1989).

Primary and direct data sources are the preferred basis for accurately determining personnel needs. Secondary data sources provide evidence for critical needs for all types of early intervention personnel in the absence of primary sources. Perceptions of state and local program administrators concerning availability of personnel constitute one such secondary data source. For example, extreme needs for well-trained personnel across various disciplines were reported in a survey of states' early intervention activities and plans conducted by Meisels et al. (1989) through questionnaires completed by directors of state planning grants. Almost 90% of the state respondents described shortages for all types of professionals in early intervention and even more dramatic shortages of well-trained personnel. Similar shortages of appropriately trained early childhood personnel also were reported by McLaughlin, Smith-Davis, and Burke (1986) and by Walsh et al.

(1988) who interviewed state education agency staff to determine their perspectives on the current and future status of special education personnel. Weiner and Koppelman (1987) also documented perceived shortages in a brief survey of states concerning personnel issues. Concerns about the availability of sufficient numbers of personnel have been expressed by Congress in the House of Representatives Report accompanying the Education of the Handicapped Act Amendments of 1986, as well as through position papers and other informational documents released by the major organizations (e.g., Dunn, Campbell, Otter, Hall, & Berger, 1989; Smith, 1987; Wilcox, Bashir, Iglesias, Liebergott, & Snyder-McLean, 1989).

The needs for specially trained personnel in any of the early intervention service disciplines are difficult to document. Needs for personnel prepared to provide special instruction for infants and toddlers have not been determined since most states have not provided early intervention services under the auspices of state education agencies. According to McLaughlin et al. (1986), only 16 (32%) of the states had standards for certification of early childhood special educators in place in 1986 and, for the most part, these standards related to special educators for children within the 3- to 5-year age range. Interestingly, only four of the six states with special education mandates to serve children from birth (or point of diagnosis) have adopted certification standards. Four of the states with mandates were included in a total of 20 (40%) states that reported shortages in early childhood special education personnel. Two of the states with mandates (Michigan, South Dakota) reported no personnel shortages for early intervention or preschool programs.

Personnel needs in all disciplines must be considered in early intervention. The majority of reports concerning personnel shortages have focused on needs for increased numbers of personnel for early intervention programs (e.g., Bailey et al., in press; Meisels et al., 1989). Less attention has been directed toward personnel needs in specific early intervention disciplines. There are severe and persistent national personnel shortages in several disciplines, particularly occupational and physical therapy. Shortages, of therapists in general, and of school-based therapists in particular, were identified by 85% of states in the survey conducted by McLaughlin et al. (1986).

Projecting Future Numbers of Needed Personnel

Widespread acknowledgment of personnel shortages by state agency personnel and by professional organizations clearly indicates anticipated needs for increased numbers of personnel in early intervention. Part H legislation allows states to expand existing early intervention services in two ways. States are encouraged to develop service-delivery systems that include a range of service options. States also are required to establish definitions of "at risk," thereby defining state-specific program eligibility requirements. Increased numbers of infants and toddlers may become eligible for services when states adopt less restrictive definitions than are currently in place (Walsh et al., 1988). States with partially established statewide systems of early intervention services are likely to require additional personnel to expand existing services to all infants and toddlers throughout a state.

Definitions adopted by states and the range of service-delivery options made available as part of statewide systems of early intervention services will have a significant impact on the numbers and types of personnel required as well as the roles that will be fulfilled by those personnel within the system. States that have relied on home-based, special instruction models, for example, will require additional personnel from other disciplines to implement team-based service-delivery models. Those that have provided once-per-week intervention will require increased numbers of trained personnel to implement, for example, 2-day-per-week infant-toddler classroom models or integrated day care systems that, by design, require increased numbers of personnel.

ACHIEVING A GOAL OF QUALIFIED
EARLY INTERVENTION PERSONNEL

Providing sufficient numbers of personnel to meet demands for services for infants and toddlers with disabilities is only a starting point in providing comprehensive services. Ensuring quality services requires definition of the particular competencies that will be required to implement the components of the statewide system described in the legislation and closer evaluation of the actual skills and competencies of personnel employed in service-delivery systems (Bailey, 1989). The need for well-trained personnel across numerous and varied professional disciplines is particularly important in programs for infants and toddlers. A number of diverse professional services for families and infants are included under the global label of early intervention services in the federal regulations.

Existing EHA provisions for preschool (3–5 years) and school-age children mandate special education and related services. Early intervention services are to be delivered through the IFSP. Establishing family-centered *systems* (rather than *programs* for infants and toddlers with various disabilities) requires varied approaches that allow for systematic retraining of currently employed personnel, training of new personnel, and ongoing training designed to keep all personnel updated on emerging research trends concerning families and infant intervention approaches and strategies (Bailey, 1989; Shelton, Jeppson, & Johnson, 1987). Well designed training approaches focus not just on personnel shortages, but also on the quality of personnel by providing: 1) longitudinal, sequenced, ongoing, and varied training activities; 2) a dual focus on attitudes and skills; 3) translation of research into practice; and 4) direct linkages between professional training and program implementation and monitoring standards (Winton, 1988).

Professional Roles and Competencies

Competencies required by professionals involved in delivering early intervention services are both generic across disciplines and specific to particular disciplines. For the most part, the range of competencies required are not likely to be fully addressed in preservice training programs (Gilkerson, Hilliard, Schrag, & Shonkoff, 1987; Trohanis, 1986). Skills required for personnel to work with infants and toddlers with disabilities are different from those required to work with children from 3 through 5 years (Mc-Collum, 1987; Weiner & Koppelman, 1987). Each professional must function as an integral part of a comprehensive service system that encompasses health, education, and family services. No one professional discipline can meet the unique needs of families and their children (Campbell & Hanson, 1987).

Family Focus A focus on families is a relatively new but essential feature of service delivery for infants and toddlers with disabilities (Healy, Keesee, & Smith, 1985). Family-centered intervention systems not only reflect best practice, but also form the basis of the statewide early intervention system outlined in the new federal program. Many individuals who are working currently with infants and toddlers, although experienced in working with young children, may require retraining to address the needs of the families. First, professionals need to have knowledge of family functioning and the impact of disability on family systems. Second, specific training in developing and writing an IFSP will be an important first step in ensuring that family and infant needs are addressed fully. Third, staff will require training in principles and practices of case management in order to fulfill responsibilities in conjunction with designated families. Fourth, knowledge of the comprehensive services available within a community, a region, and the state will be essential in designing services that meet unique family and child needs.

Parent-Professional Collaboration Family and child outcomes are enhanced when parents and professionals collaborate in providing comprehensive services. Parents are team members in programs for infants and toddlers and have an equal right to information and to have input in decisions concerning their children. Professionals must be competent in providing parents with information and in empowering parents to make informed decisions on behalf of their infants and toddlers. The most important of the generic competencies are skills necessary to work effectively with families. One mechanism for providing professional training is to use parents to train professional personnel (Gilkerson et al., 1987; Klein &

Campbell, 1990). Preservice programs must include content on family systems theory and its implementation in practice, co-taught by a professional and parents of children with disabilities. At the least, parents must be involved in some way as instructors in preservice and in-service training programs for all disciplines.

Team Collaboration   The multiple discipline approach used within most programs for infants and toddlers with disabilities presents unique challenges for professional training. Many professionals have received discipline-focused training that has not included team interaction skills for working with other professional disciplines or with families (Bailey et al., in press). These professionals require retraining to develop skills necessary to work as integral members of the comprehensive team. Working effectively as a member of a team requires skills different from those associated with the practice of a particular discipline; those different skills include adult teaching and learning, understanding of group process, and knowledge of essential information from other disciplines and families (Campbell, 1987). Well-designed preservice training programs provide newly trained professionals with information about other disciplines, as well as opportunities to practice team collaboration skills as part of basic training. Multidepartmental university training programs or those that collaborate with local hospitals or medical facilities are likely to provide students with appropriate levels of comprehensive knowledge and team-based experience (Bricker, 1987; Bricker & Slentz, 1989).

Infant Development and Programming   Knowledge of normal and atypical development and of the impact of various disabilities on both development and family functioning underlie the application of each discipline with infants and toddlers with disabilities. Each professional needs a working knowledge of various disabilities and their impact on the developmental process in order to implement interventions that enhance the development of infants and toddlers (Dunn et al., 1989; Gilkerson et al., 1987). Comprehensive early interventions are team-based and logically derive from an overall knowledge of the developmental process and its impact on family functioning without being totally directed toward remediation of atypical development (Turnbull & Turnbull, 1987). Interventions that alleviate the impact of disability on development through promoting infant-toddler and family functioning enhance the well-being of professionals, children, and families (Campbell, in press).

Nonremedial approaches to programming for infants and toddlers with disabilities are developed on the basis of assessment of infant-toddler and family functioning. Yet many professionals have been trained only to assess development of infants within the context of acquisition of developmental milestone skills and have received little information on assessment of family needs. Training opportunities that provide information on state-of-the-art infant-toddler and family assessment practices and intervention approaches are required for existing personnel to support families in ways that enable them to promote the growth and development of their children.

Professional Growth The early intervention field is one that is continuing to change as new knowledge is gained about programming, families, and infants and toddlers. Professionals who commit to an ongoing plan of professional growth and development are likely to remain current in the practice of their professions and competent as early intervention service providers (e.g., Dunn et al., 1989). Primary among these responsibilities for ongoing professional development is evaluation of the currency and efficacy of approaches being used with families and their infants and toddlers. Professionals must be knowledgeable about current research, legislation, and public policy to remain competent in their work and committed to practicing the most up-to-date methods and approaches.

PROFESSIONAL STANDARDS

Professional standards for all early intervention services must be established by states that participate in the federal Program for Infants and Toddlers with Handicaps. Several professional organizations have taken long-term positions that support training for various personnel beyond the basic preservice or bachelor's degree level (Dunn et al., 1989; Smith, 1987; Wilcox et al., 1989). State agencies, on the other hand, have primary concerns about recruiting sufficient *numbers* of personnel to meet potential demands for services for infants and toddlers. It is likely that new and existing personnel of all disciplines will be certified with limited course work and training specific to families and their infants and toddlers with disabilities (Weiner & Koppelman, 1987). Certification systems designed to allow personnel with limited skills to work in early intervention programs while pursuing additional training to acquire needed competencies will allow states to meet demands for sufficient numbers of personnel immediately while developing appropriate and well-trained personnel over time (Bailey, 1989). In this way professional standards for all disciplines are systematically linked to a concept of ongoing and longitudinal training opportunities.

A multi-level system of professional standards enables states and individuals to work toward achieving and maintaining standards of competence. A system with three levels, for example, allows provisional, basic, and permanent certification (e.g., McCollum et al., 1989). Provisional certification allows employment of personnel who have completed basic preparation in an early intervention field (e.g., education, occupational therapy) and fulfilled requirements of competency in a minimum of one early intervention content area (i.e., family-focus, teaming). A basic certificate is granted to personnel who demonstrate competence in several areas. Individuals with master's degree specialization that included generic early intervention coursework, in addition to training in the application of the individual's discipline, qualify for permanent certification. Occupational therapists, for example, would complete specific training to apply principles of occupational therapy to infant sensory functioning and posture and movement skills, whereas speech and language pathologists' training experiences would include emphasis on speech and language with infants and toddlers.

A multi-level system of standards allows for growth and development within the system but does not specifically facilitate ongoing professional responsibility for continued development. Linking professional standards to continuing education requirements is one method to encourage ongoing and individualized training. Professionals can design systematic and longitudinal learning opportunities that reflect individual learning needs and ensure use of state-of-the-art practices when continuing education is guided by an individual plan of staff development.

RESPONSIBILITIES FOR PERSONNEL TRAINING

Ensuring an adequate supply of well-qualified professionals of numerous and varied disciplines is one of the major challenges in establishing successful statewide systems of early intervention services. The realization of high-quality services delivered by appropriately trained and skilled personnel requires actions at both the federal and state levels as well as activities of professional associations and professionals themselves. The major responsibility for implementing high-quality services for infants and toddlers and their families lies primarily with professionals and secondarily with state agencies and each state's Interagency Coordinating Council (ICC). Policies established and actions taken by professional associations and the federal government will be instrumental in guiding the direction of the Program for Infants and Toddlers with Handicaps.

Professionals have an ethical responsibility to provide the highest quality services possible for families and their infants and toddlers with disabilities. Professionals' efforts to acquire and use best practices in early intervention as a whole and within individual disciplines may be supported by carefully designed state policies for professional standards, an accurate statewide Comprehensive System for Personnel Development (CSPD), and creative options for preservice and in-service training opportunities. Professional associations on both a national and state level can be effective in assisting states to develop policies, in encouraging appropriate preservice training programs, and in establishing quality in-service training activities. Policy statements and position papers prepared and distributed by professional associations provide a foundation for individual professional development and communicate information about skills and competencies needed by particular disciplines (e.g., Dunn et al., 1989; Smith, 1987; Wilcox et al., 1989).

Overriding any state level and professional activities are actions taken by the federal government in support of high-quality services for families and their infants and toddlers. Of critical importance are the Part H regulations, which describe minimal activities that must be undertaken by the lead agency to implement the personnel standards and CSPD components of the statewide system of early intervention. Monitoring of each state's plans and activities in these two areas by the Office of Special Education Programs will be instrumental in facilitating the development and maintenance of a sufficient pool of appropriate and well-trained personnel. The federal government has direct responsibility for allocating sufficient levels of funding to enable lead agencies and their Interagency Coordinating Councils to undertake responsibilities for implementing quality early intervention systems. Numerous agencies of the federal government can have an impact on the implementation of the early intervention program through cooperative interagency agreements, sponsorship of task forces and working groups, and other similar activities. Health and human services agencies on both state and federal levels must collaborate to address the comprehensive needs of families and their infants and toddlers (Department of Education and Department of Health and Human Services, 1989). Federal agencies provide a vehicle for coordinating efforts across states to ensure a nationwide program of comprehensive statewide early intervention systems.

COMPREHENSIVE PERSONNEL DEVELOPMENT ACTIVITIES

Preservice preparation, in-service training, and technical assistance are the most common approaches used to train personnel (McLaughlin et al., 1986). Episodic training that is not linked to direct and hands-on application with families and children is likely to result in limited impact on service-delivery systems (see Chapter 15, Fredericks & Templeman, this volume). Commonly used approaches for training personnel can be reduced to a series of episodic activities when didactic presentations are not well linked to practicum experiences. In-service training and technical assistance activities are particularly susceptible to becoming episodic events. Large group in-service activities often are the easiest in-service training activities to implement with large numbers of people. These activities have particular appeal for administrators whose primary concerns may lie with the numbers of people who attend training sessions rather than with the benefits and outcomes of that training.

Long-Range Commitments to Quality Personnel

A variety of training programs that address short- and long-term personnel needs for *numbers* of personnel required to implement early intervention services and the *quality* of those personnel are needed. The best preservice training programs are designed and coordinated by leadership personnel and include an interdisciplinary focus of integrated coursework and related field-based training, delivered by instructional teams that include families and medical, educational, and therapeutic personnel (Weiner & Koppelman, 1987). Doctoral level training of sufficient numbers of personnel who are prepared to perform research, teaching, administration, and service in universities and within state lead agencies must precede or occur simultaneously with the development of graduate level training for clinical practitioners. Establishing sufficient numbers of geographically distributed preservice training programs is a long-term process, at best; in states with special education mandates, such as Nebraska and Iowa, the process has required a 5- to 7-year development of sufficient numbers of well-trained and qualified personnel but has had little effect in addressing *immediate* needs for sufficient numbers of well-trained personnel.

Short-Term Commitments for
Sufficient Numbers of Personnel

The most immediate short-term personnel needs are likely to be met through a variety of in-service training mechanisms to retrain professionals from other, related disciplines to work in early intervention (Bailey, 1989). States with existing special education mandates have used in-service training mechanisms to allow education personnel with certification in any special education category or in early childhood education to be "waived" from fully meeting certification standards, due to severe personnel shortages (Weiner & Koppelman, 1987). Such strategies are appealing and often seem necessary to enable states to meet immediate demands for personnel. Such approaches, while addressing an immediate need, result in authorizing unqualified personnel and, subsequently, dramatically lower the quality of services provided (Smith-Davis, Morskink, & Wheatley, 1984). These and other "bandaid" approaches are best used only on a very temporary basis with well established linkages to long-term requirements for full certification and continued professional development.

The extent to which immediate steps to provide additional early intervention personnel are needed is impossible to determine accurately because of the lack of data describing the numbers of personnel who currently are employed or needed in early intervention programs throughout the United States. These needs are likely to be differentially distributed among various disciplines and within particular geographical areas of the United States rather than uniformly widespread. Accurate personnel needs data and implementation of a long-term plan for development of appropriate and well-trained personnel of various disciplines will decrease the need for states to waive existing personnel standards or use other superficial strategies that result in provision of services by unqualified personnel. In the absence of precise needs data, we must continue to be concerned by the perceptions of state agency personnel and professional organizations that support dramatic needs for additional numbers of early intervention personnel.

Recruitment Efforts

Waiver from certification standards, retraining of other personnel, and pre-service or in-service training activities will have limited effects in increasing the numbers of personnel within specific disciplines, such as occupational and physical therapy, where long-standing personnel shortages have existed. In addition, creative approaches to attract personnel into early intervention and to support the intensive training (or retraining) required to ensure expertise are necessary.

Combined master's degree programs that provide eligibility both for licensure examination and advanced level degrees have developed in physical and occupational therapy. Combined programs that train personnel in basic therapy skills and provide intensive training in working with families and their infants and toddlers with disabilities attract new personnel into early intervention while providing appropriate specialized training. Programs developed by lead agencies to financially support professionals during completion of advanced training in return for a defined period of work within the early intervention system provide incentives for completion of training while alleviating personnel shortages. Lead agency collaboration with university training programs within their states encourage public awareness and other efforts to recruit qualified applicants into undergraduate (or basic) educational programs. Similar programs of financial incentives can be used to support basic education in the final years of study in return for a commitment to work in early intervention while jointly pursuing advanced training.

Comprehensive System for Personnel Development (CSPD)

States are required to address training needs defined in their Comprehensive System for Personnel Development (CSPD) for early intervention. Significant experience in the use of such a system has been acquired by state education agencies (SEAs) in connection with implementation of the EHA mandates for school-age students. Past experience has indicated that the system is effective in states where additional collaborative methods are used to collect data that accurately reflect the needs of personnel for ongoing (rather than episodic) training activities. For example, states that conduct a year-by-year assessment of personnel development needs through written questionnaires, are less likely to rely exclusively on their CSPD as their sole basis for developing well-qualified and appropriate personnel throughout a state.

State personnel initiatives are the result of the CSPD process. Approximately one-third of the lead agencies designated to operate the federal Program for Infants and Toddlers with Handicaps for fiscal year 1987 are state education agencies. For SEAs, the most expedient strategies may be to link the CSPD required for early intervention to the existing CSPD used to comply with Part B requirements for programs for school-age students. The quality of personnel development systems for early intervention within these states will be dependent on the quality of each state's existing CSPD. The CSPD can be designed to coordinate statewide personnel preparation efforts, including data collection, recruitment, preservice and in-service training, ongoing professional development and retention, and dissemination activities (Smith-Davis et al., 1984).

The best designed statewide personnel development systems are based on accurate data collection methods that separately address quantity and quality issues and propose short-term strategies that will be undertaken within the long-term context of a commitment to providing quality personnel throughout a state. Collaborative systems, developed on the basis of participatory planning and implementation among state agencies, local service providers, and university personnel, link needs with methods for addressing those needs on a long-term basis (Smith-Davis et al., 1984).

Such collaboration efforts are essential to successful implementation of the federal Program for Infants and Toddlers with Handicaps because of the need for appropriately-trained and well-trained personnel from a variety of health, education, and social service professions and the potential shortages in both quantity and quality of personnel that may exist during initial implementation of this program. The Interagency Coordinating Council provides a vehicle for planning and implementing statewide personnel development systems that result in quality early intervention personnel. ICCs can authorize (and financially support) ongoing, interdisciplinary, statewide personnel development task forces with responsibility for developing: 1) accurate ongoing personnel data systems, 2) plans for addressing immediate needs for sufficient numbers of personnel, and 3) preservice and in-service training activities linked to ongoing and continuing needs for quality personnel. Task forces may be drawn from membership in the ICC itself or include appointed members from outside the ICC's membership. At the least, membership must include parents and university faculty representing health (e.g., physical therapy, occupational therapy, nursing); education (e.g., early childhood, special education); and rural and urban service-delivery providers.

Programs for In-Service Training

A number of options exist to provide in-service training that is linked to practical experience and results in change in service-delivery systems and in outcomes for children with disabilities (Blackhurst, 1980). Many of the existing models were developed to meet demands for qualified personnel to serve children with severe handicaps that resulted from the original EHA legislation and can be implemented to address needs that have resulted from the 1986 amendments to that legislation. Quality in-service training programs are the result of: 1) delineation of specific training needs, including relevant and realistic objectives for training; 2) qualified in-service training staff often resulting from linkages with university level personnel; 3) incentives for personnel to participate in training; 4) clear identification and evaluation of expected outcomes for families and children; and 5) supervised application of content information for families and children (Brinkerhoff, 1980; Browder, 1983). In addition, the most successful in-service training programs have been those to which the lead agency and local service providers have committed resources necessary to support longitudinal and planned training activities (Crossland, Hasselbring, & O'Brien, 1980) and that have involved institutions of higher education (Beck, Harris, Johnson, Van Duyne, Johnson, & Fiscus, 1982). Mass training programs, such as statewide conferences, meet few, if any, of these criteria for success.

Graduate level courses that are practicum-based or linked to field experience are an immediate possibility for in-service training of professionals who live near a college or university program that trains professionals to work with infants. Colleges and universities need to alter typical training programs to better address retraining of practicing personnel. Scheduling coursework during late afternoon and evening hours or during summer months, in convenient locations, such as program offices or schools rather than university campuses, and linking quality instructors to supervised, on-site, practical applications of course information constitute one successful approach to providing training that may be used by program personnel to address family and infant needs (Kelley & Van Vactor, 1982). Linking attention to training content to statewide systems of personnel development through collaborative efforts between state level agencies and universities enables institutions of higher education to play an integral role in developing a pool of highly qualified personnel (Browder, 1983).

Several models of in-service training rely on a productive and collaborative relationship between state agencies and institutions of higher education and offer creative approaches for developing qualified personnel. Summer training institutes, taught by university level faculty and providing specific information with on-site supervision of participants for at least one semester in their programs of employment, have been more successful than isolated didactic experiences or similar training provided by faculty who are less than well trained (Crossland et al., 1980). Field-based summer training institutes, taught at program locations to allow for practicum experiences with families and children, have also effected positive changes in both personnel trained and participant children (Crain, 1980). In another model, a series of university courses, provided at convenient community locations, with accompanying weekly seminars and regularly scheduled on-site visits by faculty, resulted in trainees achieving stated competencies and children reflecting educational gains.

Combined coursework and practicum experiences, however, are not the only effective options for in-service training. Organizing content information into written instructional modules that include both informational content and examples of self-study activities for application of information has been used, followed by on-site evaluation of trainees' application skills. A variation of this approach uses audio-visual materials to supplement instructional modules (Brown, 1987). Somewhat futuristic extensions of this approach rely on interactive television segments to allow trainees to explore instructional situations and make methods application choices (Hofmeister & Thorkildsen, 1987).

A supervised period of clinical application has been used by the American Speech and Hearing Association (ASHA) to provide additional training for recent program graduates. A variation of this model has been proposed to meet needs for in-service training by the American Occupational Therapy Association's Task Force on Early Childhood Programs (Dunn et al., 1989). In this approach, practicing therapists obtain mentor relationships with individuals recognized for their expertise with infants and children. A staff development plan is formulated, stating the goals and objectives for the supervised time period. The skilled professional's participation is supported through payment from his or her employing agency and practicing therapists are provided release time from job responsibilities to work with the mentor. Evaluation of the success of this training experience is assessed in terms of: 1) attainment of professional staff development goals, 2) change in competencies of practicing therapists, and 3) positive changes in outcomes for families and children. This approach is particularly useful for training recent graduates who are likely to have had limited experiences with families and children because it is more individualized than other in-service training activities.

Quality Early Intervention Systems

A variety of longitudinal and planned training experiences, taught by knowledgeable and competent interdisciplinary faculty, linked to state level assessments of personnel training needs, and supported by state and local service-delivery providers can be the result of collaborative efforts among state agencies, institutions of higher education, and professional organizations. The benefits of such collaborative efforts have been demonstrated in states such as Iowa that have successfully overcome the numerous obstacles to effective collaborative relationships (see Robinson, Chapter 14, this volume).

Infants, toddlers, and their families are particularly vulnerable to poorly designed or fragmented systems that deliver services through less than adequately trained personnel. Authorization of the federal Program for Infants and Toddlers with Handicaps establishes a basis for comprehensive services for all infants, but it also potentially places a generation of young children and their families at-risk for receiving less than quality services. This situation is understandable since service systems must be at least minimally in place before quality features can be designed and implemented. However, federal and state policy-makers, state administrative units, local service providers, institutions of higher education, and early intervention personnel themselves have a responsibility for implementing and supporting activities to bridge the gap between minimum and exemplary quality service systems as quickly as possible. Collaborative commitments that ensure a well-trained pool of personnel are an important and significant first step.

REFERENCES

Bailey, D.B. (1989). Issues and directions in preparing professionals to work with young handicapped children and their families. In J.J. Gallagher, P.L. Trohanis, and R.M. Clifford (Eds.), *Policy implementation and PL 99-457: Planning for young children with special needs* (97–132). Baltimore: Paul H. Brookes Publishing Co.

Bailey, D.B., Palsha, S.A., & Huntington, G.S. (in press). Preservice preparation of special educators to work with handicapped infants and their families: Current status and training needs. *Journal of Early Intervention*.

Beck, C., Harris, J.D., Johnson, R., Van Duyne, H.J., Johnson, A.B., & Fiscus, E. (1982). The liaison model: An approach to cooperative inservice program planning. *Teacher Education and Special Education, 5*(2), 50–52.

Blackhurst, E. (1980). Program evaluation through learner change. *Teacher Education and Special Education, 3,* 13–20.

Bricker, D. (1979). Educational synthesizer. In M.A. Thomas (Ed.), *Hey, don't forget about me!* (pp. 84–98). Reston, VA: Council for Exceptional Children.

Bricker, D. (1987). Comments on personnel preparation. In R. Weiner & J. Koppelman (Eds.), *From birth to five: Serving the youngest handicapped children.* (pp. 69–84). Alexandria, VA: Capitol Publications.

Bricker, D., & Slentz, K. (1989). Personnel preparation: Handicapped infants. In M.C. Wang, M.C. Reynolds, & H.J. Walberg (Eds.), *The handbook of special education research and practice: Low incidence conditions* (Vol. 3, pp. 319–345). Elmsford, NY: Pergamon Press.

Brinkerhoff, R.O. (1980). Evaluation of inservice programs. *Teacher Education and Special Education, 3*(3), 27–37.

Browder, D. (1983). Guidelines for inservice planning. *Exceptional Children, 49*(4), 300–307.

Brown, C. (1987). *The neonatal experience.* Washington, DC: George Washington University.

Bruder, M.B., & McLean, M. (1988). Personnel preparation for infant interventionists: A review of federally funded projects. *Journal of the Division for Early Childhood.*

Campbell, P.H. (1987). The integrated programming team: An approach for coordinating professionals of various disciplines in programs for students with severe and multiple handicaps. *Journal of The Association for Persons with Severe Handicaps, 12*(2), 107–116.

Campbell, P.H. (in press). Service delivery approaches. In M.J. Wilcox & P.H. Campbell (Eds.), *Communication programming from birth to three: A handbook for public school professionals.* San Diego: College-Hill Press.

Campbell, P.H., Bellamy, G.J., & Bishop, K.K. (1988). Statewide intervention systems: An overview of the new federal program for infants and toddlers with handicaps. *Journal of Special Education, 22*(1), 25–40.

Campbell, P.H., & Hanson, M.J. (1987). Early intervention guidelines. Seattle, WA: The Association for Persons with Severe Handicaps.

Crain, E.J. (1980). A generic practicum: A seven week program for mildly handicapped learners. *Teacher Education and Special Education, 3*(4), 33–36.

Crossland, C.L., Hasselbring, T.S., & O'Brien, K. (1980). Project IMPACT: Inservice plan assisting classroom teachers. *Teacher Education and Special Education, 5*(2), 53–58.

The Department of Education and the Department of Health and Human Services. (1989). *Meeting the needs of infants and toddlers with handicaps.* A report to Congress. Washington, DC: Government Printing Office.

Dunn, W. (1989). Integrated related services for preschoolers with neurological impairments: Issues and strategies. *Remedial and Special Education, 10*(3), 31–39.

Dunn, W., & Campbell, P. (in press). Designing pediatric service provision. In *Pediatric occupational therapy: Facilitating effective service provision.* Thorofare, NJ: SLACK.

Dunn, W., Campbell, P.H., Otter, P., Hall, S., & Berger, E. (1989). *Guidelines for the practice of occupational therapy in early intervention.* Rockville, MD: American Occupational Therapy Association.

Gallagher, J.J., Harbin, G., Thomas, D., Clifford, R., & Wenger, M. (1988). *Major policy issues in implementing Part H—P.L. 99-457 (infants and toddlers).* Chapel Hill, NC. Carolina Institute for Child and Family Policy.

Gallagher, J.J., Trohanis, P.L., & Clifford, R.M. (Eds.). (1989). *Policy implementation and PL 99-457: Planning for young children with special needs.* Baltimore: Paul H. Brookes Publishing Co.

Gilkerson, L., Hilliard, A.G., Schrag, E., & Shonkoff, J.P. (1987). *Report accompanying the education of the handicapped amendments of 1986 and commenting on P.L. 99-457* (House report #99-860). Washington, DC: Available from National Center for Clinical Infant Programs.

Healy, A., Keesee, P.D., & Smith, B.S. (1985). *Early services for children with special needs: Transactions for family support.* Iowa City: University of Iowa Hospitals and Clinics.

Hofmeister, A., & Thorkildsen, R. (1987). Interactive videodisc and exceptional individuals. In J.D. Lindsey (Ed.), *Computers and exceptional individuals* (pp. 189–205). Columbus: Charles E. Merrill.

Humphrey, R., & Link, S. (1989). *Entry level preparation of occupational therapists to work in early intervention programs.* Unpublished manuscript, University of North Carolina, Chapel Hill.

Johnson, B., McGonigel, M., & Kaufmann, R. (1989). *Guidelines and recommended practices for the individualized family service plan.* Washington, DC: Association for the Care of Children's Health.

Kelley, E.J., & Van Vactor, J.C. (1982). Inservice in remote, sparsely populated schools: A comparative analysis for four instructional approaches. *Teacher Education and Special Education, 5*(2), 24–32.

Klein, N., & Campbell, P.H. (1990). Preparing personnel to serve at-risk infants, toddlers, and preschoolers. In S.J. Meisels & J.P. Shonkoff (Eds.), *Handbook of early childhood intervention* (pp. 679–699). New York: Cambridge University Press.

McCollum, J. (1987). Early interventionists in infant and early childhood programs: A comparison of preservice training needs. *Topics in Early Childhood Special Education, 7*(3), 24–35.

McCollum, J., McLean, M., McCarten, K., Odom, S., & Kaiser, A. (1989, April). *Recommendations for certification of early childhood special educators.* Position paper prepared for the Division of Early Childhood, Council for Exceptional Children, Reston, VA.

McCollum, J., & Thorpe, E. (1988). Training in infant specialists: A look to the future. *Infants and Young Children, 1*(2).

McLaughlin, M.J., Smith-Davis, J., & Burke, P.J. (1986). *Personnel to educate the handicapped in America: A status report.* College Park: University of Maryland.

Meisels, S.J., Harbin, G., Modigliani, K, & Olson, K. (1988). Formulating optimal state early childhood intervention policies. *Exceptional Children, 55*(2).

Shelton, T.L., Jeppson, E.S., & Johnson, B.H. (1987). *Family centered care for children with special health care needs.* Washington, DC: Association for the Care of Children's Health.

Smith, B.J. (Ed.). (1987, March). *Position statements and recommendations relating to P.L. 99-457 and other federal and state early childhood policies.* Division of Early Childhood.

Smith-Davis, J., Burke, P.J., & Noel, M. (1984). *Personnel to educate the handicapped in America: Supply and demand from a programmatic viewpoint.* College Park: University of Maryland.

Smith-Davis, J., Morskink, C., & Wheatley, F.W. (1984). *Quality in personnel preparation for education for the handicapped: The baseline book.* Vienna, Virginia: Dissem/Action.

Tenth annual report to Congress on the implementation of the Education of the Handicapped Act. (1988). Washington, DC: United States Department of Education.

Tjossem, T.D. (Ed.). (1976). *Intervention strategies for high risk infants and young children.* Baltimore: University Park Press.

Trohanis, P. (1986). *Agenda, participants, and minutes from first meeting of OSERS task force on early childhood futures.* Chapel Hill: University of North Carolina, START Program, FPG Child Development Center.

Turnbull, A.P., & Turnbull, H.R. (1987). *Families, professionals, and exceptionality: A special partnership.* Columbus: Charles E. Merrill.

Walsh, S., Campbell, P.H., & McKenna, P. (1988). First year implementation of the federal program for infants and toddlers with handicaps: A view from the states. *Topics in Early Childhood Special Education, 8*(3), 1–22.

Weiner, A., & Koppelman, J. (1987). *From birth to five: Serving the youngest handicapped children.* Alexandria, VA: Capitol Publications, Inc.

Wilcox, M., Bashir, A., Iglesias, A., Liebergott, J., & Snyder-McLean, L. (1989). Communication-based services for at risk and handicapped infants, toddlers, and their families. *ASHA, 31,* 32–34.

Winton, P.J. (1988). Effective communication between parents and professionals. In D.B. Bailey & R.J. Simeonsson (Eds.), *Family assessment in early intervention* (pp. 207–228). Columbus: Charles E. Merrill.

7

Preparation of Personnel to Work with Students with Complex Health Care Needs

Donna H. Lehr

The newest and greatest challenge for school administrators may be providing educational services to students who have complex health care needs or who are medically fragile (Lehr, in press; Lehr & Noonan, 1989; Viadero, 1987). These children, who in the past have not survived long enough to become students, are now, in some cases, being educated in regular schools alongside peers who do not have medically complex conditions. Their presence has spurred a flurry of activity among professional groups and federal offices seeking to address their needs. The Council for Exceptional Children (CEC) has developed a task force report on the education of children considered to be medically fragile (1988). The Association for Persons with Severe Handicaps (TASH) has formed a Critical Issues subcommittee to collect and disseminate information on this topic. Surgeon General C. Everett Koop has developed a campaign designed to ensure the development of family-centered, community-based care for children with special health care needs (1987). Congress's Office of Technology Assessment has completed a study on technology dependent children (1987).

While there has been considerable activity focusing on the needs of children with special health care needs, little of this activity has specifically addressed the preparation of personnel to work with these children from an educational perspective. To understand personnel training needs, it is necessary to begin with an understanding of the unique needs of these children and the issues surrounding the delivery of services to them. Thus, this chapter focuses initially on these areas and continues with a discussion of personnel preparation for various individuals working with these children within an educational framework.

THE CHILDREN

The students who are the focus of this chapter have been variously described as being technology dependent, being medically fragile, and as having special health care needs (Lehr & Noonan, 1989). The United States Congress Office of Technology Assessment defines a technology dependent child as, "one who needs both a medical device to compensate for the loss of a vital body function and substantial and ongoing nursing care to avert death or further disability" (1987, p. 3). The Task Force on Technology Dependent Children (1988) identifies the individuals in their target group with the following characteristics: "a person from birth through 21 years of age; has a chronic disability; requires the routine use of a specific medical device to compensate for the loss of use of a life sustaining body function; and requires daily, ongoing care or monitoring by trained personnel" (p. vii–1). Surgeon General Koop (1987) indicates that the term "children with special health care needs" refers to children with a wide range of disabilities and illness whose health care needs might be mild or severe, short-term, intermittent, or chronic. He clearly states his preference, however, not to strictly define the group. CEC (1988) uses the term "medically fragile" to describe a population of students who ". . . require specialized technological health care procedures for life support and/or health support during the school day" (p. 1). Lehr (in press) has used a widely encompassing term of "complex health care needs" to refer to children who may be described in the literature as: 1) having chronic illnesses, 2) being technology dependent, or 3) being medically fragile, but furthermore uses it to describe students "when the delivery of education and health care services to meet their needs raises new issues for the school district and requires other than traditional care provided in the schools" (p. 8).

The emergence of this group of students is easily traceable to several sources (Lehr & Noonan, 1989). First, changes in medical technology have enabled persons who previously died at or shortly after birth to live long enough to become students. Second, the equipment they may need for survival or support, such as suctioning machines or respirators, are now small and portable enough to be transported outside the hospital to their homes, in their family cars, on school buses, and into their schools. Second, preschool incentives of PL 94-142 (the Education for All Handicapped Children Act, 1975) and reinforcements by PL 99-457 (the Education of the Handicapped Act Amendments, 1986) mandating the provision of educational programs to children ages birth to 3, have resulted in a greater number of programs available for these young children who have been the beneficiaries of the improved medical technology. The third reason for the increase in students with complex health care needs in our schools stems from the change from institutional care to community care for increasing numbers of individuals, including these children. This movement can be traced in part to society embracing the concept of least restrictiveness and in part to the economics of lower costs for care in nonhospital settings. The net effect is a greater number of school-age students with needs for health related services who are the responsibility of local education agencies.

INCIDENCE

There are no precise data on the number of children with complex health care needs who receive or are in need of educational services. The Office of Technology Assessment 1987 estimates are shown in Table 7.1. They indicate that anywhere from 17,000 to over 30,000 children may be considered to be technology dependent, depending upon the definition used. However, in one state, Wisconsin, it is estimated that as many as 10%–15% of the state's children (227,000) have chronic or disabling health conditions, some of which may be mild (Wisconsin Maternal and Child Health Coalition, 1989). Furthermore, as many as 30,000 children are considered to have "severe conditions which create special burdens for the child and family" (Wisconsin Maternal and Child Health Coalition, 1989, p. 3). It is also estimated that 32,633 children in Wisconsin are affected to some degree by chronic diseases including asthma, leukemia, cystic fibrosis, and spina bifida.

While variability exists in the estimate of incidence, it is clear that the numbers of children in need of specialized health care are increasing. The Office of Technology Assessment (1987) states that:

> the population of technology-dependent children has increased in both size and visibility over the past 25 years, and it will probably continue to increase for several more. . . it is likely that the incidence of dependence on the technologies used by children in Groups I, II, and III [see Table 7.1] may as much as double in the next few years, stabilizing or even declining somewhat in later years. Long survival of those who are dependent, however, means that the total number of technology-dependent children will probably not decline. (p. 5)

Table 7.1. Summary of OTA estimates of the size of the technology-dependent child population, 1987

Defined population	Estimated number of children		
Group I			
Requiring ventilator assistance	680	–	2,000
Group II			
Requiring parenteral nutrition	350	–	700
Requiring prolonged intravenous drugs	270	–	8,275
Group III			
Requiring other device-based respiratory or nutritional support	1,000	–	6,000
Rounded subtotal (I + II + III)	2,300	–	17,000
Group IV			
Requiring apnea monitoring	6,800	–	45,000
Requiring renal dialysis	1,000	–	6,000
Requiring other device-associated nursing	Unknown, perhaps 30,000 or more		

From: United States Congress, Office of Technology Assessment (1987). *Technology dependent children: Hospital v. home-care—A technical memorandum.* (OTA-TM-H-38). Washington DC: Government Printing Office. Reprinted with permission.

THE NEEDS OF STUDENTS

Considerable variability is demonstrated among students with special health care needs. Wide differences in cognitive abilities, motor abilities, language abilities, and social skills can be observed. All, however, share some common needs which include the following:

1. The need to be provided with a free, public educational program
2. The need to be provided with an education in the least restrictive environment
3. The need to have as a part of their educational plan a health care plan
4. The need to be treated as a child first, then a student, and not as a patient
5. The need to interact with other children with and without similar health care needs (Lehr, in press, p. 10–11)

ISSUES IN EDUCATIONAL SERVICE DELIVERY

Since educational service delivery to students with complex health care needs is relatively new, very difficult case by case decisions are being made regarding service-delivery models. Few state guidelines exist to aid districts in determining the best methods for providing services (Palfrey, DiPrete,

Walker, Shannon, & Maroney, 1987), and few administrators have had longitudinal experience with this group. Consequently, considerable variability in service delivery can be found across districts even within the same state (Lehr & Noonan, 1989). This lack of policy and lack of longitudinal experiences has led to the existence of a number of as yet unresolved issues. Those include issues related to placement and personnel responsible for provision of health care.

Placement Issues

In the past, students who survived the neonatal period and lived to school age were provided educational services in their homes, residential facilities, or hospitals. While these options remain, no longer are they the exclusive options. For some students with unstable medical conditions, hospital or home settings are the most appropriate educational settings. It is no longer the case, however, that students are automatically excluded from the school when they require health care service beyond that which typically has been provided in school settings (Lehr, in press). Now students with complex health care needs are being provided with services at every point along the classic placement continuums. Sirvis (1988) describes a fourth grade student with minimal head control and requiring ventilator assistance attending a regular school and enrolled in a regular fourth grade class. A survey of Wisconsin schools (Lehr & Haubrich, 1988) reveals that in some districts students requiring health services, such as tube feeding, are not provided those services at school; rather, they are provided a home program, while in other districts they are educated in their local public schools.

In one case on the issue of least restrictive placement of a student with complex health care needs (*Department of Education, State of Hawaii v. Dorr*), the school district offered a home-based education program for Katherine, a student with cystic fibrosis and tracheomalacia. Appeals of this case resulted in a ruling that, in fact, for this child, home-based instruction was not the most appropriate, least restrictive environment, and the district was ordered to provide an educational program in a school.

While decisions regarding the most appropriate placement for students with complex health care needs should be based on the individual needs of students, unfortunately, often the variability in placements is not due to the unique needs of students; rather, it is due to administrative attitude, availability of services, and costs involved (Lehr & Noonan, 1989).

Regardless of the placement, however, appropriate educational services should be provided. The Task Force on Technology Dependent Children (1988) points out that:

> the developmental/educational needs of infants and children in acute facilities are often overlooked by professional staff who focus on the child's medical problems. Attention should be given to assuring access to appropriate services

in acute care hospitals as soon as the child's condition permits. Furthermore, technology-dependent children should have access to home programs regardless of the anticipated time out of school. (p. 42)

PERSONNEL ISSUES

A considerable number of issues related to personnel arise concerning the delivery of educational programs to students with special health care needs. Among them are questions regarding who will be responsible for providing the necessary health care procedures and who will be responsible for coordinating the child's program and ensuring the development and delivery of a quality program.

One of the most controversial issues in the area of educational service delivery to children with complex health care needs is that of identifying who is responsible for providing the necessary health care services to the children and, furthermore, who will pay for the provision of the services. The basis of the issue is the lack of clarity in PL 94-142 regarding the provision of medical versus related services. PL 94-142 states that related services are those services necessary for a child to benefit from special education, while medical services are defined as evaluations essential for diagnostic purposes. While many nursing services are viewed as related services, questions arise as to whether catheterization, tracheostomy care, and suctioning are what is meant by nursing care (Task Force on Technology Dependent Children, 1988).

The *Tatro* case (*Tatro v. Texas,* 1980) determined that a school district must provide clean intermittent catheterization for a student in order to enable her to benefit from special education services, but it did not specify who must perform the procedures. In the *Department of Education, State of Hawaii v. Dorr* (1983) case, it was concluded that the school district was responsible for implementing health care procedures, including maintenance of a tracheostomy tube. This decision was based on the reasoning that, if parents could implement the necessary procedures, the procedures could not be considered so complex that school personnel could not learn to implement them. In *Detsel v. Ambach* (1986) and *In re Bevin H.* (1986), it was concluded that the school districts were *not* responsible for providing health care procedures such as monitoring use of a respirator, checking of vital signs, and suctioning.

Clearly, the courts have demonstrated differences of opinion regarding the interpretation of medical versus related services (Lehr, in press; Lehr & Noonan, 1989). Consequently, there remain substantial differences in how these questions are resolved in individual cases. In some districts, teachers and aides routinely perform procedures such as tube feeding and suctioning, while in other districts, students attend schools with private nurses to attend to their needs or students are assigned to schools with full-time school nurses and those nurses provide all the necessary services.

Beyond these basic issues of where children with complex health care needs should be educated and who will provide the services, there are a number of other issues surrounding the delivery of services to these children, including how the students will be transported to school (e.g., school buses with other children, specially equipped buses to enable transportation of the necessary equipment, ambulances); who will attend to their needs in transit; and who will be responsible for the coordination of services for the students (i.e., parents, school nurse, social worker, or teacher).

Again, while many different answers to these questions are being generated, each has implications for the preparation of personnel to meet the needs of students with complex health care needs. Different answers to the questions result in the identification of different training targets and different training needs.

The Personnel

To date little attention has been paid to the preparation of personnel to meet the needs of students with complex health care needs in educational settings. The limited studies available on this topic reveal that even school nurses responsible for implementing health related procedures, such as gastrostomy feedings or tracheostomy care, often do not feel competent in doing so (Hester, Goodwin, & Igoe, 1980). Such procedures had not been a part of "typical" school nursing. While some special educators are trained to work with students with severe disabilities, Sirvis (1988) points out that ". . . even the most skilled special education teacher may be somewhat reticent to provide educational services for students with special health care needs" (p. 42).

Typically, the key to increased competence and comfort is training. Little data exist indicating the current training efforts for personnel working in educational settings with students with complex health care needs. In one study, Mulligan-Ault, Guess, Struth, and Thompson (1988) asked teachers in Kansas to identify how they received training for implementing health care procedures in their classrooms. The teachers indicated that formal in-service training was provided 51% of the time, informal in-service training 43% of the time, the family was the source 36% of the time, and university course offerings provided training 27% of the time.

Students with special health care needs are increasing in number, and it follows that there will be an increased need for training personnel to work with them. The remainder of this chapter focuses on the need for trained personnel, the personnel requiring training, and the nature and content of their training.

The Need

Education for students with complex health care needs is a new and growing area. In the past these children did not attend schools, and consequently, educators, with the exception of teachers in hospital settings, did not need the skills necessary to work with them. That is no longer the case, and now, not only are these students in public schools, but they are in least restrictive environments, requiring that a wide range of individuals in school settings have skills in working with them. No studies providing data on the number of personnel specifically or even generally trained to work with these students or on the number of training programs providing specific course content on this topic were found in the literature. However, the need for trained personnel is expressed in much of the literature on the topic.

The Council for Exceptional Children (CEC) (1988) provides specific recommendations for including appropriate information about students with specialized health care needs as one of the legislative issues. The Iowa State Department of Education has adopted guidelines developed by the Task Force on Children with Special Health Care Needs (1988) that clearly specify training recommendations, which are discussed under the Training Content and Nature section of this chapter. The Task Force on Technology Dependent Children (1988) included as one of its five recommendations regarding education that:

> Congress should provide funding, through the Department of Education, Office of Special Education with assistance from Title V, Maternal and Child Health, to assist states in identifying and developing appropriate inservice training for all school personnel who interact with the technology-dependent child. (p. 43)

All of these reports underscore the need for trained personnel to meet the special health care needs of students in the schools.

The Trainees

Deciding who should receive the training begins with a look at the special health care needs of the students. Surgeon General C. Everett Koop (1987) describes their need for family-centered, community-based, coordinated care. Fulfilling these needs necessitates a system that includes many individuals from many perspectives, including the parents and social, medical, and educational services. Figure 7.1 provides an illustration of the elements of comprehensive care for children with special health care needs (Wisconsin Maternal and Child Health Coalition, 1989). While Figure 7.1 shows the interrelationships necessary to serve the child in the community in general, this approach should include considering the student as a part of a regular education environment. The people included in the early identification and intervention services and educational and vocational services may include: 1) the principal; 2) the special education teacher; 3) the regular education teacher; 4) the speech, occupational, and physical therapists; 5) the school psychologists; 6) the school social workers; 7) the school nurse; 8) the physical education teacher; 9) the secretary; 10) the cafeteria staff; 11) the building maintenance staff; and 12) the bus driver.

All these people will interact with and provide services to the student with complex health care needs and must understand their unique needs for best interaction. However, in most school districts, few of the individuals in any of these roles have had opportunities to have contact with children who have complex health care needs. The author has made presentations on the topic of students with complex health care needs to many groups of school

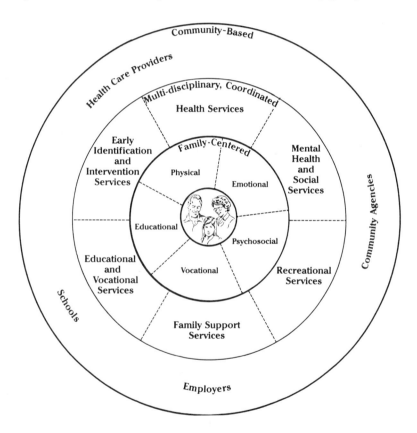

Figure 7.1. Elements of comprehensive care for children with special health care needs. From: Wisconsin Maternal and Child Health Coalition. (1989). *Mothers and children: The bridge to comprehensive care for children with special health care needs.* Madison: Author. Reprinted with permission. (This figure was adapted from an original concept in "Comprehensive Care for the Person with Hemophilia," The National Hemophilia Foundation, 1977.)

administrators. Typically, the presentations have been descriptions of children and, in some cases, videotapes of the children in public schools. The overwhelming reaction has been one of amazement that these students are included in public schools elsewhere and realization that these children may become a part of their own school programs in the future.

The target populations for training are obvious and extensive. If school administrators are to be responsible for educational programs for students with special health care needs, they need to be prepared to do so. Teachers, psychologists, therapists, nurses, social workers, and support personnel must be prepared to meet the student's needs. If these children are to become students in the schools, all persons interacting with them need to be prepared to do so.

While differences of opinion continue to exist regarding whose responsibility it is to administer health related procedures, whoever is responsible must be appropriately and specifically trained. As discussed, one cannot automatically assume that the responsibility should be placed upon the school nurse and that because the nurse has medical training, she or he will feel competent to implement the necessary procedures. Procedures such as tube feeding and suctioning may be quite different from those procedures typically administered as a part of standard school nursing practices.

Training Content and Nature

Just as with identifying trainees, the skills and knowledge individuals involved in educational service delivery must have is best understood after considering the special health care needs of the students. The students are first of all children, with needs like all other children. Although these children have special needs, it is not true that only personnel with very specific, very different training can interact with them. In fact, most of the skills and knowledge needed to work with children with complex health care needs is exactly the same as those needed by all individuals working directly in, or as a support to, other programs for children with and without special educational needs. For children with complex health care needs, however, it is possible that a professional's lack of knowledge or skills could have more serious consequences than for other children. For example, all personnel working in schools should have ability to work as a team to best provide educational programs for students. However, when the child has special health care needs, lack of teaming could result in the inappropriate provision of critical health related care for that child. As another example, consider the need for everyone to have basic knowledge of what to do in case of an emergency. The knowledge is necessary; fortunately, however, with most children the odds of needing to apply it are small. In contrast, consider the odds of needing to act in an emergency when the student has apnea or experiences life threatening seizures. Again, the information needed is the same, but the likelihood of needing to use the information is much greater, and the consequences of failure to use the information correctly may be more serious.

Consequently, training must be designed in a manner to ensure that each child's needs are met. The CEC Ad Hoc Committee on Medically Fragile Students (1988) recommends that:

> Personnel who might have contact with students requiring specialized health care needs [*sic*] should demonstrate:
>> awareness and understanding of students' health care, emotional, and educational needs
>> knowledge of common medical and health terms
>> knowledge of medical characteristics including etiology and implications
>> knowledge of physical, developmental, and emotional characteristics
>> knowledge of appropriate curricular and environmental modifications
>> knowledge of the roles and responsibilities of the health care professional in the classroom
>> knowledge of the importance and necessity for establishing support systems for personnel, students, and families
>> knowledge of resources for families (pp. 5–6)

The Iowa State Department of Education has adopted guidelines suggested by the Task Force on Children with Special Health Care Needs regarding training (1988). Emphasized are recommendations that the Department of Education develop standards for preservice training and encourage area education agencies to provide in-service training in specified areas. The recommendations relating to training are included in Table 7.2.

It should be noted that specifications are included in the Iowa recommendations for both preservice and in-service training. Obviously, including information about individuals with complex health care needs is desirable for all future teachers, therapists, psychologists, and administrators. Building an awareness of the existence of these students in our school system is essential to ensure acceptance and the development of appropriate programs. There is a clear need for two specific groups of individuals to receive training to meet the needs of students with special health care needs. Many of these children are the beneficiaries of advances in medical technology and are very young (Lehr & Noonan, 1989) or are children with other severe disabling conditions (Hotte, Monroe, Philbrook, & Scarlata, 1984). Frequently, these children are taught by teachers with early childhood, special education training or training to work with students with severe disabilities. Thus, these particular groups of teachers or students preparing to become teachers should be specially prepared to work specifically with children with special health care needs.

Targeting preservice personnel exclusively has several obvious limitations. First, many professionals already holding degrees are having their initial experiences with children with complex health care needs, and they did not receive training during their preservice years. Second, some training

Table 7.2.   Iowa Department of Education training recommendations

1. The Department of Education should develop standards that would require preservice institutions to include the following information in their preparation programs:

   a. Didactic and practicum experiences for school administrators should include information and training in the following areas:
      - Children with special education and health needs
      - Special education entitlement, rules, and regulations
      - Interagency and interdisciplinary communication
      - Community resources and how to gain access to them

   b. Didactic and practicum experiences for special education instructional and support personnel should include information and training in the following areas:
      - Certification in first aid and CPR
      - Physical care of the child with disabilities, general health information and nutrition, infection control, skin care, elimination, oral hygiene, common childhood diseases, and commonly occurring disabling conditions
      - Community resources and how to gain access to them
      - Team approach to service provision, confidentiality, and dealing with sensitive information
      - Effective IEP (individualized education program) writing for children with special health care needs

2. The Department of Education should require that human relations staff training include information on persons with disabilities and children with special health care needs.

3. The Department of Education should encourage AEAs (area education agencies) to provide periodic in-service training in the following areas:
   - Certification in first aid and CPR
   - Stress management
   - Grief process
   - Health care practices
   - Legal implications and ethical dilemmas
   - Interaction and communication with parents and other family members
   - Administration of medications for noncertified staff and teachers
   - Interdisciplinary group decision-making
   - Family systems
   - Teaming with the family and other service providers

4. The Department of Education should promulgate rules requiring all persons providing services to a child with special health care needs to receive training in first aid and CPR and be recertified as recommended by the certifying agency.

5. The Department of Education should develop standards and training experiences for those staff who transport children with special health care needs. Training should cover:
   - First aid and CPR
   - Evacuation procedures in case of accident or fire
   - Use of medical equipment
   - Positioning for safe transportation
   - Signs and symptoms of distress

From: Task Force on Children with Special Health Care Needs. (1988). *Recommendations: Services for children with special health care needs.* Des Moines: Iowa Department of Education. Reprinted with permission.

cannot be provided in the abstract. That is, while one can receive general training in providing tube feeding in a preservice training program, specific information is required about each individual child and must be provided by the child's physician. Prior background training is helpful, but in-service training is still necessary to individualize the procedures.

Particular note must be made of one essential training focus: the family. The Surgeon General's Campaign on Children with Special Health Care Needs (1987) emphasized the importance of family care coordination for these children. Shelton, Jeppson, and Johnson (1987) have translated this need to maintain a family focus into a checklist for professional training programs which is shown in Figure 7.2.

The ideal training program designed to prepare personnel to provide appropriate educational programs for students with special health care needs would be multifaceted. It would have the following characteristics:

1.   The training program would be designed to meet the needs of a wide range of personnel in the schools, including the principals and other building administrators; regular and special education teachers, including those having direct contact with the students and those who may have only indirect contact; related service personnel; clerical, maintenance, and transportation personnel; the other students in the school; the families of the children with special health care needs; and the families of the other students in the school.

2.   The training program design would identify different training goals for people in different roles. Obviously, not everyone has to be trained to administer the specific health care procedures. All school employees should be knowledgeable of appropriate procedures of obtaining medical assistance in the event of an emergency.

3.   The training program would be designed to utilize a variety of methods for meeting the training goals. During the 1980s a number of very useful training materials have been developed in the area of the education and care of children with special health care needs. Some of these are provided in the Appendix to this chapter. These materials, as they stand, will be sufficient to meet some training goals, while for others they will not be sufficient. For example, viewing the tape from Learner Managed Designs on tracheostomy care might be appropriate to meet the goal of developing an awareness of the process of implementing procedures for building administrators and other personnel in the school not directly responsible for implementing the procedures. However, it is not enough to meet the goal of training someone to actually implement the procedures. For those personnel, viewing the tape might be just the first step. Additional training might include:

A.   Reading appropriate sections of the Larson book referenced in the Appendix

B.   Obtaining instructions from the child's physician

C.   Observing the parent implement the procedure
D.   Implementing the procedure while being observed by a trainer
E.   Repeated practice until mastery
F.   Periodic monitoring to ensure continued appropriate implementation

4.   Training would be timely, systematic, and comprehensive, not sporadic or episodic. Careful thought would be given to the timing of training. While it may be obvious that training in implementing specific health care procedures should be provided prior to a child's arrival at school, the author has heard numerous reports of teachers being responsible for implementing procedures without the benefit of formalized training until several weeks

Are there opportunities for professionals to learn directly from parents about their perspectives and support needs?

Do parents participate in the development of training programs for professionals?

Do preservice and in-service training programs provide instruction in the following areas?

  Effective communication skills and methods for working collaboratively with families

  Skills in working collaboratively as a team member with professionals of other disciplines

  Service delivery models that provide a mechanism for coordinating care among agencies in the community and for developing linkages to and from primary, secondary, and tertiary care settings

  Planning care in the home and community

  Financing options for families

  Normal and atypical child development

  Support needs of families

  Family dynamics

  Effectiveness of parent-to-parent support

  Advocating for comprehensive community resources

  Research methodology examining the cost and emotional effectiveness of family-centered care policies and programs

  Techniques for conducting research in a way that respects the rights of the children and families and reflects a balanced approach, focusing on family strengths as well as needs

Figure 7.2.   A checklist for professional training programs.   From: Shelton, T.L., Jeppson, E.S., & Johnson, B.H. (1987). *Family centered care for children with special health care needs.* Washington, DC: Association for the Care of Children's Health. Reprinted with permission.

later or not at all. Training must be designed in a manner to ensure that goals are met through careful planning, implementation, and monitoring of training effectiveness.

5.   Training would be sensitive to the needs of the student as a child. Decisions regarding what information is provided to whom, in what manner, with who present, must be made in the best interest of each specific child. Some children may want to tell their peers about why they must be tube fed or catheterized. Others may not want or be able to do so. Some children might wish to be present during discussion of their needs, while others may not. Discretion must be used at all times regarding what information is appropriate to share and what will be kept confidential. Parental involvement in the decision-making in this area is critical.

SUMMARY

Along with the emergence of a new population of students with complex health care needs a need for personnel trained to meet their unique needs has developed. Professionals are finding that their current repertoire of skills from previous training does not adequately meet the needs of these students. Professional need for in-service training to expand current knowledge and skills bases is critical. For students preparing to enter the profession we can anticipate the likelihood of encountering students with special health care needs in the schools, and we must redesign our courses to incorporate information regarding this new group of students.

Training design must recognize the multitude of involved personnel and their varying levels of involvement. It must be systematic and individualized. But most important, it must be sensitive to the fact that children with special health care needs are first of all *children.*

REFERENCES

Council for Exceptional Children. (1988). *Report of The Council for Exceptional Children's Ad Hoc Committee on Medically Fragile Students.* Reston, VA: Author.

Department of Education, State of Hawaii v. Katherine D. Dorr, 1983, 727, F.2d 809 (9th Cr. 1983).

Detsel v. Ambach (ND NY 1986, 1985–86 EHCR DEC, 557:335).

Hester, H.K., Goodwin, L.D., & Igoe, J.B. (1980). *The SNAP School Nurse Survey: Summary of procedures and results* (Project #1846002597A1). Washington, DC: United States Department of Maternal and Child Health.

Hotte, E.A., Monroe, H.S., Philbrook, D.L., & Scarlata, R.W. (1984). Programming for persons with profound retardation: A three year retrospective study. *Mental Retardation, 22*(2), 75–78.

In re Bevin, H. EHLR 508: 134, 1986.

Koop, C.E. (1987). *Surgeon General's report: Children with special health care needs—Campaign, '87.* Washington, DC: U.S. Government Printing Office.

Lehr, D.H. (in press). Students with complex health care needs in today's schools. In E.L. Meyen (Ed.), *Exceptional children in today's schools* (2nd ed.). Denver: Love Publishing Co.

Lehr, D.H., & Haubrich, P. (1988). [Service Delivery Models for Students with Special Health Care Needs.] Unpublished raw data. University of Wisconsin-Milwaukee.

Lehr, D.H., & Noonan, M.J. (1989). Issues in the education of students with complex health care needs. In F. Brown & D.H. Lehr (Eds.), *Persons with profound disabilities: Issues and practices* (139–160). Baltimore, Paul H. Brookes Publishing Co.

Mulligan-Ault, M., Guess, D., Struth, L., & Thompson, B. (1988). The implementation of health related procedures for classrooms for students with severe multiple impairments. *Journal of The Association for Persons with Severe Handicaps, 13*(2), 100–109.

Palfrey, J., DiPrete, L., Walker, D., Shannon, K., & Maroney, E. (1987). *School children dependent on medical technology,* Washington, DC: ATA Associates.

Shelton, T.L., Jeppson, E.S., & Johnson, B.H. (1987). *Family centered care for children with special health care needs.* Washington, DC: Association for the Care of Children's Health.

Sirvis, B. (1988). Students with special health care needs. *Teaching Exceptional Children, 20*(4), 40–44.

Task Force on Children with Special Health Care Needs. (1988). *Recommendations: Services for children with special health care needs.* Des Moines Iowa Department of Education.

Task Force on Technology Dependent Children. (1988). *Fostering home and community-based care for technology dependent children.* Washington, DC: United States Department of Health and Human Services.

Tatro v. Texas, 625 F.2d 557 (5th Cir. 1980), 703 F.2d 823 (5th Cir. 1983).

United States Congress, Office of Technology Assessment. (1987). *Technology dependent children: Hospital v. home care—A technical memorandum (OTA-TM-H-38).* Washington, DC: Government Printing Office.

Viadero, D. (1987). Medically fragile students pose dilemma for school officials. *Education Week, 1,* 14.

Wisconsin Maternal and Child Health Coalition (1989). *Mothers and children: The bridge to comprehensive care for children with special health care needs.* Madison, WI: Author.

APPENDIX

Training and Resource Material

Video training tapes

Clean Intermittent Catheterization
Includes information on benefits of and procedures for performing CIC, as well as how to instruct others—25 minutes

CPR and Emergency Choking Procedures for Infants and Young Children
Introduction and review of procedures to prevent and provide emergency treatment—37 minutes

Home Oxygen for Infants and Young Children
Demonstrates use of three commonly used home oxygen systems, emphasizing precautions for use—30 minutes

Home Tracheostomy Care for Infants and Young Children
Reviews physiology of infant airways and procedure for caring for the child with a trachea tube—40 minutes

Infection Control in Child Care Settings
Addresses necessary concerns regarding prevention of spread of contagious diseases in group care settings and provides instruction on effective control techniques—30 minutes

These tapes are available from Learner Managed Designs, 2201 K West 25th Street, Lawrence, Kansas 66046.

Books and manuals[1]

California State Department of Education (1980). *Guidelines and procedures for meeting the specialized physical health care needs of students.* Sacramento: Author.
A manual that includes specific information on how to implement specialized health care procedures in the schools

Graff, C., Mulligan Ault, M., Guess, D., Taylor, M., & Thompson, B. (1990). *Health care for students with disabilities: An illustrated medical guide for the classroom.* Baltimore: Paul H. Brookes Publishing Co.
A manual designed for teachers to provide them with relevant information regarding health related procedures received by their students

Larson, G. (Ed.). (1988). *Managing the school age child with a chronic health condition.* Wayzata, MN: DCI Publishing.
A book designed for all personnel in the schools working with students with chronic health conditions, it includes practical how-to-do information on planning and implementing health care procedures

---

[1]From: Lehr, D.H. (in press). Students with complex health care needs in today's schools. In E.L. Meyen (Ed.), *Exceptional children in today's schools* (2nd. ed.). Denver: Love Publishing Co. Reprinted with permission.

8

Training Needs of Physical and Occupational Therapists Who Provide Services to Children and Youth with Severe Disabilities

Jennifer York
Beverly Rainforth
and Winnie Dunn

People with severe disabilities are increasingly integrated into regular home and community life. Large residential facilities close as more typical, family size living options develop in neighborhoods. Large numbers of families of children with severe disabilities and complex health care needs receive the support necessary to care for their children at home. In some school districts, children with even the most severe disabilities attend their local schools and age-appropriate classes with typical peers from their neigh-

The development of this chapter was supported in part by Grant Nos. G008730009 and G008630347-88 from the United States Office of Special Education and Rehabilitative Services of the United States Department of Education to the University of Minnesota, Departments of Communication Disorders and Educational Psychology; and by Grant No. G008730057-89 to the University of Kansas, Occupational Therapy Education Department. Points of view or opinions stated in this chapter do not necessarily represent the official position of the United States Department of Education. No official endorsement should be inferred.

borhoods. Supported employment efforts continue to expand, and many individuals with severe disabilities work in integrated community settings alongside co-workers who do not have disabilities. As these integrated life outcomes are sought and realized, physical and occupational therapists have a greater opportunity than ever before to effect this greater degree of participation by people with disabilities in their homes, at school, in the community, and at work.

Capitalizing on the expertise of therapists to facilitate integrated life outcomes requires a substantial modification of traditional service provision and personnel preparation models. As the locations where people with disabilities live, work, and play change, so too must the locations in which therapists provide service. Flexible approaches to service provision are required if therapists are to work in community settings with individuals who have severe disabilities, and with their families and friends who can provide ongoing support in these typical environments. Such a change in service provision presents a significant challenge to therapists, therapist educators, public schools, human services agencies, and professional organizations. Can personnel preparation programs expand their already intensive curricula to include yet another area of specialization? How do public school and human service agencies support existing therapists and other team members during the change to a more integrated model of service provision? Can continuing education networks and local therapy associations collaborate to offer courses related to persons with severe disabilities?

The professions of physical and occupational therapy were established in response to rehabilitation and habilitation needs of persons with both acute and chronic disabilities. These professions are grounded in the pursuit of improved functional sensorimotor abilities, which enable individuals to learn, work, play, communicate, socialize, and perform daily living activities. Because therapy services originated in medical models and settings, a major assumption underlying therapeutic intervention has been that improved performance in clinical settings (e.g., therapy areas) will result in improved functioning in daily life outside the clinical setting. For many individuals with severe disabilities, this is an incorrect assumption. Adaptive functioning at home, school, work and in the community depends largely upon the demands, opportunities, and characteristics of the individual's specific natural daily environments and activities. For example, use of a wheelchair may be very efficient in a home that has firm wall to wall carpeting, large open spaces, wide doorways, and institutional size bathrooms. In a home with narrow door frames, multiple levels, throw rugs, and furniture filled rooms, use of a wheelchair may be nearly impossible. Alternative mobility methods such as cruising along the furniture, kneewalking, scooting along the floor, or even being physically assisted to walk may prove much more efficient (Wiemann & York, 1990; York, 1989).

It is difficult to determine appropriate intervention strategies to improve motoric functioning without knowledge of the demands and opportunities that exist in the daily, real world environments encountered by the individual with disabilities. Isolated therapy (e.g., working with students in a separate room or a corner of a classroom) does not allow the therapist to make an accurate determination of needs or current functioning abilities. It is equally difficult to determine acceptable performance criteria unless competencies are environmentally referenced. For example, in an interview session with adults who have severe physical disabilities, one of the authors was informed that it was peers with disabilities and not therapists who were the most helpful in identifying adaptive strategies for using restrooms, carrying personal belongings, and storing a wheelchair in a car during transport. In addition, one of the adults reported learning to transfer from her wheelchair to a toilet in the "world's largest bathroom" located at a clinic. She went on to explain that there were grab bars at every possible height and location and enough space to turn the wheelchair 360 degrees on either side of the toilet. Not surprisingly, this individual found that none of the transfer strategies learned in the clinic were useful in any bathroom at home or in the community. Similarly, results of a survey of physical therapists who work in clinical settings indicated a lack of uniform or environmentally-referenced criteria for classifying patients as "functional community ambulators" (Lerner-Frankiel, Vargas, Brown, Krussell, & Schoenberger, 1986). The increasing pressure for accountability and for validating outcomes of interventions makes it more important than ever that educational team members, including physical and occupational therapists, carefully reference and validate performance objectives to demands and outcomes in natural environments.

The goal of therapeutic interventions always has been to improve clients' functioning; however, as numerous philosophical and programmatic changes in educational service provision systems have occurred, there has been a corresponding need to change the framework for recommending, designing, and implementing therapeutic interventions. First, expected life outcomes for persons with disabilities have changed. Individuals with severe disabilities and their families expect a life that includes growing up in a regular community with supports provided in normal, daily environments. Second, a more holistic and environmentally-referenced view of individuals has replaced a disability, dysfunctional focus. That is, educational teams are beginning to identify integrated school and community environments in which students can learn to participate. Teams then assume a problem-solving stance to decide how to enhance functioning in each of the identified integrated environments. This is in direct contrast to old curricular models of focusing on skill deficits and setting criteria that must be met before inclusion in regular home, school, community, and work life. To a greater extent, instruction is being provided in regular education and community environments. Third, there has been a shift beyond mere physical integration in regular schools to an emphasis on including students with severe disabilities in all aspects of regular school life and on facilitating relationships among students with disabilities and their classmates who do not have disabilities. Regular education students and teachers are becoming more involved in the lives of children and youth with severe disabilities. Fourth, the movement toward greater decentralization of programs (i.e., students attending the home/neighborhood schools they would attend if not labeled as having a disability) requires far more flexible models of teamwork to support personnel in local schools to meet the varied and complex needs of students who have severe and multiple disabilities. Professionals who have worked in collaborative team models and realized the benefits are among the strongest advocates for collaborative teams and integrated therapy. Many therapists have seen the results of their efforts multiply when they work more closely with family members, teachers, and others on the educational team. Fifth, more is known about learning characteristics of persons with severe disabilities. One of the most important findings is that skill generalization (transfer of training) cannot be assumed from one context to another context (Haring, 1988). Maintenance and generalization of skills rarely occurs if not required for daily functioning. This makes it critical that educational teams identify skills required in natural, daily environments for present and future functional skill development. In sum, there has been a shift to more integrated service provision as professionals and parents have observed the positive effects of integrated life outcomes, interpersonal relationships with peers who do not have disabilities, effective collaborative teaming models, and knowledge of learning facilitators. The momentum is continuing to grow in support of more inclusive life in the community for people with severe disabilities.

The purpose of this chapter is to identify critical areas of knowledge and skill development for physical and occupational therapists who work with school-age individuals who have severe disabilities. Strategies for addressing these needs are discussed also. The majority of the content relates specifically to physical and occupational therapy services provided to school-age children and youth with severe disabilities in educational environments.

CRITICAL AREAS OF KNOWLEDGE AND SKILL DEVELOPMENT

In order for therapists to work successfully in educational environments with students who have severe disabilities, several areas of specialized knowledge and skill development are necessary. Although some of the concepts described here may be introduced in preservice experiences, preser-

vice training programs must prepare therapists to provide services to all age groups and a wide range of physical and psychological conditions. It is most likely that the majority of the specialized areas of knowledge and skill development will be addressed in post graduate learning experiences.

In a survey of related services personnel who are members of The Association for Persons with Severe Handicaps (TASH) (York & Rainforth, 1989), physical and occupational therapists identified neurodevelopmental treatment (including positioning and handling), educational curricula, teamwork, and adaptive equipment as the most valuable areas of previous training related to persons with severe disabilities. Interestingly, they identified educational curricular areas (especially vocational); behavior analysis (including data collection); adaptations (including orthotics, computers and related technology, and instructional adaptations); and teamwork as priority areas in which additional training would be beneficial. Therapists also indicated that continuing education courses and workshops were the primary means by which they had developed competencies related to working with students who have severe disabilities. The TASH related services survey indicates that therapists recognize the specialized skills and many pragmatic needs that are necessary to work successfully in school programs but do not seem to be receiving training in these areas in preservice experiences.

The training needs for physical and occupational therapists who provide services to school-age individuals with severe disabilities can be organized into four areas of knowledge and skill development: 1) assumptions underlying service design for people with severe disabilities, 2) knowledge and skills in educational models of service provision for people with severe disabilities, 3) knowledge and skills related specifically to the disciplines of occupational and physical therapy, and 4) collaborative teamwork knowledge and skills. Each training need is discussed below. Table 8.1 provides a summary of specific competency areas and resources.

Assumptions Underlying Service Design

When working with individuals who have severe disabilities, there are at least five assumptions that serve as the basis for integrated service design and intervention. These are assumptions regarding: 1) a "person first" orientation, 2) recognition of similarity of needs, 3) the value of interdependence, 4) a shared vision of participation in ordinary environments with extraordinary supports, and 5) learning and performance characteristics of learners with severe disabilities.

"People First" Orientation   A person first orientation as an assumption underlying service design emphasizes that each individual who happens to have a disability is first and foremost a person (Perske & Perske, 1988). Furthermore, each person is an individual with unique interests,

Table 8.1.   Physical and occupational therapy in education settings for students with severe disabilities: Competency areas and resources

Competency area	Resources
Legislation and professional guidelines •State, federal and special education laws (PL 94-142, PL 99-457) •Guidelines for physical and occupational therapy in educational settings	American Occupational Therapy Association (1987, 1989); American Physical Therapy Association (in press); The Association for Persons with Severe Handicaps (TASH)
Educational best practices for students with severe disabilities •Curriculum and instruction	Falvey (1989); Ford, Schnorr, Meyer, Davern, Black, and Dempsey (1989); Snell (1987); Wilcox and Bellamy (1987)
•Measurement/research (specific to physical and occupational therapy practice)	Ottenbacher (1986)
•Integration	Gaylord-Ross (1989); Stainback, Stainback, and Forest (1989)
•Collaborative teamwork and integrated therapy	Campbell (1987); Dunn (in press); Giangreco (1989); Orelove and Sobsey (1987); Rainforth and York (in press)
Physical and occupational therapy expertise •Normal and abnormal development of movement	Bly (1984); Slaton (1980)
•Therapeutic interventions	Campbell (1984); Connelly and Montgomery (1987); Finnie (1975); Jaeger (1987); Levitt (1986)
•Mobility	Trefler (1984)
•Positioning (including positioning equipment)	Bergen and Colangelo (1982); Ward (1982)
•Hand use	Erhardt (1982)
•Adaptations (not including positioning equipment)	Webster, Cook, Tompkins, and Vanderheiden (1985); York and Rainforth (1987)
•Orthopedics	Fraser, Hensinger, and Phelps (1987)
•Oral motor	Morris and Klein (1987)
•Sensory integration	Ayres (1980)

assets, and difficulties. If it is necessary to label an individual at all, the label follows the noun. For example, John is a "student with a disability" instead of a "disabled student." Best of all would be "John is a fourth grader." Adopting "person first" language can be particularly difficult for health professionals who have experienced and been required to use, in both spoken and written communications, a multitude of diagnostic labels.

Similarity of Needs   Therapists must adopt the assumption that people with disabilities have needs similar to those of people who do not have disabilities. By viewing a person with a disability as sharing many of the same life goals and needs as people who do not have identified disabilities, there is a common ground for working together. Therapists offer valuable knowledge of sensorimotor functioning and interventions to assist persons with severe disabilities in meeting their identified priority goals and needs. Physical and occupational therapists design interventions to address sensorimotor strengths and difficulties to facilitate accomplishment of priority life goals determined by the individuals, their friends and family, and others who care about them. Occupational therapists also contribute to cognitive and psychosocial components of performance. It is in the context of addressing priority needs and accomplishing priority life goals that the need for therapy expertise is identified and integrated.

Interdependence   The underlying service design assumption regarding interdependence is essential, especially in a society in which independence is the lauded aspiration of many people. Independence is a misnomer. Very few, if any, individuals are truly independent, or would be happy in such a state of isolation. "It is a mistake to have INDEPENDENCE as a goal, because we cannot exist without others. We thrive in INTERDEPENDENCE. This is community. It is not a goal to strive for. It is a gift to receive from everyone we meet" (Lynch, 1989, p. 1). Independence was once the ultimate qualifier for each objective on an individualized education plan (IEP). Emphasis on independence, however, combined with the inability for many individuals with severe disabilities to achieve independence across life functioning areas, resulted in exclusion from a variety of natural environments.

The concept of interdependence has expanded the concept of partial participation (Baumgart et al., 1982). Interdependence serves to emphasize the positive and normalized aspects of requiring assistance in certain aspects of our daily lives. Independence as a focus of intervention, therefore, should be considered carefully, given the specific environmental demands and supports of each student. Some people with the most severe sensorimotor difficulties cannot achieve physical independence in daily activities. Others can be independent in some aspects of sensorimotor functioning, but the amount of energy required to do so results in a diminished capacity to perform in other areas. For example, one elementary school student could independently wheel her wheelchair to the playground for recess. By the time she reached the playground, however, recess was half over and she was exhausted. In this situation, independent mobility resulted in isolation from peers. For each individual, the educational team makes decisions about when independent motoric functioning is more important and when interdependence is more appropriate. In many situations these are difficult determinations to make. Only the individual and those who know him or her best can make the most appropriate decisions.

Ordinary Environments with Extraordinary Supports

Therapists must adopt the underlying service design assumption that people with disabilities can and should participate in typical home, school, community, and work environments and recognize that doing so may require individualized support. This principle is the basis for a new design of services. Previously, the predominant models of service provision were centralized services in which students with severe disabilities were assigned to special environments (e.g., institutions, special schools, special education classroom, therapy rooms) in which professionals with expertise in specialized areas provided services. Institutions, large group homes, day activity centers, sheltered workshops, handicapped-only schools, and even special education classes are results of a centralized, clustered service design. The challenge now is to mobilize specialized supports, such as physical and occupational therapists, from centralized locations to decentralized, more integrated environments in which students with severe disabilities are learning alongside peers who do not have disabilities in regular school and community environments. As therapists modify their assessment and intervention practices to be carried out in a wide array of natural environments, they can be sure that their expertise will be most useful to the students with whom they work.

Learning and Performance Characteristics

The underlying service design assumption regarding learning and performance characteristics of individuals with severe intellectual disabilities is based on expanded knowledge of these characteristics. When compared to individuals who are not so labeled, people with severe intellectual disabilities tend to require a greater number of instructional trials to acquire new skills, tend to learn fewer skills, have greater difficulty with skill maintenance and generalization, and learn less complex skills (Brown et al., 1983; Zanella Albright, Brown, VanDeventer, & Jorgensen, 1987). These characteristics make it critically important for therapists to prioritize in collaboration with other members of educational teams. Teams always identify more skills for which instruction is needed than can be taught in the number of hours, days, and years available. The highest priorities for instruction, therefore, are those skills that allow the learner to participate in integrated settings, and those skills whose use will be encouraged by the people and activities that occur naturally in those settings.

Educationally Related Models of Service Provision

In order for physical and occupational therapists to function effectively within educational environments, a basic understanding of an educational model of service provision is required. This includes knowledge of state and federal laws governing practice in educational settings, an educational as opposed to a medical orientation to services, what are considered educational best practices for students with severe handicaps, and models of therapy service provision.

Laws Governing Therapy in Educational Settings   Public Law 94-142, the Education for All Handicapped Children Act (EHA) of 1975, requires the provision of "related services," including physical and occupational therapy services, as "required to assist a handicapped child benefit from special education" (Sec. 3, 20 U.S.C. Sec. 1401 [17]). The implication is that therapists are included as educational team members so they can contribute expertise that results in improved educational performance by children labeled as handicapped. Even though mandates that promote an integrated approach to the provision of physical and occupational therapy services have existed since 1975, there remains considerable difficulty in designing and adopting models of integrated and educationally related services. Mandates were provided with little direction or support guiding implementation. In the late 1980s, however, both the American Occupational Therapy Association (AOTA) (1987) and the American Physical Therapy Association (APTA) (1981, in press) undertook initiatives to provide specific guidelines for therapy practice in educational settings. In both of these documents, there is an emphasis on addressing educationally relevant skills, the need for therapists to work collaboratively as members of educational teams, the need to develop a better understanding of the role of therapists in educational settings, and the need for educational personnel, administrators, parents, and other team members to understand how to use related services. Therapists in educational settings must make interventions relevant to educational performance and promote a better understanding of their role in educational settings.

Public Law 99-457, the Education of the Handicapped Act Amendments of 1986, modify the requirements of Public Law 94-142. Children from birth through 2 years of age may receive physical and/or occupational therapy as a primary service, while children ages 3–5 may receive physical and/or occupational therapy as a related educational service. Infants, toddlers, and their families do not have to meet the qualifications of educational handicap to receive physical and occupational therapy services through public education and may receive these services alone or in conjunction with other needed services. These revisions related to physical and occupational therapy services for infants and toddlers currently are the focus of many interagency efforts at local, state, and national levels. The practical implications of therapy as primary service for infants and toddlers, paid for by education monies will require continuing efforts to develop, demonstrate, and disseminate effective models of service provision. The American Occupational Therapy Association has provided guidelines for early intervention and preschool services to assist in these efforts (Dunn, Campbell, Oetter, Hall, & Berger, 1989).

Medical Versus Educational Models of Service Provision   An important area of understanding for physical and occupational therapists in educational settings lies in the distinction between medical and educational models of service provision. Most therapists have been trained predominantly in medical models of service provision. Adapting to an educational model, especially when the differences are not delineated and described, can be a difficult transition at best and an impossible one at worst. A physical therapist told one of the authors about 2 frustrating years with a special education teacher: "I think she's a good teacher, but she doesn't think I support her; I would be happy to do whatever it is she wants, if only I could figure out what it is!" Medical and educational service orientations differ in several ways (Ottenbacher, 1982). Medical models focus on identifying and remediating underlying causes of dysfunction. Current educational models are based on a more behavioral approach in which interventions are directed at changing behaviors that are observable and measurable. Another difference is that medical interventions frequently are short term. Educational interventions are longitudinal because the nature of the disabilities is long-term. Finally, medical interventions sometimes focus on isolated body parts or functions because dysfunction relates to only certain parts of the body. Most school-age children with severe disabilities with whom therapists work have difficulties in more than one part of the body and more than one area of functioning. There is one area that should be common ground of both medical and educational models. This common ground relates to outcomes.

Educational Best Practices   Educational best practices for students with severe disabilities promote inclusion in regular school and community life (see Chapter 16). The involvement of physical and occupational therapists is not limited to narrowly defined areas of service provision, but is essential to each of the educational best practices. Given that most school districts have not fully implemented educational best practices, therapists can be involved along with other school personnel in efforts to adopt these practices and to modify existing service provision models for implementation.

Models of Service Provision   The processes by which physical and occupational therapists effect student change include both direct and indirect therapy. Direct therapy refers to direct "hands-on" interactions between the therapist and the student, during which the therapist analyzes student interactions with the environment and uses specific therapeutic techniques to develop or improve particular movement, sensory, or perceptual skills. Direct therapy services can be provided in a variety of settings, including the classroom, the playground, physical education class, the home, the school bus, community environments, and other places where the student functions during the school day. When the therapist provides direct therapy, he or she must also provide ongoing consultation to teachers and other team members so that effective interaction strategies can be incorporated into activities throughout the school day.

Indirect therapy refers to teaching, consulting with, and directly supervising other team members (including paraprofessionals) for the purpose of integrating therapeutic interventions into daily activities. The AOTA (1987) uses the term "monitoring" to describe this array of service provision options. Specifically, monitoring occurs when the therapist creates an individualized plan for a student but trains someone to carry out the plan in the natural environment on a regular basis. The therapist maintains regular contact with the person who carries out the plan and shares responsibility for student outcomes. The therapist also interacts directly with the student on a regular basis in order to appropriately monitor and modify intervention procedures. Many states and the AOTA (1987) require that there be at least two contacts per month with the responsible therapist.

The type of therapy services provided is related to the larger issue of criteria for therapy services of any kind. Eligibility criteria have been suggested in an effort to identify students in need of therapy services, as well as to determine the type and intensity of services. In some situations, need for therapy and potential to benefit from therapy have been equated, with the result that some students with severe disabilities receive no or very limited therapist involvement in educational programming. Dunn and Campbell (in press) present a model in which therapists recommend to the team how they might be involved in educational programming given the degree to which sensorimotor dysfunction interferes with specific educational activities. The five steps in this model are: 1) team identifies general educational priorities for the student (e.g., leisure, activities of daily living, work; 2) therapists assess students to determine sensorimotor strengths and difficulties; 3) therapists present the degree to which sensorimotor dysfunction appears to be interfering with educational performance; 4) therapists suggest interventions (e.g., adapt materials, adapt posture/movement, teach and supervise others); and 5) team decides whether and how to integrate therapy interventions.

In making the decision as to the type of intervention that might be most appropriate for an individual student, therapists consider the least restrictive, that is, most integrated, approach first (Giangreco, York, & Rainforth, 1989). As much as possible, service decisions made should keep the student involved in the regular daily school routines with his or her peers. If therapy expertise can be successfully integrated into regular school activities, the student should not be removed from the classroom. The team, which includes parents, decides the most appropriate type and intensity of service for each student, with those recommendations changing over time as students' needs change. It is important to remember that direct services are not automatically preferred over or considered better than other service provision models. Indirect service does not have to mean less service or less intensive service. One model is not necessarily better than the other, they simply are different.

Physical and Occupational Therapy Areas of Expertise

Working in educational settings is a new area of practice for many physical and occupational therapists. Furthermore, students with severe disabilities are only a small percentage of children served by therapists in educational settings. Specific therapy competencies for working with these children relate to the pediatrics area of specialization. In general, the roles of physical and occupational therapists working in educational settings can be identified as follows: 1) participating in the team process for identifying educational priorities, designing instructional interventions (including integration of therapy methods), solving problems, and supporting other team members; 2) contributing therapy information and skills (e.g., hands-on interventions, equipment) that facilitate student success in educational programs, which includes training other team members to implement positioning and handling procedures and use of adaptive equipment; 3) addressing sensorimotor needs in naturally occurring educational contexts; and 4) collaborating with the team to develop strategies for students with severe disabilities to be integrated into all aspects of regular school life, including regular classes and extracurricular activities.

Although there may be many differences in the skills of individual physical and occupational therapists, there are many areas in which the expertise of physical and occupational therapists overlaps. Both occupational therapists and physical therapists have expertise in the areas of sensorimotor development, gross motor skill development, positioning, and certain types of adaptive equipment (e.g., wheelchairs). Physical therapists generally have additional expertise in use of ambulation, modalities, and cardiorespiratory functioning. Occupational therapists generally have additional expertise in fine motor and perceptual skills; sensory integration; cognitive, psychosocial aspects of performance; and adaptive devices related to daily activities. The expertise of a specific therapist will vary depending on his or her training, work experiences, and continuing education. Because of varied experiences and the fact that therapists in different school systems assume varying roles given their individual interests and the needs in their local circumstances, no attempt is made here to draw distinct lines of discipline boundaries. Some individuals with severe disabilities require physical therapy or occupational therapy or both. (See York & Rainforth [1989] for a sample job description for physical and occupational therapists who work with students with severe disabilities in educational settings.)

Functional Sensorimotor Components of Daily Activities

In an effort to promote a functional orientation for integrating physical and occupational therapy expertise into daily activities and natural environments for individuals with severe disabilities, the following model has been promoted (York & Rainforth, in press; York, Rainforth, & Wiemann, 1988). For each daily activity, there are three major components for which therapists can contribute information on ways to improve learner performance. The first component is a *mobility* component, which refers to how the individual travels to the designated environment and activity. Relevant to the mobility component, therapists determine the mobility methods (e.g., scooting, kneewalking, assisted walking, motorized scooter) most appropriate for the individual's motoric capabilities and environmental demands. The second component is a *positioning* component, which refers to how the learner's body is positioned to allow efficient access to and involvement in the activity. Therapists have extensive expertise related to efficient methods for assuming, maintaining, and changing positions to promote task efficiency. Sitting, lying, and upright weightbearing positions are but a few of the options. A wide variety of equipment options are available to assist students in maintaining well aligned and stable postures that facilitate functional participation. Also relevant to positioning, therapists consider times during the day when alternatives to sitting can be employed in age-appropriate and functional ways (e.g., lying down to watch television at home or kneeling at the kitchen table to make cookies). Many students spend most, if not all, of their school day in a seated position. Although sitting is particularly problematic, prolonged use of *any* position promotes the development of contractures and deformities, decubitus ulcers, respiratory difficulties due to immobility, and digestive dysfunction. Positions should be varied and balanced across the day. The third component is a *sensorimotor competence for participation* component in which specific body parts (e.g., hands, eyes, mouth) are used to participate in the activity. Therapists can determine ways in which body parts can move most efficiently to enable participation in the activity. They also may design hands-on interventions and environmental adaptations that allow greater participation. By conducting a functional sensorimotor analysis of a student's day, therapists can identify numerous opportunities throughout the day in which therapeutic interventions could be integrated, providing a greater number of opportunities to develop more efficient motor competencies.

Merging Developmental and Environmental Orientations

Many of the approaches to assessment and intervention used by therapists for individuals with severe disabilities are grounded in theories of normal development. Developmental constructs, however, must not serve as the only basis of intervention design. Rigid adherence to a developmental approach severely limits the range of potentially constructive interventions. It fails to account for an individual's history of adaptive sensorimotor functioning. It focuses on skill deficits instead of on abilities and adaptive functioning. In addition, adaptive equipment (e.g., wheelchairs, splints, microswitches) that might replace the need for specific sensorimotor skills is not referenced in developmental constructs. While patterns and sequences of normal sensorimotor development have been researched extensively and provide a rich source of information about efficient movement for individuals who do not have sensorimotor dysfunction, there has been much less study of abnormal patterns and sequences of motor development. Furthermore, there is a very limited empirical basis for either supporting or refuting popular therapy intervention approaches. This is not meant to imply that clinicians have not been successful in their interventions, only that an empirical basis for success is lacking. Clearly, more study is needed. Preliminary investigations support combining therapeutic and systematic instruction methodologies (Campbell, McInerney, Cooper, 1984; Giangreco, 1986).

Developmental, adaptive, and environmentally-referenced orientations to intervention can be integrated. This is accomplished when therapists determine intervention needs based on an environmental analysis by observing children function in different daily environments and by talking with family members and others involved with the individual in home, school, and community environments. This is referred to as an ecological inventory approach (Brown, Branston-McLean, Baumgart, Vincent, Falvey, & Schroeder, 1979; Falvey, 1989). Physical and occupational therapists have an important role in the ecological inventory process. Therapists identify mobility, positioning, and other sensorimotor demands encountered in daily environments. In Table 8.2 an example of how therapists can analyze needs and possibilities in daily activities is provided. The specific activity analysis occurred in a regular education kindergarten class during free time. Once environmentally-referenced analysis occurs, physical and occupational therapists assist in designing appropriate interventions by applying their knowledge of how to facilitate more efficient participation derived from their knowledge of both developmental references and adaptive resources. An environmental analysis, therefore, serves to identify and validate important targets of intervention, or *what* to teach. A developmental and adaptive functioning analysis assists in determining *how* instruction might be designed. For example, an environmental analysis might indicate that a student

Table 8.2. Sample ecological inventory for determining acceptable mobility, positioning, and participation demands in daily activities

	Environment:	Kindergarten room	
	Period:	Free play	
	Typical methods and acceptable alternatives		
Activities of peers without disabilities	Transitions/Mobility	Positions	Participation/Adaptations
Looking at/reading books	TYP: Walk to shelves. ALT: Scoot, crawl, roll; not much space but small equipment OK	TYP: Sit on carpeted steps, sit or lie on floor; children are physically very close, usually touching. ALT: avoid use of equipment that isolates	TYP: Manipulate books with hands, read/comment out loud. ALT: Most would be OK; book holders, sticks to turn pages, taped books
Talking with friends	TYP: Walk, run to carpeted steps, room corners; small groups may change location to exclude peers or increase privacy. ALT: Floor method OK, small equipment OK	TYP: Same as above; positions may change to exclude peers or be more private. ALT: Avoid use of equipment that isolates; may need to work in position changes	TYP: Talk, whisper, giggle, point, watch others, interrupt; leave if not included. ALT: Show pictures, activate prerecorded taped messages
Showing toys to friends	TYP: Walk, skip to cubbies then return to play area. ALT: Floor method OK; scooter board difficult on surface change; wheelchair OK; friend could get toy	TYP: Stand or sit on floor or steps, usually very close to each other and touching. ALT: Most upright positions OK	TYP: Hold, show, exchange, manipulate items. ALT: Point to items, have friend help show item
Climbing on carpeted stairs/seats	TYP: Walk, skip to steps. ALT: Any method OK; small equipment OK	TYP: Stand to step, sit to scoot up/down. ALT: Could lie to roll down deep steps	TYP: Stepping in standing position, scooting seated. ALT: Rolling down deep steps

TYP indicates typical methods displayed by peers without disabilities.
ALT indicates alternatives that may be acceptable.

Reprinted with permission from York, J., & Rainforth, B. (in press). Enhancing recreation/leisure participation by individuals with severe intellectual and physical disabilities. In L.H. Meyer, S.J. Schleien, & B. Biel (Eds.), *Lifetime leisure skills and lifestyles for persons with developmental disabilities*. Baltimore: Paul H. Brookes Publishing Co.

has difficulty walking to lunch alongside classmates who do not have disabilities. Using knowledge of efficient movement (developmentally referenced), while also considering potential adaptations (e.g., a wheeled mobility device), therapists make recommendations to the team about how the student could be taught to travel to lunch more efficiently. Providing physical assistance (i.e., hands-on therapeutic interventions) designed to facilitate improved gait might be deemed appropriate for short transitions in the classroom, while use of a wheelchair might be most appropriate for longer transitions, such as going out to lunch or out to recess.

Specific Discipline Competencies If physical and occupational therapists are to function effectively in educational settings, they first must have competence within their own disciplines (Hutchinson, 1978). Competency areas specific to the fields of physical and occupational therapy compiled from several sources (American Occupational Therapy Association, 1987; American Physical Therapy Association, in press; Madison Metropolitan School District, 1984) include: 1) general sensorimotor functioning relating to muscle strength, muscle tone, interfering patterns of movement (reflexes), joint movement, coordination, balance, endurance, motor planning and reception, and use of sensory information; 2) efficient assumption and maintenance of positions for daily activities; 3) daily living skills (e.g., eating, dressing), involving functional use of arm, leg, and trunk movement, functional oral movement for eating, and use of utensils and other adaptive equipment; 4) hand use involving reach, grasp, manipulation, release, visual motor skills, hand-eye coordination, and cooperative use of hands; 5) mobility skills involving use of varied mobility methods (e.g., scooting, kneewalking, walking, use of wheelchair), use of mobility equipment, body transfers, and traversing varied terrains and levels; 6) respiratory function related to patterns of breathing, effective coughing and postural drainage, and activity tolerance; 7) development and use of perceptual, psychosocial, and cognitive skill components; and 8) design and use of adaptive equipment including orthotics, prosthetics, and instructional devices designed to improve functioning in daily routines. (Resources related to each of these topical areas are summarized in Table 8.1).

Collaborative Teamwork

Paramount to the success of physical and occupational therapists working in educational settings is their ability to collaborate with other team members. A transdisciplinary model of teamwork has been promoted in this regard. In promoting a transdisciplinary model of teamwork, Dorothy Hutchinson (1978) defined this intensive team model as "committing oneself to teaching, learning, and working together with other providers of services across traditional disciplinary boundaries" (p. 68). Given the many varied and intensive needs of individuals with severe disabilities and the increasing number of natural environments in which these individuals are participating on a daily basis, a collaborative team approach is essential. In some school districts, the use of the term transdisciplinary has been used inaccurately to imply that agencies do not need to hire multiple professionals. That is, one person with continuing educational training in specific areas could be considered the "transdisciplinary team." This is inaccurate, inappropriate, and illegal. Effective transdisciplinary teamwork requires ongoing collaboration among professionals of different disciplines.

It is interesting to note that the transdisciplinary model of service provision has its origins in nursing related to practice in neonatal intensive care nurseries where there was the need to restrict the number of people who interacted with the infants. Just as a transdisciplinary approach to services to infants in the neonatal intensive care unit may be critical, it is also a logical model to adopt when working with older children, youth, and adults. Therapists cannot be present on a regular basis in all natural environments that are relevant to each individual with severe disabilities. Furthermore, upon graduation from public school, individuals with severe disabilities frequently lose access to physical and occupational therapists, making it particularly important to integrate effective interventions into a whole life-style routine so that maintenance of efficient movement in adulthood can be achieved.

Exchanging Information and Skills among Team Members Adopting a transdisciplinary approach is difficult for many team members. Few teachers and therapists acquired experience in intensive, collaborative teamwork during their preservice training (Rainforth, 1985). Although therapists may excel at designing and implementing therapeutic interventions with individual students, they may be less skilled at transferring skills to other team members. The success of collaborative teamwork depends to a large extent upon the exchange of information and skills among team members. This has been referred to as role release (Lyon & Lyon, 1980), but might better be considered role expansion, as accountability is not relinquished. In this process, all team members are teachers and learners.

Shared Decision-Making and Problem-Solving Perhaps the greatest difficulty for individual members of educational teams is to be committed to team decision-making, particularly for determining priorities in the educational program. When functioning in relative isolation from one another, decisions are made from a single discipline perspective. In a team approach, *relative* priorities are discussed. The team may determine that the recommendations from one discipline have lower priority than those from other disciplines. The focus is on the greatest student needs overall. Some team members have difficulty relinquishing decisions to the team. Given the large number of potential instructional targets, however, a team decision is the best safeguard for ensuring attention to the highest priorities for an individual child. Furthermore, it is only through a team process that the benefits of group problem-solving can be realized.

Scheduling Time in Natural Environments   One final competency that facilitates efficient functioning in educational settings relates to scheduling therapy time. Scheduling strategies that allow therapists to work with individual learners in multiple environments is essential for an integrated and collaborative team approach to service provision. Two strategies that can be considered as alternatives to traditional approaches to scheduling are block scheduling and a primary therapist model. These strategies were designed in an effort to increase the flexibility of related services personnel to better meet the needs of children, *not* as an administrative ploy to reduce the number of therapists needed or to cut costs.

Traditionally, therapists schedule individual students for half hour- to hour-long periods of time, two or three times a week, at times that remain consistent throughout the school year. A block scheduling approach (Rainforth & York, 1987; York et al., 1988) designates longer periods of time, such as 2–6 hours of a school day, to work with numerous learners. In school systems where five to eight students with severe disabilities are assigned to one building, a therapist could allocate half or full days to this building on a weekly or biweekly basis. The specific time allocations and places targeted for block scheduling vary depending on the number of learners, the complexity of learner needs, and the environments in which instruction is provided.

In the primary therapist model, teams decide to assign either the physical or occupational therapist as the primary therapist for individual learners. This strategy has been used in an effort to minimize overlap and inefficiency between therapist roles and to increase flexibility by increasing the amount of time available to individual learners by one therapist. For situations in which both a physical and an occupational therapist provide services to the same students, caseloads can be effectively reduced by half. This allows longer time blocks; enables work in a greater number of environments; and reduces the number of child teams in which intensive, regular involvement is required by both a physical therapist and occupational therapist. Successful implementation, however, requires regular collaboration between the physical and occupational therapists and depends on individual therapists' areas of expertise. In a primary therapist model, physical and occupational therapists continue to conduct assessments, design interventions, and do problem solving in difficult situations together. Consultation between therapists can be accomplished by scheduling one block a week together.

An essential component of an integrated model for therapy services is time to communicate with other team members. Much of this communication occurs on the block scheduled therapist days and during the educational activities. Over time, as strategies for working together on the IEP development and sharing information and skills become more efficient, less time is required.

STRATEGIES FOR ADDRESSING CRITICAL AREAS OF KNOWLEDGE AND SKILL ACQUISITION

Preservice preparation programs in occupational and physical therapy address training related to individuals of all ages and conditions, resulting in little or no opportunity to specialize in one specific area of interest (Effgen, 1988). Given the extreme diversity of practice in the field of physical therapy, physical therapists can graduate from entry-level programs without experience in pediatrics or public school settings (Effgen, 1988). In addition, very few therapists and educators have the opportunity to collaborate during preservice training (Rainforth, 1985). Approximately one third of occupational therapists take jobs in pediatrics. Public school therapy is the second most frequently held job of occupational therapists (American Occupational Therapy Association, 1985). There continues to be, however, a varying amount of attention to pediatric content in preservice programs (AOTA Pediatric Task Force, 1989). The diversity in these therapy fields may eventually lead to specialized areas of concentration at a preservice level similar to the way in which both regular and special education training programs have diversified to focus on children of specific age ranges and abilities. Although preservice training programs should make every attempt to continue to expand in order to include preparatory experiences related to practice in educational settings, trying to address training needs from a preservice level only is likely to have a limited impact, since ultimately therapists must be certified to practice across the life span. Considerable emphasis is needed on in-service training for the specialized skills needed to practice in public schools.

The difficulty in recruiting and retaining physical and occupational therapists to work in educational settings is a major concern for the therapy fields, as well as for the public schools. The problem of recruiting therapists with experience working with individuals who have severe disabilities is compounded by the nationwide shortage of therapists that is projected to continue for some time (American Society of Allied Health Professionals [ASAHP], 1988; Davis, 1988; Simonton, 1988). Working with school-age children who have severe disabilities comprises a very small percentage of practice in the fields of physical and occupational therapy; therefore, ways in which school districts can recruit, support, and retain therapists are emphasized below.

Numerous factors that influence therapists' decisions to work in educational settings have been identified (Ciccione & Wolfner, 1988; Effgen, 1985; Effgen, Bjornson, Deubler, & Kaplan, 1987; Lundy, 1988; Rainforth, 1985, 1988). One preservice influence is an emphasis on pediatrics and work in educational settings through academic coursework and clinical affiliations (i.e., practica). A report by Ciccione and Wolfner (1988) indicated that 51% of therapists seek immediate post graduation employment in one of their clinical education sites. Therefore, public schools might improve recruitment by establishing clinical education experiences (i.e., practica) for therapists in their school programs. Other influences on the decision to work in educational settings include a competitive salary and continuing educational opportunities (Effgen, 1985; Effgen et al., 1987; Kaplan, 1984; Rainforth, 1988). Isolation from other therapists was identified as a concern of therapists considering employment in educational settings (Effgen, 1985; Rainforth, 1988). Public school administrators should consider that continuing education opportunities serve to train therapists for work in educational settings (Effgen, 1985; Langdon & Langdon, 1983) as well as provide therapists with opportunities to network with other therapists. Assurances of continuing education opportunities are an important recruitment tool.

Once they are employed in the public schools, efforts must be made to train and support therapists on the job. Essentially there are three approaches to in-service training: 1) on-the-job training, 2) continuing education workshops and coursework, and 3) graduate study in programs with specialized areas of interest. On-the-job training accounts for a majority of training in specialty areas (Effgen, 1988; Rainforth, 1988; York & Rainforth, 1989). One strategy for on-the-job training to support new therapists is to implement a mentoring program (Effgen, 1988). In small school districts, opportunities to observe and talk with therapists working in surrounding districts should be provided. Districts can hire therapists with experience working in educational settings to provide short-term, technical assistance to new therapists also. Therapists must be supported in the change process as they learn new roles and responsibilities. An initial investment to support therapists can have the long-term pay off of retention and effectiveness of a school-based therapist.

A second approach to in-service training is continuing education opportunities, which can take the form of short or extended courses; participation in local, regional, and national conferences; and in-service training sponsored by local school districts. A large percentage of therapists have identified continuing educational experiences as the major avenue through which they have developed expertise related to the pediatric and developmental disabilities specialty areas of practice.

Third, graduate programs in special education, physical therapy, and occupational therapy can address the training needs of therapists for working with individuals who have severe disabilities. There are numerous programs throughout the country with advanced special education graduate training programs related to the area of severe disabilities. There are no physical or occupational therapy graduate programs specific to this area, but there are several programs with pediatrics as a specialization option. (Contact the

American Physical Therapy Association and the American Occupational Therapy Association about current programs.) Furthermore, the United States Office of Education funds approximately five projects each year to prepare related services personnel, including occupational and physical therapists, for work in special education. In addition to the related services grants, other special education funded projects have included occupational and physical therapists as part of teams involved in service, demonstration, and research activities. (Contact the U.S. Office of Education for specific information about current related services training programs.)

Interdisciplinary efforts among national organizations can facilitate training. Just as effective service provision for persons with severe disabilities is dependent upon collaboration among team members who have varied areas of expertise, addressing the training needs of therapists for working most effectively with people who have severe disabilities requires collaboration among individuals in various professional organizations, training programs, and service-provision systems to ensure an interdisciplinary consensus on issues and on strategies for solving the problems of designing and implementing training. The Association for Persons with Severe Handicaps, the American Physical Therapy Association, and the American Occupational Therapy Association are very much aware of therapist training needs for working with students who have severe disabilities. For the therapy associations, these needs are part of the greater issue of training for therapists to work in educational settings with students having a variety of disabilities, of which learners with severe disabilities comprise a small percentage. Since 1986, the TASH Related Services Subcommittee (York & Rainforth, 1989) has focused on: 1) developing a series of sessions at the annual conference directed at occupational therapy, physical therapy, and speech issues in providing services to persons with severe disabilities; 2) developing a position statement on the role of related-services personnel in working with individuals who have severe disabilities and their families (see Figure 8.1); 3) developing a resource list on team models and integrated therapy; and 4) conducting a survey of the related-services members of TASH to determine training needs and strategies. This subcommittee is composed of physical therapists, occupational therapists, speech therapists, special educators, and parents, many of whom also are involved in national therapy associations. Participation by therapists in the related services series at the TASH annual conference has grown, and discussion during crackerbarrel sessions has served as a forum in which to share practical strategies, raise and address issues, connect with other therapists, and generally provide support. School district and interdistrict efforts might be directed at developing task forces and critical issues discussion groups for physical and occupational therapists at the local level. The position statement has been published in topical newsletters of both APTA and AOTA. The resource list and complete results of the survey are available from TASH.

Position Statement of the
Related Services Subcommittee of the TASH Critical Issues Committee

The Association for Persons with Severe Handicaps (TASH) is an international organization whose primary purpose is to advocate and support exemplary models of service delivery for persons with severe handicaps.

Many persons with severe handicaps have complex and challenging needs. The expertise of related services professionals, such as physical therapists, occupational therapists, and speech and language pathologists is frequently required.

TASH believes that related services personnel have expertise and can contribute in the process of integrating persons with severe handicaps into typical home and community life. A high degree of collaboration and sharing of information and skills must occur among families, direct service providers, and related services personnel.

The provision of integrated services requires that related services personnel:

1. Establish priorities with parents/advocates and other team members;
2. Observe and assess persons with handicaps in natural settings;
3. Collaborate with family and other team members to provide intervention strategies and adaptations that optimize participation in natural settings;
4. Teach specific and individualized procedures to enhance functional positioning, movement, and communication abilities in natural settings;
5. Evaluate the effectiveness of intervention procedures based on performance outcomes in natural settings.

Figure 8.1. TASH statement on the role of related services personnel in working with persons with severe disabilities and their families (adopted by TASH Board, November, 1986).

Both the American Occupational Therapy Association (1987) and the American Physical Therapy Association (in press) have written and revised guidelines for practice in educational settings. While not specific to students with severe disabilities, educationally-relevant therapy and collaborative teamwork are emphasized. Also, in 1988, the American Occupational Therapy Association received funding for a 3-year interdisciplinary training program focusing on preparation of occupational therapists to work with infants, toddlers, and their families. Program faculty will include occupational therapists and parents of children with disabilities. These collaborative efforts related to addressing the personnel preparation needs of physical and occupational therapists to work with individuals who have severe disabilities are very positive first steps. Just as the problems have been longstanding, addressing them on a large scale cannot be done within a short period of time, especially since addressing training needs specific to individuals with severe disabilities is only one piece of the larger picture of needs related to other client groups. The strategies employed will need to be multifaceted and longitudinal.

CONCLUSION

Physical and occupational therapists have a tremendous opportunity to affect integrated life outcomes for persons with severe disabilities by working as collaborative team members in educational settings. As educational service provision systems continue to change so that children are included to a greater extent in regular school life and receive instruction in off campus, community environments, models of therapy service provision must change also. Instituting more integrated models of therapy will require participation and support by the therapists, educators, and parents on the teams; by district administrators; and by therapy and education training programs and organizations. Key to the success will be designing and implementing training and technical assistance models that provide "how-to" information and that support the individuals in educational systems who are learning new roles and responsibilities.

REFERENCES

American Occupational Therapy Association. (1985). *Occupational therapy manpower: A plan for progress.* (Report of the Ad Hoc Commission on OT Manpower). Rockville, MD: American Occupational Therapy Association.

American Occupational Therapy Association. (1987). *Guidelines for occupational therapy services in school systems.* Rockville, MD: American Occupational Therapy Association.

American Occupational Therapy Association Pediatric Task Force. (1989). (Anne Henderson [Chair], Winnie Dunn, Charlotte Exner, Jane Koomar, Elizabeth Murray, Charlene Pehoski, Stephanie Hoover). Ad Hoc Committee to Evaluate Pediatric Content in Entry Level Education, Boston. *Survey of pediatric occupational therapy entry level practice and education.* Submitted to the Commission on Education of AOTA.

American Physical Therapy Association. (1981). *Physical therapy practice in educational environments: Policies, guidelines, and background information.* Washington, DC: American Physical Therapy Association.

American Physical Therapy Association. (1986). Educational programs leading to postgraduate degrees for physical therapists. *Physical Therapy, 66,* 1616, 1618.

American Physical Therapy Association (in press). *Physical therapy practice in educational environments (revised).* Alexandria, VA: American Physical Therapy Association.

American Society of Allied Health Professionals. (1988, March). ASAHP study foretells serious shortage of PT. *PT Bulletin,* p. 6.

Ayres, J. (1980). *Sensory integration and the child.* Los Angeles: Western Psycholog-
ical Services.
Baumgart, D., Brown, L., Pumpian, I., Nisbet, J., Ford, A., Sweet, M., Messina,
R., & Schroeder, J. (1982). Principle of partial participation and individualized
adaptations in educational programs for severely handicapped students. *Journal of
The Association for the Severely Handicapped, 7*(2), 17–27.
Bergen, A., & Colangelo, C. (1982). *Positioning the client with central nervous system
deficits.* Valhalla, NY: Valhalla Rehabilitation Publications.
Bly, L. (1984). *The components of normal development during the first year of life and
abnormal motor development.* Chicago: Neurodevelopmental Treatment Association.
Brown, L., Branston-McLean, M., Baumgart, D., Vincent, L., Falvey, M., &
Schroeder, J. (1979). Utilizing the characteristics of current and subsequent least
restrictive environments as factors in the development of curricular content for
severely handicapped students. *AAESPH Review, 4*(4), 407–424.
Brown, L., Nisbet, J., Ford, A., Sweet, M., Shiraga, B., York, J., & Loomis, R.
(1983). The critical need for nonschool instruction in educational programs for
severely handicapped students. *Journal of The Association for Persons with Severe
Handicaps, 8*(3), 71–77.
Campbell, P. (1987). The integrated programming team: An approach for coordinating professionals of various disciplines in programs for students with severe and
multiple handicaps. *Journal of The Association for Persons with Severe Handicaps,
12*(2), 107–116.
Campbell, S.K. (1984). *Pediatric Neurologic Physical Therapy.* New York: Churchill
Livingstone.
Campbell, P.H., McInerney, W.F., & Cooper, M.A. (1984). Therapeutic program-
ming for students with severe handicaps. *American Journal of Occupational Therapy, 38*(9), 594–602.
Ciccione, C., & Wolfner, M. (1988). The relationship between clinical education and
post-graduate job selection by physical therapists. *Clinical Management, 8*(3),
16–17.
Connelly, B.H., & Montgomery, P.C. (1987). *Therapeutic exercise in developmental
disabilities.* Chattanooga, TN: Chattanooga Corp.
Davis, K. (1988, February). U.S. demand for physical therapists outweighs supply.
Progress Report, p. 5.
Dunn, W. (in press). Integrated related services. In L. Meyer, C. Peck, & L. Brown
(Eds.), *Critical issues in the lives of people with severe disabilities.* Baltimore: Paul
H. Brookes Publishing Co.
Dunn, W., & Campbell, P. (in press). Designing pediatric service provision. In W.
Dunn (Ed.), *Pediatric occupational therapy: Facilitating effective service provision.*
Thorofare, NH: Slack Publishers.
Dunn, W., Campbell, P., Oetter, P., Hall, S., & Berger, E. (1989). *Guidelines for
occupational therapy services in early intervention and preschool services.* Rockville,
MD: American Occupational Therapy Association.
Education for All Handicapped Children Act, 1975, Sec. 3, 20 U.S.C. Sec. 1401
(17).
Effgen, S. (1985, November). *Recruitment and retention of pediatric physical and
occupational therapists.* Paper presented at the meeting of The Association for
Persons with Severe Handicaps, Chicago.
Effgen, S. (1988). Preparation of physical therapists and occupational therapists to

work in early childhood special education settings. *Teaching Early Childhood Special Education, 7*(4), 10–19.

Effgen, S., Bjornson, C., Deubler, D., & Kaplan, S. (1987, February). *Recommendations from the Task Force on Recruitment and Retention of Pediatric Physical Therapists.* (Available from Susan Effgen, Department of Physical Therapy, Hahnemann University, Philadelphia.)

Erhardt, R. (1982). *Developmental hand dysfunction: Theory, assessment, treatment.* Laurel, MD: RAMSCO Publishing Co.

Falvey, M.A. (1989). *Community based curriculum: Instructional strategies for students with severe handicaps.* Baltimore: Paul H. Brookes Publishing Co.

Finnie, N. (1975). *Handling the young cerebral palsied child at home.* New York: E.P. Dutton.

Ford, A., Schnorr, R., Meyer, L., Davern, L., Black, J., & Dempsey, P. (1989). *The Syracuse community-referenced curriculum guide for students with moderate and severe disabilities.* Baltimore: Paul H. Brookes Publishing Co.

Fraser, B.A., & Hensinger, R.N. (1983). *Managing physical handicaps: A Practical Guide for Parents, Care Providers, and Educators.* Baltimore: Paul H. Brookes Publishing Co.

Fraser, B.A., Hensinger, R.N., & Phelps, J.A. (1987). *Physical management of multiple handicaps: A professional's guide.* Baltimore: Paul H. Brookes Publishing Co.

Gaylord-Ross, R. (Ed.). (1989). *Integration strategies for students with handicaps.* Baltimore: Paul H. Brookes Publishing Co.

Giangreco, M.F. (1986). Effects of integrated therapy: A pilot study. *Journal of The Association for Persons with Severe Handicaps. 11*(3), 205–208.

Giangreco, M. (1989). Making related services decisions for students with severe handicaps in public schools: Roles, criteria and authority. Unpublished doctoral dissertation, Syracuse, NY: Syracuse University.

Giangreco, M., York, R., & Rainforth, B. (1989). Providing related services to learners with severe handicaps in educational settings: Pursuing the least restrictive option. *Pediatric Physical Therapy, 1*(2), 55–63.

Haring, N. (Ed.). (1988). *Generalization for students with severe handicaps: Strategies and solutions.* Seattle: University of Washington Press.

Hutchinson, D. (1978). The transdisciplinary approach. In J.B. Curry & K.K. Peppe (Eds.), *Mental retardation: Nursing approaches to care.* St. Louis: C.V. Mosby.

Jaeger, L. (1987). *Home program instruction sheets for infants and young children.* Tucson: Therapy Skill Builders.

Kaplan, S. (1984). *Why aren't there more of you? A descriptive and correlational study of physical therapists in Ohio's developmental settings.* Unpublished master's thesis, Ohio State University, Columbus.

Langdon, H.J.U., & Langdon, L.L. (1983). *Initiating occupational therapy programs within the public school system: A guide for occupational therapists and public school administrators.* Thorofare, NJ: Charles B. Slack.

Lerner-Frankiel, M.B., Vargas, S., Brown, M., Krussell, L., & Schoenberger, W. (1986). Functional community ambulation: What are your criteria? *Clinical Management in Physical Therapy, 6*(2), 12–15.

Levitt, S. (1986). *Treatment of cerebral palsy and motor delay.* Boston: Blackwell Scientific Publications.

Lundy, M. (1988, July 18). The relative importance of continuing education in job selection and job satisfaction for PTs: A pilot study. *Physical Therapy Forum,* p. 7.

Lynch, B. (1989, March). Barriers to community. *ARC News for Colorado.* Denver: ARC Colorado.

Lyon, S., & Lyon, G. (1980). Team functioning and staff development: A role release approach to providing integrated educational services for severely handicapped students. *Journal of The Association of the Severely Handicapped, 5*(3), 250–263.

Madison Metropolitan School District. (1984). *Occupational and physical therapists' role descriptions.* Madison, WI: Author.

Morris, S.E., & Klein, M.D. (1987). *Pre-feeding skills.* Tucson: Therapy Skill Builders.

Orelove, F.P., & Sobsey, D. (1987). *Educating children with multiple disabilities: A transdisciplinary approach.* Baltimore: Paul H. Brookes Publishing Co.

Ottenbacher, K. (1982). Occupational therapy and special education. Some issues and concerns related to Public Law 94-142. *American Journal of Occupational Therapy, 36*(2), 81–84.

Ottenbacher, K.J. (1986). *Evaluating clinical change: Strategies for occupational and physical therapists.* Baltimore: Williams & Wilkins.

Pediatric Speciality Council, American Physical Therapy Association (1985). *Physical therapy advanced clinical competencies: Pediatrics.* Alexandria, VA: Author.

Perske, R., & Perske, M. (1988). *Circles of friends.* Nashville: Abingdon Press.

Rainforth, B. (1985). *Preparation of physical therapists and teachers of students with severe handicaps.* Unpublished doctoral dissertation, University of Illinois at Urbana-Champaign.

Rainforth, B. (1988). *Recruitment and retention of occupational and physical therapists in Southern Tier special education programs.* Unpublished report, State University of New York at Binghamton, School of Education and Human Development.

Rainforth, B., & York, J. (1987). Integrating related services in community instruction. *Journal of The Association for Persons with Severe Handicaps, 12*(3), 190–198.

Rainforth, B., & York, J. (in press). *Integrated therapy: Strategies for educational teams serving learners with severe disabilities.* Baltimore: Paul H. Brookes Publishing Co.

Simonton, T.E. (1988, November). Shortage of physical therapists reaching crisis stage. *Progress Report,* p. 11.

Slaton, D.S. (Ed.). (1980). *Development of movement in infancy.* Chapel Hill, NC: University of North Carolina, Division of Physical Therapy.

Snell, M. (Ed.). (1987). *Systematic instruction of persons with severe handicaps* (3rd ed.). Columbus, OH: Charles E. Merrill.

Stainback, S., Stainback, W., & Forest, M. (1989). *Educating all students in the mainstream of regular education.* Baltimore: Paul H. Brookes Publishing Co.

Trefler, E. (Ed.). (1984). *Seating for children with cerebral palsy: A resource manual.* Memphis: University of Tennessee, Rehabilitation Engineering.

Ward, D. (1982). *Positioning the handicapped children for function:* Chicago: Phoenix Press.

Webster, J.G., Cook, A.M., Tompkins, W.J., & Vanderheiden, G.C. (Eds.). (1985). *Electronic devices in rehabilitation.* New York: John Wiley & Sons.

Wiemann, G., & York, J. (1990). *Mobility, positioning and participation in daily activity at home: Three case studies.* Manuscript submitted for publication.

Wilcox, B., & Bellamy, G.T. (1987). *The activities catalog: An alternative curriculum for youth and adults with severe disabilities.* Baltimore: Paul H. Brookes Publishing Co.

York, J. (1989). Mobility methods selected for use in home and community environments. *Physical Therapy, 69*(9), 736–747.

York, J., & Rainforth, B. (1987). Developing instructional adaptations. In F.P. Orelove & D. Sobsey (Eds.), *Educating children with multiple disabilities: A transdisciplinary approach* (183–217). Baltimore: Paul H. Brookes Publishing Co.

York. J., Rainforth, B., & Wiemann, G. (1988). An integrated approach to therapy for school aged learners with developmental disabilities. *Totline, 14*(3), 36–40.

York, J., & Rainforth, B. (1989). *Related educational services for individuals with severe disabilities: A report from the Related Services Subcommittee.* Seattle: The Association for Persons with Severe Handicaps.

York, J., & Rainforth, B. (in press). Enhancing recreation/leisure participation by individuals with severe intellectual and physical disabilities. In L.H. Meyer, S.J. Schleien, & B. Biel (Eds.), *Lifetime leisure skills and lifestyles for persons with developmental disabilities.* Baltimore: Paul H. Brookes Publishing Co.

Zanella Albright, K., Brown, L., VanDeventer, P., & Jorgensen, J. (1987). *What regular educators should know about students with severe intellectual disabilities.* Madison: Madison Metropolitan School District.

9

Teaching Personnel to Use State-of-the-Art, Nonaversive Alternatives for Dealing with Problem Behavior

Ian M. Evans

It is somewhat discouraging to have to accept that there is a need for a chapter such as this one. One might have expected that after so many years of theoretical, empirical, and technical refinement in behavioral intervention, we would now be able to focus on a new phase of sophisticated treatment design, one that is oriented toward primary prevention, complex response repertoires, and the forging of meaningful life outcomes for persons with severe disabilities. Instead, however, it still seems necessary to examine the training of personnel in what *not* to do, and to consider alternatives for aversive intervention procedures that never should have been promulgated in the first place. In this chapter I consider such training issues while continuing to assert that finding alternatives to aversive treatments is an inversion of the real priority—the design and implementation of constructive opportunities for those with severe disabilities.

Argument over the use of physical punishment in behavior modification has existed ever since electric shock and other aversive stimuli were intro-

I would like to thank Luanna H. Meyer for helpful suggestions regarding this chapter and for stimulating many of the ideas expressed herein.

duced into treatment protocols in the late 1960s. The controversy has revolved around technical issues such as safety and efficacy, as well as ethical and moral concerns, particularly when punishment involved clients unable to give informed consent. In the 1980s, however, interest in non-aversive behavior management has greatly intensified, largely as a result of two things. First, there was wide publicity given by the popular media to the procedures used by programs of the Behavior Research Institute in Providence, Rhode Island when in July of 1985 a young man with autism died while undergoing what was referred to as "aversion therapy." By the end of the following year, several major professional and advocacy organizations had followed TASH's (The Association for Persons with Severe Handicaps) lead and adopted resolutions against the use of aversives with persons who have developmental disabilities. Second, a variety of positive techniques of behavior change have emerged in the 1980s that seem to be effective in reducing severe behavior problems. Closely related to such developments has been the need for more natural, normalized interventions that can be blended into community settings, public schools, and other contexts where individuals with severe disabilities receive services alongside their peers who do not have disabilities (Evans, in press).

This chapter examines the implications of these developments for personnel preparation and training. Two general issues concerning attitudes and prevention are considered first. Then, some current trends in conceptualizing problem behavior are presented because these theoretical developments set the stage for reviewing training needs. In order to demonstrate the need for sophisticated professional training, the next section surveys some of the misuses of behavioral principles involving aversive contingencies. That, in turn, leads to a critique of the possible side effects of learning behavior modification techniques. These concerns should not be construed as criticism of behavioral principles in general. Rather, I am arguing that to deal with the most serious problem behaviors requires very specialized personnel training. Finally, I comment on the evaluation of personnel training in this important and complex area.

BASIC ISSUES IN TRAINING PERSONNEL

Treatment As Abuse

A number of reasons for being interested in training personnel in nonaversive behavior management have already been mentioned. However, first, at the most basic and practical level, the major training issue is the possible parallel between treatment abuses and aversive interventions. If we consider the field of child abuse, we now know that parents who are abusive are not necessarily psychiatrically disturbed or somehow unusually cruel. Incidents of violence towards children can emerge from a variety of natural contexts, including frustration and anger in parents with poor self-control skills, lack of knowledge of more effective behavioral management strategies, and being convinced of the value of punishment as a disciplinary technique (Dubanoski, Evans, & Higuchi, 1978). Direct care staff, classroom aides, and other paraprofessionals who come in contact with persons with severe disabilities and severe behavioral problems would seem to be at risk for being abusive if they have poor anger control, lack effective positive methods, and have punitive practices legitimized by professionally designed treatment plans. Thus, the availability of specially designed aversive treatments, especially if they are touted as ethically undesirable but extremely effective from a practical standpoint (which is exactly the way the applied behavior analysis literature has conceptualized punishment), encourages direct service personnel to think of aversive methods. Guess (1989) has labelled this the "spread effect."

Examples of this effect have been substantiated in the literature. Leduc, Dumais, and Evans (in press) have described in detail a behavior modification program in a Canadian facility that served persons with both psychiatric disorders and developmental disabilities. Supposedly based on sound behavioral principles, the program involved a token economy that became increasingly restrictive, serving only to control clients' behavior. A formal investigation of the program was interpreted by those running it as an attack on behavior modification per se. However, when a really broad range of behavioral methods was introduced (including a focus on teaching functional skills and other concepts from social behaviorism [Staats, 1975]), the program became not only more acceptable to lay evaluators but also much more successful.

Another case study has been carefully documented by the New York State Commission on Quality of Care for the Mentally Disabled (1987). They report on a facility called Opengate, an ICF-MR (intermediate care facility for the mentally retarded) serving 30 adults. The program for one client involved earning tokens for periods of silence and then using them to purchase time to talk—what Guess (1989) has referred to as "procedural decay." For another woman, screaming behavior resulted in her being bound hand and foot in a restraint chair with a helmet over her head. A behavioral intervention plan involving contingent ammonia and water spray was introduced for one client's self-stimulatory behaviors on the first day he was admitted, so that less intrusive methods were neither considered nor tried. As the Commission commented:

> In each of the four case records examined, Opengate had moved beyond using a single aversive to reduce a maladaptive behavior to the use of multiple aversives. This phenomenon demonstrated the reinforcing nature of the aversives on the person administering them. The absolute power of the staff and the

reciprocal powerlessness of the client, combined with the apparent success of aversives in reducing the targeted behaviors, easily leads to the "more is better" way of thinking. As commonly recognized, aversives are potentially reinforcing to the person administering them. (p. 9)[1]

An interesting element of these examples is that, as with child abuse, it is naive to think the perpetrators were somehow evil people. However, it does seem that having a positive attitude towards persons with severe disabilities and behavioral excesses is of overriding importance. This means recognizing the significance of an orientation toward the normalization ethic and recognition of the rights, worth, and humanity of the client. Certainly, misplaced sympathy or the need to protect and control may be as damaging to respect as active dislike, fearfulness, or anger towards persons with severe behavior problems. And yet, simply liking one's clients and students is surely a powerful antidote to abusive treatment.

Focus on Prevention

A second very general training issue relates to teaching those positive standards or practices that seem particularly important for the prevention of more serious behavior problems. It has already been argued that positive attitudes are preventative for treatment abuse; however, there may also be some general attitudes that are preventative for behavior problems in the first place. One of these seems to be the important skill to be able to separate oneself emotionally from threatening, aggressive, or annoying incidents. The professional or other caregiver must respond to such incidents with professional detachment rather than with natural personal reactions. Personnel training should pay special attention to the interpretation of negative behavior by staff.

Caregivers must also be able to set up a positive environmental atmosphere so that they are able to anticipate the settings likely to exacerbate excess behavior and to find appropriate ways to circumvent these situations. Ecological interventions (Evans & Meyer, 1985) influence the setting "atmosphere" variables and represent a key characteristic of effective parenting and effective teaching. A related skill is being able to make appropriate decisions in crisis or unexpected situations. Caregivers must have a conceptual framework for dealing with problem behaviors of long standing,

---

[1]It is important to provide some follow-up information on these events. A new director for Opengate was hired and the staff re-educated in "sound pedagogical principles, behavior modification through positive reinforcement, and the building of open and trusting relationships between staff and residents . . . . Those professionals who could or would not abandon punitive treatment measures were terminated" (p. 10). In a subsequent review by the Commission, "residents' behaviors were continuing to respond to the emphasis on skill-building, the focus on appropriate behavior and *the sense of being valued which came from interacting with caring staff*" [italics added] (p. 11).

which is why Evans and Meyer (1985) stressed the decision-making role of the effective teacher. Not all behaviors are equally serious. Sometimes, it is the best policy to ignore undesirable behaviors or accommodate them in some way. Such judgment calls and a strategy for decision-making are not adequately covered in training manuals that concentrate only on contingency management principles.

The third training issue concerns being able to design and implement meaningful programs. Having this general ability is vital to caregivers in preventing excess behaviors. Meaningful programs are educational activities that are motivating, age-appropriate, and tailored to the unique preferences and needs of the individual student (Meyer, Eichinger, & Park-Lee, 1987). Failure to provide such programs appears to be a major factor contributing to excess behaviors. The relationship between excess behavior and specific instructional method has been documented. Winterling, Dunlap, and O'Neill (1987) demonstrated that a varied sequence of tasks produced significantly lower levels of self-stimulatory and disruptive behavior by students with autism than did a constant task approach. Task variation, in this case, simply involved mixing mastered and unmastered tasks during teaching sessions. A preventative program goes well beyond instructional technique and includes all facets of a meaningful curriculum.

UNDERSTANDING EXCESS BEHAVIOR

The broad issues just mentioned are really the general skills of good teaching. These skills are preventative in focus an thus, they represent the field's most promising future options for dealing with excess behavior. However, there are two realities that must be accepted. First, for some time to come, educational service providers are going to be inheriting clients and students who have already developed serious behavior problems. This is particularly true in those classrooms, group homes, or alternative living situations where people with the most difficult behaviors are being placed after living major portions of their lives in large residential facilities. Personnel preparation must focus training on skills for dealing with such behavior.

The second reality is that not all excess behavior is a reactive consequence of inappropriate environments, poor teaching, or monotonous and silly programs. While most incidence studies of self-injurious and similar behaviors have been conducted in large institutions, there are at least some reports of excess behavior in more benign settings. Evans and Voeltz (1982), basing their findings on direct observation of a statewide population, reported a wide range of excess behavior in young children with severe disabilities living at home and attending integrated public schools with well-trained teachers and an exemplary curriculum.

The implication for training is that the knowledge base for educators and other service personnel must include some understanding of the nature of excess behavior. While it is beyond the scope of this chapter to provide an overview of contemporary understanding of excess behavior and the reader must be referred to other sources (e.g., Barrett, 1986; Meyer & Evans, 1989), there are three aspects of excess behavior that would be worth focusing upon in any professional training curriculum. These are outlined briefly.

First, much excess behavior can be understood best in terms of its function for the individual, such as being self-stimulatory, getting the attention of others, serving to influence others, or communicating wants. The work of Durand and Carr (e.g., Durand & Carr, 1985) has been especially important for clarifying the possible communicative function of excess behavior. The implications of a functional orientation to excess behavior are: 1) that excess behaviors can be seen to be meaningful, not bizarre or "psychotic" as they are sometimes called; and 2) excess behaviors reveal critical cues as to the student's needs and wants and thus, have importance for individual program development.

Second, although the function of excess behavior must be considered, there seem to be many inappropriate behaviors that do not have "intent" and that are components of long established behavior patterns. Such behaviors may be dynamically related to emotional or mood states, such as aggressive behavior being triggered by anger or fear. The interrelationship among behaviors in the individual students' repertoire is now much better understood and has considerable significance for the design of therapeutic interventions (Evans, Meyer, Kurkjian, & Kishi, 1988; Scotti, Evans, Meyer, & DiBenedetto, in press; Voeltz & Evans, 1982).

A third consideration is that a significant number of excess behaviors can be traced to direct, and sometimes indirect, organic causes. Disorders such as Lesch-Nyhan syndrome and Tourette syndrome give rise to highly specific patterns of excess behavior. Indirect physiological causes are multitudinous and include responses to pain, reactions to allergies, and secondary sequelae of metabolic disorders such as difficulty in temperature regulation causing children to strip off their clothes. A very useful discussion of medical factors in persons with severe disabilities and behavior problems is found in Gourash (1986). Obviously non-medical personnel cannot be expected to have the background to recognize organic disorders or to appreciate their full implications. Thus, training needs to emphasize the value of collaboration with specialists in neuropsychology, neurology, internal medicine, and pediatrics. Outside the excellent training of the University Affiliated Programs (UAP) network, physicians may not have much background in developmental disabilities.

THE MISUSE OF PRINCIPLES OF AVERSION

Given the complexity of the origins of excess behavior, including organic etiologies, the simple manipulation of consequences (whether reinforcement or punishment) would appear to be the most superficial treatment approach possible. That is not to say that contingencies of reinforcement do not *influence* all behavior—there are many examples in behavior therapy of organic problems being altered by environmental contingencies. In such cases, the contingencies may have their effect through indirect means. For example, reinforcing a client for not having seizures might actually work by means of encouraging the person to avoid becoming overtired, or helping the person learn to relax as a mediator to reduce stress and, therefore, seizures. Behavior problems that may have an organic origin in persons with severe disabilities are equally amenable to environmental contingency control.

Successfully reducing a behavior that is intrinsically reinforcing—such as grabbing food—by means of a negative contingency—such as removal of all available food for that meal—probably has its effect not through the direct suppression of stealing but through the pupil learning to exercise some kind of self-control. Thus, the success of a punishment strategy is not contained only in the contingency rule, but is dependent upon the availability, or emergence, of a more general skill (e.g., self-control) in that individual.

This point is raised because the use of aversives often is defended on the grounds that it represents sound application of behavioral principles. As a result, any argument against their use would have to be made purely on values, ethical, or practical grounds. In actuality, however, the typical aversive procedures represent a limited understanding of contemporary behavioral theory. This has come about because of the narrow-band approach to behavior modification adopted by psychologists whose background is only in applied behavior analysis. They have not been exposed to the wider rubric of behavioral theory as contained in such integrative approaches as social behaviorism (Staats, 1975) or social learning theory (Bandura, 1977). For example, Staats argues from a theoretical perspective that punishment paradigms would be undesirable treatments for persons with severe disabilities because of these individuals' lack of more basic behavioral repertoires. Bandura has been particularly influential in broadening learning concepts to include attention to the self system, the power of modeling, and other aspects of vicarious learning.

Why, then, has behavior modification with clients with severe disabilities continued to use outmoded and limited Skinnerian or radical operant concepts? One important factor seems to be that behavioral researchers have been focused clinically and not influenced by the advances in educational practices during the 1980s that emphasize the similarities rather than the differences between persons with severe disabilities and those without (e.g., Horner, Meyer, & Fredericks, 1986). The researchers needed are those who not only have a broad knowledge of behavioral principles, but who also are immersed in the conceptual trends in service delivery that have emerged in the 1980s. Evans and Meyer (1985) described such a union as representing a second generation of behavior modification.

One way to achieve this much needed shift is to challenge the standards of evidence used in evaluating behavioral interventions. Two methodological papers (Evans & Meyer, 1987; Voeltz & Evans, 1983) have proposed new assessment criteria of the efficacy of a given intervention to include the impact of the intervention not just on an isolated target behavior but on the person's life-style. Continued critical evaluation of contemporary standards of educational validity is recommended.

Critically evaluating outcomes usually results in refinement of intervention methods or innovations. For instance, in adult behavior therapy, systematic desensitization certainly was successful in treating phobias. When interest expanded to long-term prevention and clinically meaningful change, clinical applications extended to new methods for teaching coping, self-modification, and other cognitive skills. Similar developments have been slow in being introduced into interventions for persons with severe disabilities. For instance, Azrin (1987) provided some interesting material on the efficacy of brief interruption in dealing with excess behavior. His data showed that the method was more effective than punishment, but his introduction to the method emphasized not the limitations of punishment but how it is becoming harder to use punishment in institutions and thus, new procedures are required.

Training programs for doctoral and postdoctoral level clinical researchers should be designed to encourage continued expansion of the full range of behavior therapy techniques into areas of concern for persons with severe disabilities. Many innovations in practice come from the educational arena. While training behavioral researchers in sophisticated experimental design is still important, it is crucial that a new generation of researchers be educated in policies and human values (Guess, 1989).

LIMITATIONS OF BEHAVIOR MODIFICATION TRAINING

Practical Problems in Staff Training

It should be clear that these concerns with certain behavioral approaches are not criticisms of behavior modification in general. Behavior analysis, by its empirical nature, should be self-correcting, especially if continued attention is paid to appropriate outcome measures. Similarly, criticisms of training paraprofessionals in behavior modification is not a repudiation of the principles of behaviorism or the employment of paraprofessionals. Rather, it reflects concern for the translation of behavioral principles into educational or clinical practice.

One of the earliest concepts in behavior modification was that in order to effect change in inappropriate behavior, the persons interacting with the client on a day-to-day basis would have to begin to plan and design these interactions in accordance with basic contingency principles. One of the earliest discussions of this notion was in Ayllon and Michael's (1959) classic article, "The psychiatric nurse as a behavioral engineer." A very thoughtful perspective was provided in Tharp and Wetzel's (1969) book, *Behavior Modification in the Natural Environment*, which described a program to train peers, parents, college students, and any other members of a community to be the behavior change agents under the consultative direction of a clinical psychologist. Before long, parents were being trained as behavior modifiers, as were teachers, people with milder disabilities, siblings, and others. A quick glance at the many manuals, books, and other training materials commercially available will show clearly that constructing formal baselines, learning about reversal designs, and variable ratio schedules of reinforcement were all part of the recommended curriculum. Everyone was being trained as a mini behavior modifier.[2]

In hindsight, however, we realize that the approach was misguided. From the very first there was evidence that nonprofessional staff were not able to generalize principles. Also, direct service staff typically come into institutional settings with little or no prior training. The verbal behaviors or technical knowledge acquired in a workshop are not potent enough to influence actual behaviors in the facility. The trainees fail to generalize workshop skills to the real setting. Or, if trainees do acquire specific applied skills, use of these skills does not continue when the supervisor or consultant is no longer demanding them. In an excellent summary of generalization and maintenance issues, Reid and Schepis (1986) reviewed the numerous studies that have assessed direct care personnel's very limited use of sound behavioral principles after training. As a result, Reid and his colleagues advocated a behavioral supervision model in which the behaviors of staff members themselves become the targets of intervention. There is experimental evidence of the effectiveness of the model at least in changing staff behavior. The model involves defining specific staff performance; monitoring that performance by time sampling techniques; teaching specific skills if staff appear to have difficulty implementing procedures; providing rewards such

---

[2]Between about 1970 and 1974 I myself gave weekly workshops and participated in the training of almost 600 direct care staff at Waimano Training School and Hospital in Honolulu. While I remember fondly the warmth of those involved, and while I learned much about the needs of clients and staff in such settings, the basic strategy seems flawed.

as praise, salary bonuses, and release time; and ongoing evaluation (reviewing data collected by the monitoring procedures) to ensure correct staff response.

Conceptual Limitations

While there are training developments that are likely to make the application of behavioral principles a little more effective, the more fundamental question is whether applied behavioral principles are indeed the appropriate skills for the task at hand. The various objections that can be raised against these behavioral skills often have been couched in humanistic terms easily discounted in behavior modification. For instance, *Gentle Teaching* (McGee, Menolascino, Hobbs, & Menousek, 1987) contains some excellent suggestions for nonaversive intervention, but all of behavior therapy is presented as a dehumanizing technology. There *are* some important concerns and caveats regarding behavior modification that can be derived from behavioral principles themselves and certainly from other well-established psychological concepts.

One of these is that if taught behavior modification techniques, direct care staff learn to interact with clients according to a pre-planned formula, thus reducing the naturalness of their day-to-day interactions. Behavior principles relate to static descriptions of events, not new procedures to be added to the ongoing social stream. Even if staff members learn these concepts rather than specific artificial techniques, their normal interactions often violate general behavior principles. A good example is laughing with a student or client who has done something wrong but is being funny at the same time. Such natural events may be inhibited by a rigid concern for reinforcement principles. Yet, they may represent the types of reactions that other people will provide, so that clients need to learn appropriate behavior *despite* social contingencies that are less than "ideal" in reinforcing this learning.

Other concerns are similar. For example, teachers and nonprofessional staff have a nurturing role in addition to an instructional one. Natural emotional behaviors in social interactions, such as displays of affection, may be reduced when trying to follow a behavioral program. Also, behavioral change techniques may exaggerate the importance of control (as in generalizing compliance training). Staff using these techniques may emphasize power rather than rehabilitation. Furthermore, as traditionally taught, behavioral methods place too much stress on immediate contingencies, and do not include more complex ideas such as long-term setting influences, coping, cognition, choice, and self-control. Finally, as mentioned earlier, the careful ethical guidelines that have been developed within behavior therapy (Favell et al., 1982) imply that punishment methods can be used only as the last resort—when all else has failed. This ethical restriction creates the impression for direct care staff that aversives are powerful and will really solve the problem when introduced, thus reducing their motivation to give other methods a chance. Unfortunately, there are few available data to support these concerns and no comparative studies.

A new type of personnel training is needed that emphasizes normalized social interactions between clients and direct care staff. An important variable in this training would be examination of the social expectations of the staff: do they interpret clients as friends, or patients, or enemies? Equally significant might be consideration of the social attributions of the clients: do they confuse direct care staff with personal friends, or are staff, in fact, the only persons with whom clients have a social relationship? Training in this area might examine the social cognitions of staff and the kinds of attributions they make about clients or students and their behaviors. These cognitions go beyond positive attitude to include examination of how the staff interpret client behavior and understand problem behaviors from the client's perspective.

Training in a conceptual framework is essential in limiting the risk of mistranslating research findings into practice. For example, the work on the communicative function of excess behavior (Durand & Carr, 1985) has resulted in the assumption that when clients use unacceptable behaviors to communicate, the required treatment is to teach the client a specific communicative skill. The more basic issue in designing the intervention should be to determine what has gone wrong in the relationship between client and staff member to have generated inappropriate communication in the first place. In behavior therapy, when we teach communication skills in dysfunctional marriages we assume that the communication is a two-way process. Missed communications are the result of complex processes, not simply a deficit in one member of the dyad. A similar view of dyadic process must be incorporated into training staff to interact with clients. Furthermore, research findings regarding the "treatment" of excess behavior need to be placed in a broader interactional perspective. Training in this perspective far exceeds procedures for teaching staff new techniques to manage behavior.

SOLVING THE MOST SERIOUS PROBLEMS

Although much of what has just been argued applies to teachers, the reasoning is most applicable to direct care staff. Direct care staff, like parents, should not be thought of as providing formal instruction to students, although we know that effective parents and other adults can structure their interactions such that learning can take place naturally. Teachers also structure situations to encourage interaction-based learning. In addition, teachers are responsible for direct instruction, which leads them to two very direct points of contact with students' behavior problems. First, in accordance with an educative model of managing excess behaviors, teaching certain specific alternative skills (e.g., leisure skills, social skills) is the primary intervention for these behaviors. Second, certain types of teaching situations and teaching styles may evoke excess behaviors. These two points of contact pose major dilemmas for teachers and must be considered in training them.

Some modifications in teaching strategy are likely to be effective in quickly reducing excess behavior. Weld and Evans (1990), for instance, showed that students with severe disabilities exhibited fewer disruptive and other excess behaviors when taught according to part learning strategies than did those taught according to whole routines. Ecological classroom factors that seem to minimize behavior problems have already been discussed.

Some of the behaviors that are thought to interfere with teaching and learning are not particularly severe. In our early studies, Meyer and I often coded examples of a category called "on task/excess," in which the students were simultaneously performing the task assigned by the teacher and engaging in some excess behavior, usually self-stimulation. The more disruptive behaviors, of the kind that in the literature have resulted in an array of mild but punitive procedures like overcorrection, squirts of lemon juice, and facial or visual screening, almost always occur against a backdrop of poor quality instructional programs. Replacing punitive methods with good teaching practices should be a realistic expectation for teacher training.

What will be much harder is training teachers to deal with behavior problems that have become so completely out of control that instructional programming is impossible. In intervening successfully with these few but severe behaviors, teachers or other community service personnel cannot be expected to deal with excesses that have already been a major challenge to other professionals. For teachers to be effective in dealing with such excess behaviors, an alternative model is needed in which the primary emphasis is on interdisciplinary collaboration to support management of excess behavior. One or more highly skilled behavioral intervention experts would serve as consultants in a particularly severe problem situation. For this model to work, teachers need collaboration skills including: 1) the ability to implement planned interventions with high standards of treatment integrity, 2) willingness to make major modifications in classroom procedures or curriculum, and 3) the ability to make positive and constructive contributions to the planning process. Whenever a consultation model is used, the teacher must be especially flexible. The consultants will need a sound background in behavior disorders and their etiology settings. This would seem to require postdoctoral training geared to the actual conduct of technical assistance (see Durand & Kishi, 1987, as an example), and the integration of clinical psychology (or an allied field) with special education and rehabilitation.

Large scale interventions almost always are needed to effectively manage the most serious problems. When punishment procedures are being relied upon, agencies are willing to spend large sums of money on national consultants, elaborate equipment, and so forth. A similar commitment of resources must be made for positive interventions, which inevitably are multifaceted and require extensive cooperation from many people. Resources will be needed to implement round-the-clock plans and radically alter environments. In a case study describing such a positive program, Berkman and Meyer (1988) described it as "going all out" (p. 76) nonaversively. Another model for this general approach has been described by Donnellan, LaVigna, Zambito, and Thvedt (1985).

INTEGRATION

Thus far I have concentrated training on three key personnel: direct service staff (such as the staff of group homes), teachers, and psychologists (or at least experts in behavioral management—a term and role for which, hopefully, need will steadily decline). Many other people come into direct contact with persons exhibiting severe behavior disorders, and in the ecological or systems model all these individuals must be involved in a coherent effort to prevent and change excess behavior. Meyer, Evans, Horner, Schreibman, and Williams (1987) defined eight distinct and mutually exclusive roles occupied by those who interact and work with people having severe disabilities and excess behavior. These are: 1) family members, such as parents and siblings; 2) community people with no formal training but who have regular contact, such as friends, neighbors, co-workers, and employers; 3) specialized personnel with limited contact, like police, emergency medical personnel, lawyers; 4) trained and certified personnel with regular direct contact, for example, teachers, speech/language therapists, and occupational therapists; 5) trained noncertified individuals with direct contact, such as residential staff, job coaches, and educational assistants; 6) local experts providing limited technical assistance, such as psychiatric social workers, school psychologists, and neurologists; 7) case managers or administrators; and 8) expert consultants and researchers, and exemplary service providers.

In the more traditional clinical perspective, in which "treatment" for behavior problems is planned by a professional specialist and administered by direct service staff, most of these eight roles are irrelevant. In an ecological perspective, it is assumed that the student or client will come into contact with a wide range of people in the natural environment as well as in professional roles. The eight roles specified differ considerably in degree of regular contact with the target population, as well as in the adequacy of existing training programs, expected expertise with behavior problems, and

Table 9.1. Training priorities for local experts

Content	Importance (high, medium, low)	Rationale
1. Descriptive information	H	Expert problem solver needs extensive background knowledge regarding behavior problems and developmental disabilities.
2. Values/expectation	H	It is important to have positive expectations and knowledge of successful outcomes possible.
3. Policy/systems variables	L	Intervention plans should be based on expectation that immediate context can be changed rather than total system changing.
4. Basic principles of behavior	H	Consultant needs to be able to derive flexible treatment suggestions from first principles.
5. Principles of behavioral intervention	H	This content area represents the criteria for the role—it is the task they are called on to perform.
6. Crisis management	M	Experts in crisis management procedures need to train those in Roles 4 and 5, but local consultant need not be that expert.
7. Advanced treatment technologies	H	Local experts should at least have book knowledge of techniques in current literature.
8. Research methodology	M	Role requires consuming of research information but not generation of new knowledge.
9. Decision-making	H	Including all staff, in addition to client, in planning and decision-making is crucial.
10. Legal/ethical	M	Other administrative roles will be more concerned with legal issues, but professional ethics are very important.
11. Design of active treatment/instruction	M	Service provider should have basic knowledge and be able to call on instructional/curriculum experts.
12. Advocacy	L	While not primary role, local experts do need to be able to advocate for better services and be willing to report problems.

(continued)

Table 9.1. (*continued*)

Content	Importance (high, medium, low)	Rationale
13. Social interaction/relationship skill	M	Local experts do not have regular or direct contact, so needs are greater in respect to numbers 2 and 14.
14. Practical knowledge	H	Suggested interventions should reflect both respect for individual's human rights as well as practical knowledge of integrated environments and possibilities for the person.

(Adapted from Meyer, Evans, et al. [1987].)

degree to which the system will hold the individual accountable. As a result, it would not be sensible to train everyone the same way or in the same content areas. Yet individuals in all eight roles might benefit considerably from training in values that raise expectations for the normalization of service strategies. In order to clarify which personnel might benefit from which content, Meyer, Evans, et al. (1987) suggested 14 content areas that are equally important for designing effective prevention and intervention plans. These content areas are briefly outlined in the following paragraphs and summarized in Table 9.1.

The first area covers descriptive information about severe disabilities. This is not technical information about syndromes and etiologies; it is positive information designed to remove myths and stereotypes by focusing on how individuals with severe disabilities function in society. This area overlaps somewhat with the second, an understanding of contemporary values and expectations concerning the civil rights of people with severe excess behavior to participate fully in society. Teachers, for example, would need to know the importance of teaching functional skills that promote community living, employment, recreation, and social integration. A third content area incorporates the systems perspective that has guided this chapter (see also Meyer & Evans, 1989). Systems at various levels (e.g., the classroom schedule, the degree to which the school is integrated) are all variables that have an impact on our ability to resolve excess behavior problems in a meaningful way.

The next set of content areas is more conventionally a part of the technology for successful behavior change: four—the basic laws and principles of behavior; five—the translation of these principles into socially valid interventions; and six—how to respond appropriately when a serious behavior does occur, that is, crisis management. The seventh area might be called something like advanced treatment technologies. The application of cognitive principles of self-control for individuals with limited cognitive skills, the introduction of novel instructional strategies that focus on outcomes, or sophisticated pharmacological trials are examples of advanced treatments. Advanced treatment, no matter how ingenious, is valuable only if proven effective, and knowledge of scientific methods for research and evaluation is essential to determining the effectiveness of treatments. Thus, research skills is the eight area.

The ninth content area covers decision-making and team collaboration skills, which seem to be especially important if nonaversive management plans are to be effectively implemented. The 10th area is knowledge of legal rights and ethical guidelines. Professional knowledge of legal rights are converted into action content through the ability to individualize instructional programs, area 11, and through the ability to use information regarding rights to advocate for needed changes in services, programs, and local policies, area 12. Often clients with excess behaviors are particularly discriminated against. Thus, knowledge of their rights and willingness to advocate on their behalf is essential.

Content area 13 addresses the development of relationship skills. It is the saliency and demandingness of some excess behaviors that often force societal response out of balance. Disruptive, aggressive, and self-injurious behavior become the overriding feature of the client's persona. Some clients experience only professional interactions—they are being treated or being educated. Social interaction training needs to be developed to assist families, teachers, and direct service staff to normalize their relationships with the people in their lives who are described euphemistically as "challenging." Finally, area 14 reflects the need to design treatment in the context of consideration for a person's long-term life situation. Neglect of "futures planning" (O'Brien, 1987) can be seen clearly in reports of research on excess behavior reduction in which the outcome is reported in terms of change in rate of the excess behavior, not the improved quality of life for the person. (See Evans and Meyer, 1987, for a further discussion of these concerns.) Practical knowledge about persons with disabilities, about their daily experiences and their basic human needs that are shared by those who do not have disabilities is required.

Training in all 14 content areas is not needed by persons in each of the different roles outlined earlier. Tables 9.1 and 9.2 indicate the degree to which those in two different roles (local experts and family members) might require training in the 14 content areas. A brief rationale explaining why they would need this content is also provided. This matrix is an example of the type of framework for evaluation that might be used for all possible personnel roles. Constructing such a matrix would allow expert judges to rate the discrepancy between what personnel now know in these content areas and what they should know, thus providing a systematic agenda for training.

Table 9.2. Training priorities for family members

Content	Importance (high, medium, low)	Rationale
1. Descriptive information	H	Families will be involved in all aspects of person's life
2. Values/expectation	H	Will affect motivation of family members for treatment implementation
3. Policy/systems variables	M	Information useful in pursuing services in community
4. Basic principles of behavior	M	Useful for understanding rationale of program and for guiding conduct at home
5. Principles of behavioral intervention	H	Essential to implementation of treatment programs
6. Crisis management	H	Crises bound to occur; family needs to know how to handle effectively or run risk of harm
7. Advanced treatment technologies	L	May not be involved in highly specialized treatments that would be provided by clinician
8. Research methodology	L	Will not be designing research to contribute to scholarly knowledge
9. Decision-making	H	Should be involved in decision on treatment targets and school programs
10. Legal/ethical	M	Need to know basic rights and ethical concerns but not details of specific legal issues
11. Design of active treatment/instruction	L	May be involved in designing general instruction strategies but likely to be concerned in specifics only of treatment they implement
12. Advocacy	H	Are primary advocates for person's rights; also, need to know their own rights and how to effect change in community services
13. Social interaction/relationship skill	H	Need to normalize their interactions with individual with disability as much as possible, also need to enhance social skills of the individual
14. Practical knowledge	H	Inevitably, they are in the environment with individual with disability on a regular and frequent basis

(Adapted from Meyer, Evans, et al. [1987].)

CONCLUSION:
THE EVALUATION OF PERSONNEL PREPARATION

The most general position argued in this chapter is that there is no need for specialized training in state-of-the-art, nonaversive interventions. While there are useful intervention strategies that are nonaversive (e.g., DRO [differential reinforcement of other behavior], reinforcing positive alternatives, aggression replacement training, and certain ecological manipulations), the true antidote to excess behavior lies in excellent programming. This requires suitable living arrangements and life-styles, in addition to exemplary curricula and effective instructional strategies. Hence, personnel preparation for dealing with behavior problems should not be very different from personnel preparation in general. In a sense, the presence of excess behaviors is a barometer for how well we are doing in personnel training: negative behaviors in persons with severe disabilities reflect bad programs and inadequate training.

Nonaversive behavior management has become a rallying cry for positive reform. Most service providers are enthusiastic about the possibilities for nonaversive behavior management. In New York State, for instance, we are working on a training program for residential staff within the Office of Mental Retardation and Developmental Disabilities that avoids debate over whether or not to use punishment and simply focuses on methods that should enhance the quality of programs and services within the state system. As we come to evaluate such training, however, it will be critical to measure outcomes in three domains: whether the trainees acquired the skills taught (treatment integrity), whether programs and services changed as a result (direct outcome), and whether excess behaviors subsequently declined (indirect outcome).

Although it has been argued in this chapter that decreasing excess behavior is an indirect consequence of personnel preparation, there are few empirical data directly supporting the recommendations made. The rationale for these recommendations is extrapolated from treatment studies where there has been an attempt to show a direct causal connection between a specific treatment and the decrease in some excess behavior. The traditional experimental approach may not represent a good standard for *evaluation* (Voeltz & Evans, 1983). A documented decrease in an excess behavior does not indicate whether other negative behaviors have replaced it (side effects), or whether positive behaviors were enhanced, or whether the person's life situation improved in a meaningful way. Standards developed from a broader-based analysis of the impact of the intervention on the life of the person exhibiting excess behavior must be the basis for evaluating treatment outcomes. These same standards should be used in judging the effectiveness of personnel preparation.

Comparative studies along these lines might be particularly interesting at this stage of our development. It is time to directly examine the atmosphere (as well as the specific rate of excess behavior) in group homes where the staff have been trained with an emphasis on values as well as behavioral principles, as compared with the atmosphere in settings where staff have been trained in behavior modification techniques alone.

Behavior modification has not really envisaged such studies. Staff training has been cast in terms of the implementation of a specific intervention plan. For many serious excess behaviors that have been allowed to develop in persons with severe disabilities there *will* be a need for intensive formal intervention plans. However, these interventions are best designed and implemented by well-trained experts familiar with current scholarship concerning excess behavior, including physiological and medical information. Thus, the task of the direct service staff, both professional and paraprofessional, is to be flexibly involved in change and collaboration.

Evaluation designs for such consultant models are beginning to appear in the literature (Donnellan et al., 1985; Durand & Kishi, 1987). Within these evaluation models, we must elaborate on the basic systems model to reflect positive life-styles. We must focus on our clients' lives, experiences, and their future opportunities. If we simply took all the aversive programs written for these clients and rewrote them as positive ones, we would be doing something worthwhile. But we would be failing to make available to persons with severe disabilities the *full* range of social and educational opportunities that already are well within the boundaries of our scientific knowledge.

REFERENCES

Ayllon, T., & Michael, J. (1959). The psychiatric nurse as a behavioral engineer. *Journal of the Experimental Analysis of Behavior, 2,* 323–334.

Azrin, N.H. (1987). *Self-injurious behavior: How to treat without mistreating.* Paper presented at the annual meeting of the American Psychological Association, New York.

Bandura, A. (1977). *Social learning theory.* Englewood Cliffs, NJ: Prentice-Hall.

Barrett, R.P. (Ed.). (1986). *Severe behavior disorders in the mentally retarded: Non-drug approaches to treatment.* New York: Plenum.

Berkman, K.A., & Meyer, L.H. (1989). Alternative strategies and multiple outcomes in the remediation of severe self-injury: Going "all out" nonaversively. *Journal of The Association for Persons with Severe Handicaps, 13,* 76–86.

Donnellan, A.M., LaVigna, G.W., Zambito, J., & Thvedt, J. (1985). A time-limited intensive intervention program model to support community placement for persons with severe behavior problems. *Journal of The Association for Persons with Severe Handicaps, 10*(3), 123–131.

Dubanoski, R.A., Evans, I.M., & Higuchi, A.A. (1978). Analysis and treatment of child abuse: A set of behavioral propositions. *Child Abuse and Neglect, 2,* 153–172.

Durand, V.M., & Carr, E.G. (1985). Self-injurious behavior: Motivating conditions and guidelines for treatment. *School Psychology Review, 14,* 171–176.

Durand, V.M., & Kishi, G. (1987). Reducing severe behavior problems among persons with dual sensory impairments: An evaluation of a technical assistance model. *Journal of The Association for Persons with Severe Handicaps, 12*(3), 2–10.

Evans, I.M., Meyer, L.M., Kurkjian, J.A., & Kishi, G.S. (1988). An evaluation of behavioral interrelationships in child behavior therapy. In J.C. Witt, S.N. Elliott, & F.N. Gresham (Eds.), *Handbook of behavior therapy in education.* New York: Plenum.

Evans, I.M., & Voeltz, L.M. (1982). *The selection of intervention priorities in educational programming of severely handicapped preschool children with multiple behavior problems* (Final Report, Grant # G00-790-1960). Honolulu: University of Hawaii Departments of Psychology and Special Education.

Favell, J.E., Azrin, N.H., Baumeister, A.A., Carr, E.G., Dorsey, M.F., Forehand, R., Foxx, R.M., Lovaas, O.I., Rincover, A., Risley, T.R., Romanczyk, R.G., Russo, D.C., Schroeder, S.R., & Solnick, J.V. (1982). The treatment of self-injurious behavior. (AABT Task Force Report, Winter, 1982). *Behavior Therapy, 13,* 529–554.

Gourash, L.F. (1986). Assessing and managing medical factors. In R.P. Barrett (Ed.), *Severe behavior disorders in the mentally retarded: Nondrug approaches to treatment* (pp. 157–205). New York: Plenum.

Guess, D. (1989). *Transmission of behavior management technologies from researchers to practitioners: A need for professional self-evaluation.* Unpublished manuscript, Department of Special Education, University of Kansas, Lawrence.

Horner, R.H., Meyer, L.H., & Fredericks, H.D.B. (Eds.). (1986). *Education of learners with severe handicaps: Exemplary service strategies.* Baltimore: Paul H. Brookes Publishing Co.

Leduc, A., Dumais, A., & Evans, I.M. (in press). Social behaviorism, rehabilitation, and ethics: Applications for people with severe disabilities. In G.H. Eifert & I.M. Evans (Eds.), *Unifying behavior therapy: Contributions of paradigmatic behaviorism.* New York: Springer.

McGee, J.J., Menolascino, F.J., Hobbs, D.C., & Menousek, P.E. (1987). *Gentle teaching: A nonaversive approach for helping persons with mental retardation.* New York: Human Sciences Press.

Meyer, L.M., Eichinger, J., & Park-Lee, S. (1987). A validation of program quality indicators in educational services for students with severe disabilities. *Journal of The Association for Persons with Severe Handicaps, 12*(4), 251–263.

Meyer, L.M., & Evans, I.M. (1989). *Nonaversive intervention for behavior problems: A manual for home and community.* Baltimore: Paul H. Brookes Publishing Co.

Meyer, L.M., Evans, I.M., Horner, R.H., Schreibman, L., & Williams, R. (1987). *Personnel preparation.* Study Group report presented at the State of the Art Conference on Treatment of Behavior Disorders, Kansas City, MO.

New York State Commission on Quality of Care for the Mentally Disabled. (1987). *Abusing the unprotected: A study of the misuse of aversive behavior modification techniques and weaknesses in the regulatory structure.* Albany: Author.

O'Brien, J. (1987). A guide to life-style planning: Using *The Activities Catalog* to integrate services and natural support systems. In B. Wilcox & G.T. Bellamy (Eds.), *A comprehensive guide to The Activities Catalog: An alternative curriculum for youth and adults with severe disabilities* (175–189). Baltimore: Paul H. Brookes Publishing Co.

Reid, D.H., & Schepis, M.M. (1986). Direct care staff training. In R.P. Barrett

(Ed.), *Severe behavior disorders in the mentally retarded: Nondrug approaches to treatment* (pp. 297–322). New York: Plenum.

Scotti, J.R., Evans, I.M., Meyer, L.H., & DiBenedetto, A. (in press). Individual repertoires as behavioral systems: Implications for designing and evaluating interventions. In R. Remington (Ed.), *The challenge of severe mental handicap: A behaviour analytic approach.* London: Wiley.

Staats, A.W. (1975). *Social behaviorism.* Homewood, IL: Dorsey Press.

Tharp, R.G., & Wetzel, R.J. (1969). *Behavior modification in the natural environment.* New York: Academic Press.

Voeltz, L.M., & Evans, I.M. (1982). The assessment of behavioral interrelationships in child behavior therapy. *Behavioral Assessment, 4,* 131–165.

Voeltz, L.M., & Evans, I.M. (1983). Educational validity: Procedures to evaluate outcomes in programs for severely handicapped learners. *Journal of The Association for the Severely Handicapped, 8*(1), 3–15.

Weld, E.M., & Evans, I.M. (1990). Effects of part versus whole instructional strategies on skill acquisition and excess behavior. *American Journal on Mental Retardation, 94,* 377–386.

Winterling, V., Dunlap, G., & O'Neill, R.E. (1987). The influence of task variation on the aberrant behaviors of autistic students. *Education and Treatment of Children, 10,* 105–109.

10

Preparing Personnel to Work in Community Support Services

Julie Ann Racino

The field of community living for people with disabilities is undergoing tremendous changes in philosophy and in practice. Many new challenges in training personnel are being posed. Deinstitutionalization is no longer our primary issue. We must now focus our training efforts on how best to support children with the most severe disabilities in families and adults with severe disabilities to live in their own homes (Taylor, Racino, Knoll, & Lutfiyya, 1987).

In general, personnel preparation programs at all levels—graduate, undergraduate, community college, and provider-based—have had difficulty keeping pace with the major developments in the field. The majority of literature related to community living emphasizes group home management, attitudinal barriers to community living, quality assurance mechanisms, and general community services information (Community Integration Project, 1985). New materials on family support and nonaversive approaches are

The preparation of this chapter was supported in part by Contract No. G0085C03503, awarded to the Center on Human Policy, Division of Special Education and Rehabilitation, Syracuse University, Syracuse, New York by the Unites States Department of Education, Office of Special Education and Rehabilitative Services, National Institute on Disability Research and Rehabilitation. The opinions expressed herein do not necessarily reflect the position of the United States Department of Education, and no official endorsement should be inferred. The author would like to thank Steve Taylor, Gail Jacob, Alison Ford, Dianne Apter, Bonnie Shoultz, Pam Walker, Susan O'Connor, and Dick Pratt for their contributions to this chapter.

now available; however, published resources on nonfacility-based supportive community living arrangements are limited (Nisbet, Clark, & Covert, in press).

This chapter examines critical principles and issues in the preparation of personnel for the field of community living. The chapter introduces a new way of thinking about personnel preparation that is relevant to all levels of personnel involved in residential services for people with disabilities. Major questions addressed include: What are new directions in community living for people with severe disabilities? What do personnel need to know to support people with severe disabilities in the community? How can we prepare personnel to look at what is best in the field and accordingly create changes in their daily work? What are the issues in personnel preparation emerging for the 1990s?

PROMISING NEW DIRECTIONS IN COMMUNITY LIVING

There has been a shift from a focus on residential services to a broader understanding of community living for people with severe disabilities. Community living now can be viewed from a variety of different perspectives. Each perspective raises different questions about the nature of community living and the supports required to accomplish it.

1. **An individual perspective.** What does community living mean from the viewpoint of each individual person?
2. **A family perspective.** What does community living mean from the viewpoints of individual family members and from families as units?
3. **A community perspective.** What roles do ordinary citizens play in the lives of people with disabilities? What contributions do people with disabilities make to community life?
4. **A service system perspective.** How can service systems and supports be designed to enable people with disabilities to participate fully in community life?
5. **A cross-disability perspective.** What commonalities exist across different disability groups and across social movements (e.g., independent living, disability rights) that can bring those involved in the field together?
6. **A policy perspective.** How can federal, state, and local policies be developed to support people with disabilities in order that they may live in the community?
7. **A societal change perspective.** What changes are necessary to improve the lives of all people, including people with disabilities?

While each perspective is important, this chapter examines community living primarily from a service system perspective and emphasizes the preparation of human services personnel who work in communities.

SUPPORTING FAMILIES AND THEIR CHILDREN

"There's no kid in the world who can't do better in a family than in a group home" (Nancy Rosenau, Director of Admissions and Placement, Macomb-Oakland Regional Center, Michigan, 1986).

There is a growing recognition of the importance of providing families with the support they need to maintain their children at home (Agosta, Bradley, Rugg, Spence, & Covert, 1985; Bates, 1985; Taylor, Racino, Knoll, & Lutfiyya, 1987). Promising practices in family support include: 1) an emphasis on family-centered approaches to service delivery (e.g., Nelkin, 1987); 2) the provision of individualized and flexible supports (e.g., Taylor, Racino, & Rothenberg, 1988); 3) coordination of those supports through responsive case management/service coordination, if desired by the family (e.g., Kaufmann, Lichtenstein, & Rosenblatt, 1986); 4) empowerment of families (e.g., Dunst, Trivette, Davis, & Cornwell, 1988); 5) supports based on the principle of providing "whatever it takes" to assist the family (e.g., Connecticut Developmental Disabilities Council, 1988); 6) and the importance of social relationships and informal social support (e.g., Dunst, Trivette, Gordon, & Pletcher, 1989).

Making family supports available is one aspect of efforts to ensure that all children have "a consistent and nurturing environment, an enduring, positive adult relationship and a specific person who will advocate for the child into adulthood" (Michigan, 1986, pp. 5–6). This policy translation of the belief that all children belong in families (Center on Human Policy, 1987) is called permanency planning. Permanency planning is built around three guiding principles: 1) supporting the family; 2) encouraging family reunification efforts; and 3) pursuing adoption or exploring other permanency options, such as open adoption or co-parenting when children cannot remain with their biological families (Taylor, Lakin, & Hill, 1989).

Currently, children with the most severe disabilities, including complex medical needs, behavioral challenges, and multiple disabilities, are being supported to live with families. While Macomb-Oakland, Michigan is the location of a notable example of efforts to support children with severe disabilities in families (Biklen, 1988a; Taylor, 1985b), several states and regions have made aggressive efforts to limit admission of children to state institutions and develop community supports for children, particularly in families. For example, as of spring 1989, fewer than 12 children remain in state institutions in places as diverse as Minnesota and West Virginia, with efforts underway for each of these children to move into the community.

SUPPORTING ADULTS TO LIVE IN THEIR OWN HOMES

"All people, regardless of severity of disability, can live in their own home in the community. People should have choice about where and with whom they live, control over their environment and how they spend their time" (Gail Jacob, Director, Options in Community Living, Madison, Wisconsin, 1989).

Traditionally, community living arrangements have had two primary features. First, the guiding policy for the design of these services has been the principle of the least restrictive environment, which is operationalized as a continuum of services (e.g., Castellani, 1987). People with the most severe disabilities typically have received services from the most restrictive end of the continuum (in institutions); those with the mildest disabilities have been provided services at the least restrictive end of the continuum. Second, traditional community living arrangement programs have been facility-based; programs have revolved around the living arrangement or facility rather than around individuals. Facility-based services inherently are limited in their flexibility and potential for individualization (Taylor et al., 1988).

In contrast, the emerging paradigm in supporting adults with developmental disabilities in the community is often called a *nonfacility-based, individualized, person-centered, or housing/support service* approach. This approach explicitly rejects the continuum of services concept and seeks to overcome many of the pitfalls associated with the traditional design of residential services (Taylor, 1988). Every adult is assumed to have the right to live in a home in the community with whatever supports are necessary. Key characteristics include: 1) separation of housing and support services; 2) home ownership; 3) individual assessment, planning and funding; 4) flexible and individualized supports; 5) consumer-directed services.

Separation of Housing and Support Services

To increase flexibility and individualization, the housing and support components of residential services must be separated. People with disabilities, whether single or married, must be able to gain access to a variety of support services, regardless of where they live (Johnson, 1986; O'Brien & Lyle, 1986; Taylor et al., 1987). Even when housing is separated from support services, support service agencies might assist people in locating housing, signing leases, negotiating with landlords, arranging for architectural adaptations, and obtaining subsidies (Taylor et al., 1988).

Home Ownership

Increasingly, home ownership and home leasing are becoming options for people with disabilities and their families (Racino, 1989b; Turnbull, Turnbull, Bronicki, Summers, & Roeder-Gordon, 1989). There are a variety of strategies to enable people with disabilities and/or their families to obtain affordable, accessible, and decent homes; however, relatively few of these strategies have been used on a large scale. Strategies include the development of private cooperatives (Co-op Initiatives Project, n.d.; Kappel & Wetherow, 1986), the use of trusts for housing (Teltsch, 1988); housing subsidies (Racino, 1989a; Taylor, Racino, & Rothenberg, 1988); the purchase of homes through housing associations (Shoultz, 1988); and the creative use low-income tax credits and other financing for housing (Laux, 1979; Randolph, Carling, & Laux, 1987). Other endeavors to promote both home ownership and the development of support services include the concomitant development of housing associations and residential support agencies (Shoultz, 1988); private cooperatives linked with circles of support or agency support services (Biklen, 1989); and efforts by parents in conjunction with existing agencies (Center on Human Policy, 1989a).

Individual Assessment, Planning, and Funding

All significant decisions about living arrangements must be based on the needs and preferences of the person with a disability. To the fullest extent possible, decisions should be made by the individual, with support from the significant people in his or her life. Thus, assessment of the individual's needs, planning for housing and support services, and funding must be closely tied (Taylor et al., 1988). This is a substantial departure from the traditional residential development process in which most of the significant decisions about housing and services (e.g., the size of the arrangement, the selection of the site, the level of disability accommodated, the number of staff, the level of supervision, and the operating budget) are made prior to the involvement of the person with a disability. The concept of individualized funding is a key component of this process, although a fully developed conceptual model and guidelines for implementation of this component are incomplete (Racino, 1989a; Salisbury, Dickery, & Crawford, 1987; Smith & Aderman, 1987; Tarman, 1989).

Flexible and Individualized Supports

An individualized approach focuses on support strategies as opposed to focusing on supervision and relying on paid staff (Taylor et al., 1988). Support strategies may include paid support, such as live-in, on-call, or drop-in staff employed by an agency and hired specifically to work with the person;

paid roommates or companions who may be self-employed; an attendant hired by a person with a disability; or a person who lives in the neighborhood and receives payment for services to the individual with a disability. Support strategies also can include the use of physical adaptations (e.g., automatic door openers, emergency response systems); routine modifications (e.g., listening to a tape recorded guide for everyday tasks); and the fostering of unpaid support (Walker & Salon, 1987).

Consumer-Directed Services

This approach promotes increased choice and self-determination in all life areas, including where and with whom people live, and represents a step toward greater control by people with disabilities of their housing and support services (Hibbard, Ferguson, Leinen, & Schaff, 1989; Johnson, 1986). The design and implementation of an *individualized* or *housing support services* approach represents the application of the fundamental premises of the independent living movement for people with severe developmental disabilities (DeJong, 1979; Frieden, 1978; Stoddard, 1978). For example, people with disabilities can be supported to hire or express preferences for the support staff who will work with them.

While the issues described above concern service directions in community living; critical themes for the 1990s may also include issues that are more fundamental and critical to people's lives than services. Among these may be the importance of living in one's own home and an increased emphasis on the broader context of community (Center on Human Policy, 1989c). The emerging service directions are important in that they seem to support, or at least not undermine, these fundamental shifts in how we understand community living.

WHAT PERSONNEL NEED TO KNOW

The description of the positive trends in community living for people with severe disabilities provides a framework for defining significant areas of training and staff development in the 1990s. The following section examines four specific areas in the preparation of personnel for community living: 1) values and commitment, 2) strategies for promoting quality lives, 3) ways of thinking about dilemmas in community living, and 4) leadership and change strategies.

VALUES AND COMMITMENT

"If decision makers believe that everyone will be served and integrated in the community, half the struggle is over" (Lyn Rucker,

Former Executive Director, Region V Mental Retardation Services, Lincoln, Nebraska, 1985).

At the heart of personnel preparation in community living is the centrality of values and commitment. As O'Brien (1987b) states, "providing direct service focused on supporting community participation for severely handicapped people is high commitment work" (p. 103). Personnel preparation must address this building of commitment and values, including translating and maintaining them in the working environment.

A national qualitative study of programs and services that support people with severe disabilities in the community, conducted by the Center on Human Policy, indicated that commitment and a strong set of guiding principles were central themes in good organizations (Taylor et al., 1987). To many of the providers in the study it was an accepted fact that people with disabilities had a right to live in the community (Knoll & Racino, 1988). Core personal and organizational values identified in this study include: 1) respect for the humanness of the person (Bogdan & Taylor, 1989); 2) promotion of autonomy and choices (Walker & Salon, 1987); 3) an appreciation of people as individuals (Bogdan & Taylor, 1989); 4) the importance of relationships (Lutfiyya, 1988); 5) celebration of successes or accomplishments (Biklen, 1989); and 6) a spirit of mutual growth and learning (Racino, 1989a). These core values are based in part on principles of normalization (Nirje, 1969; Thousand, Burchard, & Hasazi, 1986; Wolfensberger, 1972; 1983), which are frequently included as a module in staff training curricula (e.g., Cohen & Gothelf, 1988).

Although belief in a set of guiding principles or core values is foundational to further staff development, there has been no systematic use of these principles or values in recruiting, hiring, or personnel preparation (Burchard & Thousand, 1988). Organizations promoting community integration for people with severe disabilities must select staff who respect people with disabilities, are optimistic and creative, have a sense of humor, value equality, and are good at building a sense of community, among other characteristics. In addition, organizations may need to provide information about values and support staff in acquiring new principles for working with people with disabilities. Increasingly, organizations must also support people with disabilities in selecting and educating their own staff (Johnson, 1986). Including people with disabilities on screening/admissions committees for all types of training programs (including graduate and undergraduate programs) and systematically providing personnel with information about a values framework are essential first steps to ensuring the quality of personnel.

Many staff members develop and maintain their commitments to people with disabilities through one or a combination of experiences: a discussion with a leader in the field (Biklen, 1987); a visit to an institution or what was considered a demeaning environment (Racino, 1987); an intense training experience; a personal relationship with a person with a disability (Racino, 1989a); visiting programs or places where individuals with severe disabilities are well-supported in the community (Racino, 1987); or camaraderie (Provencal, 1987). Each of these experiences reflects potential strategies for developing and maintaining commitment and enhancing the articulation of values.

On an ongoing basis, agencies or organizations promote values through a variety of different mechanisms, which include: participation by staff members in formalized values-based training, such as PASS (*Program Analysis of Service Systems*) (Wolfensberger & Glenn, 1975); PASSING (*Program Analysis of Service Systems' Implementation of Normalization Goals*) (Wolfensberger & Thomas, 1983); or *Framework for Accomplishment* (O'Brien & Lyle, 1987); informal discussions and brainstorming sessions at staff and team meetings (Shoultz, 1988); day-to-day supervision or problem solving; mission statements, goal setting, and evaluations based on their principles (Taylor, 1985a); and modeling or teamwork with other people in the organization (Johnson, 1986). Values must be incorporated into all day-to-day aspects of the organization to maintain the spirit and energy of its staff.

STRATEGIES FOR PROMOTING QUALITY LIVES

Strategies represent today's understanding of how best to support people with severe disabilities in the community. While strategies may change, the fundamental questions remain basically the same: How do we get to know people? How do we support people with disabilities to live full and meaningful lives? How do we work with others in these endeavors? The way we answer these questions depends largely upon how we think about people with severe disabilities and the possibilities for their lives.

Getting to Know People

> If you view me and other people with disabilities as disabled first, then your vision of our needs will focus on fixing and alleviating our problems through paid services, and you will overlook opportunities to involve families, friends, neighbors and coworkers. (Brost & Johnson, 1984, p. 6)

One of the most important aspects of personnel preparation is helping a person to understand the process of how to get to know another person. If a person is involved with a service system, this process is called assessment (Browder, 1987). Traditionally, assessment focused on the identification of deficits or problems to be alleviated, on the determination of eligibility for services, and on matching people with available services. In contrast, new approaches to assessment create a picture of the uniqueness of the person "in order to determine what forms of help the community needs to plan, arrange, provide and monitor to meet his/her individual or human needs" (Brost & Johnson, 1984, p. 14).

The assumptions underlying this new approach to assessment include: 1) all people can be served in the community, if adequate supports are arranged; 2) planning and supports must be unique for each person; and 3) relationships with others are at least as important as the need to learn specific tasks. As information relevant to the field of severe disabilities expands, it is increasingly important to assist personnel to integrate useful but diverse approaches into a broader framework as one basis for promoting quality lives. Useful perspectives can be found in the literature, for example, on active listening and other communication facilitation strategies (Rogers & Stevens, 1967); relationship building (Perske, 1988; Strully & Strully, 1985); ecological strategies, including functional assessment (Brown et al., 1978); the meaning of behaviors (Donnellan, Mirenda, Mesaros, & Fassbender, 1984; Lovett, 1985; McGee, Menousek, & Hobbs, 1987); nonverbal communication (Siegel-Causey & Guess, 1989); family assessments (Deal, Dunst, & Trivette, 1989; NEC*TAS, 1989); and assessments of people with medical needs (Green-McGowan, 1987). Each approach provides tools to achieve a better understanding of a person and ways of developing a relationship with a person. In addition, community living personnel may need specific opportunities to discuss these strategies and their relationship to people with severe disabilities.

Supporting People to Lead
Full and Meaningful Lives

> **"This is highly creative work. We need to find people who can look at the world through others' eyes. People must have confidence to represent the person in the community and be tenacious in figuring out how systems work"** (Gail Jacob, Options in Community Living, Madison, Wisconsin, 1989).

The way we think about supporting people to lead full and meaningful lives continues to evolve and change. This section discusses four major elements that must be a focus in personnel preparation: creating a vision, supporting children and their families, supporting adults to live and participate in the community, and helping people to meet the challenges of everyday life. Another essential element, making systems responsive to the needs of individuals, will be discussed in the section on leadership and strategies to promote change.

Creating a Vision

To support people with severe disabilities, it is important to create a shared vision of the valued possibilities in the life of each individual. Such a vision includes a focus on the presence and participation of the person in the community, on the promotion of choice, on the encouragement of valued social roles, and on supporting people's contributions (O'Brien, 1987a). The personal futures planning process (Mount & Zwernik, 1988) is one valuable way to help personnel develop such a new way of thinking about the lives of people with disabilities (Minnesota Council on Developmental Disabilities, 1987). While this is only one of many approaches to creating a vision (Deshler, 1987), it is an important tool because it: 1) helps people confront the fact that not all issues can or should be addressed through services; 2) vividly creates a picture of the individual as a person first; 3) builds on the creativity and resourcefulness of the group; 4) places decision-making substantially back into the hands of the person with a disability and the people close to the person; and 5) changes the fundamental question from "How does the person need to change?" to "What can we all to do support these positive things in the person's life?"

Supporting Children and Their Families

Currently, there is a growing emphasis in the field on two primary areas: 1) family supports, with parallel developments occurring for children with developmental disabilities and children with technological needs, and 2) the perspectives, issues, and training of families (usually meaning parents and siblings). To support children and their families, several important changes must occur in the area of personnel preparation. First, there must be a move toward more cross-disciplinary training (Center on Human Policy, 1989a), including, among other areas, family studies, social work, child development, and community living. Second, the content of existing residential services training programs must be revised to: 1) differentiate more clearly between the needs of children and adults; 2) integrate the issues of family support and out-of-home placement through incorporation of concepts such as permanency planning; and 3) include information on family empowerment and family perspectives, relationships, and roles across the life span. Third, training must be reframed to ensure that the families and children remain central and the tools to accomplish the support (e.g., service coordination, family assessment) remain secondary. Fourth, training must prepare personnel to provide support that includes the full participation of children and their families in the community. Thus, new personnel should have exposure to materials on integrated education (Stainback, Stainback, & Forest, 1989); integrated recreation (Lord, 1981); gaining access to and building community supports; relationships (Shearer, 1986); and other aspects of being a family with a child with a disability in this society (Featherstone, 1980).

Supporting Adults to Live and Participate in the Community

There are several major aspects of supporting adults to live and participate in the community. First, adults participate in life at home, in mutually established routines, in relationships with others in the home, and in making the home a comfortable place in which to live. Second, adults are increasingly having a substantial role in selecting the housing and services that affect their lives. Third, adults participate in community life outside the home, including work, recreation, and relationships, and often need support to do so.

These aspects of adult life create certain clear implications for personnel preparation. First, residential services training courses must be expanded to include information on supportive community living arrangements for adults and on the differences between emerging and traditional approaches. Second, consideration must be given to moving from a narrow view of "residential services" to a broader view of life in the community for people with disabilities. Third, the content of courses should include, among other concerns, information about generic housing and home ownership strategies; understanding the choices and preferences of people with severe disabilities in both major and minor life areas (Guess, Benson, & Siegel-Causey, 1985); planning, developing, providing, and monitoring individualized and flexible supports (Johnson, 1986); tenets of the independent living movement and personal assistance strategies (Nosek, Potter, Carol, Quan, & Zhu, 1988); responsive case management or service coordination (Lippert, 1987); the meaning of home (Center on Human Policy, 1989c); the changing role of residential staff (Knoll & Ford, 1987); the importance of relationships and community building strategies (Perske, 1988); and supporting adults' varied life-styles (Boles, Horner, & Bellamy, 1988).

While aspects of the housing/support approach are incorporated into existing training programs (Taylor, 1988), there are few written resources on this approach to community living for adults. A notable exception is *Belonging in the Community* (Johnson, 1986). This book describes an innovative support agency in Madison, Wisconsin and provides an excellent discussion of principles and dilemmas in community living. Selected portions of other curricula designed for use in training group home personnel (e.g., Cohen & Gothelf, 1988) can also be adapted for use in training personnel in supporting people to live in their own homes.

Helping People to Meet the Challenges of Everyday Life

Helping people to meet the challenges of everyday life is one of the major purposes of support. This discussion highlights the context for teaching, for meeting people's special needs, and for incorporating the growing technology in this field to support people with disabilities and their families.

Strategies such as partial participation (Baumgart et al., 1982) and task analysis (Gold, 1980) have had a marked impact on the expectations for involvement of people with severe disabilities in decisions for their own

lives. Much of the literature in the area of personnel preparation in community living for people with severe disabilities stresses the importance of the
selection of instructional strategies or step-by-step teaching techniques:

> We must prepare professionals . . . for the complex step-by-step work of
> teaching severely and profoundly handicapped individuals: to learn basic func-
> tional behavior, to use functional behavior purposefully, to use purposeful behav-
> ior to master the environment, to understand and use the resources of the
> environment, to contribute to the environment, and to attain one's full potential
> for autonomy and self-determination. (Perske & Smith, 1979, p. 9).

There is considerable literature (e.g., Gaylord-Ross & Holvoet, 1985;
Horner, Meyer, & Fredericks, 1986; Sailor & Guess, 1983) and there are
many curricula (e.g., Falvey, 1989; Ford et al., 1989) available on teaching
people with severe disabilities. Most of this information, however, is based
on educational or vocational models as teachers extend their school efforts
in the preparation of students to use the skills necessary for functioning as
adults in this society. With few exceptions, this material is not designed to
address the complexity and challenges of the day-to-day environments of
home and community.

With advances in technology, new avenues are opening in the lives of
people with disabilities. Children with complex medical needs (who as late as
the 1970s did not survive because the technology did not exist) are now
moving out of hospitals and living in the community (United States Congress, 1987). New technology has brought about an increased need for
information about programming for people with movement difficulties
(Campbell, 1983); the use of communication systems (Yoder, 1980); medications (Merker & Wernsing, 1984); and in-home medical supports (Lawson
& Pierce, 1984).

Most assessments of the needs of staff for training include supporting
people with behavioral challenges as a central priority. Curricula now exist
on training staff in nonaversive interventions (Meyer & Evans, 1989). A
new research center established in Oregon is investigating this area, and
newly published approaches to nonaversive treatment increasingly are relationship or life-focused (Hitzing, 1987; Lovett, 1985).

As the complexity of information increases, it becomes important that
community living personnel (who typically are generalists) are trained to
view technology and teaching strategies as tools for achieving the goal of
fuller participation in home and community life for people with severe disabilities. More important than a specific teaching strategy or tool are the
"dynamics of people growing, changing, interacting with each other and
meeting the challenges of everyday life" (Jacob, personal communication,
1989).

HOW CAN WE WORK WITH OTHERS IN THESE ENDEAVORS?

"Opportunities for people with disabilities to be involved in community life can only be provided on a partnership basis" (Frankie Lewis, Macon-Bibb Citizen Advocacy, Macon, Gerogia, 1989; Center on Human Policy, 1989a).

In the 1970s and 1980s, working in collaboration with interdisciplinary or transdisciplinary teams and developing parent-professional partnerships were central themes in the personnel preparation literature. These themes remain important, but as the 1990s begin, three new themes are emerging, each with implications for training support staff:

1. *Partnerships between people with disabilities and people in human services.* With the advent of self-advocacy (i.e., people with disabilities speaking out on their own behalf), there is a growing recognition that parent-professional partnerships are insufficient to represent the interests of people with disabilities. The 1990s may bring new issues, including increasing litigation by adults with disabilities contesting guardianship arrangements.

2. *Partnerships between community members and people with disabilities.* Increasingly, the emphasis on the role of community members in the lives of people with disabilities will become more prominent (Mount, Lutfiyya, & Kiracofe, 1988). This will be accompanied by a need to understand such areas as the relationship between formal and informal supports, how communities work, and strategies for developing community connections (Bulmer, 1987).

3. *Partnerships between human service agencies and organizations outside the disability field.* As more focus is placed on the community, new partnerships will be needed with business, state and local governments, and private and public associations. Increasingly, study tours, workshops, and policy academies should target leaders outside the disability field, and information materials should be adapted for use by the general public (Center on Human Policy, 1989a).

WAYS OF THINKING ABOUT
DILEMMAS IN COMMUNITY LIVING

"Leaders who embrace ignorance, error and fallibility in the design and governance of community services develop important competencies" (John O'Brien, Responsive Systems Associates, Georgia, 1987; O'Brien, 1987b).

People working in the area of community living are constantly faced with questions of values, which often create tensions for individuals, groups, and systems. On the individual level, appropriate choices vary between individuals and even for the same individual at different points in time. On the service level, today's solutions will generate new issues and problems; the way we understand problems today will be different tomorrow. On the societal level, values represented in policies and legislation affecting people with disabilities may conflict and cause tension for individuals working in the field as well as for people with disabilities.

Listed below are several dilemmas in the area of community living that personnel must be prepared to face:

1. *Autonomy and safeguard.* How can people take direction from the person with a disability and his or her family and yet have safeguards in place for people who may be particularly vulnerable in this society? (See Johnson, 1986, for a good discussion on this issue).

2. *Home and program.* How can a place be a person's own home and also a place where services and supports are provided (Knoll & Ford, 1987)?

3. *Quality and quantity.* How can people develop high quality integrated services for individuals and also depopulate the institutions at a rapid pace (Taylor et al., 1987)?

4. *Control over and power with.* How can people with disabilities have control over their services and housing and still move toward a society where power is shared (Center on Human Policy, 1989c)?

5. *Family supports and the role of women.* How can we support children to remain in families without further supporting stereotypic roles of women? (Traustadottir, 1988).

6. *Traditional and individualized integrated services.* How can we support the development of more person-centered approaches and still pay attention to the quality of life of people in traditional services?

7. *Independence and interdependence.* How can we move toward independence for people with disabilities while recognizing that all of us are interdependent?

8. *Legal authority and creativity.* How can we encourage creativity in a society that is increasingly legalistic and rules-oriented (Center on Human Policy, 1989b)?

9. *Rights of parents and their adult children.* How do we resolve tensions between the rights of parents (including those who may have legal guardianship) and the rights of their adult children (Gunnar Dybwad, personal communication, 1988)?

10. *Quality assurance and quality lives.* How can we support quality lives for people with disabilities without establishing mechanisms that decrease the very quality we wish to ensure?

11. *Community and service system solutions.* How can we move toward community solutions to problems and issues when this conflicts with service system solutions?

These issues are faced by community living personnel on a daily basis in their work, have an impact on the individual with a disability, and exist on organizational and systems levels. Personnel need preparation in ways of thinking about these types of dilemmas and training that provide an orientation for action without eliminating the struggle with the gray areas inherent in these dilemmas.

LEADERSHIP AND STRATEGIES TO PROMOTE CHANGE

"Bureaucracies are run by well meaning people who often are caught in rules, procedures and ways of doing things that other well-intentioned people have put in place. When rules stand in the way of full citizenship, they can be adapted, modified or changed. Think always with creativity and innovation, and above all, start by focusing on the individual rather than the system." (Cory and Ralph Moore, Leadership Institute, Washington, DC , 1988; Center on Human Policy, 1989b)

No matter where in the United States or in what position a person enters this field, personnel will be interfacing with a traditional residential service system. Personnel, thus, need to know about the history of this field; how the service system is designed; the political, economic, and social context; and how the system can be adapted, modified, and changed to be more responsive to the needs and preferences of people with disabilities and their families.

History of Services

Most personnel preparation courses already include information on the history of developmental disabilities. This information should be expanded to include how reform movements often have bypassed people with severe disabilities (Ferguson, 1988).

Design of the Service System

Texts clearly describe the traditional design of services, including the continuum-based approach, the development and management of group homes, and the growth in the 1980s in apartment programs (e.g., Halpern, Close, & Nelson, 1986; Janicki, Krauss, & Seltzer, 1988). Training curricula (e.g., Cohen & Gothelf, 1988) and excellent community residence management simulation models (House, Adams, Caruso, Goodwin, & Schwartz, 1986) are also available to prepare people to work in these group living environments. More information is needed on emerging issues and approaches in the field.

Social, Economic, and Political Context

Many social, economic, and political issues have a tremendous impact on the lives of people with disabilities. For example, personnel need to understand issues of poverty, segregation, and discrimination and how these affect the lives of people with disabilities.

Making the System Responsive to Individual Needs

For families and individuals to be better supported in the community, personnel need to know how to influence or change systems to be more responsive to the needs of individuals. "Human service organizations have been widely criticized for their seeming inability to change" (Hasenfeld, 1983, p. 218), but evidence suggests they do, in fact, change. There is rich literature on individual, organizational, and systems change (e.g., Zaltman, 1973); courses on systems change often are included in the fields of social work and administration. Personnel need strategies for problem-solving to deal with the barriers to community services they will inevitably face no matter where or in what roles they work.

Developing Leadership Capabilities

Personnel in this field need a vision of the future and an understanding of the leadership role each person can play in creating that future. They need the confidence to represent persons with disabilities and/or their families (when representation is desired) and they need the personal support system to maintain their values in the face of constant pressures.

KEY ISSUES FOR THE FUTURE

> "What we have learned is to put the person with needs in the foreground" (Gunnar Dybwad, Boston, Massachusetts; Center on Human Policy, 1989a).

Several key issues are emerging in the preparation of personnel to support people with severe disabilities in community living: teaching about people's lives, developing individualized training strategies, re-evaluating personnel preparation models, and re-examining directions in professionalization.

First, courses and training must be redesigned to shift from teaching by service categories (e.g., residential services, vocational services) and problems (e.g., behavior management, meeting people's physical needs) to teaching about people's lives. This is critical because training strategies must model the individual approaches personnel will use on a daily basis. Many of today's major barriers in the lives of people with disabilities include problems that cross service categories (e.g., lack of flexibility of residential programs to adapt to changes in the work hours of people in supported employment). Increasingly, key issues are becoming more community- and individual-oriented and less service category- and problem-focused. In addition, personnel throughout their careers are likely to work in a variety of different areas; broad based preparation will better prepare them for these different areas.

Second, greater emphasis must be placed on individualized personnel training strategies (Miller & Verduin, 1979). It is ironic that one of the current issues in the field of disability is how to individualize services and supports for people with disabilities, while the major issues in personnel preparation revolve around standardized curriculum and competencies. Strategies for teaching individual staff how to work with individual people with disabilities must extend beyond practices in good agencies (e.g., Johnson, 1986; Walker & Salon, 1987) and be modeled at every level of personnel preparation. To develop and support staff who will address the individual needs of people with disabilities, it is important to work collaboratively with staff to address their individual learning needs.

Third, the major model for personnel preparation reflected in the literature is a vocational-technical-generic, competency-based training model (Langenbach, 1988), emphasizing results. According to Blank (1982), the underpinnings of this model are the belief that "human competence is the ability to perform" and that almost anyone can learn almost anything well if given quality instruction and sufficient time. In contrast, good organizations in this field rely more heavily on approaches resembling a social action model or a self-directed learning model (Langenbach, 1988). Many aspects of these latter models better reflect the roles and context of community living personnel. For example, the rationales for self-directed learning models include their adaptability in times of rapid change, their reflection of the progression from dependence to independence, and their emphasis on capitalizing on life experiences, while the social action model assumes a change agent working within a social system.

Fourth, given the increasing complexity of our service systems, there is a tendency toward the professionalization of staff, reflected in an increased emphasis on professional expertise, degrees, requests for wages, and competency/training trends. In some ways, this trend is in fundamental conflict with other directions in the field, including the empowerment of families and people with disabilities (Biklen, 1988b); the growing use of paraprofessionals in performing tasks previously done by professionals; and the involvement of community members in providing supports. In addition, this trend does not adequately take into account current projections regarding the future labor force and the changes these will require in staffing (Smull, 1989).

In his analysis of directions in professionalization in adult education, Cervero (1987) suggests six assumptions that need to be the basis for an examination of any model of professionalization:

1. The learner should be involved, both personally and collectively, in determining both needs and solutions.
2. Learning needs should not be treated as deficiencies of the individual that can be treated and remedied. Learning should be viewed as the adults' right to know.
3. The larger portion of adults' learning does not require assistance. Educators should not seek to destroy the beauty of friends teaching friends or of self-directed learning.
4. Educators are not value neutral.
5. Problems that require learning usually do not develop within the individual, but rather are a function of the individual within the social-political-economic environment.
6. Educators exist in a symbiotic relationship with adult learners. (pp. 75–76)

These assumptions are consistent with other work in improving teaching (e.g., Raskin, 1975) and can also serve as the foundation for examining current directions in professionalization in this field. A closer examination of this issue is necessary if we are to support a good quality of life for people with disabilities in the 1990s.

FUTURE DIRECTIONS IN PERSONNEL PREPARATION

In summary, future directions in personnel preparation in community living should include movement from:

1. Primarily skills-based to values-based training
2. Group training to individual curricular designs
3. Trainer-trainee to a facilitator-learner approach
4. An emphasis on a technical focus to one of support
5. Rigid models of personnel roles to flexible and changing roles
6. Teaching how to teach to a greater emphasis on how to approach problems, issues, challenges
7. A focus on service categories and disabilities to an emphasis on the lives of individual people
8. Expert opinion in competency development to identification of important areas by people with disabilities, their families, and actual practitioners
9. A human service focus to a cross-disciplinary and general public focus
10. Research in institutional and semicontrolled environments to longitudinal studies of people living in small homes
11. A service orientation to a life/community orientation

We are at the crossroads of change in this field. We now have an opportunity to build on the experience of the 1980s and to move toward new efforts to enhance the community participation and integration of individuals with disabilities and their families in this society.

REFERENCES

Agosta, J., Bradley, V., Rugg, A., Spence, R., & Covert, S. (1985). *Designing programs to support family care for persons with developmental disabilities: Concepts to practice*. Cambridge, MA: Human Services Research Institute.

Bates, M.V. (1985). *State family support/cash subsidy programs*. Madison: Wisconsin Council on Developmental Disabilities.

Baumgart, D., Brown, L., Pumpian, I., Nisbet, J., Ford, A., Sweet, M., Messina, R., & Schroeder, J. (1982). Principle of partial participation and individualized adaptations in educational programs for severely handicapped students. *Journal of The Association for Persons with Severe Handicaps, 7*(2), 17–27.

Biklen, D. (1987). *Small homes: A case study of Westport Associates*. Syracuse: Center on Human Policy, Syracuse University.

Biklen, D. (1988a). *In support of families: A case study of the family support program of Macomb-Oakland, Michigan*. Syracuse: Center on Human Policy.

Biklen, D. (1988b). The myth of clinical judgment. *Journal of Social Issues, 44*(1), 127–140.

Biklen, D. (1989). [Site visit to New Hampshire]. Unpublished field notes and draft report.

Blank, W.E. (1982). *Handbook for developing competency-based training programs*. Englewood Cliffs, NJ: Prentice-Hall.

Bogdan, R., & Taylor, S.J. (1989). Relationships with severely disabled people: The social construction of humanness. *Social Problems, 36*(2), 135–148.

Boles, S., Horner, R.H., & Bellamy, G.T. (1988). Implementing transition: Programs for supported living. In B.L. Ludlow, A. Turnbull, & R. Luckasson (Eds.), *Transitions to adult life for people with mental retardation: Principles and practices* (pp. 101–177). Baltimore: Paul H. Brookes Publishing Co.

Brost, M.M., & Johnson, T.Z. (1984). *Getting to know you: One approach to service assessment and planning for individuals with disabilities*. Madison: Wisconsin Department of Health and Social Services.

Browder, D. (1987). *Assessment of individuals with severe handicaps*. Baltimore: Paul H. Brookes Publishing Co.

Brown, L., Branston, M.B., Hamre-Nietupski, S., Pumpian, I., Certo, N., & Gruenewald, L. (1978). A strategy for developing chronological age-appropriate and functional curricular content for severely handicapped adolescents and young adults. *The Journal of Special Education, 13*, 81–90.

Bulmer, M. (1987). *The social basis for community care*. London: Allen & Unwin.

Burchard, S.N., & Thousand, J. (1988). Staff and manager competencies. In M.P. Janicki, M.W. Krauss, & M.M. Seltzer (Eds.), *Community residences for persons with developmental disabilities: Here to stay* (pp. 251–266). Baltimore: Paul H. Brookes Publishing Co.

Campbell, P. (1983). *Teaching self-care to severely handicapped students*. Akron: Children's Hospital Medical Center. (ERIC Document Reproduction Service No. 231-126).

Castellani, P.J. (1987). *The political economy of developmental disabilities*. Baltimore: Paul H. Brookes Publishing Co.

Center on Human Policy. (1987). *A statement in support of children and their families.* Syracuse: Author.

Center on Human Policy. (1989a). *From being in the community to being part of the community: Summary of the proceedings and recommendations of a leadership institute on community integration for people with developmental disabilities.* Syracuse: Author.

Center on Human Policy. (1989b). *Moving into the 1990's: Supporting individuals with developmental disabilities in Minnesota: A planning retreat.* Syracuse: Author.

Center on Human Policy. (1989c). *Summary of proceedings of a national policy institute on community living for adults.* Syracuse: Author,

Cervero, R. (1987). Professionalization as an issue in continuing education. *New Directions for Continuing Education, 36*(Winter), 67–78.

Cohen, S., & Gothelf, C. (1988). *A modularized curriculum for training administrators of community-based residential programs for persons with developmental disabilities.* Unpublished manuscript. (Available from NARIC, Order No. 07645).

Community Integration Project, Center on Human Policy. (1985). *Review of the literature on community integration: Report to NIDRR.* Syracuse: Author.

Connecticut Developmental Disabilities Council. (1988, December). *Proposed legislative platform.* Hartford: Author.

Co-Op Initiatives Project. (n.d.). *Introduction to cooperative housing.* Unpublished manuscript. Belchertown, MA: Author.

Deal, A., Dunst, C., & Trivette, C. (1989). A flexible and functional approach to developing individualized family support plans. *Infants and Young Children, 1*(4), 32–43.

DeJong, D. (1979). *The movements for independence: Origins, ideology and implications for disability research.* East Lansing, MI: University Center for Instructional Rehabilitation, Michigan State University.

Deshler, D. (1987). Techniques for generating future perspectives. *New Directions for Continuing Education, 36,*(Winter), 79–92.

Donnellan, A.M., Mirenda, P.L., Mesaros, R.A., & Fassbender, L.L. (1984). Analyzing the communicative functions of aberrant behavior. *Journal of The Association for Persons with Severe Handicaps, 9*(3), 201–212.

Dunst, C., Trivette, C., Davis, M., & Cornwell, J. (1988). Enabling and empowering families of children with health impairments. *CHC, 17,*(2).

Dunst, C., Trivette, C., Gordon, N., & Pletcher, L. (1989). Building and mobilizing informal family support networks. In G. Singer & K.L. Irvin (Eds.), *Support for caregiving families: Enabling positive adaptation to disability* (pp. 121–141). Baltimore: Paul H. Brookes Publishing Co.

Falvey, M.A. (1989). *Community-based curriculum: Instructional strategies for students with severe handicaps.* Baltimore: Paul H. Brookes Publishing Co.

Featherstone, H. (1980). *A difference in the family.* New York: Basic Books.

Ferguson, P. (1988). *Abandoned to their fate: A history of social policy and practice toward severely retarded people in America, 1820–1920.* Unpublished doctoral dissertation, Syracuse University.

Ford, A., Schnorr, R., Meyer, L., Davern, L., Black, J., & Dempsey, P. (1989). *The Syracuse community-referenced curriculum guide for students with moderate and severe disabilities.* Baltimore: Paul H. Brookes Publishing Co.

Frieden, L. (1978). Independent living: Movement and programs. *American Rehabilitation, 3*(6), 6–9.

Gaylord-Ross, R., & Holvoet, J. (1985). *Strategies for educating students with severe handicaps.* Boston: Little, Brown.

Gold, M. (1980). *Try another way training manual*. Champaign, Illinois: Research Press.

Green-McGowan, K. (1987). *Functional life planning for persons with complex needs*. Peachtree City, GA: KMG Seminars.

Guess, D., Benson, H.A., & Siegel-Causey, E. (1985). Concepts and issues related to choice-making and autonomy among persons with severe disabilities. *Journal of The Association for Persons with Severe Handicaps, 10*(2), 79–86.

Halpern, A.S., Close, D.W., & Nelson, D.J. (1986). *On my own: The impact of semi-independent living programs for adults with mental retardation*. Baltimore: Paul H. Brookes Publishing Co.

Hasenfeld, Y. (1983). *Human service organizations*. Englewood Cliffs, NJ: Prentice Hall.

Hibbard, M., Ferguson, P., Leinen, J., & Schaff, S. (1989). Supported community life and mediating structures: Joining theory to practice in disability reform. In P. Ferguson & D. Olson (Eds.), *Supported community life: Connecting policy to practice in disability research* (pp. 1–21). Eugene: Specialized Training Program, University of Oregon.

Hitzing, W. (1987). Community living alternatives for persons with autism and related behavioral problems. In D.J. Cohen & A.M. Donnellan (Eds.), *Handbook of autism and pervasive developmental disorders*. New York: John Wiley & Sons.

Horner, R.H., Meyer, L.H., & Fredericks, H.D.B. (Eds.). (1986). *Education of learners with severe handicaps. Exemplary service strategies*. Baltimore: Paul H. Brookes Publishing Co.

House, R., Adams, N., Caruso, G., Goodwin, W., & Schwartz, D. (1986). *Community residence management simulation*. Ithaca: Cornell University, Human Services Administration Program.

Janicki, M.P., Krauss, M.W., & Seltzer, M.M. (1988). *Community residences for people with developmental disabilities: Here to stay*. Baltimore: Paul H. Brookes Publishing Co.

Johnson, T.Z. (1986). *Belonging to the community*. Madison: Options in Community Living and the Wisconsin Council on Developmental Disabilities.

Kappel, B., & Wetherow, D. (1986). People caring about people: The Prairie Housing Cooperative. *Entourage, 1*(4), 37–42.

Kaufmann, J., Lichtenstein, K.A., & Rosenblatt, A. (1986). *The family as care-manager: Home care coordination for medically fragile children*. Millersville, MD: Coordinating Center for Home and Community Care, Inc. (CCHCC).

Knoll, J., & Ford, A. (1987). Beyond caregiving: A reconceptualization of the role of the residential services provider. In S.J. Taylor, D. Biklen, & J. Knoll (Eds.), *Community integration for people with severe disabilities* (pp. 129–146). New York: Teachers College Press.

Knoll, J., & Racino, J. (1988). *Community supports for people labeled by both the mental retardation and mental health systems*. Syracuse: Center on Human Policy, Syracuse University.

Langenbach, M. (1988). *Curriculum models for adult education*. Malabar, FL: Robert F. Krieger Publishing Co.

Laux, R. (1979). *The use of private investment sources to create residential alternatives*. Falls Church, VA: National Association of Private Residential Facilities for the Mentally Retarded.

Lawson, C., & Pierce, P. (1984). Continuing education for health care providers. In Association for the Care of Children's Health. *Home care for children with serious handicapping conditions*. Washington, DC: Author.

Lippert, T. (1987). *The case management team: Building community connections.* St. Paul: Metropolitan Council.

Lord, J. (1981). *Participation: Expanding community and leisure experience for people with severe handicaps.* Toronto: The G. Allan Roeher Institute.

Lovett, H. (1985). *Cognitive counseling and persons with special needs: Adaptive approaches to the social context.* New York: Praeger.

Lutfiyya, Z. (1988). *"Goin' for it": Life at the big harbor group home.* Syracuse: Center on Human Policy.

McGee, J.J., Menousek, P.E., & Hobbs, D. (1987). Gentle teaching: An alternative to punishment for people with challenging behaviors. In S.J. Taylor, D. Biklen, & J. Knoll (Eds.), *Community integration for people with severe disabilities* (pp. 147–183). New York: Teachers College Press.

Merker, E.L., & Wernsing, D.H. (1984). Medical care of the deinstitutionalized mentally retarded. *American Family Physician, 29*(2), 228–233.

Meyer, L.H., & Evans, I.M. (1989). *Nonaversive intervention for behavior problems: A manual for home and community.* Baltimore: Paul H. Brookes Publishing Co.

Michigan Department of Mental Health. (1986). *Permanency planning for children with developmental disabilities in the mental health system.* Lansing, MI: Author.

Miller, H.G., & Verduin, J.R. (1979). *The adult educator—A handbook for staff development.* Houston: Gulf Publishing Co.

Minnesota Council on Developmental Disabilities. (1987). *A new way of thinking.* St. Paul: Author.

Mount, B., Lutfiyya, Z., & Kiracofe, J. (1988). *Building community: A two day celebration and examination of what we are learning.* Syracuse: Center on Human Policy.

Mount, B., & Zwernick, K. (1988). *It's never too early, it's never too late: A booklet about personal futures planning.* St. Paul: Metropolitan Council.

National Early Childhood Technical Assistance System (NEC*TAS). (1989). *Guidelines and recommended practice for the individualized family service plan.* Chapel Hill, North Carolina and Washington, DC: NEC*TAS and Association for the Care of Children's Health.

Nelkin, V. (1987). *Family-centered health care for medically fragile children: Principles and practices.* Washington, DC: The National Center for Networking Community-Based Services, Georgetown University Child Development Center.

Nirje, B. (1969). The normalization principle and its human management implications. In R. Kugel & W. Wolfensberger (Eds.), *Changing patterns in residential services for the mentally retarded.* Washington, DC: President's Committee on Mental Retardation.

Nisbet, J., Clark, M., & Covert, S. (in press). Is one enough? Six too many? Our analysis of research on community living. In L. Meyer, C. Peck, & L. Brown (Eds.), *Critical issues in the lives of people with severe disabilities.* Baltimore: Paul H. Brookes Publishing Co.

Nosek, M., Potter, C., Carol, G., Quan, H., & Zhu, Y. (1988). *Personal assistance services for people with disabilities: An annotated bibliography.* Houston: The Independent Living Research Utilization.

O'Brien, J. (1987a). A guide to life-style planning: Using *The Activities Catalog* to integrate services and natural support systems. In G.T. Bellamy & B. Wilcox (Eds.), *A comprehensive guide to The Activities Catalog: An alternative curriculum for youth and adults with severe disabilities* (pp. 175–189). Baltimore: Paul H. Brookes Publishing Co.

O'Brien, J. (1987b). Embracing ignorance, error and fallibility. In S.J. Taylor, D.

Biklen, & J. Knoll (Eds.), *Community integration for people with severe disabilities* (pp. 85–108). New York: Teachers College Press.

O'Brien, J., & Lyle, C. (1986). *Strengthening the system: Improving Louisiana's community residential services for people with developmental disabilities.* Decatur, GA: Responsive Systems Associates.

O'Brien, J., & Lyle, C. (1987). *Framework for accomplishment: A workshop for people developing better services.* Decatur, GA: Responsive Systems Associates, Inc.

Perske, R. (1988, January). Friends circle to save a life. *TASH Newsletter,* 1–2.

Perske, R., & Smith, J. (Eds.). (1979). *Beyond the ordinary: The preparation of professionals to educate severely and profoundly handicapped people.* Parsons, Kansas: Words and Pictures Corporation.

Provencal, G. (1987). Culturing commitment. In S.J. Taylor, D. Biklen, & J. Knoll (Eds.), *Community integration for people with severe disabilities* (pp. 67–84). New York: Teachers College Press.

Racino, J.A. (1987). [Minnesota site visit]. Unpublished field notes.

Racino, J.A. (1989a). *Community living for adults in North Dakota: A case study of an apartment program.* Syracuse: Center on Human Policy.

Racino, J.A. (1989b). New directions in community living. *New Ways,* Fall, 25.

Randolph, F., Carling, P., & Laux, R. (1987). *In search of housing, creative approaches to financing integrated housing.* Burlington, VT: University of Vermont, Center for Community Change through Housing and Support.

Raskin, N.J. (1975). Learning through human encounters. *Improving College and University Teaching, 23*(2), 71–74.

Rogers, C., & Stevens, B. (1967). *Person to person: The problem of being human.* California: Real People Press.

Sailor, W., & Guess, D. (1983). *Severely handicapped students: An instructional design.* Boston: Houghton Mifflin.

Salisbury, B., Dickery, J., & Crawford, C. (1987). *Service brokerage: Individual empowerment and social service accountability.* Toronto: The G. Allan Roeher Institute.

Shearer, A. (1986). *Building community with people with mental handicaps, their families and friends.* London: Campaign For People With Mental Handicaps.

Shoultz, B. (1988). [Residential Services Inc.]. Unpublished field notes.

Siegel-Causey, E., & Guess, D. (1989). *Enhancing nonsymbolic communication interactions among learners with severe disabilities.* Baltimore: Paul H. Brookes Publishing Co.

Smith, G.A., & Aderman, S. (1987). *Paying for community services.* Alexandria, VA: National Association of State Mental Retardation Program Directors, Inc.

Smull, M. (1989). *Crisis in the community.* Alexandria, Virginia: National Association of State Mental Retardation Program Directors, Inc.

Stainback, S., Stainback, W., & Forest, M. (1989). *Educating all students in the mainstream of regular education.* Baltimore: Paul H. Brookes Publishing Co.

Stoddard, S. (1978). Independent living: Concepts and programs. *American Rehabilitation, 3*(6), 2–5.

Strully, J., & Strully, C. (1985). Friendship and our children. *Journal of The Association for Persons with Severe Handicaps, 10*(4), 224–227.

Tarmon, V. (1989). *Client to consumer: An assessment of individualized funding projects in the United States.* Canada: Social Planning Council of Metro Toronto.

Taylor, S.J. (1985a). *Site visit report: Region V Mental Retardation Services, Nebraska.* Syracuse: Center on Human Policy, Syracuse University.

Taylor, S.J. (1985b). *Site visit report: State of Michigan.* Syracuse: Center on Human Policy, Syracuse University.

Taylor, S.J. (1988). Caught in the continuum: A critical analysis of the principle of the least restrictive environment. *Journal of The Association for Persons with Severe Handicaps, 13*(1), 41–53.

Taylor, S.J., Lakin, K.C., & Hill, B.K. (1989). Permanency planning for children and youth: Out-of-home placement decisions. *Exceptional Children, 55*(6), 541–549.

Taylor, S.J., Racino, J.A., Knoll, J.A., & Lutfiyya, Z. (1987). *The nonrestrictive environment: On community integration for people with the most severe disabilities.* Syracuse: Human Policy Press.

Taylor, S.J., Racino, J.A., & Rothenberg, K. (1988). *A policy analysis of community living arrangements in Connecticut.* Syracuse: Center on Human Policy.

Teltsch, K. (1988, April 4). Illinois project gives families a new way to aid disabled kin. *The New York Times,* P1(N), PAI(L).

Thousand, J., Burchard, S., & Hasazi, J. (1986). Field-based determination of manager and staff competencies in small community residences. *Applied Research in Mental Retardation, 7,* 263–283.

Traustadottir, R. (1988, August). *Women and caring: On the gendered nature of caring.* Paper presented at the First International Conference on Family Supports, Stockholm, Sweden.

Turnbull, H.R., Turnbull, A.P., Bronicki, G.J., Summers, J.A., & Roeder-Gordon, C. (1989). *Disability and the family: A guide to decisions for adulthood.* Baltimore: Paul H. Brookes Publishing Co.

United States Congress, Office of Technology Assessment. (1987). *Technology-dependent children: Hospital v. home care—A technical memorandum.* Washington, DC: United States Government Printing Office.

Walker, P., & Salon, R. (1987). *Report on Centennial Developmental Services, Inc., Weld County, Colorado.* Syracuse: Center on Human Policy.

Wolfensberger, W. (Ed.). (1972). *The principle of normalization in human services.* Toronto: National Institute on Mental Retardation.

Wolfensberger, W. (1983). Social role valorization: A proposed new term for the principle of normalization. *Mental Retardation, 21,* 234–239.

Wolfensberger, W., & Glenn, L. (1975). *Program analysis of service systems, PASS 3.* Toronto: National Institute on Mental Retardation.

Wolfensberger, W., & Thomas, S. (1983). *PASSING: Program analysis of service systems' implementation of normalization goals.* Toronto: National Institute on Mental Retardation.

Yoder, D. (1980). Communication systems for nonspeech children. *New Directions for Exceptional Children, 2,* 63–78.

Zaltman, G. (1973). *Processes and phenomenon of social change.* New York: John Wiley & Sons.

11

Preparation of Supported Employment Personnel

Paul Sale

The 5-year period between 1983 and 1988 has been described as an "era of major vocational breakthrough for persons with severe disabilities" (Wehman, 1989, p. 6). During this period a new vocational rehabilitation model, supported employment, has emerged as a viable rehabilitation alternative for persons with severe disabilities. Access to valued, integrated community-based employment for persons with severe disabilities has increased with the emergence of supported employment. Thousands of individuals with severe disabilities are obtaining and maintaining jobs via this new model.

Traditional vocational rehabilitation models for adults with disabilities have focused on a time-limited "train and place" approach in which consumers are declared eligible for services after standardized evaluations; go through some type of vocational training or work adjustment at a training center such as a sheltered workshop; and after work deficits are remedied, are placed in real work settings. Supported employment differs from the traditional model in several ways, First, supported employment is not time-limited but continues indefinitely. Second, supported employment utilizes a "place and train" approach through which jobs are located and employment for consumers is obtained before training begins, without regard to performance on standardized evaluations. Third, all training is conducted *in vivo* under real work and social conditions as opposed to occurring in centers or facilities where consumers have few real work demands and little or no interaction with peers who do not have disabilities. The federal regulations

The development and dissemination of the material in this chapter was supported in part by United States Department of Education grants # G008715006 and # H129T80016; however, no official endorsement should be inferred.

define supported employment in terms of real work in integrated settings and on-going services to consumers with severe disabilities (Federal Register, August 14, 1987).

The components of the supported employment model are frequently described as:

1. *Job placement.* Comprehensive assessment of consumers (primarily using situational assessments as opposed to standardized evaluations) to learn about their interests and abilities, and locating an employment situation that matches those interests and abilities.
2. *Job site training and advocacy.* Providing individually designed instruction that results in the acquisition of job duties and other skills requisite for independence from the service provider.
3. *Ongoing monitoring.* Obtaining performance information from the consumer and significant other individuals at the job site and home.
4. *Ongoing follow-up and advocacy.* Working with the consumer, employer, and family to ensure job retention and/or a new job if necessary (Wehman & Kregel, 1985).

Implementation of supported employment occurs through one of four approaches: 1) individual placements, 2) enclaves, 3) mobile work crews, or 4) small business options. The latter three supported employment approaches provide services to groups of eight or fewer consumers with disabilities at a given job site. The primary direct service staff implementing supported employment are known as job coaches or employment specialists. The model has been described extensively elsewhere, for example, Bellamy, Rhodes, Mank, and Albin (1988); Kiernan and Stark (1986); Rusch (1986); Wehman and Moon (1988). The reader is directed to these comprehensive descriptions for an expanded explanation of the model in its various implementation forms.

NEEDS FOR PERSONNEL

Supported employment is expanding rapidly and this rapid expansion is creating a dearth of qualified personnel who are trained to implement supported employment adequately and efficiently. Wehman, Kregel, and Shafer (1989) document the expansion of supported employment in their analysis of 27 states that received federal monies to stimulate the growth of supported employment. They reported that almost 25,000 persons with disabilities received supported employment in fiscal year 1988 (a 250% increase from FY 1986). Over the same 3-year period, 1,393 *new* supported employment programs evolved. A major recommendation resulting from this study calls for the immediate development of preservice training (i.e., training of personnel prior to employment, usually through a degree or certificate program) and in-service training (i.e., training of personnel as they perform the roles for which they are being trained, usually through workshops, seminars, and other nondegree activities) (Kregel, 1989).

Discretionary funding has stimulated an increase in the numbers of training programs designed to meet these training needs. These discretionary programs are administered through the Office of Special Education and Rehabilitative Services (OSERS) in the United States Department of Education. Both special education and rehabilitation training funds across CFDA (Catalog of Federal Domestic Assistance) subcategories have been used to accelerate supported employment in-service and preservice personnel preparation activities. The National Institute on Disability and Rehabilitation Research (NIDRR) has established a research and training center that provides multiple supported employment in-service trainings annually.

Given the growth of supported employment programs and the concurrent acceleration of concentrated supported employment training opportunities, it is important to examine several issues associated with the growing supported employment training movement. For example, what is the role of supported employment personnel in the model, and does this role change as the model is applied to different consumer groups? What curriculum content can assist personnel in fulfilling these roles? And, finally, what methods of curriculum delivery are useful in the provision of supported employment training? The remainder of this chapter discusses these issues.

ROLE DEFINITION

The first issue to address relates to the duties and activities to be performed by recipients of supported employment training as they engage in the provision of supported employment. Two roles have been identified: supported employment specialists who provide direct service to individuals with disabilities, and program managers who supervise the supported employment specialists (Harold Russell Associates, 1985). Both are hybrid roles—a mix of case manager, rehabilitation counselor, and special educator roles. The actual mix of these roles varies by agency structure and target consumer groups receiving supported employment services. For example, although a "holistic" employment specialist staffing configuration (one employment specialist performing assessment, job development, training, and follow-along with a given client or clients) is the configuration of preference (Sale, Wood, Barcus, & Moon, 1989), some programs divide responsibility for these components among several staff members. In this "partitioned" configuration, the employment specialist must be fully knowledgeable about only selected supported employment components (e.g., job development or job site training). In addition to this variation, many program managers also provide direct services to consumers, thus fulfilling a dual role. These and other programmatic differences between supported employment providers make role generalization difficult. The following section describes the *general* duties associated with many programs.

General Duties Associated with Supported Employment

Buckley, Albin, and Mank (1988) present the notion that *an outcome orientation* to developing desired employment specialist traits is helpful in beginning to understand the duties associated with supported employment service provision. They suggest examining the organizational outcomes that must be achieved to make supported employment successful. These outcomes include making paid employment opportunities available, analyzing work, training supported employees, ensuring integration, and meeting individual service needs. Specific job duties can be delineated from these desired outcomes. Similarly, others have tied training competencies to supported employment model components (Kregel & Sale, 1988; Wehman, 1988). It is noteworthy that, to date, there have been no empirical data that validate the actual duties performed by employment specialists. Table 11.1 provides an illustration of a sample job duty description for an employment specialist.

Brooke (1988) has studied duties associated with supported employment program managers. She asked program managers in Virginia to record time spent in each of their daily activities. On the average, these managers spent over 16% of their time (just under 1 day per week) providing direct training to consumers at their job site. Directing activities (hiring staff, supervision, and communications) accounted for almost one-third of the program manager's time. Brooke's study is interesting in that it docu-

---

Table 11.1.   Supported employment specialist job duty description

1. Meets with potential employers to secure job placements for persons with disabilities and discuss the benefits of supported employment

2. Analyzes job history and previous evaluations of persons with disabilities and conducts situational assessments to determine strengths and interests

3. Provides on-site training and related skills development to persons with disabilities

4. Conducts follow-along activities and advocacy to ensure maintenance of employment and related performance

5. Works with families, schools, and related adult service agencies to facilitate adequate delivery of services across life areas

6. Conducts extensive program effectiveness documentation, such as job screening, consumer assessment, and intervention time reporting procedures

7. Performs other related duties as required to ensure and maintain integrated employment for persons with disabilities

Table 11.2. Supported employment program manager job duties

1. Develops and implements program policies and procedures related to supported employment

2. Supervises and evaluates employment specialists in individual and group placements

3. Monitors program outcomes and initiates procedures to remediate deficiencies

4. Places, trains, and provides follow-along to consumers with disabilities as needed

5. Serves as program liaison to local interagency transition team and consortium of supported employment providers

6. Performs other program development and implementation duties, such as external funding proposal development, as needed

ments the supervision/training role of program managers. Additionally, the design of the study is one that could be applied to employment specialists who serve various consumer groups so that an empirical documentation of actual duties could be obtained. Table 11.2 provides an illustration of a program manager's job description.

Differences Among Consumer Groups

Supported employment was designed originally to serve persons with mental retardation. Systematic application of the model to persons with other severe disabilities (e.g., traumatic brain injury, cerebral palsy, chronic mental illness) is now beginning as the model becomes increasingly accepted. The duties performed by employment specialists and managers implementing supported employment with each of these new consumer groups are similar in most respects given the common desired consumer outcome of employment. Consumer assessment, job placement and training, and follow-along duties are still completed, regardless of the disability of the group served.

An examination of the employment specialists' activities within each of the major components of supported employment will reveal that activities (and required competencies) vary as supported employment is implemented among these new consumer groups. For example, as compared with employment specialists working with persons with mental retardation, employment specialists working with consumers who have sustained a traumatic brain injury must be competent in many more compensatory strategies (Kreutzer & Morton, 1988) and may use fewer extrinsic reinforcement procedures. Employment specialists working with persons with chronic mental illness need to become proficient in intensive follow-along procedures designed to manage crises at the job site.

It is evident that traditional, disciplinary training programs (e.g., in special education, rehabilitation counseling) are not designed to provide, by themselves, the competencies needed by personnel to fulfill their critical roles in supported employment. If supported employment is to continue to be a viable service option to persons with severe disabilities, then training programs must be designed to deliver the needed curriculum content.

CURRICULA FOR SUPPORTED EMPLOYMENT TRAINING

Curricula for supported employment personnel must be competency-based and consist of both didactic and field-based coursework (Kregel & Sale, 1988; Renzaglia, 1986). As discussed earlier, the core content can be delivered through preservice or in-service training.

Curriculum Areas

The curriculum areas in a supported employment curriculum should include foundations, core, and speciality areas. Table 11.3 shows the content of these areas and the topics within each. In the *foundations* area, the curriculum should include information and competencies related to the philosophical, constitutional, and legal issues related to persons with disabilities, employment, and employment of persons with disabilities. This content area should cover normalization theory, equal access to valued work issues, and the current statutory and regulatory provisions applicable to persons with disabilities and employment of persons with disabilities. Additionally, information relating to service system function, organization, and interrelationships should be contained in this foundation area (e.g., vocational rehabilitation, mental health, education systems). Finally, information related to family relationships in families of persons with disabilities would be provided in this area.

The *core* area of the supported employment curriculum should include specific information related to supported employment and behavioral training strategies. A thorough explanation of the structure and implementation strategies for each supported employment implementation model (i.e., individual placement, enclave, mobile crew, and small business option) should be provided. It is within this area that personnel would be trained to perform specific job duties (e.g., job development strategies and job duty analysis) associated with each model. Supported employment personnel also should receive training in the application of behavior analysis and behavior change strategies. This information should include analysis of behavior, using prompting hierarchies, using reinforcement theory and strategies, and behavioral contracting procedures. Supported employment models were built on these behavioral practices (Wehman, 1988), and the knowledge and skills associated with these practices must be conveyed to employment specialists, regardless of the consumer population with whom they work.

Finally, a *specialty area* should be included in a supported employment curriculum. It is within this area that personnel receive information and

Table 11.3. Program areas and topics

Foundations

Normalization theory	Transition processes
Integration values	Real work values
Constitutional rights	Zero exclusion theory
Carl D. Perkins Act (PL 98-524, 1984)	Education for All Handicapped Children Act (PL 94-142, 1975)
Vocational Rehabilitation Act (PL 93-112, 1973, Sec. 503, 504)	Adult service systems
Civil Rights Act of 1964 (PL 88-352)	Family and interpersonal relationships
School systems	

Core

Overview of supported employment models	Job development strategies across models
Consumer assessment strategies	Application of reinforcement procedures
Job site orientation and training	Development of systematic instructional programming
Application of prompting strategies	
Differential reinforcement procedures	

Specialty management

Topics related to consumer population	Supervision and evaluation of staff
Developing in-service and staff training	Policy and procedure development
Proposal development	Program evaluation

develop competencies related to specific consumer populations. For example, personnel currently or prospectively working with consumers with traumatic brain injury should receive instruction in brain physiology, neurobehavioral sequelae of brain injury, and perhaps, information relating to substance abuse. Personnel preparing to work with consumers with chronic mental illness should receive information relating to the psychodynamics of mental illness, counseling, and pharmacological approaches to treatment. Advanced behavioral instructional information and strategies should be provided to persons working with consumers who have mental retardation. Personnel working with consumers with physical disabilities should obtain information and competency in general physiology and biomechanics, principles of orthotics and prosthetics, and the role of the rehabilitation engineer in job site modifications. It is important to note that the specialty areas are not necessarily discrete. For example, counseling information and competencies may be needed by personnel who work with either persons with chronic mental illness or persons who have traumatic brain injury.

Personnel who are aspiring to be or who currently are supported employment program managers should develop the foundation and core competencies and one speciality area competency. Additionally, program managers need information and competencies in program development, including organizational design and proposal development. These personnel also need supervisory and management information and competencies.

Field-Based Instruction

Field-based instruction must be a significant component of the supported employment curriculum. This type of instruction should occur in two ways. First, didactic work should be interfaced with field activities from the onset of personnel training. Didactic instruction in each topical area within each of the foundation, core, and speciality areas should culminate in active utilization of the information by personnel in real settings. At the completion of instruction on job development, for example, personnel should observe and conduct job development activities with exemplary employment specialists. The outcome of the activity should be both increased competency of the personnel being trained and enhanced employment opportunities for the persons with disabilities. In the job development example, the desired outcome would be the securing of a job site.

An intensive, end-of-training, field-based component constitutes the second type of field experience needed. This would take the form of a paid or unpaid internship. Duration of this internship should be no less than 480 hours. Again, the personnel are paired with exemplary employment specialists and assume service provision responsibilities to consumers with disabilities. The informational competencies obtained through didactic work and practiced during the initial field exercises are synthesized within this final field experience. The outcomes should be positive for the personnel being trained (integration and application of skills) and the consumers with whom they work (employment in real, integrated settings performing valued work for fair wages).

STRATEGIES FOR PERSONNEL TRAINING

The demand for trained employment specialists is great and is expanding. Both preservice and in-service training programs are needed to meet the demand (Buckley et al., 1988; Inge, Barcus, & Everson, 1988). Preservice training is useful in providing in-depth training to entry level professional personnel. In-service training can provide the lifelong retooling required in any profession, along with providing initial training to employment specialists who enter supported employment with little or no related experience. Irrespective of whether training is in-service or preservice, three questions merit discussion: who should train, what training formats should be utilized, and what criteria should be used to evaluate the effectiveness of training?

Who Should Train

The implementation of supported employment transcends disciplinary lines within the human service field and crosses into the business and marketing arenas. Interagency collaboration is crucial both to the implementation of supported employment and in the training of supported employment personnel. Effective training of supported employment personnel should utilize specialists from a variety of disciplines and fields who hold the values of real work for equal pay in integrated employment settings for all Americans, regardless of disability. It is imperative that current and former employment specialists, employers, and consumers be involved actively in the training of supported employment personnel. It is unlikely that a single trainer has the experiential background prerequisite for supported employment training.

The role of the professional supported employment trainer (who may be titled professor, consultant, or training specialist) is similar to that of all other personnel trainers. That is, the trainer will synthesize and present new information related to supported employment and will arrange efficiently the delivery of training to persons who are or will be involved in the implementation of supported employment. Because of the diversity of people involved in supported employment, this arrangement of many knowledgeable individuals is particularly challenging.

Training Formats

Supported employment personnel preparation should be arranged in a variety of formats to meet the needs of current and prospective employment specialists and managers who often have a variety of educational and experiential backgrounds. Commonly used formats include workshops or seminars and degree or certificate programs. Workshops last from several hours to several days and may provide broad based (e.g., overview training) or focused (topically narrow but exhaustive in scope) training. These workshops typically do not result in a certificate. The *Employment Network* at the University of Oregon and the *Rehabilitation Research and Training Center on Supported Employment* at Virginia Commonwealth University are two of the many organizations currently conducting workshop-type training.

Certificate or degree programs are by nature more intensive and require longer term participant commitment than workshops. This factor tends to limit attendance since personnel may not be willing or able to make a relatively large time investment in training. Additionally, because certificate or degree programs can train relatively few people at one time, their impact on personnel shortages is limited. As stated earlier, the number of these programs is increasing as a result of the impetus of increased federal funding. Among others, the Universities of Illinois, San Francisco, and New Orleans, along with Virginia Commonwealth University, offer preservice programs related to supported employment training. Regardless of format, the training should include the content areas and field experiences described earlier in this chapter under Curriculum Areas. EPA format new to supported employment training, live interactive video telecourses, has emerged as a new training format. One example, the Supported Employment Telecourse Network (SET NET), creates a national classroom and reaches several hundred personnel simultaneously. Instruction (packaged in 2- or 3-hour, bi-weekly sessions) is prepared at a central point, transmitted to a satellite, and received at prearranged down link sites. Instruction is provided by exemplary trainers, employment specialists, employers, and consumers. Participants have the opportunity to ask questions and share their ideas with the presenters and their colleagues around the country. Each down link site has an on-site trainer who facilitates course sessions, conducts discussions and activities after the televised portion of each session, and evaluates the field-based assignments completed between sessions. Although still in the demonstration phase at Virginia Commonwealth University, this type of training already has reached many states and should be useful in providing quality training to large numbers of personnel.

Criteria for Effective Training

Supported employment training should be evaluated by examining whether the training cost-effectively resulted in increased (quantity or quality) employment in real and integrated work settings for persons with severe disabilities. Quantifying, or for that matter qualifying, the answer to this seemingly simple question presents a major challenge to trainers and funding agencies. There is a paucity of evaluation methodologies designed to measure the increase in real work attributed to a specific training program. In lieu of these methodologies, there has been a heavy reliance to date on participant satisfaction and short-term participant performance data acquired through tests, projects, and direct observation of performance. Evaluation of any supported employment training must use both formative and summative techniques (Inge et al., 1988) that collect evaluation data from participants, human service organizations, businesses, and consumers (Buckley et al., 1988). Evaluation of training is a critical issue and is discussed again below.

UNRESOLVED ISSUES AND FUTURE DIRECTIONS

Supported employment and the training of supported employment personnel are relatively new phenomena and are still evolving. Many issues related to supported employment personnel and their training remain unresolved. Several of these issues are presented below. The issues are indicative of future directions for research and demonstration in supported employment personnel preparation.

1. *The roles of supported employment personnel must be more clearly delineated.* To date, most descriptions of job duties have been based on unsystematic observation and/or theoretical roles in implementation models. It is not known, for example, how frequently behavioral training skills are needed by employment specialists serving persons with traumatic brain injuries. Without empirical description, personnel may receive training that is inappropriate to their job performance and to their consumers' needs. Role definitions are more critical as supported employment is applied across consumer populations. One task for the future is to utilize qualitative and quantitative research methodologies to document the duties and activities of employment specialists and their managers.

2. *A consensus regarding the level of training needed by supported employment specialists must be reached forthwith.* There continues to be a debate as to whether employment specialists should be trained at least at the bachelor's level in a field closely related to supported employment. On the one hand, it can be argued that attainment of a 4-year degree presupposes a level of skill in written and oral communication and a basic understanding of human behavior (given a related field of study). It has long been recognized that students with disabilities receiving services through school systems require skilled teachers who at least possess a bachelor's degree. Indeed, several states require master's level training for teachers of students with severe disabilities. It is not appropriate to create a dual credentialing standard based largely on consumer age, service provider agency, or funding stream. To perpetuate such a discrepancy devalues both the personnel providing supported employment services and the primary recipients of supported employment—the consumers with disabilities.

On the other hand, it can be argued that other direct service personnel working within adult service systems frequently are not required to possess a bachelor's degree, that there are many good employment specialists without a degree, and that to establish such a criterion would significantly reduce the pool of potential personnel, while not significantly increasing the outcomes of supported employment. Tied to this credentialing issue are the issues of salary and the status of employment specialists and their managers. These issues are at once philosophical and economic, as well as empirical. Is the value of an employment specialist (and the consumers they serve) associated, in whole or in part, to a degree or salary? Are there differences in consumer outcomes based on the degree level of employment specialists? These questions must be answered as supported employment expands in the 1990s.

3.   *Personnel training for supported employment must keep pace with the expansion of the model.* Those associated with personnel training must focus on several interrelated issues. First, curriculum content must be dynamic and responsive to local, state, and regional supported employment systems. The curriculum must be designed to rapidly disseminate large quantities of new information as it becomes available from ongoing research and demonstration projects that implement and evaluate supported employment in various ways and with differing consumer groups. Second, employment specialist and manager exemplars must be identified or developed and utilized as a critical training component within the curriculum. Third, cost-effective training methodologies should be developed in order to meet the training needs of personnel who are geographically distributed across urban and rural settings. Traditional methodologies must be augmented with new-ways of training in order to reach personnel optimally. These new ways of training will rely heavily on telemedia training modalities. And finally, local, state, and federal funding levels for supported employment programs must continue to increase in order to stimulate supported employment training programs. New funding priorities should address both in-service and preservice training formats.

4.   *New evaluation methodologies must be designed to demonstrate the impact of personnel training on increased employment for persons with severe disabilities.* As fiscal resources become more scarce, funding agencies will increasingly desire cost-benefit data that demonstrate training effectiveness. Trainee satisfaction measures should be de-emphasized. Instead, there needs to be a concerted effort to measure the impact of training on consumer wages, integration, and overall level of functioning. These newly developed evaluation methodologies will require a strong partnership between organizations whose personnel receive training and the providers of training.

SUMMARY

The rapid implementation of supported employment for persons with severe disabilities has outpaced the training of supported employment personnel, creating a dearth of qualified personnel. As with any systems change effort, personnel training is a crucial element. Proposed curriculum content and delivery mechanisms have been presented in this chapter to provide information on increasing the quality and quantity of supported employment personnel. However, many issues remain unresolved. If the expansion of quality supported employment is to continue, these issues must be adequately addressed in a timely fashion.

REFERENCES

Bellamy, G.T., Rhodes, L.E., Mank, D.M., & Albin, J.M. (1988). *Supported employment: A community implementation guide.* Baltimore: Paul H. Brookes Publishing Co.

Brooke, V.A. (1988). *An analysis of job duties performed by supported employment program managers.* Unpublished master's thesis, Virginia Commonwealth University, Richmond.

Buckley, J., Albin, J.M., & Mank, D.M. (1988). Competency-based staff training for supported employment. In G.T. Bellamy, L.E. Rhodes, D.M. Mank, & J.M. Albin (Eds.), *Supported employment: A community implementation guide* (pp. 229–245). Baltimore: Paul H. Brookes Publishing Co.

Federal Register, *52,*(15), 30546–30552, August 14, 1987. Washington DC: United States Government Printing Office.

Harold Russell Associates. (1985, January). *Development of staff roles for supported and transitional employment programs.* Technical proposal. PR1330CS0080, Cambridge, MA.

Inge, K.J., Barcus, J.M., & Everson, J.M. (1988). Developing inservice programs for supported employment personnel. In P. Wehman & M.S. Moon (Eds.), *Vocational rehabilitation and supported employment* (pp. 145–161). Baltimore: Paul H. Brookes Publishing Co.

Kiernan, W.E., & Stark, J.A. (1986). *Pathways to employment for adults with developmental disabilities.* Baltimore: Paul H. Brookes Publishing Co.

Kregel, J. (1989). Opportunities and challenges: Recommendations for the future of the national supported employment initiative. In P. Wehman, J. Kregel, & M. Shafer (Eds.), *Emerging trends in the national supported employment initiative: A preliminary analysis of twenty-seven states* (pp. 128–136). Richmond, VA: Rehabilitation Research and Training Center, Virginia Commonwealth University.

Kregel, J., & Sale, P. (1988). Preservice personnel preparation of supported employment professionals. In P. Wehman & M.S. Moon (Eds.), *Vocational rehabilitation and supported employment* (pp. 129–143). Baltimore: Paul H. Brookes Publishing Co.

Kreutzer, J.S., & Morton, M.V. (1988). Traumatic brain injury: Supported employment and compensatory strategies for enhancing vocational outcomes. In P. Wehman & M.S. Moon (Eds.), *Vocational rehabilitation and supported employment* (pp. 291–311). Baltimore: Paul H. Brookes Publishing Co.

Renzaglia, A. (1986). Preparing personnel to support and guide emerging contemporary service alternatives. In F.R. Rusch (Ed.), *Competitive employment issues and strategies* (pp. 303–316). Baltimore: Paul H. Brookes Publishing Co.

Rusch, F.R. (1986). *Competitive employment issues and strategies.* Baltimore: Paul H. Brookes Publishing Co.

Sale, P., Wood, W., Barcus, J. M., & Moon, M. S. The role of the employment specialist. In W.E. Kiernan & R.L. Schalock. *Economics, industry, and disability: A look ahead.* Baltimore: Paul H. Brookes Publishing Co.

Wehman, P. (1988). Supported employment: Toward zero exclusion of persons with severe disabilities. In P. Wehman & M.S. Moon (Eds.), *Vocational rehabilitation and supported employment* (pp. 3–14). Baltimore: Paul H. Brookes Publishing Co.

Wehman, P. (1989). Supported employment implementation in 27 states: An introduction. In P. Wehman, J. Kregel, & M. Shafer (Eds.), *Emerging trends in the national supported employment initiative: A preliminary analysis of twenty-seven states* (pp. 1–14). Richmond, VA: Rehabilitation Research and Training Center, Virginia Commonwealth University.

Wehman, P., & Kregel, J. (1985). A supported work approach to competitive employment of individuals with moderate and severe handicaps. *Journal of The Association for Persons with Severe Handicaps, 10*(1), 3–11.

Wehman, P., Kregel, J., & Shafer, M. (Eds.). (1989). *Emerging trends in the national supported employment initiative: A preliminary analysis of twenty-seven states.* Richmond, VA: Rehabilitation Research and Training Center, Virginia Commonwealth University.

Wehman, P., & Moon, M.S. (1988). *Vocational rehabilitation and supported employment.* Baltimore: Paul H. Brookes Publishing Co.

III

MODELS OF PERSONNEL PREPARATION THAT WORK

III

12

An Applied Research Model for Teacher Preparation in the Education of Persons with Severe Disabilities

David L. Gast and Mark Wolery

This chapter describes the personnel preparation program in the education of persons with severe disabilities at the University of Kentucky. The program has existed for 11 years and has been sponsored by several grants from the United States Department of Education. Included in this chapter is a historical perspective of the program, a description of the program as it currently exists, a review of data on enrollment of students, a review of data on the follow up of graduates, and summary statements and recommendations.

This chapter is based on a description of the personnel preparation program in the education of students with severe handicaps at the University of Kentucky. Preparation of this chapter was supported, in part, by the United States Department of Education, Office of Special Education and Rehabilitative Services (Grant Number G008715055). However, the opinions expressed do not necessarily reflect the policy of the United States Department of Education, and no official endorsement of the United States Department of Education should be inferred.

HISTORICAL PERSPECTIVE

In 1975, the University of Kentucky, Department of Special Education, received funding under its block grant from the Bureau of Education for the Handicapped to develop a graduate-level program to prepare persons to work with individuals with severe disabilities. The program was conceptualized by faculty to prepare special education teachers as well as other service providers such as group home managers, early childhood teachers and directors, and adult service providers. At this time the departmental faculty was recognized in the field of special education for their Competency Based Teacher Education (CBTE) model (e.g., Blackhurst, 1977) and its behavioral orientation. Insufficient faculty time was available to coordinate the development and implementation of the program; therefore, a new faculty member was hired who was philosophically compatible with the departmental mission statement. The first project year (1975–1976) was a planning period.

Several contextual factors influenced the design of the program. These included passage of PL 94-142, the Education for All Handicapped Children Act, 1975; parent initiated litigation related to individualized programs for persons with severe disabilities; the accountability movement; lack of readily available curricula; limited applied research base; heterogeneity of the population labeled "severely/multiply handicapped;" few personnel preparation programs; and few specially prepared doctoral-level personnel. It was apparent that the training program would have to prepare graduates to be:

1. Familiar with current best practices
2. Analytical in their teaching and approach to problem behaviors
3. Engaged in formative evaluation of their teaching practices
4. Knowledgeable of current legislation and litigation
5. Able to advocate for more appropriate educational and residential services
6. Able to work in relative geographic and professional isolation

Much of the original University of Kentucky program was based on the Personnel Training Program for the Education of the Severely Handicapped Student at the University of Kansas. The Kentucky model can best be described as behavioral in terms of methods of instruction; empirical in its emphasis on accountability; and ecological in that graduates would be expected to advocate for better services for students and parents.

Several important positions were taken by departmental faculty during the developmental period. First, the program should exceed the minimum credit hour requirement (12 hours) above a bachelor's degree specified by the State Department of Education, Office of Teacher Preparation and Certification. The rationale was that 9 hours of didactic coursework and 3 hours of practicum were deemed inadequate to prepare a "professional" special educator to serve persons with severe disabilities. Second, persons graduated from fields related to special education (e.g., speech/language pathology, psychology, social work, regular education) should be admitted to the program and upon completion should be eligible for teacher certification and employment in a public school system. This provision was intended to address the teacher shortage, particularly in rural districts, and was considered appropriate because of the relevance of those disciplines to the education of students with severe disabilities. Third, students should have field experiences with clients each semester they are enrolled in coursework. The purpose of this component was to provide students with a broader experience base and the opportunity to apply the information from didactic courses immediately and under supervision. Fourth, prior to certification, students should complete a 1-year internship. This was to ensure maintenance and generalization of competencies acquired during the program. Fifth, all students should complete an applied research thesis related to the education of persons with severe disabilities. The rationale for this requirement was that it would: 1) teach applied research skills that were consistent with systematic instruction (i.e., measurement and evaluation); 2) evaluate students' ability to "put it all together" in a single project (i.e., design, implement, evaluate, and modify instructional programs to meet individual student needs); 3) instill self-confidence in students' ability to teach and interact with members from other disciplines (e.g., medical and allied health professionals); 4) provide students with a heuristic for problem-solving; 5) provide students with skills for sharing and disseminating information/knowledge (e.g., professional writing and conference presentations); and 6) provide faculty who do not have federal research grants with the opportunity to have their applied research questions addressed by working with students.

Since its inception, the program has undergone several revisions as faculty, needs in the field, and funding patterns have changed. The basic foundation of the program, however, remains the same. First, the program requires 51 graduate hours (18 hours of didactic coursework in special education, 6 hours of didactic coursework outside of education, 6 hours of research preparation, and 21 hours of practicum/internship) for the master's degree and certification. Because of the large number of graduate hours required, the program is a multiyear undertaking. Full-time students typically complete the program in 2 years. Part-time students require 3–4 years of coursework. Second, an interdisciplinary approach with physical therapy and speech/communication programs is emphasized. Third, a data-based orientation to teaching and behavior management continues to be stressed. Fourth, an applied experimental thesis using single subject research methodology is required. Changes in the program also have occurred including: 1) formalizing the relationship between the program and the speech/language and physical therapy programs; 2) increasing course offerings as a result of other federally funded projects (e.g., courses in working with persons who are deaf-blind, or who have motor disabilities); 3) increasing the commitment by the SEA (state education agency) in providing student financial support; and 4) combining the preparation programs in education of persons with severe disabilities, early childhood special education, and education of persons with autism for administrative and funding purposes.

PROGRAM DESCRIPTION

The objectives and subobjectives of the program are shown in Table 12.1. Through these objectives, the program attempts to prepare professionals who can function in a variety of roles, such as classroom teacher, other direct service provider, program director, community resource, advocate, consultant, in-service trainer, and applied researcher.

By meeting the first objective (to prepare direct service providers), the project increases the number of personnel (special education teachers and related-service personnel) who are prepared to provide appropriate individualized services in integrated settings to individuals with severe disabilities. This increased number of direct service providers results in more appropriate and adequate services received by persons with severe disabilities. By meeting the second objective (to prepare personnel to provide consultation and in-service training), the project prepares competent personnel who can provide individual and group training and consultation to other professionals and paraprofessionals in local and state agencies. These personnel allow the benefits of the project to reach individuals who are not enrolled in the program. These consultation and training activities also serve as a means for recruiting new students into the program. Consultation and in-service training competencies are acquired by having students observe and assist the practicum/consultation supervisor in planning, providing, and evaluating consultation and training activities. By meeting the third objective (to prepare personnel to analyze and conduct applied research), the project teaches students to critically analyze the research literature and apply it to their instructional practices, and enables them to conduct applied research in their educational settings. Students also are prepared to conduct research related to consultation and training of others. Students are given opportunities to disseminate reports of these research activities at state and local conferences as well as through professional publications. The research orientation enables graduates to approach problems in a systematic and empirical manner and thus improve individualized instruction received by individuals with severe disabilities.

Table 12.1. Objectives and subobjectives of the personnel preparation program

Objective 1.   To prepare graduate personnel (5th-year, master's of science, and post master's level) to work in diverse settings with persons who exhibit developmental and behavior disorders

Subobjective 1.1.   To prepare special education teachers to serve elementary-age students with severe handicaps and autism

Subobjective 1.2.   To prepare preschool special education teachers to serve children with developmental and behavior disorders in integrated settings

Subobjective 1.3.   To prepare secondary and post-secondary special education personnel to provide community-based, chronological age–appropriate instruction to individuals with severe handicaps and autism, and to program for a smooth transition to adult life

Subobjective 1.4.   To prepare personnel from related disciplines, such as speech/communication pathology, allied health, physical therapy, recreation therapy, social work, family studies, and psychology, to work with individuals who exhibit developmental and behavior disorders

Objectve 2.   To prepare graduate level personnel to provide consultation, in-service training, and to disseminate information related to serving persons with developmental and behavior disorders

Subobjective 2.1.   To prepare graduate level students to provide direct consultation services to personnel in LEA and community agencies that serve persons with developmental and behavior disorders

Subobjective 2.2.   To prepare graduate level students to provide in-service training to other professionals and paraprofessionals working with persons who exhibit developmental and behavior disorders

Subobjective 2.3.   To prepare graduate level students to disseminate information at local, state, regional, and national forums concerning the education of persons with developmental and behavior disorders

Objective 3.   To prepare graduate level personnel to analyze and conduct applied research with persons who exhibit developmental and behavior disorders

Subobjective 3.1.   To prepare graduate level students to consume and conduct applied research related to effective instructional and behavior management strategies

Subobjective 3.2.   To prepare graduate level students to consume and conduct applied research related to consultation and training of others

Subobjective 3.3.   To prepare graduate level students to disseminate the results of their research through conference presentations and professional publications

A listing of specific competencies by program objective is shown in the Appendix to this chapter. Although the program has three primary objectives, most competencies are addressed in both didactic coursework and field experiences and are integrated into different courses and experiences over a student's program. The research objective (including the thesis requirement) of this program is different from traditional special education master's degree programs; therefore, we have chosen to illustrate, in Figure 12.1, the interrelationship of the research competencies to the core didactic and practicum coursework. In Figure 12.1, courses are listed across the top in the order taken, and on the left-hand side of the figure, specific activities leading to acquisition of research competencies are listed. The figure indicates which courses address each activity and whether the competencies acquired are informational (I) or performance (P) competencies.

Although emphasis is placed on preparing students, through core coursework, to conduct applied research, students may select an area of concentration that is content oriented. The purpose of the content areas of concentration is to provide students with specific expertise within the major of severe handicaps. This is an optional program component that is frequently taken to meet the Kentucky Rank I certification requirements (i.e., 60 hours past the bachelor's degree). The available areas of concentration include early childhood special education, infant/family intervention, severe communication disorders, autism, motor disabilities and programming, microtechnology, secondary transition, and family theory and dynamics. Some of these areas of concentration are made available, in part, through federally funded projects; however, all programs are staffed by state-supported faculty with the exception of one faculty member in the motor disabilities area. Federal support is used primarily for graduate assistantships and tuition payments. The content areas of concentration are available within and outside of the University of Kentucky Department of Special Education. Provision of the motor disabilities area is a cooperative effort between the Departments of Physical Therapy and Health, Physical Education, and Recreation. The family theory and dynamics area is available through the Department of Family Studies of the College of Home Economics. The severe communication disorders area of concentration is offered through the Department of Special Education, which includes Speech and Hearing Sciences. Provision of the autism area of concentration is a joint effort with the West Virginia Autism Training Institute housed at Marshall University in Huntington, West Virginia.

Persons entering the program must complete applications to the Department of Special Education and the Graduate School at the University of Kentucky. Standard admission requirements include three positive letters of reference, Graduate Record Examination, completion of a bachelor's degree

Core Coursework

Key:
I - Information Competency
P - Performance Competency

Research Activities		Year 1											Year 2		
		Survey Severe (EDS 520)	Behavior Management (EDS 601)	Practicum (EDS 532)	Assessment (EDS 620)	Language Disorders (EDS 511)	Early Childhood (EDS 621)	Curriculum Severe (EDS 631)	Instructional Methods (EDS 630)	Motor Disabilities (AHE 670)	Nonspeech (EDS 521)	Single Subject Research (EDS 633)	Physical Therapy (PT 604)	Internship (EDS 632)	Thesis Research (EDS 768)
Pre-Study	Review Literature	I/P			I/P		I/P		I	P		I/P			P
	Identify Questions	I	I		I/P	I	I	I/P	I/P	I/P	I	I/P			P
	Pinpoint/Define Behaviors		I/P	I/P	I/P	I		I/P	I/P	I/P	I	I/P	I	P	P
	Select Measurement		I/P	I/P	I/P	I		I/P	I/P	I/P	I	I/P		P	P
	Identify Task Stimuli				I/P	I	I	I/P	I/P	I/P	I	I/P	I	P	P
	Select Setting/Arrange.	I	I/P	I	I/P	I		I/P	I/P	I/P	I	I/P	I	P	P
	Describe Attention Comp.			I				I/P	I/P	I/P		I/P		P	P
	Describe Instruction Comp.	I		I	I/P			I/P	I/P	I/P	I	I/P	I	P	P
	Describe Conseq. Comp.			I	I			I/P	I/P			I/P		P	P
	Describe Behavior Mgmt.	I	I/P	I	I			I/P	I/P			I/P		P	P
	Select S-S Design		I/P					I/P	I/P			I/P		P	P
	Construct Graphs		I/P	I/P				I/P	I/P			I/P		P	P
	Write Program Proposal		I/P		I			I/P	I/P	I/P		I/P		P	P
Study	Secure Site				I/P				I/P			I		P	P
	Obtain Permissions				I/P				I/P			I		P	P
	Screen Subjects		I		I/P	I			I/P	I	I	I	I	P	P
	Assess/Select Subjects		I	I	I/P	I			I/P	I/P	I	I	I	P	P
	Identify Reinforcers		I	I/P	I/P			i	P					P	P
	Measure/Eval. Acquisition	I	I	I		I		I	I/P	I	I	I		P	P
	Measure/Eval. Fluency	I	I			I		I	I/P	I	I	I		P	P
	Measure/Eval. Maint.	I	I			I		I	I/P	I	I	I		P	P
	Measure/Eval. Generaliz.	I	i			I		I	I/P		I	I		P	P
Post-Study	Analyze Results		I		I/P				I/P			I		P	P
	Identify Future Questions				I/P		I		I/P			I		P	P
	APA (1983) Write-up	I/P	I/P		I/P	P	I/P		P	P		I/P		P	P
	Oral Presentation/Defense		I/P		I/P		I/P		P	P		I/P		P	P

Figure 12.1. The interrelationship of the research competencies to the core didactic and practicum coursework.

in special education or a related field, and an undergraduate grade point average of 2.5 or greater on a 4-point system. Persons completing undergraduate preparation in special education in Kentucky must complete a dual major in regular and special education, and are awarded a Rank III certification. Two other levels of certification are available at the graduate level: 1) Rank II, which is a lifetime certification acquired by completing a master's degree in education or a "planned fifth year program" consisting of 32 hours of planned graduate coursework, with the stipulation that 12 hours be completed outside of education; and 2) Rank I, which is acquired by completing 60 hours of planned graduate work past a bachelor's degree or a master's degree plus 30 hours of planned coursework.

The personnel program in the education of individuals with severe handicaps includes six enrollment options, which are described below:

1. *Endorsement in Severely/Profoundly Handicapped* (*Planned Fifth Year Program*). This option is open to students holding a bachelor's degree and Kentucky Rank III certification in some area of special education. Students are required to complete all courses with the exception of the research course and thesis (12 hours must be outside of the area of special education). The exact number and type of courses required is based on an analysis of the student's transcript and experience. The advisor and student develop a planned program of studies. Upon completion of this program, the student earns a Rank II classification and lifetime teaching certificate in the education of individuals with severe handicaps.

2. *Master's of Science Degree with Endorsement Plus Rank II* (*or Rank I with 9 additional hours*) *in Severely/Profoundly Handicapped.* This option is open to students holding a bachelor's degree and Kentucky Rank III (or Rank II) certification in some area of special education. The program includes completion of all coursework. Graduates receive an M.S. degree in Special Education, and Rank II or I certification, depending upon the number of hours completed.

3. *Master's of Science Degree with Certification in Severely/Profoundly Handicapped* (*Experimental Program*). This option is open to students who hold a bachelor's degree in a "special education related field" (e.g., speech pathology, physical or occupational therapy, elementary or secondary education, psychology, human development, adaptive physical education, rehabilitation counseling). Students complete the M.S. degree program in the education of individuals with severe handicaps (length = 51 hours). Students receive Rank II certification in the area of severe/profound handicaps. The purpose of this option is to encourage individuals from other disciplines to obtain teacher certification in the education of students with severe handicaps. To date, 44% of the students who have enrolled in the program have held a B.A. or B.S. degree in a related field.

4. *Master's of Science Degree without Endorsement or Certification.* This option is open to students who desire an M.S. degree in Special Education but do not want certification in the education of persons with severe handicaps. Students seeking this option include individuals from related disciplines who do not want certification but want content expertise, and special education teachers who have certification in another area of education but do not want certification in severe/profound handicaps. The exact number of hours varies from student to student based on training, experience, and career goals.

5.   *Rank I Classification and/or Educational Specialist Degree (Ed.S).* This option is open to students who hold Rank II or III certification in some area of special education. Depending upon the certification they hold, students complete 30–60 hours of approved graduate coursework in the education of persons with severe/profound handicaps.

6.   *Doctorate of Education Degree (Ed.D).* This option is open to students who hold graduate degrees in special education and related fields and who seek additional graduate degrees in the education of individuals with severe handicaps. These degrees are offered in three tracks: personnel preparation, administration, and research and development. Students declare one of these three tracks in which to focus their studies in the education of students with severe and profound handicaps.

ANALYSIS AND OUTCOMES OF PROGRAM OPERATION

The data presented in this section reflect those collected on students enrolled in the program from 1976 through 1987. The first graduates completed the programs in 1978. In 1984, the program in the education of individuals with severe/profound handicaps and in early childhood special education were combined. The data presented here reflect those collected from the portion of the program focusing on the education of persons with severe handicaps.

Enrollment Data

Over the 11 program years, a total of 63 students have completed at least 12 hours of the program. Of these, eight have withdrawn or been advised to withdraw prior to program completion. The number of persons enrolled in each option of the program are shown in Table 12.2. Of the 55 students who have been or are enrolled in the program, 47 (86%) have earned or are seeking Kentucky certification or are eligible for certification in their home state. Six of the students sought or are seeking doctoral degrees; of the 46 who were eligible for the master's degree only 10 opted to complete only the certification program.

Table 12.2.   Number of students, listed by program option

Type of enrollment	Graduate	Current students
Rank II—certification	10	0
M.S. plus certification	16	19
M.S. without certification	1	0
Rank I and/or Ed.S.	1	2
Ed.D.	2	4
Total enrollment	30	25

In 1978, the Kentucky Council on Teacher Preparation and Certification approved an Experimental Program for the University of Kentucky to prepare individuals who held degrees from related disciplines. Upon completion of the master's program, these graduates would be eligible for teacher certification in the education of students with severe/profound handicaps. Of the 55 students in the program overall, 24 (44%) were or are enrolled in the experimental program, of whom 16 are currently enrolled and eight are graduates. Their degrees were in the following areas: regular education (8); psychology (7); speech (2); deaf education (2); social work, rehabilitation counseling, recreation therapy, English, nursing (each with 1).

Enrollment data also were analyzed in terms of the number of students engaged in full-time and part-time studies. These data are presented in Table 12.3 and show that 90% of all graduates were enrolled part time 1 or more years of their program. Of the current students, 80% are anticipated (based on program plans) to be enrolled part time. The eight students who completed their entire program as full-time students were admitted with bachelor's degrees from related disciplines. Of the five currently enrolled full-time students, three are doctoral students. Of the 47 students (graduate and current) who were at least 1 year part time, 46 held or are holding positions in special education while they are part time. Forty were or are special education teachers in educational positions working with adults with severe handicaps, with one in each of the following positions: practicum supervisor, LEA (local education agency) consultant, speech therapist, regular education teacher, and research associate. Of the 18 currently enrolled part-time students, 13 are special education teachers (two of whom are not certified for the positions they hold), with one in each of the following positions: regular education teacher, speech therapist, adult educator, LEA consultant, research associate.

Table 12.3. Number of full- and part-time students

| Student status | Full-time enrollment | | Part-time enrollment— entire program taken part time |
	2 years or more of full-time enrollment	1 year of full-time and 1 or more of part-time enrollment	
Graduates (1978–1987)	3	8	19
Current enrollment	5	2	18
Totals	8	10	37

Current students' full- or part-time status is based on program plans on file with advisor.

Part-time enrollment holds disadvantages and advantages. The primary disadvantage is the length of the program. The advantages include: 1) the student can continue to serve individuals with disabilities, thus, the program does not contribute to the teacher shortage, which is particularly important for rural districts, which have difficulty identifying qualified teachers; 2) the student can immediately put to use knowledge under faculty supervision; and 3) the student has access to on-site consultation and support from program faculty and the practicum supervisor.

Location of Students

The enrollment data also were analyzed for students' addresses at date of application. This was done to determine whether the program was training students who were from urban (within 30 miles of a city with a population of 50,000), rural (31–100 miles from an urban center), remote rural (greater than 100 miles from an urban center), or out-of-state locations. These data are shown in Table 12.4. Based on the data presented in Table 12.4, it appears that the location of students enrolled in the program has shifted. Over half, 57%, of the graduates were from urban centers, while 23% were from rural locations, and none were from remote rural locations. Currently, 68% of the students are from rural or remote rural locations and only 8% are from urban centers. Explanations for this increased attraction of students from rural locations to the program are: 1) full-time graduate assistantships and federally funded tuition stipends for students who were admitted under the experimental program option; 2) a traineeship program initiated by the SEA (state education agency) in 1981 in which tuition stipends (maximum of 6 hours per semester) are available to persons who hold a Kentucky teaching certificate and are seeking endorsement in a new area; 3) full-time practicum supervisor (since 1984), available through federal funds, to provide on-site supervision of teachers and consultation to local education agencies, producing greater program visibility; 4) practicum supervisor's involvement with the SEA's statewide in-service training program for personnel to educate students with autism and severe handicaps; and 5) recommendations to LEAs, who were in violation of state regulations, by the SEA and the Office of Protection and Advocacy that they encourage interested personnel from their districts to enroll in the graduate program.

Table 12.4. Location of program students

Status	Urban	Rural	Remote rural	Out-of-state
Graduates (1978–1987)	17	7	0	6
Current enrollment	2	11	6	6
Totals	19	18	6	12

Of the 18 currently enrolled part-time students, five are providing services in urban areas, eight in rural areas, two in remote rural areas, and three out-of-state. One of the three out-of-state students commutes from an adjacent state, and two are completing their thesis research in their home state.

Financial Support for Students

Federal student support was available from 1976 through 1987. This support has been in the form of three graduate assistantships and three full-time tuition stipends per year. State support for students has been available since 1980 through the traineeship program and through the University of Kentucky Graduate School in the form of tuition waivers for out-of-state students who are on graduate assistantships. The number of students who have received financial assistance is shown in Table 12.5. Of the 49 nondoctoral students, 59% received some federal financial support. It should be noted that this percentage includes all students who received at least one semester of tuition or graduate assistantship support. Thus, this does not mean that 29 students were fully funded by federal dollars; rather, full-time assistantships and tuition stipends were distributed to deserving part-time students when qualified full-time students were not enrolled. These data do not include the 8 students who withdrew or were advised to withdraw after 1 year in the program; three of them received federal financial support for their 1 year in the program.

The SEA traineeship funds are available to any certified teacher who is seeking a new certification or endorsement and who is working or has an application on file with an LEA. The state traineeships pay for a maximum of

Table 12.5.   Financial support, listed by source and type of student recipient

| Type of student | Type of Financial Support | | |
	Federal support	SEA traineeship	University of Kentucky tuition waiver
Graduates (1978–1987)			
Number eligible for support	28	15	2
Number receiving support	19	13	2
Current enrollment			
Number eligible for support	21	8	4
Number receiving support	10	6	3
Totals (eligible)	49	23	6
Totals (receiving)	29	9	5

These data do not include doctoral students.

6 hours of coursework per semester required for certification, but not for coursework in the master's degree program beyond those required for certification (e.g., research course, thesis hours, electives). All the students who are or were eligible and applied for these funds have received them. The University of Kentucky tuition waivers are only available for out-of-state students holding graduate assistantships.

Graduate Follow-up Data

Positions Held   Data on the positions currently held by graduates were analyzed to determine whether they had remained in the field. These data are presented in Table 12.6. Based on the data presented in Table 12.6, it is clear that the vast majority (96%) of the graduates currently hold special education or related positions. One of the 28 graduates currently is not working. Furthermore, 68% are employed as special education teachers. There are some differences in terms of current position and undergraduate preparation. The students who did not have special education undergraduate degrees were much more likely to become administrators of programs. The geographic locations of graduates' current positions were also analyzed: 22 are working in urban areas, five in rural areas, and none in remote rural areas. Both of the doctoral students who have graduated with a content emphasis in the education of individuals with severe handicaps are currently employed in special education, one as a university instructor in special education and one as a special education teacher in a rural area. The positions held by all students from the time they entered the program through

Table 12.6. Number and percent of graduates, listed by their current positions

Positions	Experimental program (non-special education undergraduate degree) (n=8)	Standard program (special education undergraduate degree) (n=20)	Total (n=28)
Special education teacher	3 (38%)	16 (80%)	19 (68%)
Director of special education programs	4 (50%)	0	4 (14%)
IHE practicum supervisor	1 (13%)	0	1 (4%)
Research associate	0	1 (5%)	1 (4%)
Physician	0	1 (5%)	1 (4%)
LEA consultant	0	1 (5%)	1 (4%)
Not working	0	1 (5%)	1 (4%)

1987 shows a similar pattern. Most graduates (25) have been special education teachers, eight have directed special education programs, five have served as practicum supervisors, two have worked as SEA consultants, two as LEA consultants, one worked as a parent advocate program coordinator, one as a pediatrician, and one as a research associate. Thus, it appears that graduates have held a number of different types of jobs, continue to hold jobs similar to those held during and immediately after graduation, and tend to work in urban rather than rural or remote rural areas.

Thesis and Nonthesis Research   Of the 30 graduates, two completed the Ed.D degree, 17 completed the M.S. degree, and 11 completed planned endorsement programs. The two doctoral students and 17 M.S. students each completed an applied research thesis/dissertation. Two of the theses focused on training of paraprofessionals, and 17 focused on instructional procedures with students having severe handicaps. The results of six theses have been presented at state, regional, or national conferences. Four of the theses have been published in professional journals (Ault, Gast, & Wolery, 1988; Bennet, Gast, Wolery, & Schuster, 1986; Farmer, Wolery, Gast, & Page, 1988; Godby, Gast, & Wolery, 1987). Both doctoral students completed the program in 1987; one had his dissertation accepted for publication (Schuster, Gast, Wolery, & Guiltinan, 1988) and the other did not submit.

In addition to thesis research, master's students in the program have been engaged with faculty in nonthesis research activities. This participation has occurred during and after their completion of the program. Five students have coauthored six publications with faculty. Several other publications are in preparation. Since 1985, with federal Field Initiated Research funding of two projects (Comparison of Instructional Strategies Project and Group Errorless Teaching Strategies Project), seven former or current students who are classroom teachers have participated or are participating in research, and three students are employed as research associates with the projects. Faculty believe that students' experiences with applied thesis research facilitates participation and collaboration in later faculty research activities.

Graduate Questionnaire   The most recent follow-up data to date were collected during the 1986 calendar year. A questionnaire was sent to all graduates for whom current addresses were available; 19 responded by completing and returning the questionnaire. The program evaluation consisted of a listing of 99 competencies on which the students rated the program's effectiveness in preparing them to perform those competencies. For each competency a three-choice rating system was used: 1) adequate preparation, 2) content covered but needed more emphasis, and 3) inadequate preparation. Overall, the responses indicated that for 60.75% of all competencies there was adequate preparation; for 10.7% of the competencies preparation was inadequate. Graduates also were asked to list the strengths of the program. Major strengths included provision of knowledge of research methodology and conducting applied single subject research; other strengths included provision of instructional program planning and implementation, development and implementation of behavior management programs, curriculum development and evaluation, conducting assessments, team planning and functioning, and maintaining student records. Graduates also were asked to identify areas in which the program activities need to be expanded. Those identified included training and working with paraprofessionals, in-service training, student and program advocacy, program development and evaluation, and working with parents. These areas are being addressed in current curriculum modifications.

Data from Students' Annual Activity/Performance Logs (1984–1987) Since 1984, three major changes have occurred in the training program: 1) the program was funded by a separate grant rather than as a component of the block grant; 2) for administrative and funding purposes, the program preparing persons in the education of individuals with severe handicaps was combined with the program preparing persons in early childhood special education, and 3) a specialized area in autism was added in the 1987–1988 academic year. The combined program, called the Developmental and Behavior Disorders Program, contains three major tracks: severe handicaps, early childhood special education, and autism. Thus, students enroll in one of the three tracks, enroll in some common courses, enroll in some courses unique to their track, have practicum experiences that are unique to their track, and conduct their thesis research with students from their track.

All students in the Developmental and Behavior Disorders Program are required to complete annual activity/performance logs. The data in the following section are from the logs submitted by students since the 1984–1985 academic year. In some cases data are presented only for students in the severe handicaps track, and in others the data reflect students from both tracks (severe handicaps and early childhood special education).

Direct Services to Individuals with Severe Handicaps
The performance logs were analyzed to identify the number of individuals with handicapping conditions receiving direct services from students enrolled in the severe handicaps track of the program. These data are shown in Table 12.7 and indicate that many of the students, while enrolled in the program from 1987 through 1989, continued to provide direct service to individuals with severe handicaps (mean = 186/year). Clearly, the majority of students serve individuals in the elementary age range. This direct service is primarily a function of having a large population of part-time graduate students.

The activity/performance logs also were analyzed to identify the types of settings in which students were working or participating in practicum experiences. A variety of settings were noted, including preschool pro-

Table 12.7. Number of individuals with handicaps directly served by students in severe/profound handicaps program

Age level of students	Number of students by school year		
	1984–1985	1985–1986	1986–1987
Elementary	87	125	118
Adolescents	66	52	90
Adults	5	10	11
Total	158	187	219

grams (integrated and segregated), integrated public school kindergartens, self-contained classrooms in "regular" neighborhood schools, self-contained classrooms in "special" schools, adult day community programs, a language laboratory, and the state school for persons who are deaf. The most frequently cited settings were self-contained classrooms in neighborhood elementary, middle, and secondary schools (in order of frequency). These data have been stable across the last 3 program years to date.

In-Service Training Activities   In-service training activities have been required in the internship year since 1984, and have been given greater emphasis by program faculty since 1987. Annual activity/performance logs were analyzed to determine the number of in-service training activities conducted by students. These are shown in Table 12.8 and include students in the severe handicaps and early childhood special education programs. These data indicate that the number of in-service presentations by students in the program are increasing; this may be due to the larger number of students enrolled in the program. Sample topics included gaining access to the community for identifying training locations, myths and facts about persons with severe handicaps, legal issues and responsibilities, curricular adaptations, environmental perspective to behavior management, observational recording procedures, emergency first aid, and curriculum development.

Table 12.8. In-service activities conducted by students

Academic year	Paraprofessionals and parents		Professionals and university students	
	Number of in-services	Number attending	Number of in-services	Number attending
1984–1985	22	492	32	416
1985–1986	37	763	46	825
1986–1987	46	1,203	52	937

The numbers attending the activities are based on students' reports and do not include presentations to elementary and secondary students who do not have handicaps.

Table 12.9. Number of students attending and presenting at conferences

Conferences	1984–1985		1985–1986		1986–1987	
	Attend	Present	Attend	Present	Attend	Present
The Association for Persons with Severe Handicaps (TASH)	3	1	4	4	3	3
Kentucky Council for Exceptional Children (CEC)	7	1	19	2	11	3
Kentucky state education agency (SEA) Office of Education for Exceptional Children (OEC)	3	0	11	6	6	2
National ABA (Association for Behavior Analysis)	1	0	1	0	2	0
National DEC (Division of Early Childhood)	N/A		4	1	6	1
Kentucky DEC	N/A		N/A		2	0
National CEC	1	0	2	0	2	0
Departmental Symposia	N/A		N/A		26	2
Other	6	1	13	3	10	8

Presentations at Conferences   Students report the number of conference presentations and their attendance on the annual activity/ performance logs. These data are presented in Table 12.9 and include students from both the severe handicaps and early childhood special education tracks. Over the 3-year period, 41 presentations were made by students at professional meetings. Of these, 10 were at national conferences, 17 were at state meetings, and 14 were at local meetings. These data reflect an increasing emphasis in the program on students disseminating information at professional conferences. Sample topics included community-based instruction in rural areas, use of incidental teaching procedures, needs of preschool students with handicaps, comparison of instructional procedures, functional age-appropriate activities for adults, and managing social behavior of individuals with handicaps.

Advocacy Activities   Students enrolled in the program engaged in a variety of advocacy activities. A sample of these activities included: 1) involvement with state legislature committees on issues related to the education and services for individuals with severe handicaps (13); 2) provision of testimony at due process hearings (7); 3) involvement with the state Office of Protection and Advocacy (22); 4) involvement with legislative lobbying activities (2); 5) provision of news releases, articles, and TV media reports (10); and 6) letter writing (15). The numbers reflect the number of times students report being engaged in each activity from 1984–1987. Based on faculty knowledge of students' activities, these numbers appear to be an underestimate.

SUMMARY STATEMENTS AND RECOMMENDATIONS

Summary Statements

The following conclusions about the program are based on the data presented above and on faculty experience and perceptions:

1. The program has evolved over the last 11 years, and currently focuses on preparing personnel to engage in direct service to individuals with severe handicaps and their families; to provide consultation and in-service training to other professionals, parents, and paraprofessionals; and to conduct applied research in educational settings.
2. Students from related fields and students from special education have been admitted to the 51 credit hour M.S. plus severe/profound handicaps certification program.
3. The program has throughout its operation accommodated part-time students; 90% of all graduates were enrolled part time 1 or more years of their program, and 80% of the current students will be enrolled part time prior to program completion.

4. Including part-time students allows rural districts to retain teachers to work with students with severe disabilities; these teachers are difficult to recruit. It also allows information acquired in coursework to be applied immediately to practice under the supervision of the practicum supervisor.

5. The hiring of a practicum supervisor in 1984–1985 has permitted the program to: 1) provide consultation to LEAs, 2) provide consultation to the SEA, 3) recruit persons from rural areas who are not certified to work with the population they are currently serving, and 4) be actively involved in SEA statewide in-service training efforts.

6. The federal support has been critical to the development and operation of the program in terms of student support and hiring the practicum supervisor; however, state support through the SEA traineeship program has been important in recruiting practicing teachers into the teacher preparation program.

7. Students enrolled between 1976 and 1984 tended to be from urban centers and continue to work in such locales; however, 68% of the students admitted since 1984 are from rural or remote rural areas.

8. Of the 28 nondoctoral graduates, 96% of the graduates currently are employed in special education or special education related fields; 68% of these persons currently are classroom teachers, and 14% are currently directors of special education programs.

9. Of the 8 graduates who did not have undergraduate degrees in special education, all are currently employed in special education or related fields; three are teachers, four are program directors, and one is an IHE (institution of higher education) practicum supervisor.

10. Seventeen students have completed master's thesis research; four of the theses have been published in refereed journals since 1986; 10 master's students have participated in nonthesis research and publication activities with faculty.

11. Students have provided direct services each year to an average of 186 individuals with moderate to severe handicaps from 1987 through 1989. This is directly related to the enrollment of part-time students in the program.

12. Students have provided an average of 35 in-service training programs to paraprofessionals and parents, and an average of 43 programs to professionals and university students each year from 1987 through 1989.

13. Students have made 41 presentations at local, state, and national conferences from 1987 through 1989.

14. Students have engaged in a variety of different advocacy activities ranging from appearing before state legislative committees to letter writing.

Recommendations for Effective
Personnel Preparation Programs

1. Programs should consider adopting and implementing a research component and requiring thesis research in their curriculum. However, if this is done, emphasis should be placed on integrating research competencies into all (or nearly all) coursework rather than placing it within one or two courses. The advantages of this approach are: 1) students learn to conduct applied research, 2) students demonstrate that they can perform a number of different analytical and technical competencies while conducting a research study, 3) students learn that research is related to practice, 4) students acquire skills that allow them to participate in later faculty research, and 5) faculty can be engaged in research even in universities where the primary mission is teaching.

2. Programs should plan their curricula around what is needed by teachers in the field to be practicing professionals rather than planning to meet the minimum requirements of teacher certification. The program described here is a rigorous, 2-year, 51-semester-hour program that includes consultation and research competencies as well as direct service competencies.

3. Programs should include, teach, and assess students' acquisition and use of information and performance competencies. This can be done through inclusion of performance activities in coursework and through liberal use of practicum experiences.

4. Programs should allow enrollment of persons whose undergraduate preparation is in related disciplines. Graduates of the University of Kentucky program all continue to work in the field and have helped address the shortage of adequately prepared personnel in the state.

5. Programs should allow enrollment of part-time students, especially if the program requires multiple years for completion. Enrolling part-time students produces several desirable outcomes: 1) students are able to apply information in "real world" settings immediately after acquiring it in coursework, 2) students can continue to serve clients while they are receiving advanced preparation, and 3) rural LEAs can retain teachers while they are receiving advanced training. However, part-time students require some modifications in usual practice. First, they must frequently use their own classrooms as practicum sites. This requires that a practicum supervisor have regular contact with them during their part-time enrollment. Second, they need tuition support from state or federal sources while they are part-time students. Third, most coursework must be provided during the evenings or on weekends so that it is accessible to students who work full time.

6. When a program requires multiple years for completion, attracts part-time students from rural areas, includes consultation competencies, and uses multiple practicum experiences, the program must have adequate monitoring from a practicum supervisor. The University of Kentucky program employs, through federal funds, a full-time practicum supervisor. This person is responsible for: 1) identifying practicum sites, 2) developing syllabi for practicum experiences, 3) conducting supervisory observations, 4) monitoring acquisition of practicum related competencies, 5) recruiting students, and 6) providing consultation to LEAs, SEAs, and other relevant agencies.

7. The program should consider procuring financial support from multiple sources for graduate assistantships and tuition support for full-time and part-time students. The University of Kentucky program has used federal personnel preparation monies, SEA traineeship monies, private scholarship funds, and university tuition waivers for out-of-state students.

8. Programs should engage in regular (1–3 year) program evaluation and revision. The evaluation should include input from faculty, graduates, employers of graduates, and current students. Furthermore, the evaluation should focus on the content of the program and on the procedures by which the program is operated.

REFERENCES

Ault, M.J., Gast, D.L., & Wolery, M. (1988). Comparison of progressive and constant time delay in teaching community sign reading. *American Journal of Mental Deficiency, 93,* 44–56.

Bennett, D., Gast, D.L., Wolery, M., & Schuster, J. (1986). Time delay and system of least prompts: A comparison in teaching manual sign production. *Education and Training of the Mentally Retarded, 21,* 117-129.

Blackhurst, A.E. (1977). Competency based special education personnel preparation. In R.K. Kneedler & S.G. Tarver (Eds.), *Changing perspectives in special education* (pp. 156–182). Columbus: Charles E. Merrill.

Farmer, R., Wolery, M., Gast, D.L., & Page, J.L. (1988). Individual staff training to increase the frequency of data collection in an integrated preschool program. *Education and Treatment of Children, 11,* 127–142.

Godby, S., Gast, D.L., & Wolery, M. (1987). A comparison of time delay and system of least prompts in teaching object identification. *Research in Developmental Disabilities, 8,* 283–306.

Schuster, J., Gast, D., Wolery, M., & Guiltinan, S. (1988). Effectiveness of a time delay procedure to teach adolescents chained tasks. *Journal of Applied Behavior Analysis, 21,* 169–178.

APPENDIX

Competency List of Developmental and Behavior Disorders (DBD) Program by Project Objective

Since two levels of mastery exist (didactic coursework and practicum), each of the following competency statements should be read with two added stem statements: "During coursework, students, in writing, oral discussion, and performance, will demonstrate. . ." and "During practicum experiences, students will demonstrate. . . ."

DBD Project Objective 1: To prepare graduate personnel (5th year, master's of science, and post master's level) to work in diverse settings with persons who exhibit developmental and behavior disorders

1.0. **Screening and assessment of learner behavior**
    1.1.   Knowledge of child find activities
    1.2.   Knowledge of due process procedures and requirements
    1.3.   Use of appropriate measurement (assessment) strategies, including direct observation, interviews, and direct testing with norm- , criterion- , and curriculum-referenced tests
    1.4.   Ability to write reports of assessment results and activities
    1.5.   Ability to plan and implement assessment activities for the purpose of screening, instructional program planning, tentative diagnosis, placement, and program evaluation
    1.6.   Ability to involve parents in assessment activities
    1.7.   Ability to write yearly and short-term objectives based on assessment data
    1.8.   Ability to conduct assessments of the environment, including the use of ecological inventories and curriculum catalogs
    1.9.   Ability to conduct assessment for the purpose of instructional program planning in the following areas: motor development, perceptual development, self-care skills, communication and language, functional academics, vocational skills, social skills, social interactions, independent living and community mobility, recreation and leisure skills—including play and sensorimotor skills

2.0. **Team planning and functioning**
    2.1.   Knowledge of various team models for assessment and instruction
    2.2.   Knowledge of various professional disciplines likely to be on assessment and instruction teams
    2.3.   Ability to comply with team rules, procedures, and expectations

2.4. Ability to develop individual education programs (IEPs) with other team members

2.5. Ability to involve parents as actual participants in team activities and decisions

3.0. Instructional program planning and implementation

3. 1. Ability to plan and implement various direct instruction formats

3. 2. Ability to conduct task analyses in a variety of curricular areas

3. 3. Ability to design, select, evaluate, and adapt instructional materials to meet individual learners' needs

3. 4. Ability to select (with consultation from other professionals), evaluate, and use a variety of adaptive equipment and prosthetic devices

3. 5. Effective design and modification of the learning environment, including the schedule for and physical arrangement of the environment

3. 6. Effective design and implementation of a variety of prompting and errorless learning procedures

3. 7. Ability to plan and use a variety of data collection systems to monitor students' progress

3. 8. Ability to plan and implement instructional procedures to facilitate acquisition, fluency-building, maintenance, and generalization

3. 9. Ability to plan and implement procedures for increasing students' engaged or on-task time

3.10. Ability to involve parents in instructional program planning and, when appropriate, instructional program implementation

3.11. Ability to plan and implement developmental and functional instructional programs in the following areas: 1) prerequisites to learning (e.g., attending), 2) motor development, 3) perceptual development, 4) selfcare skills, 5) communication and language skills, 6) functional academics, 7) vocational skills, 8) social skills and social interactions, 9) independent living and community mobility, 10) play/recreation, and 11) sensorimotor skills

4.0. Curriculum development and evaluation

4.1. Ability to identify and evaluate published curricula in areas listed above on competency 3.11

4.2. Knowledge and awareness of models of curriculum development, including the developmental and functional models

4.3. Ability to select appropriate procedures, activities, and methods from published curricula to meet students' needs

4.4. Ability to describe and use developmental sequences in motor functions, sensorimotor functions, cognitive functions, self-care, social interactions, play, and communication for curriculum development and planning

4.5. Ability to develop and implement curricula to meet students' needs for functioning in specific environments including the use of ecological inventories to plan functional routines

5.0. **Planning and implementing behavior management programs**

5.1. Ability to describe the principles of human behavior

5.2. Ability to assess deficit and excessive social behaviors

5.3. Ability to select, evaluate, and modify specific behavior management procedures to control maladaptive behavior

5.4. Ability to plan and implement behavior management procedures and systems

5.5. Ability to plan and implement systems for monitoring effects of behavior management procedures and systems

5.6. Ability to use procedural safeguards when planning and implementing behavior management systems

5.7. Ability to involve parents in behavior management procedures and systems

5.8. Ability to modify learning environment (schedule and physical arrangement) to manage maladaptive behaviors

5.9. Ability to plan and implement procedures to maintain and generalize the effects of behavior management systems

6.0. **Medical and physical management**

6.1. Knowledge of the educational implications of various medical conditions and physical handicaps

6.2. Ability to seek and obtain information on various medical conditions and physical handicaps

6.3. Ability to physically position, handle, and transfer students

6.4. Ability to maintain and manage prosthetic devices and adaptive equipment

6.5. Ability to apply first aid

6.6. Ability to manage seizures

6.7. Ability to monitor the effects of medication

7.0. **Student and program advocacy**

7.1. Ability to coordinate activities with community agencies

7.2. Knowledge of various services in the community and state

7.3. Ability to seek and obtain services from a variety of community agencies

7.4. Knowledge of and compliance with state rules and regulations

8.0. **Working effectively with parents**

8.1. Ability to establish and maintain a rapport with parents

8.2. Ability to assess parent needs and abilities

8.3.   Ability to engage in shared goal setting with parents in relation to the child and parents

8.4.   Ability to plan a variety of activities to meet the goals set with parents

8.5.   Ability to assist parents in becoming advocates for their children

8.6.   Ability to provide information and training to parents

9.0.   **Maintaining student records**

9.1.   Ability to collect, organize, and maintain records of demographic, developmental, and academic performance

9.2.   Ability to develop a system for evaluation of student performance based upon direct measures and charting of student behavior

9.3.   Ability to prepare progress reports and referrals that are clear, concise, objective, and diplomatic

9.4.   Ability to develop and maintain anecdotal records pertinent to the development of the students

9.5.   Ability to maintain confidential information in a professional manner

DBD Project Objective 2: To prepare graduate level personnel to provide consultation and in-service training, and to disseminate information related to serving persons with developmental and behavior disorders

1.0.   **Training and work with paraprofessionals**

1.1.   Ability to establish and maintain a rapport with teacher aides and associates

1.2.   Ability to assess, through observation and interview, teacher aides' strengths and weaknesses

1.3.   Ability to provide ongoing training to teacher aides

1.4.   Ability to provide feedback to teacher aides on positive and negative issues and performance

2.0.   **Planning, providing, and evaluating in-service training**

2.1.   Ability to conduct needs assessment of persons requesting training

2.2.   Ability to negotiate with personnel requesting training to establish time and content of training

2.3.   Ability to plan and conduct workshop-type in-service training

2.4.   Ability to modify and adjust training to progress of trainees

2.5.   Ability to evaluate effects of training

2.6.   Ability to provide follow-up activities based on evaluation data

3.0.   **Planning, providing, and evaluating consultation**

3.1.   Ability to conduct needs assessment of persons requesting training

3.2. Ability to negotiate with personnel requesting consultation to establish method and content of training

3.3. Ability to plan and implement ongoing consultation

3.4. Ability to modify and adjust ongoing consultation to progress to problem resolution

3.5. Ability to evaluate effects of ongoing consultation

3.6. Ability to provide follow-up activities based on evaluation data

4.0. **Service planning and development**

4.1. Ability to assist agency personnel in identifying needs for services

4.2. Ability to assist agency personnel in specifying goals for program development

4.3. Knowledge of existing agencies and services and of various funding agencies

4.4. Ability to assist staff in developing plans for new services

5.0. **Participation in planning and implementing information dissemination forums**

5.1. Ability to present papers at current state and regional conferences

5.2. Ability to participate in planning and developing symposia or conferences

5.3. Ability to participate in evaluating symposia or conferences

DBD Project Objective 3: To prepare graduate-level personnel to analyze and conduct applied research with persons who exhibit developmental and behavior disorders

1.0. **Knowledge of existing research in developmental and behavior disorders**

1.1. Ability to describe research related to assessment, instruction, and management of students with developmental and behavior disorders

1.2. Ability to describe research related to selected area of concentration

1.3. Ability to evaluate and critique research in terms of adequacy of the literature review, appropriateness of the research question(s), methodology used, results, and implications of results

1.4. Ability to apply research to practice

2.0. **Knowledge of research methodology**

2.1. Ability to review existing research in developmental and behavior disorders

2.2. Ability to evaluate and critique research in terms of adequacy of the literature review, appropriateness of the research question(s), methodology used, results, and implications of results

2.3. Ability to identify and describe future research issues based on existing research

3.0. Conduct applied single subject research

3.1. Ability to identify and describe research questions

3.2. Ability to review literature and develop a rationale for research questions

3.3. Ability to describe appropriate methodology to answer research questions including subjects, settings, materials, procedures, and dependent and independent variables

3.4. Ability to obtain approval from the appropriate Human Subjects Review panels

3.5. Ability to conduct and describe a study

3.6. Ability to analyze and interpret findings from conducted research

3.7. Ability to write a report (thesis or article) describing conducted research

3.8. Ability to orally defend and describe a thesis

13

Personnel Preparation for a Community Intensive Model of Instruction

Lori Goetz, Jacki Anderson, and Kathy Doering

The community intensive personnel preparation training program in the area of severe disabilities, which originated in 1976 with the arrival of Wayne Sailor, Ph.D. at San Francisco State University (SFSU), offers a master's degree and the California Severely Handicapped (SH) specialist credential, which allows teachers to provide educational programing to 3- to 21-year-old students historically labelled as having profound to moderate mental retardation, autism, severe emotional disturbances, and severe multiple disabilities.

A commitment to excellence in training special educators to implement state-of-the-art educational practices for students with severe disabilities has been key to the success of this training program. In the attempt to retain this level of excellence consistently, department staff are well aware of the need for a dynamic process of training program development, which allows for continual upgrading of the program curriculum based on: 1) innovations in the field, and 2) areas of success/failure in producing professionals able to implement best practices in their classrooms upon graduation. On-going, creative research and model demonstration efforts by professionals in the severe handicaps area at SFSU specific to service-delivery options,

The preparation of this chapter was supported in part by OSERS Grant #G0083156, the Community Intensive Personnel Preparation Project; however, no official endorsement by OSERS should be inferred.

curriculum development, instructional technology, integration and other issues in the provision of educational services to students with severe disabilities, have provided the foundation for awareness of state-of-the-art practices. In addition, information regarding both innovations and the success of the training program has been actively sought on an informal basis via regular reviews of the literature; attendance at national and local conferences; analysis of training successes and failures from supervisor input regarding student performance in fieldwork; and informal feedback regarding both needs in field and success of the training program from district personnel, program graduates, master teachers, parents of students with severe disabilities, the university curriculum committee, and course evaluations from students. To illustrate this dynamic process, a brief history of the training program is presented below.

Initially, Dr. Sailor utilized training modules developed with Doug Guess, Ed.D. at The University of Kansas, through one of the first teacher competency grants, funded by the Bureau of Education for the Handicapped (BEH), for students with low-incidence, severe, multiple disabilities. The primary focus was systematic, data-based instructional strategies (or *how* to teach).

In 1977, the San Francisco State program was at the forefront of the personnel training movement toward a functional life skills model of curriculum and program development for students with severe handicaps (or *what* to teach). Prior to this time the content of the training program was largely developmental in nature, with emphasis on curricular areas such as cognition, motor function, social skills, communication, and/or language skill development. Teachers identified target skills for instruction through assessments of the developmental levels of the students with severe disabilities by comparison of their developmental levels against checklists for development of students who do not have disabilities, and developed programs based on the discrepancies that showed up in these skill areas for their students. Student groupings reflected the developmental approach; classes in special centers often were composed of students ages 3–22, who were considered to be of similar "mental ages." One obvious outcome of this approach was a lack of attention to students' chronological age (e.g., age-inappropriate, kindergarten level activities for secondary school-age pupils). Additional problems with the model included its readiness orientation, which excluded students' participation in vocational and other community-based activities; a lack of effective alternative communication systems for students considered to be in "pre-language" stages; and a lack of skill generalization and utilization (because of repeated practice of isolated, nonfunctional tasks) in the actual environments where the skills were needed. Like the staff of many other research and demonstration projects throughout the United States, the SFSU model program staff were recognizing the failure of the developmental model as a basis for functional curriculum content and skill development for students with severe handicaps.

The BEH award of an in-service training grant to SFSU in 1977 enabled the program to shift its emphasis to the development of a functional life skills model for personnel preparation. The grant, which targeted existing teachers in Development Centers for the Handicapped (DCHs), included funds for both new course content and supervised fieldwork experiences for teachers updating their credentials. By this provision of funds for working with the teachers in their classrooms, a direct major impact was made on hundreds of students with severe handicaps. The personnel preparation program, both preservice and in-service, began to incorporate curriculum content based on the "criterion of ultimate functioning" (Brown, Nietupski, & Hamre-Nietupski, 1976), or those skills and activities which would allow the individual ". . . to function as productively and independently as possible in socially, vocationally and domestically integrated adult community environments" (p. 8).

The relationships established with San Francisco Bay Area school districts/LEAs (local education agencies) through the in-service training grant led to the cooperative exploration of service-delivery options in accordance with the least restrictive environment principle, and the award of Project REACH (Regular Education for All Children with Handicaps) to SFSU and the San Francisco Unified School District (SFUSD) in 1980. This 3-year contract provided funding for the development of an integrated educational service-delivery model and the facilitation of system-wide change from special centers to chronological age-appropriate integrated placements for all SFUSD students with severe disabilities within SFUSD's regular elementary, middle, and high schools.

Project REACH developed specific strategies to facilitate effective integration and ongoing interaction of students with their nondisabled peers (Doering & Hunt, 1983; Murray & Porter-Beckstead, 1983; Piuma, Halvorsen, Murray, Porter-Beckstead, & Sailor, 1983), as well as strategies for the involvement of parents in the integration process (Halvorsen, 1983). Teacher competencies in these areas were incorporated into the SFSU personnel training program as they were field-tested and validated through Project REACH.

In 1982, it became obvious that additional revisions in course content and practicum experiences were needed in order to keep abreast of the trend in the field toward conducting instruction in natural environments (cf. Falvey, 1986). Federal funds were sought and obtained to support SFSU's special education department in the development of a preservice training program to prepare teachers to implement a community intensive instructional model (Sailor, Goetz, Anderson, Hunt, & Gee, 1988; Sailor et al., 1986) for students with severe disabilities.

The Community Intensive Personnel Preparation Project of San Francisco State University, San Francisco Unified School District, Alameda Unified School District, and San Mateo County Office of Education was funded to develop a preservice teacher training program to prepare teachers to provide a community intensive model of instruction for students with severe disabilities. This model is based on the belief that every individual has the right to successfully live, work, and recreate in community settings and that the purpose of education is to facilitate each student's ability to participate in a variety of settings outside the school environment, as discussed in detail in Sailor et al. (1986). In the model, instruction is centered around skills that are essential to success in natural environments and is provided in the context in which those skills will ultimately be used by the student. Instruction takes place across three environmental settings: classroom, nonclassroom (integrated school settings outside the special education classroom), and in the community at large. The major focus for elementary age students is on nonclassroom, in-school instruction that is geared toward the facilitation of interaction with peers who do not have disabilities, as well as successful participation across a variety of school environments. As the students grow older, the major focus moves to the community, with corresponding decreases in classroom and nonclassroom instruction until ideally, by age 19, the student is able to spend the entire day in the community with instruction centering primarily on work.

COMMUNITY AND CONSUMER IMPACT

Before providing some evidence that the community intensive personnel preparation model works, discussion of some components of the preservice training model that seem to contribute to its effectiveness is needed. One component is reflected in the history of the training program, which illustrates the dynamic interaction process between OSERS (Office of Special Education and Rehabilitative Services), IHEs (institutions of higher education), and LEAs (local education agencies), which is critical to effective personnel preparation. The development of demonstration classrooms in SFUSD that were integrated onto regular education campuses, for example, was made possible in part because of Project REACH. In addition, a number of specific strategies were developed to facilitate communication between universities, LEAs, and consumers. Each of these is described below.

Demonstration Sites

A critical component of the training model is a three-semester-long practicum experience that allows trainees to participate and provide supervised instruction in district operated classrooms exemplifying current best practices. A network of classroom sites were identified and developed to serve as models of community intensive instruction. Collaborative efforts by project and classroom staff resulted in the development of community intensive programs and the identification of competencies needed for implementation. Subsequent placement of credential trainees in demonstration sites for practicum experiences provided an avenue for evaluating the impact of training content related to these competencies.

Community Intensive (CI) Task Force

A community intensive task force composed of demonstration site teachers, university training personnel, and program trainees met on a monthly basis throughout the project. The task force served as a means to raise issues and discuss concerns related to community intensive instruction for students with severe disabilities, to identify strategies to resolve the issues, and to provide in-service support to demonstration site personnel.

Advisory Council

An advisory council composed of district administrators, parents, project staff, Community Advisory Council (CAC) representatives, and state department in-service training personnel was developed as a means of providing input on a regular basis regarding administrative concerns related to transferring to a community intensive model. The information generated in these meetings included strategies for resolving administrative and logistical issues (e.g., policy and procedures, staff/student ratio, job descriptions) and for identifying specific skills needed by classroom staff, while conducting community programming in compliance with administrative guidelines. Administrative evaluation of graduates employed by their districts provided additional input regarding the effectiveness of the training program.

Supervisor Committee

A committee composed of university supervisors, course instructors, and project staff met regularly to: 1) gather input regarding the effectiveness of revised course content and practicum requirements, 2) ensure consistency in the implementation of revised practicum requirements and, 3) develop evaluation strategies that reflected revisions in course content and practicum experiences. In addition, supervisor committee meetings provided the opportunity for project staff to receive input regarding both resources needed by master teachers in implementing the community intensive instructional model and the unique experiences each practicum site had to offer future trainees.

Practicum Experience Evaluation (by Trainee)

Trainees, as the primary consumers of the training program, are a critical source of information regarding the effectiveness of their field-based training experiences. To formalize input from trainees regarding practicum experiences, an instrument was developed to reflect the adequacy of the field work site, the master teacher, and the university supervisor. This instrument is now completed every semester by each student in the Severe Handicaps training program.

Graduate Survey

A survey was designed to assist university personnel in obtaining input from program graduates regarding the degree to which the training program addresses course content, the degree to which graduates apply course content, and recommendations for additional or revised content, assignments, and practicum experiences in the training program.

Annual Curriculum Retreat

In order to synthesize input obtained via the strategies described above, and to make needed changes throughout the credential and master's program, 2 days have been set aside each summer for a severe handicaps curriculum retreat. Representatives from each course and the supervisors committee convene to analyze all feedback and recommendations and develop needed revisions in the overall training sequence, individual courses, and practicum experiences.

REVISIONS IN TRAINING CONTENT

The information gathering and analysis process described above resulted in a number of additions and revisions in the pre-1983 training content. The updated training program is composed of: 1) content from the earlier training model, which remains essentially intact due to direct applicability in a community intensive model (content maintained); 2) content from the earlier model which has been revised to reflect different strategies for application in community settings (content revised); and 3) additional content that has been developed to address new issues arising from the implementation

Table 13.1.   Content components of the preservice curriculum

Program philosophy
Instructional techniques
Behavior management
Assessment
Curriculum development
IEP development
Instructional program development
Ongoing family/school interaction
Managing resources
Integrated school and community site development
Professional role of teacher

of a community intensive model of instruction (content newly developed). Each of the broad content areas of the preservice curriculum is shown in Table 13.1. To illustrate the process of content revision based upon community and consumer input, several examples are presented below.

Program Philosophy

Content Maintained The commitment to the provision of appropriate, effective educational programming that is based upon the principles of systematic data-based instruction and functional age-appropriate curriculum provided in integrated school settings remains the basis for overall program philosophy.

Content Revised The construct of integration has been expanded to more actively address the integration of persons with severe disabilities into the community at large. Although the concept of integration at SFSU historically included community integration in terms of the students' right to participation, course content has been revised to address the need for instruction within the community context in order to ensure full advantage of that right.

Content Newly Developed New content related to program philosophy centers around longitudinal educational planning, which takes into account all transitions individual students will undergo throughout the educational process. Such transitions include movement from one school setting to another, as well as transitions in the areas of recreational, domestic, and vocational activity, which occur as a function of increasing chronological age. The ultimate objective in the area of transition is a successful move from the world of education to the world of adult services and competitive employment (cf. Wehman, Moon, Everson, Wood, & Barcus, 1988).

Instructional Techniques

Content Maintained Basic behavioral principles and instructional strategies traditionally utilized in teaching students with severe disabilities, along with data collection and analysis techniques, continue to be included as core components of the training program (Snell, 1987).

Content Revised Revisions in the area of instructional techniques have been developed to address the selection and application of these techniques across a variety of school and community environments in order to ensure effective, efficient intervention. Considerations in the application of such instructional strategies as prompting, errorless learning, reinforcement, task analysis, chaining, and shaping, include the following:

Massed versus distributed trials
Obtrusiveness or potential stigmatizing impact of intervention and data collection techniques (social validity)

Use of natural cues and consequences and manipulation of environmental
    stimuli (Ford & Mirenda, 1984)
Individual versus group instruction (including heterogeneous group arrange-
    ments)
Portability of intervention and data collection techniques

Content Newly Developed   Natural environments provide opportunity for instruction not available in contained classroom settings. As a
result, techniques are being developed to maximize effective use of all
instructional options. Training content has been added to incorporate such
methods as incidental or ecological teaching techniques (Halle, 1982), inter-
rupted chain strategies (Goetz, Gee, & Sailor, 1985), and general case
programming and error analysis (Horner, Sprague, & Wilcox, 1982).

Ongoing Family/School Interaction

Contact Maintained   The need for close contact and ongoing
communication with families has always been emphasized in the training
program.

Contact Revised   The joint parent-teacher development of educational programs requires not only greater ongoing communication, but also a
change in the nature of that communication. The purpose of community
intensive instruction is to facilitate students' participation in environments
outside the school day. Thus, teachers must rely more heavily on parents
regarding evaluation of the impact of intervention. This results in ongoing
interaction in which teachers are as much in the role of receiving information
as they are in providing it. To ensure optimal parent-teacher interactions,
training content in this area has been revised to address needed skills in
listening and actively recruiting information from parents regarding present
level of performance, student needs, and evaluation of the success of the
students' educational program (cf. Turnbull & Turnbull, 1985).

Content Newly Developed   Transfer from a classroom to a community-based model of instruction, along with the accompanying change in
the orientation and nature of IEP (individualized education program) objectives, requires that trainees learn to: 1) present information regarding this
model in a clear, accurate, and nonthreatening manner, and 2) skillfully
negotiate to develop community IEP objectives that are satisfactory to all
IEP team participants. New content has been developed for these skills
areas, as well as for strategies for acquiring information from families as a
part of IEP development. In addition to forming partnerships for developing
and monitoring intervention, trainees will be using these strategies to pool
resources with parents to bring about changes in service-delivery systems,
educational policy, and other services provided to persons with severe
disabilities.

Integrated School and Community Site Development

Content Maintained SFSU has been in the forefront of the movement to integrate *all* students with severe disabilities. Both the commitment to integration and the content developed in this area remain current and are considered to be state-of-the-art practices.

Content Revised Application of social integration and site development strategies to a community intensive model has required expansion to address issues in the development of community instructional sites, such as integrated experiences and systematic instruction across domestic, vocational, recreational, and community domains.

Content Newly Developed The process of implementing community intensive instruction in demonstration classrooms has revealed specific competencies and standards of etiquette needed by teachers in interacting with members of the community. Thus, project activities have generated an abundance of information related to site development, which addresses issues such as the following:

The need for emergency and safety procedures, which are delineated for each community environment (cf. Doering & Lee, 1985)

The resolution of community programming logistics including liability, permission, fund raising, scheduling, transportation, and administrative support (cf. Doering & Lee, 1985)

The use of peer tutors in community training

A process for analyzing and developing community instructional sites (Anderson & Doering, 1985)

The public relations and negotiation skills necessary for successful acquisition and maintenance of community environments

Considerations specific to the selection and development of vocational training sites that lend themselves to incorporation into a rotational job sampling model (Graff & Farron-Davis, 1987) and/or to potential employment

A similar general content revision process occurred in each of the remaining content components shown in Table 13.1. For each of the 11 content components, some competency areas were maintained, some were revised, and new competencies were added in order to reflect the changing role of the special education teacher in a new model of service delivery (see Anderson & Doering, 1987 for comprehensive discussion).

EVALUATION

What does it mean to say that the community intensive model of personnel training described above works? For whom does it work? By what criteria is it evaluated? Changing competencies and content implies, of course, that evaluation standards also will need to be modified. Typical evaluation measures of personnel training effectiveness include consumer (trainee) satisfaction measured during and after the training experience; follow-up surveys to determine job placement success; employer satisfaction; and, of course, competence as implied by passing grades in university preservice training courses. What, however, are valued outcomes of personnel preparation? Is a trainee's satisfaction or dissatisfaction with a university training program necessarily indicative of how that training program ultimately will influence the educational program and quality of life of a student with severe disabilities?

As part of evaluation activities for the Community Intensive Personnel Preparation grant, which has funded development of the model, two additional outcome measures have been used to evaluate program effectiveness: quality of IEP objectives developed by program graduates for students with severe disabilities, and amount of instruction occurring as determined by direct observation of instruction in classes (not just class-*rooms*) of students with severe disabilities.

The first measure, quality of IEP objectives, was assessed using an instrument developed by the California Research Institute (CRI), a 5-year (1982–1987) federally funded research institute at San Francisco State University that studied the integration process. This instrument was developed and used by CRI investigators in evaluating integration outcomes, and detailed development data are reported in Hunt, Goetz, and Anderson (1986). (This is a further example of the benefits of interaction among OSERS, IHEs, and the LEAs. Such collaboration among research, model demonstration, and personnel preparation projects enabled additional evaluation efforts to be carried out at no cost beyond that covered by the grant.)

The IEP instrument rates IEP objectives on the basis of the degree to which they include seven components that current literature suggests may be identified as indicators of best practices (Brown, Branston, Hamre-Nietupski, Johnson, Wilcox, & Gruenewald, 1979; Falvey, 1986; Sailor & Guess, 1983). These seven specific components fall within three general categories: age-appropriateness (of the materials and the task), functionality (a basic skill, a critical activity, or an interaction activity), and potential for generalization to a variety of environments (teaching across a variety of settings and materials). Summary measures of the degree of the presence of these indicators of best practices were used as a basis for rating the caliber of educational programs as a function of model implementation.

Figure 13.1 presents a sample data collection sheet. In the far left column is a list of the seven indicators of best practices within the three areas of age-appropriateness, functionality, and potential for generalization to a variety of environments. A definition is given for each indicator. A set of guidelines and examples (not shown here) that clarify the definitions are

IEP ANALYSIS

Student _____   Teacher _____
Birthdate _____

INDICATORS OF BEST PRACTICES	DEFINITION		OBJECTIVE — CURRICULUM AREA(S) 1 2 3 4 5 6 7 8 9 10 11 12	TOTAL #	%
AGE-APPROPRIATE					
1) Materials	It would be appropriate for a ND peer of the same chronological age to use the materials.	1)			
2) Task	It would be appropriate for a ND peer of the same chronological age to perform the task.	2)			
FUNCTIONAL					
3) Basic Skill	The skill is based on needs identification in 1 of 5 areas: Communication, social, behavior, motor and pre-academic/academic.	3)			
4) Critical Activity	The task must be performed for the S if she can't do it for herself.	4)			
5) Interaction Activity	The activity necessitates the mutual participation of a ND and a SD person.	5)			
WILL GENERALIZE TO A VARIETY OF ENVIRONMENTS	The skill facilitates the S's ability to function in a variety of environments; specifically, a basic skill taught within and across critical activities, or a critical activity trained across settings and materials.				
6) Taught across settings and materials		6)			
7) Taught in the natural setting	The skill is taught in a way that reflects the manner in which the skill will be used in the natural environment.	7)			
TOTAL POINTS PER OBJECTIVE					

SUMMARY	#	%
# of objectives		
% points obtained from total points possible		
average # of points per objective		
#/% use age-appropriate materials		
#/% use age-appropriate tasks		
#/% are Basic Skills		
#/% are Critical Activities		
#/% are Interaction Activities		
#/% will generalize to a variety of environments		
#/% occur in the natural setting		

DIRECTIONS

1) Next to the objective #, indicate the curriculum area(s) with the appropriate letter(s): Communication (C); Social (S); Behavior (B); Motor (M); Domestic (D); Vocational (V); Community (CM); Recreation/Leisure (L); Pre-academic (Pre); Academic (A).

2) Score 1 point for each Indicator included in an objective; 7 points are possible for each objective.

Figure 13.1.   IEP data collection sheet.

281

included with each data sheet. A data sheet provides space to rate 12 objectives. One point is scored for each of the indicators included in an objective, with a total of seven points possible per objective.

On the lower right corner of the data collection sheet is an area to record summary scores on the following variables:

1. Number of objectives
2. Percentage of points obtained out of the total points possible
3. Average number of points per objective
4. Number/percentage of objectives using age appropriate materials
5. Number/percentage of objectives using age appropriate tasks
6. Number/percentage of objectives that are basic skills
7. Number/percentage of objectives that are critical activities
8. Number/percentage of objectives that are interaction activities
9. Number/percentage of objectives that will generalize to a variety of environments
10. Number/percentage of objectives that will be taught in the natural setting

Item number 2, the percentage of points obtained across all objectives on a single IEP out of the total points possible, is the score that is used to determine the overall quality of the IEP objectives.

IEP Evaluation Procedures and Results

Five students were selected at random in each of three classrooms participating in model development activities. IEPs for these students were rated prior to project implementation. On the anniversary date for each IEP, new IEPs were rated, resulting in a comparison between the IEP developed after model implementation and the most recent IEP prior to commencement of the personnel preparation project. IEP ratings were conducted by a trained rater who had participated in scoring IEPs for CRI studies utilizing this instrument (Hunt et al., 1986).

Results were analyzed utilizing the Wilcoxen Matched Pairs Signed Ranks test for small group research (Siegel, 1956). The results indicated significantly more ($p = .01$) indicators of best practices in the IEPs developed by demonstration site IEP teams after model implementation than in those developed prior to model implementation ($t = 6.5$; $n = 15$).

Observational Evaluation Data

IEP data provided one measure of effectiveness of the personnel training project by evaluating performance of practicing teachers in the field who served as master teachers for student practica and student teaching experiences. A second selected measure of effectiveness was the amount of instruction occurring across classroom, school, and community environments. Instruction in multiple natural environments is an integral component of the model, so two external evaluators were asked to collaborate with project staff to develop an instructional observation procedure that evaluated the types of environments used for instruction (classroom, nonclassroom but within school, and nonschool) and the types of activities students with severe disabilities engaged in within these environments. This procedure was used to evaluate performance of program graduates.

Instructional observations were conducted for program graduates who were working as classroom teachers in the greater San Francisco Bay Area. Three students (oldest, youngest, and middle) were selected from each classroom, and observations were conducted for four 15-minute sequences, with sequences alternated across all three students in each class. This resulted in 60 minutes of observation for each student or 180 minutes per classroom. The observer followed one of the three selected students and rated both the type of setting (class, nonclass, nonschool) and activities (functional/nonfunctional) engaged in by the student. (Definitions were taken from the IEP instrument.)

Results are presented in Figure 13.2. At the elementary level, project graduates engaged in instruction 34% of the time in classroom settings, 45% of the time in nonclassroom school settings, and 21% of the time in community settings. At the middle school level, students of project graduates spent

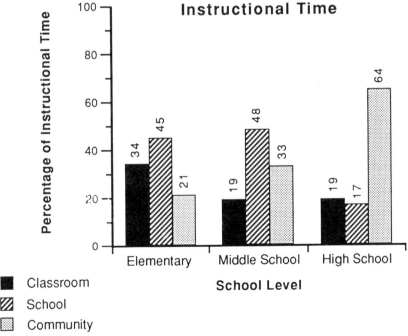

Figure 13.2. Observational evaluation data for program graduates working as classroom teachers.

less time in instruction in the classroom (19%), increased time in the school (48%), and spent 33% of the time in the community. At the high school level, project graduates' students spent the same amount of time in the classroom (19%), substantially less time in the school (17%), and substantially more time in the community (64%) than at the middle school level.

Analysis of the proportion of time spent engaged in functional activities indicated that project graduates provided time engaged in functional activities 88% of the time at the elementary level, 80% at the middle school level, and 87% at the high school level.

Similar data were collected in classrooms used as model demonstration sites, resulting in a total of 15 classrooms (model teachers and project graduates). A summary of all observational data collected across these classrooms is presented in Table 13.2.

These data suggest a general trend of providing more instruction within the school setting during the early elementary school years, with gradually more and more time spent in the community throughout the middle and high school years, consistent with recommendations for implementation of a community intensive model (Sailor & Guess, 1983; Sailor et al., 1989).

Does the community intensive personnel preparation model at San Francisco State University work? Taken together, the IEP data from model teachers and the observational data from program graduates suggest that the training model does have some direct impact upon the quality of educational services provided to students with severe disabilities: there are indications that students of teachers trained in this model are meeting objectives consistent with current best practices in the field (according to the IEP data), and there is some evidence that implementation of IEPs does actually occur in multiple natural environments (based on observational data).

The global question, however, of what type of outcome data best measure the effectiveness of training programs still remains. Meyer and Eichinger (1987) discuss five levels of evaluation relative to in-service or staff development: 1) participant satisfaction, 2) pre- and posttest of knowledge acquired, 3) utilization or application of new knowledge, 4) changes in the overall educational program, and 5) child change data. With few modifi-

Table 13.2. Observational evaluation data

| Population age | Percentage of school day | | |
| | | Nonclassroom | |
	Classroom	School	Community
4–7	40	56	4
8–11	30	44.8	25.2
12–15	31	30	39
16–22	19	23	53

cations, these categories could also be applied to preservice training programs. Posttests (if not pretests) of knowledge acquired are standard procedure in university coursework, and skill application is the underlying basis of practicum, internship, and student teaching experiences; the final evaluation is the student grade in the course.

The two measures used by the Community Intensive Model—IEP quality and time spent in different instructional environments—reflect the fourth level of evaluation: changes in educational programs. This level of evaluation currently is not typical, but perhaps it should become more typical. Documentation of *program* change as a function of preservice training provides evidence that personnel preparation programs do have the ability to change actual service delivery. This ability puts those in the field in a better position to consider the educational and social validity of these changes for students with severe disabilities and their families, and to evaluate child change data (level 5) as a function of personnel preparation programs.

The changing of teacher competencies in response to changes in quality practices, as documented above in examples of the three content types (maintained, revised, newly developed), also suggests the need for innovation and growth in evaluation standards applied to personnel training programs. Competency in using a specific prompting strategy to teach a classroom skill can be readily observed and evaluated. Competency in approaching a local storekeeper to negotiate use of the shop as a regular training environment, or competency in responding to an intensive behavioral crisis while using public transportation is less readily evaluated, in part because the field has no history of instruction in natural environments to fall back upon.

SUMMARY

Development and application of evaluation standards that: 1) are appropriate to the changing teacher competencies required by emerging best practices, and 2) are reflective of changes in quality of life for students and their families is an ongoing concern for the field. The community intensive model reviewed in this chapter reflects an initial attempt to respond to these concerns: evidence suggests it trains teachers to develop instructional programs consistent with "promising practices" and to implement these programs in multiple natural environments. Some of the possible contributions to the effectiveness of the model were addressed earlier: interaction and communication among OSERS projects, IHE training programs, and LEAs through task forces, advisory councils, and ongoing formative evaluation from consumers; a year-long supervised practicum experience in demonstration classrooms; and a strong summative evaluation component that structures all training activities with an awareness of the outcome standards of quality IEPs and community instruction across different kinds of environments. Continued use of these strategies as part of ongoing personnel training should result in further changes and refinement in the training model that are consistent with other newly emerging "promising practices" in education of students with severe disabilities.

REFERENCES

Anderson, J., & Doering, K. (1985). *The changing role of teachers and administrators.* San Francisco: San Francisco State University, Nonschool Personnel Preparation Grant.

Anderson, J., & Doering, K. (1987). *Nonschool personnel preparation manual.* San Francisco: San Francisco State University, Department of Special Education.

Brown, L., Branston, M.B., Hamre-Nietupski, S., Johnson, F., Wilcox, B., & Gruenewald, L. (1979). A rationale for comprehensive longitudinal interactions between severely handicapped students and nonhandicapped students and other citizens. *AAESPH Review, 4*(1), 3–14.

Brown, L., Nietupski, J., & Hamre-Nietupski, S. (1976). The criterion of ultimate functioning and public school services for severely handicapped students. In M.A. Thomas (Ed.), *Hey, don't forget about me: Education's investment in the severely, profoundly, and multiply handicapped* (pp. 197–209). Reston, VA: Council for Exceptional Children.

Doering, K., & Hunt, P. (1983). *Inventory processes for social interaction (IPSI).* San Francisco: San Francisco State University, Project REACH. (ERIC Document Reproduction Service No. ED 242 181)

Doering, K., & Lee, M. (1985). *Administrative guidelines for a community intensive model of instruction.* San Francisco: San Francisco State University, CIPSSI Project.

Falvey, M.A. (1986). *Community based curriculum: Instructional strategies for students with severe handicaps.* Baltimore: Paul H. Brookes Publishing Co.

Ford, A., & Mirenda, P. (1984). Community instruction. A natural cues and corrections decision model. *Journal of The Association for Persons with Severe Handicaps, 9,* 79–87.

Goetz, L., Gee, K., & Sailor, W. (1985). Using a behavior chain interruption strategy to teach communication skills to students with severe disabilities. *Journal of The Association for Persons with Severe Handicaps, 10*(1), 21–30.

Graff, S., & Farron-Davis, F. (1987). [Comparison of student placement in postschool environments from the 1986–87 school year.] Unpublished raw data. San Francisco: San Francisco State University, Department of Special Education, Community Transitional Services Project.

Halle, J.W. (1982). Teaching functional language to the handicapped: An integrative model of natural environment teaching techniques. *Journal of The Association for the Severely Handicapped, 7*(4), 29–37.

Halvorsen, A. (1983). *Parents and community together (PACT).* San Francisco: San Francisco State University, San Francisco Unified School District. (Eric Document Reproduction Service No. ED 242 183)

Horner, R.H., Sprague, J., & Wilcox, B. (1982). General case programming for community activities. In B. Wilcox & G.T. Bellamy (Eds.), *Design of high school programs for severely handicapped students* (pp. 61–98). Baltimore: Paul H. Brookes Publishing Co.

Hunt, P., Goetz, L., & Anderson, J. (1986). The quality of IEP objectives associated with placement on integrated versus segregated school sites. *Journal of The Association for Persons with Severe Handicaps, 11*(2), 125–130.

Meyer, L.H., & Eichinger, J. (1987). Program evaluation in support of program development: Needs, strategies, and future directions. In L. Goetz, D. Guess, & K. Stremel-Campbell (Eds.), *Innovative program design for individuals with dual sensory impairments* (313–346). Baltimore: Paul H. Brookes Publishing Co.

Murray, C., & Porter-Beckstead, S.P. (1983). *Awareness and inservice manual (AIM)*. San Francisco: San Francisco State University, San Francisco Unified School District. (Eric Document Reproduction Service No. ED 242 182)

Piuma, C., Halvorsen, A., Murray, C., Porter-Beckstead, S., & Sailor, W. (1983). *Project REACH administrator's manual (PRAM)*. San Francisco: San Francisco State University, San Francisco Unified School District. (Eric Reproduction Service Document No. ED 242 185)

Sailor, W., Anderson, J.L., Halvorsen, A.T., Doering, K., Filler, J., & Goetz, L. (1989). *The comprehensive local school: Regular education for all students with disabilities*. Baltimore: Paul H. Brookes Publishing Co.

Sailor, W., Goetz, L., Anderson, J., Hunt, P., & Gee, K. (1988). Research on community intensive instruction as a model for building functional, generalized skills. In R. Horner, G. Dunlap, & R.L. Koegel (Eds.), *Generalization and maintenance: Lifestyle changes in applied settings* (pp. 67–98). Baltimore: Paul H. Brookes Publishing Co.

Sailor, W., & Guess, D. (1983). *Severely handicapped students: An instructional design*. Boston: Houghton Mifflin.

Sailor, W., Halvorsen, A., Anderson, J., Goetz, L., Gee, K., Doering, K., & Hunt, P. (1986). Community intensive instruction. In R.H. Horner, L.H. Meyer, & H.D.B. Fredericks (Eds.), *Education of learners with severe handicaps: Exemplary service strategies* (pp. 251–288). Baltimore: Paul H. Brookes Publishing Co.

Siegel, S. (1956). *Nonparametric methods for the behavorial sciences*. New York: McGraw-Hill.

Snell, M. (1986). *Systematic instruction of persons with severe handicaps* (3rd ed.). Columbus: Charles E. Merrill.

Turnbull, A.P., & Turnbull, H.R. (1985). *Parents speak out* (rev. ed.). Columbus: Charles E. Merrill.

Wehman, P., Moon, M.S., Everson, J.M., Wood, W., & Barcus, J.M. (1988). *Transition from school to work: New challenges for youth with severe disabilities*. Baltimore: Paul H. Brookes Publishing Co.

14

The Iowa Model of Personnel Preparation

Greg A. Robinson

Iowa has achieved a level of excellence in the provision of services for students with severe or profound disabilities through the combination of strong leadership at the state level and the development of a comprehensive statewide network of services and personnel in the intermediate area education agencies and local school districts. This chapter begins with an overview of the situation in the state of Iowa and then examines factors that have contributed significantly to improving Iowa's service-delivery system, including: 1) in-service training and technical assistance, 2) curriculum, 3) integration efforts, 4) teacher certification, 5) cooperation, and 6) educational publications. The chapter concludes with a review of unresolved issues requiring future action.

To assist the reader in contrasting Iowa with his or her own state, a brief statistical overview is provided for background information related to special education services in general and to specific information pertaining to services for students with severe or profound disabilities.

BACKGROUND

In 1989, the state of Iowa consisted of 436 local school districts serving a population of 524,243 students. The largest district had a student population of slightly more than 30,000, while Iowa's smallest K–12 district had an enrollment of 91 students.

The PL 94-142 (the Education for All Handicapped Children Act, 1975) special education child count for 1989 totaled 58,072 (11%). Of that total,

698 were identified as students with a severe or profound disability. This group of students represented .13% of the total students enrolled in public and nonpublic schools in Iowa and 1.2% of the total of students with disabilities being served.

Iowa special education instructional services are, for the most part, provided by local school districts. Iowa is divided into 15 area education agencies (AEA), which are charged with providing local school districts with support services such as psychological services, speech therapy, social work, instructional consultation, audiology, and occupational and physical therapy. These disciplines within each AEA receive technical assistance through the Bureau of Special Education of the Iowa Department of Education. The Bureau consists of 18 consultants who facilitate a variety of services to AEAs and local school districts. The consultants are able to provide these types of services through on-site visitations, workshops, or special projects. These special projects are funded through the discretionary funds (approximately 20%) provided by Part B of PL 94-142.

Special education in Iowa is funded through a weighted index system. For the majority of students with severe or profound disabilities the instructional program will be in a self-contained classroom. If the average cost per student in general education is $2,778, the cost for a student in a self-contained classroom would be $9,306 for special education programming, with an additional $695 flowing back to general education for administrative costs, regular transportation, integration, and operation and maintenance of facilities. The student to teacher ratio in a self-contained classroom is five to one, with one paraprofessional. If the class size increases from six to nine students, an additional paraprofessional is employed.

HISTORY OF SERVICES FOR STUDENTS WITH SEVERE DISABILITIES

The first positive signs in the direction of services for students with severe or profound disabilities in Iowa preceded the passage of PL 94-142. Iowa already had committed to serving all children with disabilities (ages birth through 21) prior to the federal mandate.

In 1976, the Bureau of Special Education employed Steve Maurer to serve as the consultant in the area of severe and profound disabilities. Maurer designed the blueprint for what now has become known as the "Iowa Model" for preparing those who work with students with severe disabilities. Since the university and college programs in the state were not addressing the training of personnel in this area, even when the passage of the federal law was imminent, Maurer conducted a statewide assessment of the needs of the educators working in this area.

Because local districts did not have funds to send their educators to national meetings, Maurer formulated a series of summer workshops involving national leaders in the area of mental retardation and low-incidence disabilities. Beginning in 1976, these 5-week in-service programs took place for the next three summers, providing the necessary training for educators and support service personnel assigned to low-incidence programs. The bureau continued to provide technical assistance through in-service training even when universities expressed interest in establishing preservice teacher training programs. In retrospect, this decision allowed the development of the in-service training and technical assistance network that formed the backbone of Iowa's personnel preparation model.

The provision of in-service training and technical assistance would have been quite limited without the aid of consultants from outside the bureau. The use of these professionals for the purpose of providing short-term in-service training or long-term technical assistance has become the primary strategy used to keep personnel in Iowa knowledgeable about current research, technology, and expertise in the area of mental retardation.

During the 1980s, an impressive list of professionals have provided technical assistance in Iowa in the field of mental retardation:

Paul Alberto
Paul Bates
Tom Bellamy
Fredda Brown
Kat Campbell
Ann Casey
Meg Cooper
Ian M. Evans
H.D. Bud Fredericks
Doug Guess
Joy Kataoka
Kathleen Marshall
Luanna H. Meyer
John Nietupski
Ernie Panscofar
Debby Petty
Ian Pumpian
Daniel Reschly
Frank Rusch
Michael Shafer
Tom E.C. Smith
Dick Sobsey
Scott Sparks

Donald Armstrong
Mark Batshaw
Felix F. Billingsley
Lou Brown
Philippa Campbell
John Cawley
Anne Donnellan
Alison Ford
Lori Goetz
Rob Horner
Donna Lehr
Karen Green McGowan
Pat Mirenda
Jan Nisbet
Terry Page
Edward Polloway
Tip Ray
Adelle Renzaglia
Gary Sasso
Ellin Siegel-Causey
Marti Snell
Jeff Strully

Don Baer
Diane Baumgart
Doug Biklen
Bruce Buehler
Irene Carney
Mary Cronin
June Downing
Alan Frank
Susan Hamre-
    Nietupski
Brian Iwata
Linda Higbee
    Mandlebaum
Celane M. McWhorter
Dennis Mithaug
Fred Orelove
James Patton
Beverly Rainforth
Joe Reichle
Suzanne Robinson
Stuart Schleien
J. David Smith
Les Sternberg

Francis Stetson   Owen White   Terri Vandercook
Paul Wehman   Dave Wacker
                      Bob York
Judy Wood   Barbara Wilcox
Jennifer York   Joyce Zachow   Kathy Zanella

In-service training and technical assistance has been successful in Iowa for two major reasons. First, many consultants have indicated that Iowa administrators ask them to provide in-service training and technical assistance in areas or on projects for which they would be unable to provide assistance in other states. Leaders in the bureau have always shown a willingness to participate in research that has implications for positive change in all areas of disability and in support services. Second, before any consultant arrives for the in-service training session, the bureau consultant and local contact persons establish a technical assistance follow-up plan to ensure that the training by the consultant will have the necessary follow through. The planning for follow through ensures that the consultants' efforts will make an impact on actual services.

Summer workshops have become a vital part of the in-service training model for personnel in the area of severe disabilities, and this aspect of our model has been used throughout the bureau in working with consultants. Successful technical assistance workshops provided in the state have focused on the use of paraprofessionals in the classroom; involving general education principles in the special education process; working with medically fragile children; and providing occupational, physical, and speech therapies in an integrated fashion.

In addition to these forms of technical assistance, an annual statewide conference sponsored by the bureau was initiated several years ago as a way to expose Iowa educators to national leaders responsible for innovations in special education. Sessions for those who work with low-incidence disabilities are always well attended. The 1989/1990 conference attracted 2000 Iowa special educators and support service personnel, approximately 35% of the state's total staff in these two groups.

CURRICULUM DEVELOPMENT

The Actualization of Mainstream Experience Skills Project (Project A.M.E.S.) (Maurer, Teas, & Bates, 1979) was developed to explore vocational training options for students with severe and profound disabilities. After initiation of the project, it became clear that all curricular or life skill areas needed to be addressed and the project became Iowa's first attempt at developing a longitudinal, age-appropriate curriculum model. Over the next 3 years, Project A.M.E.S. contributed important data for developing a model that could be replicated in other urban and rural settings across the state. By 1984, all 15 area education agencies had a replication site. Though many of the replication sites were located in segregated facilities, the use of the Project A.M.E.S. model has been successful with integrated programs in many locations throughout the state. As a result of the success of the replication sites, a curriculum guide was developed to be used across the state (Iowa Department of Public Instruction, 1984). The guide addressed program formation, program implementation, model curriculum activities, transition, and graduation. The response to the curriculum has been very positive, with teachers incorporating and adapting the information into their classroom programs. Enough new information was generated as a result of the statewide application to reconvene the task force to update and revise the curriculum guide.

Even with the success of Project A.M.E.S., there have still been questions about the sufficiency of the state's efforts with those students who have profound disabilities. The Iowa definition of profound disabilities appears to be very selective of students with the most severe disabilities. In fact, descriptions of the abilities of individuals in many research studies reportedly involving students with profound disabilities would place them within the moderate to severe range in Iowa. Attempts to focus specifically on students with profound disabilities have met with mixed results. In a special project, funded by the bureau, within the state's largest school district, several nationally recognized consultants were contracted to provide technical assistance simultaneously as a group. Although some teachers did make appropriate accommodations for their students with profound disabilities, others failed to adapt new approaches even after extensive consultation. Another concern noted was the inability of some support service personnel to agree that there is a need to provide services to students with this level of disability.

INTEGRATION

Public Law 94-142 requires that, to the maximum extent appropriate, students with disabilities are to be educated with students who do not have disabilities, and that special classes, separate schooling, or other removal of students with disabilities from the regular educational environment should occur only when the nature or severity of the disability is such that education in regular classes with the use of supplementary aids and services cannot be achieved satisfactorily.

This concept is referred to as the least restrictive environment (LRE) principle. As in other states, Iowa's applications of the concept of LRE and integration has not always been easy. Iowa administrators began by reviewing the mainstream efforts of the late 1960s and 1970s to determine where errors were made. Even though the students being mainstreamed at that time had mild to moderate disabilities, problems arose because sufficient planning was not done prior to the movement of students into general education. As a result of failure to deal with barriers ahead of time, educators and students experienced frustration, failures, and self-doubt. In order to eliminate or at least significantly reduce these effects when the new push for LRE came with the federal mandate, Iowa began an active process to remove the barriers to placements in least restrictive environments.

Having experienced success with curriculum development, or "what" to teach students with severe or profound disabilities, the next step was to examine "where" teaching occurred. Figure 14.1 illustrates the reduction in the number of segregated schools in Iowa from 1976 to 1987.

It was most difficult to convince parents that their children would not experience a lower level of services in the integrated settings than they had become accustomed to in the segregated facilities. Some of these parents who had been involved in the earlier mainstreaming effort were vehemently opposed to moving into community facilities, and their opinions remain unchanged. For others, confidence in their child's teacher and support staff gave them the courage to try an integrated program. Yet, parent concerns were a constant reminder that the level of services cannot be reduced, regardless of the location of the program. Ensuring parents that "what" is taught will not lose quality even when the "where" (location) or the "how" (e.g., direct instruction, using a consulting expert or therapist) is changed was the key to selling LRE in Iowa. Successful implementation of these services has made LRE reasonably successful.

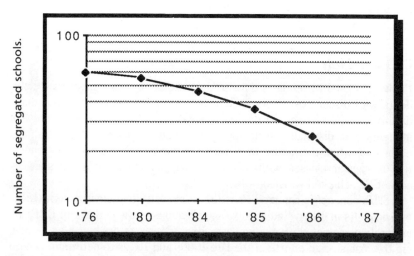

Figure 14.1.   Decline in segregated schools.

In December of 1984, the then State Board of Public Instruction unanimously passed a position statement encouraging each school district to develop policies and implement procedures dealing with the least restrictive environment requirement for all special education students, including those with moderate and severe disabilities. The statement included four of the five levels of integration (i.e., physical, functional, social, societal) that Biklen (1985) introduced in formulating a hierarchy of integrated options for programming. As a result of the position statement, each AEA and local district is now required to submit integration plans to the Bureau of Special Education. The position statement was accepted, but not without disagreement. The final version reflected a great deal of change and compromise of the original draft. Iowa has developed the philosophy of providing options for the location of programs. Parents should have a choice, and that choice must include the opportunity for their children to attend school in an integrated setting. Adapting to implement this policy has been a major factor in Iowa's ability to continue its progress toward programming in less restrictive environments, as illustrated in Figure 14.2.

Also, in 1984 the State Board of Public Instruction authorized the bureau to form the State Technical Assistance Team for Integration to assist school districts in developing their plans. The team is now in its 6th year and has as its mission to provide technical assistance to AEAs and local districts who request assistance in developing LRE options for students with moderate and severe disabilities. The team is composed of parents, teachers, administrators, and teacher trainers. Team members can: 1) assist district

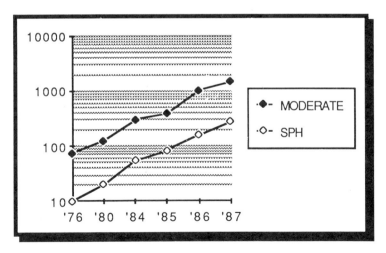

Figure 14.2. Number of students integrated. (SPH = severe/profound handicaps.)

planning teams in developing integration plans, 2) make "awareness" presentations, 3) review facilities, 4) meet with parent groups, 5) provide
written materials, and 6) conduct in-service training sessions. Since its
inception team members have provided technical assistance to 176 school
districts.

Iowa has sponsored several successful regional summer meetings on
the topic of integration. A new focus since 1986 is to bring general education
principals together from across the state to provide assistance in understanding the concepts of LRE. A brief videotape developed to illustrate this
effort has also been well received.

CERTIFICATION

In 1980, the University of Northern Iowa (UNI) began a teacher preparation
training program in the area of severe disabilities. Currently, the University
of Iowa and Morningside College, in addition to UNI, have the only teacher
preparation programs that provide course work in severe or profound disabilities. In addition, there are 13 other college or university programs in the
state that provide teacher training in the area of mental retardation. A
continuing concern is that many teacher and support service candidates who
receive training in mental retardation rarely are the recipients of any coursework or exposure in the area of low-incidence disabilities. Yet, under most
state certification programs these candidates may receive authorization to
provide instructional or support services across the continuum from mild to
profound disabilities in public school settings. State definitions across the
continuum of disability are even broader. A student may be identified as
having a mild mental disability if he or she has a general intellectual quotient
of more than one standard deviation below the mean, with a significant
deficit in adaptive behavior.

To remedy this situation, a certification approval process was initiated
to require more specialized coursework for those who would provide instructional services to students with severe and profound disabilities. This
helped the problem with in-state candidates but was an issue for those
coming to Iowa from other states. Requests for temporary certification
were not uncommon. In analyzing the skills of newly certified teachers, it
became apparent that teachers of students with severe disabilities were no
more equipped to deal with functional- and application-oriented aspects of a
curriculum than the majority of the teachers of students with mild disabilities. As a result, when the new certification standards were developed,
changes were suggested accordingly. Teachers, as of September 1988,
receive Iowa certification in mental retardation in one of two areas:
mild/moderate or moderate/severe/profound. New requirements for teachers of students with mild disabilities will include a methods course in teach-

ing students ages K–6 or 7–12 who have mild disabilities; the course will include the concepts of career-vocational education, transition, and integration, in addition to a K–12 functional, longitudinal curriculum development course. Ecological assessment techniques and systematic observation systems will be required as part of the content in the diagnostic, assessment, and evaluation courses. Behavioral intervention and parent consultation coursework also will be required. In addition, there have been changes in the requirements for student teaching assignments. If the teacher candidate selects a student teaching assignment in a program on mild mental disabilities, he or she must also have a lengthy practicum in a program on moderate mental disabilities. For moderate/severe/profound certification, two student field-based experiences also are required. The candidate selects one area (moderate or severe/profound) for the student teaching assignment and completes a practicum experience in the other area.

Requirements of support service personnel preparation programs are also changing to better prepare future providers. One example is in the School Psychology Program at Iowa State University where school psychology students must take specific coursework in functional assessment of low incidence populations. This coursework is paired with field-based practica and has been quite successful.

COOPERATION

By initiating a network of parents and professionals across the state, the Bureau of Special Education has facilitated the development and growth of several advocacy groups. The technical assistance provided in such a concentrated effort brings many national leaders into the state, and Iowa enjoys a strong state branch of TASH (The Association for Persons with Severe Handicaps). With the move to a more application-oriented curriculum for students with mild mental disabilities, a new state division of mental retardation in the Iowa Federation of the Council for Exceptional Children (CEC-MR) has also been started. In 1988, the Iowa TASH and CEC-MR joined to sponsor a conference for those involved with the instruction and care of students who have mental disabilities. Iowa also hosted the International CEC-MR teacher conference in October 1989, which featured a strong strand in the area of severe or profound disabilities.

The Association for Retarded Citizens (ARC) also has prospered in our state. With their intense lobbying, a "Bill of Rights" for persons with disabilities of all ages in our state will pass within the next legislative session. We are convinced that if our adult services do not keep pace with the developments in the school programs, the total service-delivery system will not be successful. Success requires that all of these advocacy and support groups work together towards a common goal.

COMMUNICATING IN PRINT

Individuals can attend meetings and listen but they must also have information in their hands to read in order to maintain the focus of the contemporary issues being addressed. Iowa has developed and distributed numerous publications on topics including, among many others, integration activities, exemplary curriculum, technological advancements, best practices, and decision-making.

The *Iowa News* is a monthly newsletter that is sent to 12 states. With over 2,700 copies printed, its targeted audience is specifically those who work with students with low-incidence disabilities. Since 1988 periodic newsletters for all teachers within the state who have authorization in the area of mental disabilities and who have multicategorical certification have been developed. Newsletters mailed to 3,600 teachers discussed special projects, goals, and conferences that would increase their skills in dealing with students who have mental disabilities. The feedback received indicates that people read the information and talk with others about it.

UNRESOLVED ISSUES

Even with the successes the state of Iowa has enjoyed, there are issues, such as programming for students with profound disabilities, integration, and the development of a working relationship between in-service and pre-service training programs, that need further work to be resolved. If information and assistance could be provided through attention to these areas at the federal level and among those who do research, Iowa could only benefit.

In the area of curriculum, more guidance in developing programs for students with truly profound disabilities and students who are deaf/blind is needed. Our efforts to increase least restrictive programming for these students, including promotion of social interactions with peers who do not have disabilities, will not be accepted by professionals in other areas of education unless there is data-based research to support the validity of these efforts. There are many pressing questions that need empirically based answers: Is there ever a time when the level of a student's participation is so minimal that only the educator is involved in the task? Should respite care be provided in educational settings? What types of programs are educationally appropriate? These are the questions that teachers face on a daily basis when working with students with the most severe disabilities. Providing assistance to these professionals is vital not only to their students but to the professionals as well.

In the area of integration, are more restrictive environments ever appropriate? What is the balance between advocating for placement of students with severe or profound disabilities in regular classrooms and expanding previously developed community-based programs that take students from the school environment into community settings? How can least restrictive placements for students who are medically fragile and for students who have behavioral difficulties best be managed? How can we prepare teachers to handle students with the more severe difficulties when preservice programs do not expose them to the kinds of situations they will encounter with these students? Many special education teacher candidates graduate with limited training in behavioral interventions and graduate without skills to deal with medically fragile students.

Although it would be easy to blame the inadequacies of our services on teacher preparation programs, that is not entirely fair or very helpful in improving the situation. Rather, it is time for state departments of special education to reach out and develop a better working relationship with university programs. University programs not only train future teachers, they also are a resource for the state education delivery system. As faculty are involved in the state system, the system's awareness of current needs in preparation of teachers for students with severe disabilities will improve. University faculty involvement will also allow in-service and preservice trainers to work together on projects that will promote planned longitudinal improvements in the services for students with severe or profound disabilities.

Information about education and intervention for students with severe disabilities needs to be spread to the areas outside of instruction. Support service personnel must continue to receive exposure to students with low-incidence disabilities in their training programs. Many support service personnel have difficulty understanding how these students can learn, even though they are the professionals responsible for identification and placement of these students into programs.

Fifteen years after the mandate of PL 94-142 to serve all children is past the time to dispel the fears and myths about working with students with severe disabilities. It is only through challenging ourselves further that we continue to provide quality services to students who used to be forgotten. The goal for Iowa is to make sure that students with severe or profound disabilites are always remembered. In Iowa, "expecting the best" is not a dream, but a workable objective.

REFERENCES

Biklen, D. (1985). *Achieving the complete school: Effective strategies for mainstreaming.* New York: Teachers College Press.

Iowa Department of Public Instruction. (1984). *Curriculum development for students with moderate, severe, and profound handicaps.* Des Moines: Author.

Maurer, S., Teas, S., & Bates, P. (1979). *Project A.M.E.S. (Actualization of Mainstream Experience Skills).* Des Moines: Iowa Department of Public Instruction.

15

A Generic In-Service Training Model

H.D. Bud Fredericks
and Torry Piazza Templeman

Since 1976, the education of students with severe disabilities has emerged into a major educational thrust throughout the United States. As school districts implemented programs for these students, qualified staff became a priority. However, qualified staff were not always available and a small flurry of concern in the literature was manifested in the late 1970s. Stainback, Stainback, Schmid, and Courtnage (1977) proposed a model for training teachers of students with severe and profound disabilities. Iacino and Bricker (1978) proposed another model for teacher training. Staff training continues to be a major need, but since those early writings there has been a paucity of journal articles on the subject.

One of the phenomena that has exacerbated the need for personnel training programs is rapidly changing technology and the emergence of new techniques and practices for the education of students with severe disabilities. To realize how swiftly the field is changing, one need only reflect briefly upon the major trends of the 1970s and 1980s: initiation of the process of deinstitutionalization on a large scale, followed by a strong impetus for integration in the public schools, then emergence of the need for independent living skill training and community-based vocational training. All of these trends have emerged, and, to some extent, have been opertionalized and implemented from the mid-1970s through the 1980s. Education of persons with severe disabilities is a dynamic field, and change and growth will continue as we learn more about teaching persons with severe disabilities.

The service needs of persons with severe and profound disabilities extend beyond the school years. Thus, the need for qualified personnel is not limited to those who serve in schools. There are also needs for personnel throughout the entire array of adult services, including vocational re-habilitation personnel, job coaches, residential staff, and recreation and lei-sure specialists. In addition, some people with severe and profound disabilities need long-term assistance with some specialized physical, oc-cupational, or language therapy services.

Because of the dynamic nature of special education and the extensive requirement for services beyond school, in-service training of staff is a continual need. This chapter focuses on in-service training. It documents the need for such training and offers a generic in-service training model that can be adapted for the training of all staff.

THE NEED FOR IN-SERVICE TRAINING

In early October, 1987, a conference was held in Nashville, Tennessee, to discuss personnel preparation. During that conference, educational leaders from throughout the United States discussed the needs in preparation of personnel for persons with severe disabilities. Although not all speakers focused on in-service training, a recurring theme through many of their talks was the need for a massive in-service training program to meet the needs of personnel in the field of severe disabilities:

Steven F. Warren: "In-service training needs to be considered seriously."

Philippa Campbell: "We have created for ourselves a system of retrain-ing. There is a need for well-trained personnel now. The need for in-service is now. There are a few good in-service training models."

Joleta Reynolds (Director, Special Education, Tennessee State Depart-ment of Education) as she discussed the problems of integration: "Regular classroom teachers need in-service."

Ian M. Evans: After identifying eight roles for personnel, he indicated, "Everyone in those roles needs some training."

Sam Odom: "There is a need for in-service training."

Margaret J. McLaughlin has stated that there is a lack of personnel and existing personnel are underprepared.

Although these opinions were voiced by these leaders in the final months of 1987, the need for in-service training has been constant since the passage of PL 94-142. Nevertheless, the federal government, under the Reagan administration, stopped funding in-service training programs through the special education personnel preparation program except under the category of special projects. While the federal government did initiate a program of in-service training under the auspices of the severe handicaps program, very few training programs are funded under these two categories of personnel preparation funds.

Government officials have indicated several reasons why federal fund-ing for in-service training was significantly curtailed: 1) there was no need for such training; 2) there was no money; 3) states, through their cooperative personnel preparation planning councils, could fund all the in-service training needed, especially if those funds and programs were combined with local education agency efforts; and 4) the effectiveness of in-service training that was previously funded was seriously questioned.

The purpose of this chapter is not to argue with the federal government's position regarding in-service training needs; however, response to each of the reasons for not funding in-service training is in order. Currently, there is a need to update teachers of students with severe disabilities on the latest developments in research and teaching techniques because the knowledge base related to persons with severe disabilities is changing rapidly. Not only must teachers be retrained, but there is also a need to update the training of aides and therapists. In addition, there is a new set of professionals, including job coaches and vocational trainers, who need to be taught the latest methods for community-based vocational training. The in-service training of residential care providers in community-based programs is continually an area of need.

The shortage of funds for in-service training must be recognized as a reality attributable in part to the priorities of the Reagan administration (1980–1988). Prior to 1980, federal funding was available for both preservice activities and in-service training. Since 1980, states have assumed the primary fiscal responsibility for in-service training. It is unlikely that state personnel preparation programs can provide sufficient in-service training to keep professionals and paraprofessionals abreast of current technology. While in-service training funded by the state can have an impact on these needs, states are unable to disseminate information on state-of-the-art practices. Thus, providing training in such practices appears to be a critical function of federally funded in-service training projects. Furthermore, the impact of federally funded research and model demonstration projects could be greatly enhanced if these projects were linked directly to in-service training programs. Currently, most demonstration and model projects do not have a mechanism for providing training in other developments occuring at the time of the projects.

Finally, the question of quality of in-service training is an issue of concern that needs careful attention. Quality of training is a direct function of the evaluation systems that are built into in-service training (Iacino & Bricker, 1978). Yet, few states are able or willing to provide incentives for systematic in-service training evaluation.

A GENERIC IN-SERVICE TRAINING MODEL

The Teaching Research Infant and Child Center in Monmouth, Oregon has been involved in conducting in-service training since 1973 when it moved into dissemination of its data-based classroom model for students with moderate and severe disabilities. Since then, in-service training procedures have been continually refined and modified based on input from the adopting agencies and the results of training as measured at the time of follow-up. On November 7, 1979 Teaching Research received validation by the Joint Dissemination and Review Panel (JDRP). The JDRP approval indicates that this project is a nationally recognized exemplary in-service model. The panel is composed of a number of nationally known evaluation and research experts. In order for the Teaching Research In-service Training Model to receive the panel's validation, solid evidence of effectiveness of the in-service training model procedures in changing teachers' behavior had to be submitted.[1]

Although the original in-service model focused on classroom services at the preschool and elementary levels, this same model has since been demonstrated to be effective for personnel across a variety of environments and situations, including, but not limited to, residential providers, activity center personnel, community job coaches, and paraprofessionals. Following is a brief description of the components of this generic in-service model:

The underlying thesis of the generic in-service model is that effective in-service training must be based on a strong evaluation component. The generic in-service model comprises five levels of evaluation.

The five levels of evaluation have been chosen to measure consumer satisfaction with the training presented and to provide data that demonstrate that trainees acquired either skills or knowledge or that attitudes had changed during the training session(s). The more advanced levels of evaluation measure whether the trainee implements what has been learned, whether that implementation has an impact on the trainee's students, and/or whether the training produces more global program change. A discussion of each of the five levels of training evaluation with some examples follows:

Level 1:   Trainee Satisfaction

This evaluation level determined whether a trainee believed that the training received was worthwhile and was well organized and effectively presented.

Unless a trainee enjoys the training session and believes that the instructor was well organized and presented the instructional material in an interesting manner, one cannot expect that the trainee will use and adapt what was presented. Moreover, any agency arranging for its staff to receive

---

[1]The JDRP process was established by the United States Department of Education (USDOE). Its purpose was to select from USDOE funded projects those projects that demonstrated empirically that their procedures were effective in producing the results claimed by the project. The process for obtaining JDRP approval was as follows: 1) permission to request JDRP approval was first obtained from the project officer in the federal government; 2) a 10 page report on the project was prepared according to JDRP guidelines by the project personnel and submitted; 3) the project director and selected members of his or her staff appeared before the JDRP and responded to questions about the submission; 4) the panel voted to approve or reject.

training should expect from the instructor that he or she is well organized, knows the material to be presented, and presents it in an effective and interesting manner. Thus, some measure of trainee satisfaction should be elicited from all trainees. This is the easiest type of evaluation to obtain, which is evidenced by the fact that it is used in many workshops. An example of such a measure of trainee satisfaction is shown in Figure 15.1.

Level 2: Trainee Skills or Knowledge Acquired

This evaluation level focuses on the acquisition of knowledge, skills, or attitudes during the training session. To obtain these evaluation data, measures of performances are taken during the training. Pretests and posttests and pre- and postobservations of the trainees are the preferred strategy for evaluation. However, posttests and postobservations are sometimes acceptable enough demonstrations that trainees have acquired skills, knowledge, and attitudes taught during training that it is assumed the trainee did not have prior to training.

For instance, if an instructor were teaching behavior management skills to a group of trainees, one part of the instruction might focus on terminology. To determine that the trainees acquired a knowledge of the terminology, the instructor administers a terminology test which requires that the trainee match terms to definitions. This test is administered both at the beginning of instruction and then again at the end of instruction, thus constituting a pretest and posttest of the instructional period. A comparison of the pretest and posttest scores will indicate the degree to which the students acquired a knowledge of the terminology.

Another instructor who is teaching basic sign language to classroom aides may administer a skill test at the beginning of the instructional period to determine how many signs of a certain type the members of the class know. This pretest will dictate the subject matter that the instructor must teach. At the conclusion of the instruction, a similar skill test will indicate the degree to which the trainees mastered the signs taught.

Level 3: Trainee Implementation
of Skills or Knowledge Acquired

This level of evaluation focuses on what the trainee does in the work site after training. Ideally, observations at the trainee's work site would be the most revealing based on a set list of behaviors and criterion measures taught during the previous in-service training session. When it is not possible to observe the trainee on site, reports by supervisors or self-reports by the trainee may be accepted as evidence of trainee skill acquisition and application of new information and newly-learned skills.

This is perhaps the most neglected form of in-service evaluation, and yet the one that justifies the entire in-service effort. In-service training is

WORKSHOP EVALUATION SCALE

Workshop name: _____ Date: _____

Presentor: _____

Instructions:

To determine whether or not the workshop met your needs and our objectives, we would like for you to give us your honest opinion on the design, presentation, and value of this workshop. Please circle the number which best expresses your reaction to each of the items on the following list. Space is provided for your comments.

EVALUATION CRITERIA

1.	The organization of the workshop was:	Excellent	7	6	5	4	3	2	Poor 1
2.	The objectives of the workshop were:	Clearly evident	7	6	5	4	3	2	Vague 1
3.	The work of the presenter(s) was:	Excellent	7	6	5	4	3	2	Poor 1
4.	The ideas and activities of the workshop were:	Excellent	7	6	5	4	3	2	Poor 1
5.	The scope (coverage) was:	Very adequate	7	6	5	4	3	2	Inadequate 1
6.	My attendance at this workshop should prove:	Very beneficial	7	6	5	4	3	2	No benefit 1
7.	Overall, I consider this workshop:	Excellent	7	6	5	4	3	2	Poor 1
8.	Do you feel a need for additional information about this topic?		1. Yes			2. No			

The stronger features of the workshop were: _____

_____

_____

The weaker features were: _____

_____

_____

General comments: _____

Figure 15.1. The McCallon Trainee Satisfaction Form. From: McCallon, E. [n.d.] *Workshop evaluation scale.* Austin: Learning Concepts. Reprinted with permission.

designed to change trainee behavior. There is an assumption that if the trainee's behavior changes, then the trainee will be performing his or her duties more effectively, and thus those whom the trainee is serving or teaching will benefit by that changed behavior. The crux of all in-service training lies here. If the trainee fails to change behavior at his or her work site, the in-service training does not stand any chance of having an impact on the trainee's students, residents, or workers. Yet the vast majority of in-service programs never attempt to measure this important factor.

Some measures at this evaluation level can be obtained quite easily. For instance, if a trainee were taught a new language curriculum for preschool children with severe disabilities, it could be determined from a survey completed by the trainee or the trainee's supervisor whether the trainee was implementing the curriculum. Of course, a much better set of data would come from someone observing the trainee to determine if the curriculum was being implemented according to some prescribed criteria.

Within the system of Teaching Research group homes in Oregon for students with severe emotional disturbances, all direct care staff are taught to maintain a 4–1 positive to negative feedback ratio with each student within the residence. Supervisors periodically observe the staff to ensure that the ratio is being maintained. Thus, in-service training in these environments is continuously accomplished through the observations of the supervisors and the feedback given to the staff during and after the observations.

Level 4:   Child Behavior Changes as a Result of the Skills and Knowledge Acquired by the Trainee

Increased effectiveness in teaching or service delivery is the intended outcome of in-service training. Ideally, student performance data would be acquired before the trainee received the in-service training. After training, data would be collected again for comparison. These types of data are recognized as difficult to gather and are frequently dismissed as impractical to gather. Yet, prior to the planning of every in-service program, these data should be focused upon first, and efforts should be made to design an in-service program that would gather some measure of child change.

We use the term "child change" generically. It may be students, workers, or residents who experience the change as a result of their teacher or direct care staff receiving in-service training. For instance, direct care staff at a residence received in-service training that focused on supporting residents to participate in more activities in the community. The instructor, before providing the in-service training, had the trainees fill out a checklist that indicated how often residents participated in certain community activities. A month after the in-service training was completed, those who had attended the training program completed a similar questionnaire that indicated that the residents had a 30% increase in community participation.

Level 5:   Program Change

Comparable to level 4, level 5 focuses on changes in program or philosophies. For example, integration of children with disabilities with peers who do not have disabilities where that did not occur before or the implementation of a community-based vocational program at the secondary level where none existed before would be evidence of a Level 5 change. This level of evaluation could substitute for child change data (Level 4) although child change data are still desirable even when there is evidence of program change.

We place the evaluation component at the forefront of any in-service training program. We do so for a number of reasons. When TASH's technical assistance project for deaf-blind children and youth first started in 1983 and hired renowned consultants from around the country to provide in-service training, we learned that many of these consultants delivered lectures and conducted workshops without receiving any feedback as to their effectiveness. We therefore insisted that all such consultants be required to obtain evaluation data. We did so because of the obligation we felt to account for the efficient use of public funds. We believe that same obligation exists whether the funding is provided by a local school district, a state developmental disabilities agency, or a vocational rehabilitation entity. If public funds are used for in-service training, there is an obligation to account for those funds being well spent and for achievement of the expected results. One of the major reasons why funding for in-service training at the federal level has virtually ceased is that funded projects could not document that they had been effective.

However, there is an even more important reason for evaluating the effectiveness of in-service training. Such training is undertaken because needs are perceived by administrators, direct service providers, or funding agencies. These needs generally were those of the recipients of the services—the students, the residents, or the workers. In-service training is conducted to effect improvements for them. Evaluation measures whether their situations have improved.

Other Key Components

The generic model has several other key components which are discussed below:

    1. Identification of Training Needs   This is a two-step process. The first step is an overall needs assessment. The trainers should conduct a survey among those for whom the in-service training is being planned. For this survey, precise definition of needs is necessary. Phrases such as "behavior management" are not specific enough to delineate needs.

A more specific definition might be something such as, "Needs to learn how to take data on various types of behavior programs and how to analyze that data to make decisions about the program." Although this type of needs assessment can be conducted rather formally using a checklist, most often the identification of training needs is determined through detailed conversations between those who are to be trained and those who will do the training. The second step is prioritizing the needs.

2. ***Identification of Training Competencies*** For each training need a list of behavioral competencies for staff members would be developed. These competencies would be phrased to identify the skills, knowledge, or attitudes that the trainees would manifest after training. For example, if data keeping was the identified need, the trainee first would need to know how to identify various behaviors to be observed, need to learn observation skills, need to learn how to record various kinds of data, and so forth. The question must logically arise: How does one determine the skills of those who will receive the training? Only in very rare cases will a formal process be undertaken. It would be ideal for the trainer to observe the trainees in their natural settings and from that observation develop a list of training needs. Resources and time almost invariably prevent such a formal process. Certainly, during the in-service training itself when a formal pretest or skill test is administered, the trainer will be able to determine quite precisely the skills and knowledge of the trainees. Most often, however, the needs as expressed by those who are to be trained are accepted, and no formal assessment of trainee competencies is undertaken prior to the commencement of training.

3. ***Design of Objectives*** All training needs are formulated in terms of training objectives. Figure 15.2 shows a sample set of training objectives for individuals who are to become foster parents for youth with severe emotional disturbances.

4. ***Design of Training Activities*** The next task would be to assemble a set of activities in which trainees would participate to develop the desired competencies. The selection of activities would depend on the nature and the complexity of the desired outcome. Generally for each objective there are one or more activities designed. During the course of designing training activities, a project would employ a number of training techniques: lectures, small group discussion, reading, role play, and practica. Figure 15.2 shows such a plan.

In the course of over 10 years of in-service training experience, Teaching Research has found the following techniques to be most effective in ensuring the success of training:

1. *Training at a Neutral Site* The trainee is "transplanted" from his or her work environment to a neutral training site. By removing the trainee from the work setting, a large number of potential distractors are elimi-

Objective	Activities	Evaluation
1. To train natural or foster parents to successfully manage behaviors of targeted youth.	1.1. Each set of parents will attend a 1-day workshop on behavior management technique.	1.1.1. Attendance records of parents' participation will be documented.
	1.2. Parents identify specific categories and appropriate responses to behaviors presented in role-play exercises.	1.2.1. Scores 7/8 or 85% on "rules of thumb" exercise.
	1.3. Utilizes "rules of thumb" when interacting with targeted youth in home setting.	1.3.1. Scores 80% on 10-minute observations across two different activities in home setting.
	1.4. Designs formal behavior intervention program during formal behavior exercise.	1.4.1. Designs behavior intervention program to include 8/10 or 80% of the necessary components of criterion.
	1.5. Designs and conducts formal behavior programs for targeted youth in home setting. (Each youth will be measured for baseline performance utilizing direct observational techniques.)	1.5.1. Each behavior and its subsequent objective will be measured for all youth. Behavior change from baseline conditions and a description of the activity contributing to the change will be documented. Parents will design a behavior intervention program with 60% accuracy.
		1.5.2. Update behavior intervention programs currently with 100% accuracy.
		1.5.3. Treatment strategies implemented utilize natural and age-appropriate reinforcers when possible.

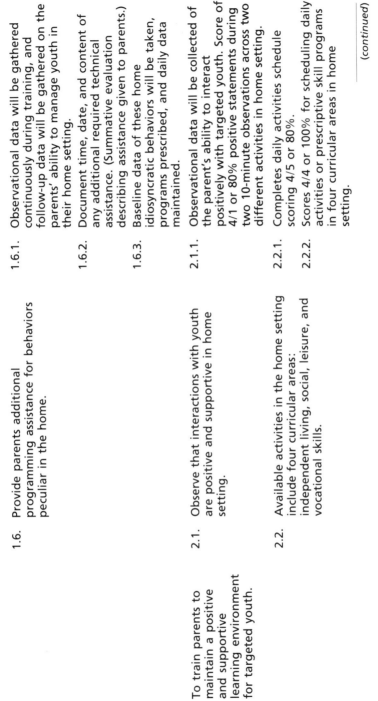

1.6. Provide parents additional programming assistance for behaviors peculiar in the home.	1.6.1. Observational data will be gathered continuously during training, and follow-up data will be gathered on the parents' ability to manage youth in their home setting.
	1.6.2. Document time, date, and content of any additional required technical assistance. (Summative evaluation describing assistance given to parents.)
	1.6.3. Baseline data of these home idiosyncratic behaviors will be taken, programs prescribed, and daily data maintained.
2. To train parents to maintain a positive and supportive learning environment for targeted youth.	
2.1. Observe that interactions with youth are positive and supportive in home setting.	2.1.1. Observational data will be collected of the parent's ability to interact positively with targeted youth. Score of 4/1 or 80% positive statements during two 10-minute observations across two different activities in home setting.
2.2. Available activities in the home setting include four curricular areas: independent living, social, leisure, and vocational skills.	2.2.1. Completes daily activities schedule scoring 4/5 or 80%.
	2.2.2. Scores 4/4 or 100% for scheduling daily activities or prescriptive skill programs in four curricular areas in home setting.

(continued)

Figure 15.2. Objectives, activities, and evaluation plans for the training of foster parents of youth with severe emotional disturbances.

Figure 15.2. (continued)

Objective	Activities		Evaluation	
	2.3.	Utilizes phase transitional system in home setting.	2.3.1.	Scores 4/5 or 80% components present in phase transitional system in the home.
3. To train parents to conduct formal skill training programs and to utilize a data-based communication system to track youth progress.	3.1.	The parents will be trained to use the *Teaching Research Curriculum for Mildly and Moderately Handicapped Adolescents and Adults Taxonomy and Assessment Tool* to gain point deficit independent living and social skills that will be taught in the home.	3.1.1.	Completes sample of Environment Characteristics form, Student Assessment form, and student priorities cover sheet during training.
	3.2.	Using data collected from assessment tool, the parent will aid in the development of the individualized education program (IEP) through joining participation of instructor and vocational trainer.	3.2.1.	Completes assessment of required skills for present and projected environments for targeted youth in home setting.
			3.2.2.	Based on current assessment information, identifies programming priorities for targeted youth, prescribes an individualized program plan (IPP) and instructs youth to make maximum gains in social/sexual, independent living, vocational, and leisure skills in the home.

3.2.3. Documents time, date, and content of parent's participation in IEP development.

3.3. Trainer models teaching and data collection technique of a required skill program; trainer and parent role-play teaching and data collection techniques of a skill program.

3.3.1. Given a sample skill program, parents will score 80% accuracy for instruction and data collection.

3.4. Conduct formal training programs with targeted youth in individual instructional home settings in the curricular areas of independent living skills.

3.4.1. Parents will score 80% accuracy in conducting program and in data collection per individualized program.

3.4.2. A data-based teaching system will be developed and utilized continuously to assess the individual progress of youth and parent program.

3.4.3. A program evaluation will be conducted that will note the number of programs each parent is conducting, how many of these are completed, how many are aborted, and how many parents are unable to conduct these programs.

3.5. Modify the programs as needed giving necessary feedback to the parent.

3.5.1. Document time, date, and content of any additional technical assistance delivered to parents.

nated. The complexity of the in-service training topic and the desired trainee outcomes must be considered in the selection of an appropriate site in which to conduct the training. For example, when the desired outcome is at the knowledge level, it is only necessary to select a site that is pleasant, comfortable, and neutral to all participants. However, when the desired trainee outcome is skill level implementation, it may be appropriate to conduct major portions of the training in a demonstration site where opportunities exist for observation, role play, and practica. Credibility of the trainer and the training process are enhanced when the trainees can see the procedures/processes in action and talk with staff who are using them. The primary determinant of the training site is the initial training outcome as determined by in-service planners.

2.   *Practica-Based Training* Practica-based training is a highly effective means of increasing trainees' skills. In closely supervised practicum experiences the trainee has a chance to try out procedures and materials while a trainer is there to encourage, correct, and assist. Trainers can observe trainee skills first hand in practica and do not have to rely on guessing at a trainee's level of mastery in a certain competency. These observations provide an occasion for trainers to give immediate feedback on the use of specified procedures and materials. During practicum experiences, trainers receive valuable feedback about the success of their training strategies. By systematically determining which competencies trainees have mastered, trainers can determine the need to concentrate on further training. The likelihood that the trainee will implement newly learned procedures is greatly increased when the trainee develops the competencies during a practicum training session.

3.   *Utilizing Multiple Presentation Formats* Using a variety of presentation approaches to provide a balance between participatory and passive activities for the trainees is highly recommended. The staff at Teaching Research has found that there is value in varying training formats to include lecture, discussion, video demonstration, live demonstration, and perhaps short written exercises. Whenever practical, it is advised that a variety of trainers be used as well. The example below, from the Teaching Research in-service model, demonstrates the effectiveness of varied training formats in: 1) the ability to train others, 2) teacher implementation, and 3) impact on students. This is taken from the submission by Teaching Research to the Joint Dissemination and Review Panel.

Fifty-one former trainees were selected for study in the example. These trainees received training within the same 12-month period. Each of these trainees received training in a management system designed for use in classes for students with moderate to severe disabilities. At the completion of training, 394 (96%) of 410 training objectives were achieved.

Of 51 trainees who received in-service training, 43 worked directly with children. In implementing the skills learned, trainees were asked to implement first one set of skills, then a second set of skills at a later date. Follow-up data for 32 individuals were gathered by 8–12 weeks after training for the first set of skills and 24–28 weeks after training for the second set. At the time of the first follow up, the first set of skills were measured and 94% were present. For these two sets of skills, respective quality levels were 97% and 98%. During the second follow-up visit, 97% of the first set of skills were present, with 82% meeting pre-established criterion level. Ninety percent of the second set of skills were present, with 93% of those skills at the pre-established criterion levels.

Impact on students was measured relative to student progress on 13 curricular areas of the *Student Progress Record* (SPR) (Oregon Mental Health Division, 1977). This test is routinely administered to all students with moderate to severe disabilities in the State of Oregon.

A random sample of 141 students (5%) was selected for study from the total pool of students whose teachers had received training and had implemented at least one set of the data-based classroom components. A comparison of mean gain scores for the 141 students across the 13 areas of the SPR revealed that the gains for students whose teachers had received training by Teaching Research were significantly higher ($p = .001$) than for a comparison group of students whose teachers had not received the training. Pretest scores for the two groups were not significantly different.

SUMMARY

This chapter has proposed that there is a major need for in-service training for professionals working in the field of severe disabilities. This need has been and is being generated by the dynamic nature of the field. Moreover, the need for in-service training is generated as new staff positions are developed, such as job coach or community trainer. Not only are personnel in public school settings in need of training, but there are also training needs within the area of adult services and within the therapeutic professions that serve persons with severe disabilities. The need is continual and had been exacerbated by the federal government's withdrawal of major in-service funding.

In addition, this chapter has presented a brief description of a generic in-service training model that includes the identification of needs and the formulation of objectives and activities to fulfill those needs. A generic in-service training evaluation plan that includes five levels of evaluation has been proposed. Finally, some data have been presented to demonstrate the effectiveness of such an in-service model.

RECOMMENDATIONS

Because of the dynamic nature of the field of severe disabilities, experienced and well-trained staff are not always available in sufficient numbers. This situation is exacerbated by the numbers of new staff required as the field expands and patterns of service delivery change, especially in the vocational and residential areas. Therefore, a greater emphasis on quality in-service training is necessary. This emphasis must come primarily from the federal government. Furthermore, states must supplement the federal government's efforts to raise the level of expertise of staff in all environments that serve persons with severe disabilities.

In order to ensure that in-service training is accomplishing its goals and objectives, greater accountability in terms of the effectiveness of the training must be required by funding agencies and administrative heads of agencies that receive the training. This chapter has discussed a five-level system of evaluation that could be applied to any in-service training program. Certainly other evaluation models can be used, but it is imperative that some system of formal evaluation be applied to in-service training.

Finally, there is a need to generate additional research regarding in-service training. The generic in-service training model proposed in this chapter is only one model of in-service training. It has been found to be effective, but it has not been compared empirically with other methods. Such scientific comparison should be undertaken. A number of questions, including the following, need to be examined systematically:

1. What are the relative effects of lecture, demonstration, and workshop training formats?
2. Is there an optimum length of time for practicum experiences for various positions?
3. What is the most effective type of feedback to give to trainees during practica—continuous feedback while the trainee is performing, intermittent feedback, or summary feedback?
4. What effect do follow-up activities have on trainee implementation and retention? What type of follow-up activities are best? What are the optimum time intervals for follow-up activities?
5. When is the most effective time to solicit trainee feedback as to the effectiveness of the in-service training—immediately after the conclusion of training, 3 weeks later, 3 months later, another time period?
6. Is it better to conduct hands-on training at the trainee's work site or in a neutral site?
7. How do we examine the cost effectiveness of in-service training?

These and many other questions are appropriate for research in the area of severe disabilities. Once again, the federal government will have to provide the initiative to implement this research.

Each year in this country billions of dollars are spent by school districts, group home organizations, vocational entities and early intervention programs on in-service training. We know very little about the effectiveness of that training or how best to conduct it. Perhaps Colleen Wieck (1979) said it best: "Because of the profit incentive and greater investment in employees, training and development specialists in business have pioneered systematic approaches to the issue of needs analysis, adult education methodology, and evaluation techniques. With some measure of creativity, these systematic approaches can be adapted by educators to improve the level of inservice training currently being offered in public schools" (p. 6).

REFERENCES

Iacino, R., & Bricker, D. (1978). The generative teacher: A model for preparing personnel to work with the severely/profoundly handicapped. In N.G. Haring & D.D. Bricker (Eds.), *Teaching the severely handicapped* (Vol. 3, pp. 62–74). Columbus: Special Press.

McCallon, E. (n.d.) Workshop evaluation scale. Austin: Learning Concepts.

Oregon Mental Health Division. (1977). *Student progress record.* Salem: Author.

Stainback, S., Stainback, W., Schmid, R., & Courtnage, L. (1977). Training teachers for the severely and profoundly retarded: An accountability model. *Education and Training of the Mentally Retarded, 12*(2), 170–173.

Wieck, C. (1979). Training and development of staff: Lessons from business and industry. *Education Unlimited, 1,* 6–13.

16

Contemporary Policy and Best Practice

Celane M. McWhorter and Ann P. Kaiser

This book is about the future, the future of disability policy and service implementation for individuals with severe disabilities. Even more important, this book is about the future of the thousands of individuals who have severe disabilities and on whose lives these policies and services will have a direct impact.

The chapters in this book describe the cutting edge of practice: the high quality, best practices in early childhood services, educational supports, and supported employment for individuals with severe disabilities; quality community care; and the realization of nonaversive behavior interventions as common procedure. In these discussions of best practice, personnel issues are so integral that the quality of services cannot be evaluated without evaluation of staff capability.

Very few of the topical issues in this book would have appeared in a book on personnel preparation in years past. In the 1970s this book would have been limited to a discussion of personnel training for special education classrooms, institutional and day activity programs, and model early intervention programs. Emerging research and technology and resultant adjustments in the service-delivery systems have opened new vistas for people with severe disabilities. As a result, there are new challenges in training professionals and paraprofessionals who will provide supports for people with disabilities.

In the 1980s, formulation of policies related to services for individuals with severe disabilities has markedly influenced our approaches to personnel preparation. Three major issues have been at the forefront of policy discussions; each has clear training implications: 1) The definitions of the least restrictive environment (LRE), 2) the development of community-based programs for adults with severe disabilities, and 3) allocations from limited funding sources to serve the extensive lifelong support needs of persons with severe disabilities.

Policy discussions have changed from a focus on access to services to a focus on the quality of the services and accessibility to these services. For individuals with severe disabilities, current policy discussions center on issues related to the locus of and strategies for the most effective service. Ensuring appropriately trained personnel is a central theme within these discussions.

LEAST RESTRICTIVE ENVIRONMENT (LRE)

Determining the definition of least restrictive environment mandated by the statutory language of PL 94-142 (the Education for All Handicapped Children Act, 1975) has proven to be one of the greatest challenges of the implementation of that law. The law provides that students shall be served in the least restrictive educational setting in which their special needs can be met. The indication that education should be provided with nonhandicapped students who do not have disabilities presumes that the regular classroom is the least restrictive setting.

The law in fact is quite clear, with the requirement that students remain in the regular setting unless "the nature or severity of the handicap is such that education in regular classes with the use of supplementary aids and services cannot be achieved satisfactorily" (Education for All Handicapped Children Act, 1975, Sec. 612[5][B]). The implementation of this requirement is uneven across states, and advocacy for strict implementation is uneven across disability groups.

There is an emerging consensus that the regular environment is the most appropriate setting (i.e., the least restrictive environment) for meeting the educational goals for students with severe and profound cognitive disabilities. Strong debates arise, however, about enforcement of LRE for students with certain other disabling conditions, such as deafness, blindness, deaf-blindness, and learning disabilities. Advocates line up on both sides of the integration argument for these students. No matter which position they take, there is concern among all advocates regarding the understanding of appropriate supports in the regular setting and the quality of individualized instruction that can currently be provided to students in the context of most regular classrooms. The latter issue is largely an issue of adequacy of personnel preparation for both the special educator and the regular educator, although it has infrequently been discussed strictly in that context.

One of the single most imposing barriers to adequate personnel preparation is a functional mandate for a level of personnel preparation that will make education in the regular classroom possible. One of the single most imposing barriers to integration of students into regular classrooms in regular schools is teacher preparation to instruct these students. And, while the field has been successful in removing many of the physical barriers to integration and in changing the attitudes of parents and children toward students with disabilities, we have been remarkably unsuccessful in having an impact on either the federal policies for enforcing the LRE requirement or the changing state certification policies that should reflect an appropriate level of teacher preparation to serve students with a wider variety of educational needs.

Alternative models for the development of a single educational system to serve students with varied educational needs have been proposed (Biklen, 1985; Sailor et al., 1989), researched (Reynolds, Wang, & Walberg, 1987), and demonstrated to be possible and effective (Brown et al., 1983). Three common theses of these proposed, researched, and demonstrated models of fully integrated education are noteworthy. First, there is a common model of a single service system for children with varied educational needs rather than the existing two track, special and regular educational systems. Second, there is a common view that special and regular educators must work together in teams with other ancillary service personnel to meet the specific needs of students on a day-to-day basis. Responsibility for student outcomes is shared by educators with expertise in different aspects of instruction. Students are neither special education students nor regular education students. Third is the assumption that all educators will require somewhat broader and continuing training in order to fulfill the roles required of them in the team approach to educating all students.

The research and policy implications from these common themes are considerable. Certainly, we need to carefully expand our information on understanding of successful models (Fuchs & Fuchs, 1988). Even more important to this discussion on personnel preparation, there are many areas that need further exploration. First, we must identify more specifically the skills required of all members of an educational team that serves children with a variety of needs and abilities. Second, we must consider how to provide effective training in these skills using both preservice and in-service strategies. The task of training personnel for a common model of education is a long-term undertaking that will require ongoing use of effective, efficient, and creative strategies to support the development of a wider range of teacher skills. Third, we must address the issue of teacher evaluation and child outcomes as they relate to standards for professional performance. Fourth, we must examine how federal, state, and local funding and certification systems must be adjusted to support the development of highly skilled teachers who can collaborate in meeting the educational needs of a range of students.

It is essential that the current discussions of educational reform include issues related to children with special needs and the development of a fully integrated, single education system. While policy debate regarding least restrictive environments has been conducted almost entirely within special education (Lipsky & Gartner, 1987), further progress toward a single educational system will be made largely through policies addressing all of the education establishment. The policy agenda for special educators and others concerned with the preparation of personnel to meet the educational needs of all students must be a broader, more public, and more systems-oriented agenda than ever proposed previously. It is no longer appropriate or ultimately functional for discussion of least restrictive environments to be strictly an issue of special education. This issue, and the attendant requirements for teacher preparation, is an immediate and continuing issue for all educators, educational administrators, and policy makers concerned with the well being of children.

COMMUNITY-BASED PROGRAMS FOR ADULTS WITH SEVERE DISABILITIES

During the 1980s, there has been increasing demand for appropriate community programs for adults with severe disabilities. This demand has emanated from two sources. First, the improvement of school-age services resulting from the passage of PL 94-142 has drawn attention to the notable lack of high-quality community services available to adults after they leave school. Second, the national movement toward deinstitutionalization has relocated many adults with severe disabilities into community living settings and prevented many others from ever being placed in an institution. The need for expanded appropriate adult services for individuals who live in communities is increasing with parent, professional, and disabled individuals' expectations that persons with disabilities will lead lives that include work, recreation, and life as a member of a community. In particular, innovations in employment accomplished through supported work initiatives have challenged communities to provide a new model of service that is outside the parameters of the typical adult-services model established before 1980. As more normalized models for adults living in communities emerge, we can expect an even larger variety of supports for daily living. Flexibility in designing appropriate individualized community life and work options is essential to both supported employment and normalized living arrangements.

The policy challenges surrounding the development of community-based services for adults are considerable because of the range of supports needed to ensure full involvement in community living by persons with severe disabilities, and because the funding for these supports derives from a variety of federal and state agencies, each serving a range of clients and designed to meet a range of client and community needs. Not only must different policies be developed for each agency, but also care must be taken to develop consistent policies across agencies so that funds may be used flexibly to achieve the desired outcomes for individuals.

Three major federal support systems for adults form a potential basis for providing community services: 1) Title XIX of the Social Security Act Amendments (PL 89-97, 1965), which authorized Medicaid; 2) Supplemental Security Income (SSI) (PL 92-603, 1972); and 3) the Vocational Rehabilitation program as authorized in the Rehabilitation Act (PL 93-112, 1973). Currently, Title XIX provides a major source of support for long-term care. While some states have used Title XIX options to create small living arrangements in the community, the law contains a bias towards large institutional care. Advocacy for policy development related to Title XIX focuses on expanding the flexibility of funds to support community living and the elimination of the bias toward funding for institutional care. Medicaid funds provide waivers for a range of services that can be provided in the community. The primary focus of the Medicaid reform legislation proposed in the late 1980s has been to broaden the range of services that can be paid for with Medicaid funds. By redirecting federal reimbursements from institutional services to community services, it would be possible to provide a stable and continuing source of funds for community programs and to allow individuals and families to choose those services most needed. The Medicaid reform legislation, introduced as the Community and Family Living Amendments in 1983 by Senator John Chafee (R.-RI), would limit the funds available for institutional services and provide for the redirection of these funds toward community-based services.

SSI benefits are an important part of funding for community services for a growing number of individuals who are living in community-based residences. Individuals who have disabilities and meet a requirement for income and resources and a requirement of severity (i.e., being unable to participate in substantial gainful activity [SGA]) that has lasted or is expected to last at least 12 months or result in death, are eligible for cash benefits. Medicaid benefits are tied to SSI eligibility.

An individual is considered to be participating in a substantial gainful activity if there is an earning of $500 or more. This figure was raised in January, 1990 from an unacceptably low level of $300. There is likely to be a push to secure an SGA level that is equitable with the $780 (1990) applicable to individuals with blindness, with the accompanying annual increases tied to the consumer price index.

If an individual meets the eligibility requirements based on severity of disability but is earning $500 or more, SSI benefits generally are not available. Fortunately, for individuals who are already on SSI, the 100th Congress adopted provisions in Section 1619 of the Social Security Act that allow an individual to earn above the SGA and still receive cash and medical benefits. There is a gradual reduction of the cash benefits as the income increases. Eligibility for medical benefits, in many cases, continues beyond the break even point for earnings that terminate the cash benefit. Section 1619 provisions have removed work disincentives for individuals who are benefitting from SSI, but no similar protections are available for individuals with severe disabilities who are instead eligible for cash benefits through Social Security Disability Insurance (SSDI) based on the Social Security work record of a parent who has retired, become disabled, or died. Policy makers are seeking access to Section 1619 protections for these individuals.

The Rehabilitation Act provides for vocational services for persons with disabilities. Under the current authorization, which expires at the end of the 1991 fiscal year, states are required to establish a priority for rehabilitation services for individuals with severe disabilities. In most states, the implementation of that priority has been difficult because programs and personnel trained to work with individuals with severe disabilities are limited. Although model programs have demonstrated that individuals with severe disabilities can be employed through supported work arrangements, unfortunately, many states have chosen to use their limited resources to serve persons with lesser disabilities first, as a means of extending funds to serve as many people as possible.

Taken together, the development of specific policies related to each of these three support systems will determine the extent to which stable, flexible, long-term appropriate programs for persons with severe disabilities will be developed in community settings. Unless stability of funding is ensured, it will be difficult to establish programs; to train personnel in the specific skills needed for these programs; and to develop standards for personnel performance in the critical areas of service, including supported work and supported living. Although there is continuing discussion regarding the specific skills needed by support personnel working in community settings (see, for example, Chapter 10 by Julie Ann Racino and Chapter 11 by Paul Sale in this volume), current policy development is focused on securing basic funding to establish community services and to allow persons with disabilities full access to generic community services. Unlike the legislation affecting school-age persons (which is largely anchored in PL 94-142 and its subsequent amendments), legislation for community services is dispersed across several different legislative mandates and is affected by funding regulations in several different federal agencies. And, since many of the regulations affecting community services for persons with severe disabilities have an impact on other persons with disabilities, changing regulations is unusually complex.

LIMITED FUNDING FOR PROGRAMS FOR PERSONS WITH DISABILITIES

Working within budgetary constraints is a familiar issue in educational policy-making. However, throughout the 1980s and into the 1990s there has been stringent budgetary context for special education services. At the same time, the numbers of persons being served are increasing. There have been major expansions in the age range for which services are provided, to include infants and toddlers and post-school–age adults. Best practices have stressed innovative supports to individuals with disabilities to provide increased involvement in everyday community life. The numbers of persons who do not have disabilities (e.g., elderly persons and children living in poverty) requiring social services has also increased. As a result, many current policy decisions revolve around the allocation of limited resources to achieve the greatest impact.

Services for persons with severe disabilities are particularly vulnerable during times of budgetary constraint. In general, it costs more to provide the extensive supports required for a person with severe disabilities than it does to provide support for persons with lesser or no disabilities. And, while the costs of providing educational and community services for persons with disabilities are far less than the provision of institutional care for these individuals, the relative costs, when compared to services for other individuals, are still high. A complex policy-making environment has resulted. In this environment, advocates for persons with disabilities sometimes must compete with each other for limited funds. There is considerable pressure to earmark funds for specific programs and to write legislation that clearly delimits the use of funding. While the pressures are understandable in times of limited resources, they may mitigate against the design of flexible programs to serve persons with a range of disabilities in individualized, appropriate ways. Policy-making in such an environment is a process of carefully negotiated compromises with long-term implications for the development of services. A specific outcome of policy-making during periods of budgetary constraint is the likelihood of underfunding of the personnel preparation required to support new programs.

SEVERE DISABILITY POLICY AGENDA FOR THE 1990S

There are five major areas of activity expected for policy of the 1990s affecting individuals with severe disabilities:

Education—Early Intervention

To address early intervention, Part H was incorporated into PL 99-457, the Education of the Handicapped Act Amendments of 1986 (which amended PL 94-142, the Education for All Handicapped Children Act, 1975 [EHA]). PL 99–457 provided start-up and implementation authority through 1991. Thus, the 1990s will begin with a very careful examination of these programs. Advocates and policy makers together will address such issues as level of funding for state implementation, interagency collaboration, family protections, least restrictive environment, procedural safeguards, and a professional understanding of case management. Legislative review likely will take up most of 1990 and 1991, with final reauthorization occurring late in fiscal year 1991.

Education—EHA Discretionary Programs

At the close of 1989, Parts C through G of the EHA, the discretionary programs, were under a 1-year emergency extension. The statutory authority under the act expired on September 30, 1989, and, as Congress had not yet completed the reauthorization, the automatic 1-year extension provided for all federal education programs under the GEPA (General Education Provisions Act) went into effect. Congress is expected to complete reauthorization in early to mid-1990. The programs will be up for review again in 3–5 years, depending on the length of the authority ultimately provided for in the 1990 reauthorization. This action, of course, provides the authority, direction, and leadership for the personnel preparation programs in the Office of Special Education Programs (OSEP), as well as research, demonstration, and other discretionary programs funded by OSEP.

Education Reform

The educational reform movement will dominate the general educational scene at least through the beginning of the 1990s, most likely focusing in Washington, D.C. on the redefinition of federal versus state responsibility. Deregulation will likely be a major reform issue; the question for special education concerns what that will mean for PL 94-142 funding and guarantees.

Medicaid Reform

Programmatic and attitudinal barriers to successful community living for people with severe disabilities are fast being removed state by state. As this occurs the major drawback to community services will be the federal funding stream, which is primarily directed to the ICF/MR (intermediate care facility for the mentally retarded). Advocates for reform are optimistic that substantial reform will occur in the 1990s, but no matter when this occurs, there will be a "tinkering" with regulations, refinements, and so forth, well into the 1990s.

Employment: Supported Employment

In 1986 the Rehabilitation Act (PL 93-112, 1973) was amended to include supported employment services as an integral part of the rehabilitation system. By definition, these services are to serve individuals who have the more severe disabilities. Data at the close of 1989 indicated that only a small percentage of these individuals were yet being served. The reasons for the low numbers most certainly will be explored during the reauthorization of the Rehabilitation Act that will occur in 1991. There is emerging consensus that major changes to the law are not necessary and likely will not be pursued during the 1991 activities. The 1991 focus probably will be on implementation refinements.

POLICY-MAKING AND BEST PRACTICES

The gap between best practices and current or even proposed policies often is apparent in the development of legislative and regulatory policy. Special education is a dynamic field in which changes in best practices are frequent. At the same time, the variability in quality of services and current practice is considerable. In the time required to ensure that a best practice becomes part of a set of regulations or is reflected in funding priorities, that practice will evolve beyond the parameters of the policy. And, at the same time, the expertise and resources required to implement the practice will not yet be accessible for many local agencies. The resulting tension between policy makers and leading practitioners and researchers frequently challenges even the most astute advocate to generate acceptable compromises that are innovative and encouraging of best practices, logistically possible, and fiscally feasible. Thus, the particular challenge in making policy related to services for persons with severe disabilities is to embody current best practices while retaining sufficient flexibility to encourage and support progressive participation by agencies and communities at various points in developing their services. Issues related to least restrictive environment and to the development of community services for adults are excellent examples of areas in which policy-making has lagged behind exemplary practice, and innovative legislation to improve policy has been difficult to achieve.

A key element in ensuring that current policy reflects best practices in the field is the specific provision for continuing personnel preparation. When systems are developed to support tranference of research and knowledge of exemplary practice to practitioners, implementation is more likely to keep pace with developments in the field than when few or no provisions for ongoing training are provided. Thus, specific policies related to personnel preparation must be included if any innovation in special education is to be implemented through the development of state or federal policies.

REFERENCES

Biklen, D. (1985). *Achieving the complete school*. New York and London: Teachers College Press.

Brown, L., Ford, A., Nisbet, J., Sweet, M., Donnilhan, A., & Gruenewald, L. (1983). Opportunities available when severely handicapped students attend age appropriate regular schools. *Journal of The Association for Persons with Severe Handicaps. 8*(1), 16–24.

Education for All Handicapped Children Act, PL 94-142, Sec. 612(5)(B).

Fuchs, D., & Fuchs, L. S. Evaluation of the adaptive learning environments model. *Exceptional Children, 55*(2), 115–127.

Lipsky, D., & Gartner, A. (1987). Beyond special education: Toward a quality system for all students. *Harvard Educational Review, 57*, 367–395.

Reynolds, M., Wang, M., & Walberg, H. (1987). The necessary restructuring of special and regular education. *Exceptional Children, 53*(5), 391–397.

Sailor, W., Anderson, J., Halvorsen, A., Doering, K., Filler, J., & Goetz, L. (1989). *The comprehensive local school: Regular education for all students with disabilities*. Baltimore: Paul H. Brookes Publishing Co.

17

National Needs and Resources

A Commentary

Steven F. Warren

Taken together, the preceding chapters provide an overview of the resources presently committed to personnel preparation for individuals with severely disabling conditions, and the challenges we face in using these resources effectively. The picture of personnel preparation presented is a mix of positive trends and perplexing problems. We are left with many questions, including some with a disheartening ring. For example, we must ask ourselves: If we have such a comprehensive system of support for personnel preparation and models for innovative training programs, why are we not making more progress?

What are we doing right? What are the *real* problems? How can we improve our personnel preparation efforts and effectiveness? These are key questions. The purpose of this chapter is to note some of the things that are working well, to discuss three major problems, and to offer some suggestions as to how we might make further progress.

The preceding chapters offer some good news. The positive trends described provide the basis for efforts to resolve the problems we face. They symbolize the commitment of the field, as represented by landmark

Preparation of this chapter was supported in part by a grant titled, "An Ecologically Oriented Educational Model for Children with Deaf-Blindness," through the United States Department of Education, #G00860417. However, the information and opinions expressed within are solely those of the author, and no official endorsement should be inferred.

legislation such as PL 94-142 (the Education for All Handicapped Children Act, 1975) and other laws, to provide effective education for individuals with disabling conditions. Four positive trends identified in the preceding chapters merit specific comment.

First, the Office of Special Education Programs (OSEP) is clearly attempting to be responsive to the personnel preparation needs of the field, as evidenced in Chapter 2. Through their discretionary training grant programs, there are clear indications that OSEP is targeting resources in a flexible manner with the intent of meeting both the general and the specific needs of the field. Grant application guidelines require a strong statement of need and a well-developed training plan. This is one of several indications of OSEP's efforts to influence the quality of personnel preparation efforts. Other attempts, most notably the establishment of a major research institute on personnel preparation at the University of North Carolina and several modifications to strengthen the grants review process, provide further evidence of OSEP's responsiveness and concern.

Second, the federal government is attempting to support a *comprehensive* system of personnel preparation, as discussed in Chapters 2, 3, and 4, which provide an overview of federal training funds provided through various agencies and authorizing legislation.

Third, advances by the field in developing effective best practices have been remarkable during the 1970s and 1980s, as noted in Chapters 11, 12, and 14. As a result, we have many effective procedures well worth the effort to prepare personnel to use. Attempts to develop effective, functional, appropriate practices are far from complete, as noted in Chapter 1. Nevertheless, we have come a long way toward developing effective personnel preparation strategies.

Fourth, there is an awareness of the problems that the field faces in personnel preparation at virtually all levels. This is demonstrated by the very fact that this book has been published and by many related activities that have occurred and are occurring.

POOR DATA

The data base on numbers of children with severe and multiple disabilities is inaccurate and misleading. An example of this problem was provided by Fredericks and Baldwin (1987). They presented some astonishing data on the numbers of children with multisensory impairments reported by various state governments for the 1985–1986 reporting year. They noted that while Maine and Oregon have almost the same number of residents, Maine reported only 9 children who were both deaf and blind, while Oregon reported 89 children with both disabilities. Populous Indiana reported 20 such children, while sparsely populated South Dakota reported 56. The megastate of

California reported 318 children who were deaf and blind, 8 less than sparsely populated Oklahoma. Fredericks and Baldwin argue that the reason for these unlikely discrepancies has to do with varying state policies and population definitions. We may assume that these discrepancies are also present in state counts of students with other severely disabling conditions. If it is unknown how many students need to be served, how can we determine the number of teachers that are needed?

There are some interesting paradoxes in this situation. Applicants for personnel preparation training grants are required by OSEP to clearly establish the need for such funds in their locale. Yet, these need statements must be based on an obviously flawed data base. Furthermore, a field that has strongly argued for data-based decision-making in the classroom, may be unable to make reliable data-based decisions beyond the classroom.

Obviously we will remain unable to determine the number of students with severe and multiple disabilities on a nationwide basis until there are identical definitional and counting procedures in use (Fredericks & Baldwin, 1987). We do not need more data, we need better, more accurate data. This is the simplest, most straightforward problem we face. However, until it is solved, we will be unable either to plan effectively or fully evaluate the effects of our efforts to address personnel shortages.

BURNOUT

Burnout and turnover occur in every profession, but Howe and his colleagues (Howe, Thomas, & Bowen, 1987) reported some particularly disturbing data:

> Despite the fact that 10 times as many teachers were hired for children with severe handicaps in 1984–85 as were employed in 1974–75, the attrition rate for these personnel is 30% compared to 6% for all teachers and 12% for special education teachers. . . . The total number of degrees awarded for special education appears to be dropping rapidly. The Association for School, College, and University Staffing reports that the areas of greatest shortage are in multihandicapped, mental retardation, and learning disabilities. . . . (p. 3)

These data show that a severe shortage of qualified teachers for students with severe disabilities is developing. With fewer students seeking preservice training and with such a high turnover rate, it is necessary to both train more teachers and find some way to decrease the attrition rate. Barring extra pay for special education teachers (the unions would fight this), the best approach may be to enhance the quality of training and support teachers receive. The premise is that a well-trained, well-supported teacher is likely to be an effective teacher. And an effective teacher is more likely to be a satisfied teacher. Finally, a satisfied teacher is, hopefully, more immune to burnout and turnover. Inversely, a poor teacher will be ineffective, quickly burn out, and so forth. Given that children with severe disabilities are very challenging to educate, teachers obviously must be well trained and well supported or they may naturally seek out less challenging students, if not a less challenging career in general.

In addition to insufficient or ineffective training, the high turnover rate may reflect the social and physical isolation many teachers face within their schools. Meaningful social integration needs to be a goal for students with severe disabilities *and* their teachers. Reynolds (1987) noted the trend of teachers within Tennessee schools moving from special to regular education teaching assignments, but points out that the reverse seldom occurs.

The problem of burnout and turnover may be the most complex of the issues we confront. It is the result of a multiplicity of variables. To solve it, or at least to lower the turnover rate to something more acceptable, will necessitate a complex strategy, as well as both hard work and long-term commitment. There is unlikely to be any complete solution. Furthermore, many potential solutions may either have little real impact if instituted, or be resisted actively or passively to such a degree that they could never be fully implemented. For example, simply training more teachers is unlikely to decrease the rate of turnover, and paying higher wages will be strongly resisted on many fronts. However, the combination of providing better training for a modest number of teachers and providing ongoing support for them in the field through a variety of mechanisms, might meet less re-sistance and have more impact. Still, this strategy may be opposed by many as too difficult and nebulous to carry out. But then, burnout and turnover are difficult and nebulous problems (Cherniss, 1980).

TOO MUCH TO DO

Snell (1987) challenges us to further consider the contents of our personnel preparation efforts. She identifies some discrepancies between most cur-rent preservice curriculums, and what many consider to be best practices. Most obvious among these discrepancies are a lack of transdisciplinary training, a lack of emphasis on training personnel to facilitate transitions into and out of the school years for very young children and young adults respec-tively, and our collective failure to translate basic human values into educa-tional approaches. Snell argues that these and other topics need to be addressed in preservice personnel preparation curricula. It is difficult to dismiss her logic. These topics do seem of sufficient importance to be formally represented in preservice curricula. To the extent that they can overlap what is already taught, additional courses, hours, and credits will not be required.

Snell's proposals implicitly raise a more puzzling question. Teachers of students with severe impairments need all the skills that any competent teacher must have plus many specialized techniques necessary to work with low-incidence conditions (e.g., cerebral palsy). How can we train teachers in all the skills they need at even a minimal level of competency within an undergraduate or master's program? This is not a new problem. The growing sophistication and effectiveness of our educational procedures may only increase the gap between what is possible and what typically is practiced unless we modify our training systems accordingly. Preservice training programs are under increasing pressure to produce certified teachers with minimal time and effort. These programs are being squeezed by the economics of higher education, the so-called educational reform movement, and the dynamics of the teacher market economy at the very time when we need both more and better trained teachers. Many deans of schools of education may regard programs to train teachers to work with persons with low-incidence disabilities as expensive and questionable investments. Thus, training faculties are being pressured to "streamline" preservice efforts.

It is highly unlikely that preservice training as presently conceived can meet all the goals set by professionals and certification agencies. Furthermore, the continuing evolution of best practices and the need for ongoing support for special education teachers in the field suggest that, under any conditions, preservice training alone will not be enough. We need a comprehensive, effective, nationwide, in-service training system. There are admittedly many problems with this proposal. Deans of schools of education may not like it any better than they do low-incidence preservice programs. University training faculty may resist it to the extent that it forces them out into the field and away from campus. Furthermore, in-service training efforts have a reputation for being ineffective. Despite these and other problems, there are also some compelling reasons why a nationwide in-service training system deserves serious consideration. First, as noted, it could have an impact on the problems of both turnover and too much to do. Second, there is, in fact, much more knowledge available on how to provide effective in-service training than many realize (e.g., Farris & Fluck, 1985; Fredericks and Templeman, Chapter 15, this volume; Glaser, Abelson, & Garrison, 1983; Neil, 1985; Wade, 1985). Finally, comprehensive, sophisticated, nationwide in-service training is an untried solution. As with any potential solution, the best way to derail it would be to implement it poorly.

THE PROCESS OF CHANGE

The problems we face include insufficient training funds, an inaccurate data base for planning purposes, an increasingly crucial shortage of trained teachers in the field, and too much to do within our present training system. Clearly, reform and change are needed.

It is widely recognized that the process of change often is threatening and painful for both individuals and the institutions with which they are connected. Thus, it is not surprising that change usually is resisted through both active and passive means. Fortunately, the process of change can be managed to some extent. There are both many ways in which it can be purposefully slowed and other ways in which it can be facilitated. To solve the problems of insufficient funds, poor data, burnout, and too much to do, we need to become experts in some new technologies. Foremost among these is the technology of systems change (Glaser et al., 1983).

There are several well-established principles of systems change. These principles may be intuitively understood by many in the field, but they are not broadly recognized or practiced. Yet, as we have come to understand how to change behavior on an individual or small group scale, our inability to manage the change process on the institutional or societal level has become an obvious limitation. Hopkins (1987) has noted that in spite of many examples of effective educational and therapeutic models, the majority of the innovative developments in the field of applied behavior analysis over the years have not resulted in systemic change, and this is precisely because we have failed to understand how to make and maintain innovations in large systems. Likewise, we may have some good ideas on how to solve the problems discussed above, but only vague ideas about how to make these innovations on a large-scale level. Until we attack these problems within a broadly conceived macrosystems change approach, we are unlikely to make much headway.

In the 1990s, as the field moves toward the year 2000, the enormous progress we have made in the 1960s–1980s may abate unless we can develop solutions to many of the insidious, more systemic problems we face. The preceding chapters provide some of the background necessary to understand the strengths and problems of a key area of special education—our system of personnel preparation as it relates to individuals with severe disabilities. Based on this understanding, we need to begin the task of devising workable and effective solutions to the problems.

REFERENCES

Braddock, D. (1987). *Federal policy toward mental retardation and developmental disabilities.* Baltimore: Paul H. Brookes Publishing Co.

Cherniss, C. (1980). *Staff burnout.* Beverly Hills: Sage Publications.

Farris, P., & Fluck, R. (1985). Effective staff development through individualized inservice. *Association of Teacher Education, 7*(4), 23–28.

Fredericks, H.D.B., & Baldwin, V.L. (1987). Individuals with sensory impairments: Who are they? How are they educated? In L. Goetz, D. Guess, & K. Stremel-Campbell (Eds.). *Innovative program design for individuals with dual sensory impairments* (pp. 3–14). Baltimore: Paul H. Brookes Publishing Co.

Glaser, E.M., Abelson, H., & Garrison, K. (1983). *Putting knowledge to use.* San Francisco: Jossey-Bass.

Hopkins, B.L. (1987). Comments on the future of applied behavior analysis. *Journal of Applied Behavior Analysis, 20,* 339–346.

Howe, N.H., Thomas, A., & Bowen, M. (1987, October). *Current personnel needs: The national data base.* Paper presented at the Conference Preparing Personnel to Work with Persons Who Are Severely Handicapped. Nashville.

Neil, R. (1985). In-service teacher education: Five common causes of failure. *Actions in Teacher Education, 7*(3), 49–55.

Reynolds, J. (1987, October). *Perspectives from the States.* Paper presented at the Conference Preparing Personnel to Work with Persons Who Are Severely Handicapped. Nashville.

Snell, M.E. (1987). *Systematic instruction of persons with severe handicaps.* Columbus: Charles E. Merrill.

Wade, R.N. (1985). What makes a difference in in-service teacher education? A meta-analysis of research. *Educational Leadership, 42*(4), 48–54.

Index

Abuse, treatment as, 182–184
Actualization of Mainstream Experi-
    ence Skills Project, *see* Pro-
    ject A.M.E.S.
Adaptive functioning, 154–155
Adult education, professionalization in,
    219–220
Adults
    community living arrangements, sup-
        port for, 206–208, 212–213
    preparation of personnel serving,
        14–16
    services for
        demand for, 322
        expansion of, 322
        personnel shortages in, 302
        policy and practice related to, 320,
            322–325
        staff turnover in, 15
        state regulation of, 15
Advocacy
    activities, of students in applied re-
        search model, 260
    professional, 19
    see also Case management
Age-based service delivery, problems
    deriving from, 10–11, 16–17,
    301–302
American Society for College and Uni-
    versity Staffing, demand data
    for teaching fields, 41–43
Appropriations, legislation for, 50
Assistive technology programs, per-
    sonnel preparation for,
    federal funding for, 29–30
Association for Behavior Analysis
    (ABA), position paper on
    rights of clients with develop-
    mental disabilities, 20
Association for Retarded Citizens
    (ARC), 297
Authorizing legislation, 50

Aversive treatment
    as abuse, 182–184
    misuse of, 187–188
    spread effect, 183

Behavior, excess
    meaningful programs for, 185
    physiological causes of, 186
    teachers and, 191–192
    understanding, 185–186
Behavior modification, 181–182
    as abuse, 183
    outcome evaluation in, 188
    personnel preparation in, 188
    evaluation of, 198–199
    limitations of, 188–191
Behavioral disorders and problems
    descriptive information about, 195
    interventions for
        elements of successful programs,
            194–195
        integration of, 193–197
        legal rights and ethical guidelines
            in, 196
        training in, 193–197
    personnel serving
        collaborative interdisciplinary train-
            ing for, 191–193
        shortfall of, 40
    prevention, 184–185, 194–195
Best practices, 9–10
    educational, 162
    policy-making and, 327–328
    progress in, 319, 330
Budgetary constraints, 325, *see also*
    Funding
Budget resolution legislation, 50
Bureau of Education for the
    Handicapped
    in-service training grant, 273
    teacher competency grants, 272

Bureau of Elementary and Secondary Education, Division of Personnel Training, 77–78
Burnout, among personnel serving those with severe disabilities, 92, 331–332

Case management, 19–20
in early intervention, 115
by teachers, 82
Census data, in needs analysis, 39
Certification, *see* Teachers, certification
Change, process of, 333–334
Child abuse, 182–183
Collaborative planning, for personnel preparation, 3, 88, 104–106
in community intensive model of instruction, 274, 280
in early intervention, 130–131
Communication, 191
in print, in Iowa model, 298
Community, collaboration with, 3
Community-based programs, 3
federal funding for, 323–324
legislation regarding, 324–325
policy and practice related to, 320, 322–325
preparation of personnel to work in, 203–220
Community intensive model of instruction, personnel preparation for, 271–287
advisory council for, 275
community and consumer impact of, 274–276
community intensive (CI) task force, 275
curriculum content, 273
revisions of, 276–279
demonstration sites, 274–275
evaluation of, 279–285
federal funding for, 273
graduate survey, 276
history of, 271–274
IEP evaluation procedures in, 282
IEP objectives in, 280–282
instructional techniques for, 277–278
integration in, 279
observational evaluation data in, 282–285

ongoing family/school interaction in, 278
outcome data, 284
practicum experience in, 274–275
evaluation of, 275–276
practicum experiences in, 273
program philosophy for, 277
site development strategies in, 279
supervisor committee, 275
Community living
for adults, support for, 206–208, 212–213
and challenges of everyday living, 213–214
for children and families, support for, 205–206, 212
collaborative programs for, 215
dilemmas in, 215–217
and home ownership, 207
new directions in, 203–205
people-oriented approach to, 210–212
preparation of personnel to work in, 203–220
future of, 219–220
knowledge base for, 208–218
and promotion of quality lives, strategies for, 210–214
values and commitment underlying, 208–210
see also Residential services
Competency, 333
evaluation of, 285
Complex health care needs, students with, *see* Medically fragile students
Comprehensive System of Personnel Development (CSPD)
and early intervention, 116, 124, 127–128
and needs data, 33, 41, 103
requirements for, 112
The Condition of Education, as needs data source, 41
Cooperative IHE-SEA-LEA arrangements, 98–100
in early intervention, 130–131
Council for Exceptional Children (CEC), Division of Mental Retardation, in Iowa, 297

Curriculum trends, in services for students with severe disabilities, 81

Daily activities
  functional sensorimotor approach to, 165
  mobility component, 165
  positioning component, 165
Data
  deficiencies in, 330–331
  on numbers of children with disabilities, 330
Deaf/blindness
  number of special education teachers employed and needed to serve children with, 37
  percentage of school enrollment served as students with, 35
  and placement in special education, 11
Deafness
  number of special education teachers employed and needed to serve children with, 36
  percentage of school enrollment served as students with, 35
  see also Deaf/blindness; Hearing impairments
Department of Education, State of Hawaii v. *Dorr*, 139–140
Department of Health and Human Services (DHHS), Division of Maternal and Child Health (MCH), 13
Detsel v. *Ambach*, 140
Digest of Education Statistics, as needs data source, 41
Direct services, 162–164
Direct services staff
  preparation of, 15
  training in behavior modification, 191–193

Early intervention
  case management in, 115
  collaborative commitments to, 130–131
  coordination of services in, 113–114

family focus of, 121
federal policy changes in, 112–113
infants and toddlers served, data on, 118–119
in-service training in, 117, 125, 129–130
interdisciplinary teams for, 113
parent-professional collaboration in, 121–122
personnel
  new roles for, 114–115
  professional growth, 123
  quality, long-range commitments to, 126
  recruitment, 127
  retention strategies, 117
  state certification standards, 117–118, 123–124
  sufficient numbers of, short-term commitments for, 126–127
personnel needs in, 112, 115–120
  determination of, 118–119
  future projections of, 119–120
  meeting, 111–131
personnel preparation
  comprehensive programs for, 125–131
  federal funding for, 26–27
  instructional modules used for, 130
  programs in institutions of higher education, 116–117
  responsibilities for, 124–125
  training for recent program graduates, 130
personnel shortages, 80, 117, 119
policy agenda for future, 326
preservice training in, 126
professional roles and competencies in, 121–123
professional standards in, 123–124
programs, and infant development, 122–123
quality service delivery, 130–131
  ensuring, 120–123
service delivery models, 111–112
  changes in, 112–113
team collaboration in, 122
Ecological inventory approach, in intervention with severe and profound handicaps, 166–168

Educational system
  evaluation of, 321–322
  models for, 321
  reform of, 12, 321–322, 326
Education and Consolidation Improve-
    ment Act, 1965, 53
Education for All Handicapped Children
    Act (PL 94-142), 11, 15, 53,
    91, 128–129, 161, 289–290,
    293, 320
  discretionary programs, policy agen-
    da for, 326
  and medical versus related services,
    140
  Part B, 113, 118, 128
  Part D program, *see* Part D program
  Part H (Program for Infants and
    Toddlers with Handicaps),
    112–113, 116, 119, 125,
    128
  see also Least restrictive environ-
    ment (LRE)
Education of the Handicapped Act (PL
    91-230), 52
  Amendments of 1986 (PL 99-457),
    12–13, 15, 19, 21, 25, 32,
    112
    Part D, 25
    physical and occupational therapy
      mandated by, 161–162
    Section 631, *see* Section 631
    Section 632, *see* Section 632
    teacher certification requirements,
      13–14
  implementation of, annual reports to
    Congress on, as data source,
    40
  Section 624, 53
EHA, *see* Education for All Hand-
    icapped Children Act
Elementary and Secondary Education
    Act Amendments (PL 89-313,
    1965), 118
Elementary and Secondary Education
    Act Amendments (PL 89-750,
    1966), 76–77
  Title VI (of Elementary and Second-
    ary Education Act Amend-
    ments, 1966), 76–77
Emotional disturbance
  number of special education teachers
    employed and needed to
    serve children with, 36

percentage of school enrollment
    served as students with, 35
Employment specialists, 228
Environment
  and behavioral interventions, 184
  in intervention with severe and pro-
    found handicaps, 166
  ordinary, with extraordinary sup-
    ports, 160
  see also Least restrictive environ-
    ment (LRE)
Everyday life, helping people to
    meet the challenges of, per-
    sonnel preparation for, 213–
    214

Families
  with at-risk infants or toddlers, ser-
    vices to, 113
  as focus of early intervention,
    120–121
    see also Individualized family ser-
      vice plan (IFSP)
  and service system, 16
  support for, 205–206, 212
  training in strategies for behavior
    change, 193–197
Federal policy
  and early intervention personnel
    preparation, 124–125
  and personnel preparation, 47–73,
    330
  in special education, 75
  see also Public policy; Regulations,
    federal
Federal policy-making, 48–52
Federal Register, 51–52
Funding
  limitations on, 325
  policy and practice related to, 320,
    323–325

Graduate education
  applied research model, 244–269
  approaches to, 84
  demographics of students enrolling
    in, 84
  leave program for, 98
Graduate fellowships, federal funding
    for, 76–78
Guess, Doug, 272

Handicapped Children's Early Education Program (HCEEP), 94
Head Start, teachers, certification requirements, 13
Hearing impairments
number of special education teachers
employed and needed to
serve children with, 36
percentage of school enrollment
served as students with, 35
personnel shortfall for, 39
*Higher Education General Information
Survey*, as needs data source,
41
Home ownership, 207

Independence, versus interdependence, 159–160
Indirect services, 163–164
Individualized education program, in
community intensive model of
instruction, 280–282
Individualized family service plan, 19,
120
requirements for, 112–114
Infants
development
assessment of, 122–123
and early intervention programming, 122–123
educational programs for, division of
responsibility for, 13
medically fragile, services for, personnel preparation for, 28
physical and occupational therapy
mandated for, 161–162
preparation of personnel serving,
12–14
federal funding for, 27
programs for, locations of, 14
at risk, 113
speech/language pathologists for,
preparation of, federal funding
for, 29
see also Early intervention
In re Bevin H., 140
In-service training, 4, 301–317, 333
design of objectives, 309
design of training activities, 309–315
for direct care personnel, 16
in early intervention, 117, 125,
129–130

evaluation of, 284–285, 303–304,
314–315
federal funding for, 88
funding of, 83–84, 303
generic model of, 303–315
identification of training competencies in, 309
identification of training needs in,
308–309
in Iowa, 292
need for, 302–303
practica-based, 314
presentation formats for, 314–315
program change, 308
recommendations for, 316–317
research about, need for, 316
site location for, 309–314
trainee skills or knowledge acquired
in, 306
child behavior changes resulting
from, 307
implementation of, 306–307
trainee satisfaction with, 304–306
Institutions of higher education (IHE)
collaboration in community intensive
model of instruction, 274,
280
contracts with, to provide training
programs, 105
cooperative agreements with LEAs
and SEAs, 98
early intervention training programs,
116–117, 129
faculty, support for, 95–97, 102–103
grants to, 76–78
and in-service training, 83–84
low-enrollment programs
arguments for support of,
101–103
duplicative, disposition of,
107–108
in meeting critical personnel needs,
103
personnel preparation programs,
versus income generation
concerns, 91, 333
programs to prepare special education teachers
arguments for support of,
101–103
collaborative, 104–106
contexts influencing, 106–108
economic context of, 106–107

Institutions of higher education
  programs to prepare special educa-
      tion teachers—*continued*
    external funding awards, 102
    federal funding of, 93–96
    geographic context of, 107
    impact of, 103
    quality of, 102
    ratio of common core courses to
        specialty courses, 101–102
    resource allocation
      and program enrollments, 101
      qualitative arguments for, 102
      university and extra-university
          contexts for, 106–108
    students
      financial support for, 94–95
      IHE-funded support for, 100–101
      support for, 102–103
Integration
  barriers to, 321
  into community, 154
  in Iowa project, 293–296
  principle of, 293
  of school programs, 9–10, 155–156
    leadership personnel training,
        federal funding for, 30
  of special education teachers, 332
  unresolved issues related to,
      298–299
Intensive special educators, prepara-
    tion of, federal funding for, 28
Interagency Coordinating Council
    (ICC), in early intervention
    personnel preparation,
    124–125, 128
Interdependence, versus indepen-
    dence, 159–160
Interdisciplinary training
  collaborative planning for, 3
  federal funding for, 28
  university-based, 17–19
Internships
  cooperative IHE-SEA-LEA arrange-
      ments for, 99
  student, state funding of, 97–98
Iowa
  programming in least restrictive en-
      vironments in, 293–295
  segregated schools in, number of,
      294

services for students with severe
    disabilities, history of,
    290–292
statewide conference on special edu-
    cation and support services,
    292
Iowa model of personnel preparation,
    289–299, *see also* Project
    A.M.E.S.
  background of, 289–290
  unresolved issues and, 298–299
Iowa News, 298

Job coaches, 228
Joint Dissemination and Review Panel
    (JDRP), 304

Koop, C. Everett, 135–136

Leadership personnel, preparation
  federal funding for, 26, 30, 76
  needs data for, 86
Learning disability
  number of special education teachers
      employed and needed to
      serve children with, 36
  percentage of school enrollment
      served as students with, 35
Least restrictive environment (LRE),
    163–164, 206, 273
  Iowa's programming in, 293–295
  placements in, 11
  policy and practice related to,
      320–322
  principle of, 12, 293–294
  for students with complex health
      care needs, 139
  unresolved issues related to,
      298–299
Legislation
  provisions for personnel preparation,
      52–72, 75–76
  types of, 50
Legislative process, 48–49
  committee system, 50–51
Local education agencies
  collaboration in community intensive
      model of instruction, 274, 280

cooperative agreements with IHEs, 98
student financial support, 95
Low-incidence handicaps, preparation of personnel serving
federal funding for, 26–27, 30, 85
and funding priorities, 333

Master's level training, 4, 247–252, 256, 260
federal funding for, 28
Maurer, Steve, 290–291
Medicaid, 68, 323
reform of, 323, 326–327
Medical model, versus educational model, 162
Medical services, definition of, 140
Medically fragile students
comprehensive care for, elements of, 142–144
definition and characteristics of, 136–137
educational service delivery to, 138–140
personnel issues, 140–149
needs of, 138
numbers of, in schools, 137–138
personnel serving, 141
need for, 142
trainees, 142–144
placement issues related to, 139–140
preparation of personnel serving, 135–149
family focus in, 147
training content and nature, 144–149
training/resource materials for, 147–148, 151
Mental retardation
number of special education teachers employed and needed to serve children with, 36
percentage of school enrollment served as students with, 35
personnel shortfall for, 39
and placement in special education, 11
preparation of personnel serving programs related to, federal funding for, 64–67, 75, 78

Mobility, in daily activities, 165
Model schools, for in-service training, 88
Monitoring, 163
Multihandicaps
data on children with, deficiencies in, 330–331
number of special education teachers employed and needed to serve children with, 36
percentage of school enrollment served as students with, 35
personnel serving, shortage of, 80
and placement in special education, 11

National Clearinghouse for Professions in Special Education, as data source, 40
National Institute for Child Health and Human Development (NICHD), grants, 95
National Institute of Mental Health (NIMH), research and training funding, 95
National Institute on Disability and Rehabilitation Research (NIDRR), 53
National Institutes of Health (NIH), grants, 95
Needs analysis, in grant applications, 32–44
requirements for new applicants, 34–44
Needs data, 85
in decision making about training priorities, 33
in early intervention systems, 118–119, 126
gaps in, 33
lack of, 331
for leadership training, 86
Nonaversive interventions, 3
collaborative interdisciplinary model for, 192–193
personnel preparation for use of, 181–199
Notice of Proposed Rulemaking (NPRM), 51

Occupational therapists, 153–175
  areas of expertise, 164–168
  collaborative teamwork by, 168–171
  critical areas of knowledge and skill
      acquisition for, 156–171
  interdisciplinary training for,
      173–174
  models of service provision for,
      162–164
  practice in educational settings,
      161–164
    continuing education for, 172
    graduate training for, 172–173
    guidelines for, 174
    in-service training, 172
    knowledge and skill acquisition for,
        171–175
    preservice training, 171
    recruitment, 171–172
    roles of, 114
    service delivery models for, 154
    shortage of, 80
    special competencies of, 168
    therapeutic interventions by, frame-
        work for, 155–156
Office of Education, Section on Excep-
    tional Children and Youth, 77
Office of Educational Research and Im-
    provement (OERI), grants,
    95
Office of Special Education and Re-
    habilitative Services
    (OSERS), 14
  collaboration with LEAs and IHEs,
      274, 280
  Division of Personnel Preparation
      (DPP), 25
Office of Special Education Programs
    (OSEP), 13
  Division of Innovation and Develop-
      ment, 40
  Division of Special Education Pro-
      grams, 96
  grants
    for personnel training, 54–59
    to state education agencies, 59
  program funding by, 94, 326
  standards, in special education per-
      sonnel preparation, 31–32
  support for personnel preparation,
      330

Office of Technology Assessment, esti-
    mates of technology-
    dependent child population,
    135–138
Orthopedic handicaps
  number of special education teachers
      employed and needed to
      serve children with, 37
  percentage of school enrollment
      served as students with, 35
  and placement in special education,
      11

Parent projects, federal funding for, 27
Part D program, 25, 44, 52
  administration of, 77–80
  commitment to increasing personnel
      supply, 85
  current directions of, 84–89
  legislative history of, 76–77
  priorities of, 84–89
People, similarity of needs of, 159
People-oriented approach, to service
    delivery, 158–159
  in community living, 210–212
Permanency planning, 205
Personnel
  needs, defining, 33
  see also Needs data
  quality of, 80–83
Personnel preparation
  age- and discipline-based, problems
      deriving from, 10–17
  challenges in, 319–320
  federal funding for, 25–44, 47,
      52–72, 76
    direct, 52–69
    discretionary, 53, 70, 326
    indirect, 68–72
    state optional programs, 53–68,
        70–72
  future of, 1–5, 21
  long-term systems for, 4
  as ongoing process, 1
  problems in, 10–17
  as public policy priority, 2–3
  recommendations for, 262–263
  shared training in, 17–19
Personnel preparation programs, eval-
    uation of, 285

Personnel shortages, 331
addressing, in federal grant applications, 32–44
in early intervention, 117, 119
for services to students with severe disabilities, 91–92
in special education, 80
Physical therapists, 153–175
areas of expertise, 164–168
collaborative teamwork by, 168–171
critical areas of knowledge and skill acquisition for, 156–171
interdisciplinary training for, 173–174
models of service provision for, 162–164
practice in educational settings, 161–164
continuing education for, 172
graduate training for, 172–173
guidelines for, 174
in-service training, 172
knowledge and skill acquisition for, 171–175
preservice training, 171
recruitment, 171–172
roles of, 114
service delivery models for, 154
shortage of, 80
special competencies of, 168
therapeutic interventions by, framework for, 155–156
Policies, and best practices, 327–328
see also Politics
Politics
of higher education and personnel preparation, 91–108
and program development, 4–5
see also Public policy
Positioning
in daily activities, 165
personnel preparation for, shared training in, 18–19
Post-doctoral study, in special education, 86
Preservice programs, curricula, 332–333
Preservice training, quality control in, 86–88
Professional staff, preparation of, 15
Professionalization, 219–220

Program Assistance Grants, 79
Program Development Priority Grant, 85–86
Project A.M.E.S., 292–293
Project REACH (Regular Education for All Children with Handicaps), 273–274
Psychologists, preparation for handicapped and at-risk infant/toddler specialization, federal funding for, 28
Public Law 85-926, 75
graduate fellowship program authorized under, 77
Public Law 88-164, 76, 77
Public Law 89-97, *see* Social Security Act Amendments
Public Law 89-313, *see* Elementary and Secondary Education Act Amendments (1965)
Public Law 89-750, *see* Elementary and Secondary Education Act Amendments (1966)
Public Law 91-230, *see* Education of the Handicapped Act
Public Law 92-602, 323
Public Law 93-112, *see* Rehabilitation Act
Public Law 94-142, *see* Education for All Handicapped Children Act
Public Law 98-221, *see* Vocational Rehabilitation Act
Public Law 99-457, *see* Education of the Handicapped Act, Amendments of 1986
Public policy, and personnel preparation, 2–3
see also Federal policy; Politics

Quality control, 86–88
Quality services, 80–83
changing teacher competencies in response to, 285
features of, 9

Recruitment, 84
of early intervention personnel, 127

Recruitment—*continued*
of physical and occupational therapists for work in educational
settings, 171–172
Regulations, federal, 51–52
Rehabilitation Act (PL 93-112), 53
323, 327
Rehabilitation Research and Training
Centers, 53
Rehabilitation services, personnel preparation for, federal funding
for, 58–67
Rehabilitation Services Administration
(RSA), 53
Related services personnel
definition of, 140, 161
grants for, 173
preparation, federal funding for, 26, 28
preparation of, 141–149
Relationship skills, 196
Reports, as needs data resources,
41–44
Requests for Proposals (RFP), 52, 96
Residential services
consumer-directed services, 208
design of services, 217–218
flexible and individualized supports
in, 207–208
future of, 218–220
history of, 217
individual assessment in, 207
individualized planning and funding
for, 207
leadership in, 218
personnel preparation for
future of, 218–220
values in, 208–214
professionalization in, 219–220
responsiveness to individual needs,
218
separation of housing and support
services, 206
social, economic, and political context of, 218
see also Community living
Resources, 329
federal, 52–72
Retraining, 83–84
Role release, 18
Rural areas
personnel shortages in, 92

preparation of personnel serving,
federal funding for, 27, 29

Sailor, Wayne, 271–272
Scheduling, of therapy, 170
School-age persons
preparation of personnel serving,
11–12
programs for, 11–12
Section 631 (of the Education of the
Handicapped Act Amend-
ments), 26–27, 53
application for funding under, 34
priority spending for, 26–27
Section 632 (of the Education of the
Handicapped Act Amend-
ments), 30–31, 53
programs under, federal funding for,
30–31
Segregation, of school programs, interstate variation of, 11
Self-care skills, personnel preparation
for, shared training in, 18–19
Sensory disabilities, personnel shortfall
for, 39
Service delivery, quality issues in,
80–83
Service groupings
inconsistencies across, 16–17
transitions between, 17
Severe and profound handicaps
adaptive functioning with, 154–155
collaborative treatment models, 156
and community living, *see* Community living
definition of, 33–34
education of persons with, personnel
preparation in, applied research model, 243
environmental integration and,
155–156, 160
functional skill development and,
156, 165
integrated therapy for, 155–156
interventions for
adaptive orientation, 166
collaborative teamwork in,
168–171

ecological inventory approach,
166–168
integrated approach to, 168–171
in Iowa, 290–292
merging developmental and
environmental orientations,
166–168
need for, 301–302
policy agenda for future, 325–327
progress in, 301
learning and performance characteristics with, 160
models of service provision for
assumptions underlying, 158–160
changing focus of, 272–273
community intensive model,
271–287
developmental model, 272–273
educational, 161–164
educational best practices, 162
medical versus educational, 162
number of children with, 290
numbers of students with, 33–34,
153–154
personnel serving
attrition among, 92, 331–332
burnout among, 331–332
increasing the supply of, 85–86
retention of, 92
shortage of, 40, 80, 91–92
physical and occupational therapists
serving, training needs of,
158–171
preparation of personnel serving, 301
enrollment of students in programs for, 92
federal funding for, 27–31, 79–80,
93–96
funding programs in IHE for,
92–93
programs serving
curriculum content, 81
placement of services, 81
quality of, 81
service delivery models for,
154–156
state funding for, 96–98
service delivery programs, people
first orientation of, 158–159
Skill generalization and maintenance,
156

Social Security Act Amendments (PL
89-97, Title XIX), 323
Social Security Disability Insurance
(SSDI), 324
Special education
data base, need for, 4
degree awards, decrease in, 40
in Iowa, 289–290
number of students enrolled in,
289–290
personnel
competency of, 80–81
enhancing the quality of, 86–87
shortage of, 80
supply and demand data for, 80
personnel preparation programs
applied research model, 243–269
activity/performance log data,
257
advocacy activities, 260
content areas of, 248–249
description of, 245–251
direct service activities,
257–258
enrollment data, 251–253
enrollment options, 250–251
federal student support in, 254
format for, 245
graduate follow-up data,
255–260
graduate questionnaire, 256–
257
in-service training activities, 258
location of students, 253–254
objectives of, 246–248
positions held by graduates,
255–256
presentations at conferences,
259–260
state student support in,
254–255
summary of, 260–261
thesis and nonthesis research
in, 256
demographics of students enrolling
in, 84
federal funding for, 26, 28, 78
ongoing support for, 332–333
recommendations for, 262–263
placement in, 11–12
policy agenda for future, 326

Special education—*continued*
  policy and practice related to,
      321–322
  versus regular education, 11
  in rural settings, personnel shortfall
      in, 40
  at secondary school level, personnel
      shortfall in, 40
  state-of-the-art practices, and per-
      sonnel preparation, 271–272
  unresolved issues related to,
      298–299
Special Education Instructional Re-
    source Network, 29
Special education teachers
  attrition rate, 40, 331
  employed and needed
      data on, 34–38
      shortage and attrition data, 39–40
  integration of, 332
  turnover of, 331–332
Special health care needs, students
    with, *see* Medically fragile
    students
Special populations, preparation of per-
    sonnel serving, federal fund-
    ing for, 27–28
Special projects, federal funding for,
    27, 29–30
Speech/language impairment
  number of special education teachers
      employed and needed to
      serve children with, 36
  percentage of school enrollment
      served as students with, 35
Speech/language pathologists, prepara-
    tion of, federal funding for, 29
Speech-language pathologists, roles of,
    114
SSI, *see* Supplemental Security Income
Staff development, evaluation of,
    284–285
State education agencies
  cooperative agreements with IHEs,
      98
  federal funding for, 29
  funding of programs in severe dis-
      abilities, 97
  funding of programs to prepare spe-
      cial education teachers, 93

  grants to, 59, 76
  preservice and in-service training
      funds, 31
  and quality preservice training,
      87–88
  student financial support, 95
State funding
  with discretionary federal flow-
      through funds, 96
  for programs in severe disabilities,
      96–98
States
  in early intervention personnel prep-
      aration, 124–125
  early intervention programs,
      115–116
Substantial gainful activity (SGA), defi-
    nition of, 323–324
Supplemental Security Income (SSI),
    323–324
Supported employment programs, 154
  components of, 227–228
  consumer groups, variation in,
      231–232
  expansion of, 228–229
  interagency collaboration for, 235
  managers, 229
  need for personnel in, 228–229
  personnel preparation for, 53,
      227–238
    criteria for effective training, 236,
        238
    curricula for, 232–234, 238
    expansion of, 238
    federal funding for, 62–65
    field-based instruction in, 234
    future directions of, 236–238
    strategies for, 234–236
    trainers for, 235
    training formats for, 235–236, 238
    unresolved issues in, 236–238
  policy agenda for future, 327
  staff
    credentialing of, 237
    general duties of, 230–231
    professional standards for, 15–16
    role definition, 229–232, 237
    salaries of, 15–16
Supported Employment Telecourse
    Network, 236

Surveys, as needs data resources, 41–44
Systems change, principles of, 334

TASH, *see* The Association for Persons with Severe Handicaps
Task Force on Children with Special Health Care Needs, 135–146
Tatro v. *Texas*, 140
Teachers
  as case managers, 82
  certification
    in area of profound impairments, 30
    policy and practice related to, in Iowa, 296–297
    programs leading to, state funding for, 97
    provisional, 83
    requirements
      in federal programs serving young children, 13
      as quality control measure, 82–83
  demand for, by teaching area and year, 42–43
  preparation of, 12
  shortage and attrition data for, 39–40, 331
    by specialty, 39
  training in behavior modification, 191–193
  turnover of, 331–332
Teaching Research Infant and Child Center, Monmouth, Oregon, in-service training program, 303–304
Team approach, to intervention with severe and profound disability, 168–171
Technical assistance, in Iowa, 292
Technology, *see also* Assistive technology programs
Technology-dependent students
  comprehensive care for, elements of, 142–144
  definition and characteristics of, 136–137
  educational service delivery to, 138–140
  personnel issues, 140–149
  needs of, 138
  numbers of, in schools, 137–138
  personnel serving, 141
    need for, 142
  placement issues related to, 139–140
  preparation of personnel serving, 135–149
    family focus in, 147
    training content and nature, 144–149
    training/resource materials for, 147–148, 151
Telecommunication network to provide coursework, state-sponsored, 104–105
The Association for Persons with Severe Handicaps
  Critical Issues Subcommittee, 135
  in Iowa, 297
  Related Services Subcommittee, position statement of, 173–174
  resolution on aversive therapy, 182
  survey of related services personnel, 158
Title XIX, 323
Toddlers
  educational programs for, division of responsibility for, 13
  physical and occupational therapy mandated for, 161–162
  preparation of personnel serving, 12–14
    federal funding for, 27
  programs for, locations of, 14
  at risk, 113
  speech/language pathologists for, preparation of, federal funding for, 29
  see also Early intervention
Training programs
  selection of, 84
  standards for, 87
Transdisciplinary team, 169
Transdisciplinary training, 332

Transition services
concept of, 17
personnel preparation for, federal
funding for, 26, 28–29
teaching, 17

University Affiliated Programs (UAP),
53
federal funding for, 66–69
University consortium, for training programs, 105
University departments, collaboration
across, 3, 17–19
University of Kentucky, personnel
preparation program in education of students with severe
handicaps, 243–269

Values, preparing professionals with,
20–21

Values-based service delivery, in community living, 208–210
Visual handicaps
number of special education teachers
employed and needed to
serve children with, 37
percentage of school enrollment
served as students with, 35
personnel shortfall for, 39
and placement in special education,
11
Vocational rehabilitation, 323
models of, 227
Vocational Rehabilitation Act
(PL 98-221), 15
Vocational services, federal policy on,
324

Workshops, summer, in Iowa, 292